# THE BOYS
# IN THE BAND

• • • • • • • • •

## CONTEMPORARY APPROACHES TO FILM AND MEDIA SERIES

*A complete listing of the books in this series can be found online at wsupress.wayne.edu.*

### GENERAL EDITOR

Barry Keith Grant
*Brock University*

### ADVISORY EDITORS

Robert J. Burgoyne
*University of St. Andrews*

Caren J. Deming
*University of Arizona*

Patricia B. Erens
*School of the Art Institute of Chicago*

Peter X. Feng
*University of Delaware*

Lucy Fischer
*University of Pittsburgh*

Frances Gateward
*California State University, Northridge*

Tom Gunning
*University of Chicago*

Thomas Leitch
*University of Delaware*

Walter Metz
*Southern Illinois University*

© 2016 by Wayne State University Press, Detroit, Michigan 48201. All rights reserved. No part of this book may be reproduced without formal permission. Manufactured in the United States of America.
20 19 18 17 16     5 4 3 2 1

Library of Cataloging Control Number: 2016941942
ISBN 978-0-8143-4153-7 (paperback) | ISBN 978-0-8143-4154-4 (ebook)

Designed and typeset by Keata Brewer, E.T. Lowe Publishing
Composed in Minion Pro

Wayne State University Press
Leonard N. Simons Building
4809 Woodward Avenue
Detroit, Michigan 48201-1309

Visit us online at wsupress.wayne.edu

# THE BOYS IN THE BAND

Flashpoints of Cinema, History, and Queer Politics

EDITED BY MATT BELL

Wayne State University Press
Detroit

*In memory of Gregory W. Bredbeck,
whose queer intellectual life
enabled me to envision my own*

# Contents

*Acknowledgments* ix

Introduction:
On Returning to *The Boys in the Band* 1
**MATT BELL**

## Cinematic Transitions

1. Let's Hear a Round of Applause
for the Camps in the Band 35
**STEVEN COHAN**

2. "Turning": Alcohol and Affect
in *The Boys in the Band* 57
**JOE WLODARZ**

3. Gothic Spatiality and the Limits of Gay Visibility
in *The Boys in the Band* 88
**RYAN POWELL**

4. Closet Dramas: Masculinity and Claustrophobia
in William Friedkin's Films 113
**NICK DAVIS**

## Historical Thresholds

5. "Who Does She Hope to Be?":
Celluloid Ghosts, Queer Utopias, and *The Boys* Onstage 141
**JAMES WILSON**

6. The Boys in the City: Disintegration, Transformation, and the Cinematic Flash in William Friedkin's New York City Films (1970–80)   163
DAVID A. GERSTNER

7. "Nobody's Goddamn Business but My Own": Leonard Frey and the Politics of Gay and Jewish Visibility in the 1970s   190
STEPHEN VIDER

## Queer-Political Crises

8. "Beware the Hostile Fag": Acidic Intimacies and Gay Male Consciousness-Raising in *The Boys in the Band*   219
RAMZI FAWAZ

9. "A Credit to the Homosexual": *The Boys in the Band* and the Appearances of Queer Debt   247
MATTHEW TINKCOM

10. The Tragedy and Hope of Love between Gay Men: *The Boys in the Band* and the Emotionality of Gay Love in the 1960s and '70s   266
J. TODD ORMSBEE

11. The Sounds of Silence: Acoustics and Politics   292
AMY VILLAREJO

*Contributors*   309

*Index*   313

# Acknowledgments

Among the many pleasures I have taken in working on this project, some of the greatest have come in communication with colleagues and friends who have generously given me their encouragement, guidance, and companionship during its development. First among these is David Gerstner, who initially invited me to take part in a workshop on *The Boys in the Band* at the 2012 Society for Cinema and Media Studies conference and afterward urged me to pursue publishing an edited collection devoted to the film. His energy and fearlessness have inspired me all along, and his shrewd advice in matters large and small has proved invaluable.

I have boundless admiration and gratitude for the contributors to this volume, all of whom not only came up with a brilliant, original approach to the film but also did the hard, long-term work of research and writing that has resulted in their finished chapters. Their conversation and correspondence have been gratifying, and I now think of them collectively as a band of good friends. I thank in particular Steven Cohan, Nick Davis, Stephen Vider, and Amy Villarejo; their timely recommendations and bits of counsel have been important aids to my efforts.

Several audiences have crucially informed this book's shape and sense of purpose. Conceiving this project in advance of certain academic presentations has helped me to clarify its significance, and individual audience members' questions and comments have prompted improvements. In addition to the highly engaged audience at the 2012 SCMS conference, audiences offered helpful comments at the 2014 SCMS conference and at the 2013 and 2015 Modern Language Association conventions. I also shared portions of my introduction with colleagues at Bridgewater State University in 2015, and I remain grateful for their generous responses. Valerie Rohy and Sean Desilets gave a draft of the introduction tough, scrupulous readings; I can't imagine a better pair of readers, and I thank them for their readiness to help with this piece and for their long-standing friendship.

Bridgewater State University has been my happy academic home over the years of this project's development. Material support has come in a variety of forms there, including a 2014 summer grant from the Center for the Advancement of Research and Scholarship to conduct research for the book's introduction. That funding made possible a visit to the Film Study Center at the Museum of Modern Art in New York; I am grateful for Ashley Swinnerton's assistance during the day I spent there. The BSU library's archivist, Orson Kingsley, did not hesitate to help with one uniquely tricky illustration for this book, and Tim Wenson's technical expertise and patient assistance made possible another two dozen illustrations. In more general ways, I have benefited from working alongside colleagues who enrich my life daily, both in and beyond my own department. It gives me great pleasure to thank Ann Brunjes, Benjamin Carson, Kimberly Chabot Davis, Anne Doyle, Kathy Evans, Diana Fox, John Hooker, Bjorn Ingvoldstad, John Kucich, Leora Lev, John Mulrooney, Erin O'Connor, Maura Rosenthal, John Sexton, Jadwiga Smith, William Smith, Lee Torda, and Sarah Wiggins.

Transforming the draft manuscript into a book has involved challenges of many sorts, and I would not have been able to meet them without a crack team at Wayne State University Press, notably production editor Carrie Downes Teefey and designer Rachel Ross. I am very thankful for Andrew Katz's excellent copyediting skills and for Rachel Lyon's meticulous work on the index. From the beginning, Annie Martin's knowledge and professionalism have kept this project on track, and her calm manner and good humor have been reliable sources of reassurance at every step.

Supportive words about this project from colleagues and mentors elsewhere have also heartened me over the past few years. William Germano, David Greven, Joseph Litvak, and D. A. Miller have all urged me on, and I hope they enjoy seeing the result. At a late stage in the book's development, I wrote to Mart Crowley, whose immediate and generous reply continues to delight me. Lee Edelman's rigorous reading practices set a standard that has improved all of my academic efforts, and I am deeply appreciative of his kind, unstinting advocacy of my work over many years.

Outside the world of academia, friends and family have given me experiences of love and laughter that have indirectly, but no less decisively, made my work possible. Among them, I want to thank especially my parents, Michael Bell and Louise Bell, who long ago made me feel free to become the person I grew up to be; Todd Anderson, who showed me the humor and affection in *The Boys in the Band*; and Michael Kaplan, whose steadfast love sustains me.

# Introduction

## On Returning to *The Boys in the Band*

**MATT BELL**

Why should a dozen scholars come together in the twenty-first century to take another look at William Friedkin's 1970 film *The Boys in the Band*? After more than four decades, audiences and commentators of various persuasions have already settled on a certain reckoning of its value for cinema, history, and queer politics: it is merely an early and minor effort in the career of a director who went on to create cinematic monuments called *The French Connection* and *The Exorcist*; merely a toxic touchstone that evinces a bygone era's homophobia; and merely a fictional group portrait of apolitical gay men gathered comfortably in an Upper East Side apartment, while other people, in their time and ours, risk their lives for the queer cause. The conventional understanding of the film may concede its important place in the history of gay male representation, but that understanding also implies an expectation that the film will know its place and dutifully stay there. So well established is the film's reputation that returning to it may therefore seem an inconsequential, indulgent, or even morbid academic exercise.

Countering the prevailing impression of familiarity with *The Boys in the Band*, this collection of new essays displays how much is to be gained by such a return. As readers of this book will discover, *The Boys in the Band* merits not only the close study that should accompany such an artfully constructed film but also recognition as a landmark ideally situated to orient us amid the highly complex, shifting cultural terrain it occupied upon its release and has occupied since. Using a variety of approaches across a range of academic disciplines, the contributors to this volume make long-overdue corrections to the ignorance and misunderstanding that have dogged the film. Among the many other insights afforded by the essays here, readers will encounter, in individual chapters or across multiple chapters, strong cases for positioning *The Boys in the Band* at the center of its director's body of work, for recognizing its shaping influence on the gay liberation movement, and for regarding its political vision as potentially transformative for our contemporary queer discourse. As these essays show, instead of languishing as an antique outlier in the interdisciplinary field of queer studies, this film has the capacity to catalyze bold, fresh, and exciting new work, both in and beyond queer studies.

Returning to *The Boys in the Band* makes possible intensive examination of what this book's subtitle calls *flashpoints*. In revisiting this film and its historical and critical contexts, each of this book's contributors has isolated a moment of crisis, contention, or transformation. Such a moment occurs midway through the action of the film itself, when an explosion of homophobic violence instantaneously alters the relationships among the characters and precipitates the unnerving tension that follows through the remainder of the film: Alan assaults Emory verbally and physically, shouting "faggot" and beating him to the floor. Because of this and other instances of conflict in the story, in fact, it makes sense to read this film as an allegory of social combustion. As the allegorical reading of the film suggests, the flashpoints observed by this book's contributors are not all contained within the content of the film. As many of the following chapters explain in various ways, the formal techniques that convey this content produce an impression of a world on the verge of explosion. Moreover, both the contentious social environment depicted within the film and the cinematic techniques used to present it also express very real conflicts that had taken place before or were taking place during the historical moment of its creation. Not least among these conflicts is the exactly contemporaneous Stonewall Riots; the cultural circumstances in which this film was made are also those of the most legendary moment of queer resistance.[1] The specific episode of violence in the film's action may also be said to prefigure moments of cultural and critical crisis that followed it, such as the heated debates about this particular film during the 1970s and the combustible arguments about queer politics and queer thought that are taking place now. What makes the film so interesting to the scholars assembled here is its exceptional combination of elements: no other film combines such an evocative formal design, such a pivotal role in history, and such powerful resonance for our contemporary queer-political discourse.

Before moving outward to the sociopolitical significance of the film, though, it will be helpful to begin by offering a brief description of it. The debut of *The Boys in the Band* was revolutionary, above all, because of the film's fictional but frank presentation of a male homosexual subculture in Manhattan. A very faithful adaptation of Mart Crowley's hit Off-Broadway play of 1968—in fact produced and scripted by the playwright himself—Friedkin's 1970 film takes place at a birthday party attended by nine men whose language, clothing, and behavior evoke a range of New York gay "types," and its two-hour running time approximates the real time of the party. Following an opening montage that shows each of the characters as he prepares, works, or plays before the party, the principal action takes place in a two-story apartment on East Sixty-Fifth Street, where the characters gradually gather. These nine characters are the host, Michael (Kenneth Nelson); the guest of honor, Harold (Leonard Frey), who is turning thirty-two; invited guests Donald (Frederick Combs), Emory (Cliff Gorman), Bernard (Reuben Greene), and the couple Hank (Laurence Luckinbill) and Larry (Keith Prentice); the street hustler identified in the script as "Cowboy" (Robert La Tourneaux), purchased for the night by Emory as a birthday gift for Harold; and Michael's former college roommate Alan (Peter White), a married party crasher who may be about to come out of the closet. The film's action and visual style are largely naturalistic, and the narrative shape follows a traditional three-act structure: the first act assembles the party guests at Michael's apartment, climaxing with Alan's assault on Emory and Harold's late arrival; the second act, most of which unfolds on the apartment's terrace, follows the conventions of a birthday party, including dining, singing "Happy Birthday," sharing birthday cake, opening gifts, and slow dancing to music; and the third act, divided from the second by a thunderous burst of rain that forces everyone indoors, centers on a cruel party game invented by Michael, in which each player must make a telephone call to confess his love to another person.[2] Following the game, the film's denouement represents the disbanding party: by this time, Larry and Hank have already retired to Michael's upstairs bedroom; Alan, Harold, Cowboy, Emory, and Bernard depart soon after the game's conclusion; the drunken Michael suffers an anguished, shouting breakdown in Donald's arms; and in the film's final moments, Michael exits to attend a midnight Mass, leaving Donald alone in the apartment's living room.

William Friedkin's 1970 film adaptation is this book's primary object of study, and it should be understood as the product of several forces over the preceding years, including not only the activity of the playwright but also the critical environment in which he wrote. Crowley's play responded directly to a notorious 1966 essay by Stanley Kauffmann in the *New York Times* called "Homosexual Drama and Its Disguises," in which Kauffmann suggested that—though he refrained from naming these well-known dramatists—Tennessee Williams, William Inge, and Edward Albee had effectively translated gay male experience into heterosexual scenarios, with the effect of producing a "distorted" view of "American women, marriage, and society" in mainstream plays. Though Kauffmann's piece is dripping with homophobic contempt, it presents the following challenge: "The homosexual dramatist must be free to write truthfully of what he knows, rather than try to transform it to a life he does not know, to the detriment of his truth and ours."[3] In response, Crowley deliberately set about writing a play with contemporary gay male subject matter as an "undisguised," realist treatment of what this "homosexual dramatist" knew, and he completed the first draft of *The Boys in the Band* in a short burst of activity during the summer of 1967.[4] After some revision, Crowley's play, under the direction of Robert Moore, made its debut in New York City in 1968 in two phases: first in a workshop at the Playwrights Unit at the Village South Theater on Vandam Street, which ran briefly in late January 1968, and then at the Off-Broadway Theatre Four on West Fifty-Fifth Street in April that year in a fully realized production that went on to run for over one thousand performances. Alluding to the dramatists not quite named in Kauffmann's article, Crowley's play refers explicitly to Williams, Inge, and Albee.[5] The play's success led to its adaptation into other media. In 1969, A&M Records released an original cast recording of *The Boys in the Band* as a double LP. Hollywood producers expressed interest in adapting it to film, but Crowley balked at the changes they proposed and decided to produce the film himself. The film-production unit of CBS in that period, Cinema Center Films, agreed to Crowley's terms: it would be shot in New York City, it would use the original cast from the play, Crowley himself would adapt the script, and no extra-diegetic song or musical score would be included. When Cinema Center refused to allow the cinematically inexperienced Robert Moore to direct, Crowley chose the thirty-three-year-old director William Friedkin, who had recently helmed a film adaptation of Harold Pinter's play *The Birthday Party*.[6]

The resulting film reached movie theaters in March 1970, and this introduction later provides more substantive discussions of its reception among different groups, including popular reviewers, historians, and academics. For now, what is most remarkable is how quickly, despite the film's pioneering treatment of male homosexuality, it became a bête noire for the emergent gay liberation movement. To put it plainly, many people have loathed this movie, and among them are a considerable number of prominent gay activists who have denounced it in the name of liberation politics. *The Boys in the Band*'s provocative subject matter itself helps to account for the activists' outrage. A good deal of the film's peculiar power, after all, comes from its disturbing showcase of what we now call *internalized homophobia*; an especially inflammatory example is the shocking bit of dialogue that has most often been adduced in arguments against the film, in which Michael remarks, "You show me a happy homosexual, and I'll show you a gay corpse." At face value, this line appears to condense multiple strands of homophobic ideology, including rather obviously the suggestion that homosexual people, when alive, must be unhappy and perhaps less obviously the persistent trope of the male homosexual as a figure of death. A certain activist gay audience has used this piece of verbal evidence to claim that the film as a whole espouses and reinforces the internalized homophobia it depicts. As Steven Cohan and Joe Wlodarz demonstrate persuasively in their respective chapters in this volume, this line has frequently been removed from its context and willfully misread, and the misreading of the film as an endorsement of the homophobia it expresses has had real and lasting consequences.

Two statements suffice to represent the political foundations of the activist reception. First, one of the most influential activists in both the mid-1960s homophile movement and in the gay liberation years after Stonewall, Franklin Kameny, described *The Boys in the Band* as the kind of work that he was fighting against. In a 1995 letter written to the historian Charles Kaiser, Kameny recalled that he had coined the gay-affirmative slogan "Gay Is Good," he wrote, "as a direct antidote to the mindset among gays epitomized by that abomination, *The Boys in the Band*."[7] Second, in an article titled "Homosexuals and Literature" that appeared in a 1974 issue of *College English*, another important gay activist and academic, Arnie Kantrowitz, reflected on his attention to the play and the film *The Boys in the Band* in a course he had taught called "Homosexuals and Literature": the characters in the film, he wrote, "pose as a complete spectrum of male homosexual behavior when in fact they represent a small part of such a spectrum, and a quickly atrophying part at that."[8] Kameny's and Kantrowitz's appraisals of the film exemplify two key components of the politics of representation that took issue with it during the early 1970s: to correct for a history of simplifying, negative, and harmful portrayals of homosexuals in both fictional and nonfictional contexts, activists called for representations that would (1) show gay people favorably, as law-abiding, sane, moral persons who are capable of happiness, and (2) reflect the wide range of lived experiences of real gay people. Given the context of a cinematic history that had regularly depicted lesbians and gay men as sinister or psychologically compromised—films including Alfred Hitchcock's *Rope* (1948), William Wyler's *The Children's Hour* (1961), and Otto Preminger's *Advise and Consent* (1962) are in different ways precursors of Friedkin's film—Kameny's and Kantrowitz's longing is surely comprehensible. According to their version of identity politics, *The Boys in the Band* was objectionable both for its exposition of hostility and self-loathing in its main character and for the highly specific constitution of the population it depicted.

The major consequence of this regard for the film has been neglect among scholars. While it has received some recognition in the form of a few academic articles and book chapters, it has not yet received the kind of sustained, complex scholarly treatment that would do it justice. Notably, however, *The Boys in the Band* has begun in recent years to enjoy something of a popular renaissance. In 2008, Friedkin's film appeared on DVD in a transfer that—to anyone who had seen it before only on videotape—is revelatory for its clarity and beauty.[9] In 2010, the director Crayton Robey's documentary feature *Making the Boys*, which combines a wealth of archival material and interviews with the surviving filmmakers, made a compelling case for revisiting the film. William Friedkin devoted a chapter of his 2013 memoir *The Friedkin Connection* to the film's production, effectively calling his readers to regard *The Boys in the Band* alongside his more well-known films.[10] Also in 2013, the Brooklyn Academy of Music included the film in its retrospective of Friedkin's great works of the 1970s. Meanwhile, the theatrical afterlives of Mart Crowley's play have included two New York revivals (in 1996 and 2010) and a sequel, titled *The Men from the Boys*, which premiered in 2002. In March 2015, the film was the subject of a brief retrospective on the website of *Time* magazine, and the film's appearance on Blu-ray midway through the same year prompted a new wave of press coverage, including a review of the disc in the *New York Times* and interviews with Friedkin about *The Boys in the Band* in the magazine *Cineaste* and on the website Fandor.[11] Renewed popular interest in the text over the past twenty years indicates an ongoing fascination that has survived the controversy that shadowed the film in the 1970s and 1980s.

It surely helps the film's case that it no longer bears the representational burden that caused Kameny and Kantrowitz to repudiate it so forcefully. In a historical appraisal of the film, John Loughery remarked succinctly on the impossible political position *The Boys in the Band* occupied: "The temper of the times demanded that Crowley's characters be taken as representatives of their kind rather than quirky, suffering individuals."[12] To point only to the most salient example of the difference made by the intervening decades of gay-themed mass media, consider the critical and popular favor that greeted another film about a highly specific subset of gay men who suffer both internalized homophobia and homophobic assault, *Brokeback Mountain* (dir. Ang Lee, 2005). There are other ways to account for the success of *Brokeback Mountain*—its pastoralizing vision likely satisfies a nostalgic longing for a closeted homosexuality in relation to which the spectator can feel pity—but it surely benefited from the fact that it did not face the kind of scrutiny that greeted earlier, more truly groundbreaking queer films.[13] No one now expects *The Boys in the Band* to prove single-handedly that Gay Is Good; now, instead, *The Boys in the Band* is perfectly poised for the substantial, wide-ranging reassessment that the chapters in this collection perform.

In pursuing this reassessment, this essay collection does not attempt to provide direct counterarguments to the objections raised by commentators like Kameny and Kantrowitz; no contributor to this volume proposes either that *The Boys in the Band* in fact envisions unequivocally positive images of gay men or that it presents a broadly representative portrayal of real queer persons. What *The Boys in the Band* affords, however, is an ideal opportunity to reconsider the foundations of the representation politics adopted by Kameny and Kantrowitz. Indeed, demands for positive, comprehensive, and accurate portrayals, whether of queer persons generally or of gay men more specifically, are based on certain evaluative criteria that *The Boys in the Band* may be most instructive for enabling us to contest. Of course, the raw material of idealized heroes or diverse populations does not necessarily translate into good movies; equating one's aesthetic principles with positive or diverse portrayals often just means subscribing to Hollywood's most lasting narrative clichés or to a utopian ideal of conflict-free multiculturalism. Demands for representations of the Good Gay and for a more inclusive spectrum of queer personhood are surely more political than aesthetic, however, and they warrant a more politically minded answer. Notably, these two demands inevitably produce an irreconcilable conflict; the fictional Good Gay could only ever be a small fraction of the full range of queer persons. Especially after the New Queer Cinema of the early 1990s, the queer-political imperative to show positive images of homosexuality has lost much of its force, and observing this shift helps to explain how a film like *Brokeback Mountain* could be financed and widely celebrated in the new century. As a result, we may be better prepared now to take stock of the Bad Gays of *The Boys in the Band*.

By contrast, demands for diverse or inclusive representation have grown more common and clamorous; while it is difficult to imagine someone taking Frank Kameny's exact position on *The Boys in the Band* today, it is not difficult at all to imagine someone condemning the film by using language identical to Arnie Kantrowitz's, especially in those areas of higher education that reflexively prescribe "diversity" in curricula and course materials to remedy both social and academic ills. Perhaps most tellingly in Kantrowitz's remarks on Mart Crowley's play and the film adaptation, what begins as mere objective description (the characters "represent a small part of . . . a spectrum") gives way immediately to something closer to schadenfreude ("and a quickly atrophying part at that"). The band of gay men in the film is a very narrow one, Kantrowitz suggests, and we should in fact take pleasure in its further diminution amid the rise of a more diverse queer population. What troubles me in this formulation is how it maintains a fantasy that has roots in a profoundly homophobic past: it depends on a familiar image of the male homosexual as insular, narrow-minded, or narcissistic, a chain of associations that, in different contexts, can spread outward to include other descriptors (bourgeois, hedonistic, politically indifferent). This pernicious image of the male homosexual has persisted over time, so that it is possible to observe its surprising continuity across such "disparate" discourses as 1960s-era American psychiatry, post-Stonewall liberationist writing, and even a prominent strain of queer theory still apparent in the twenty-first century.[14]

In response to criticism like Kantrowitz's, *The Boys in the Band* prompts a risky and difficult critical project that I wish to outline here: a defense *in the name of queer politics* of the narrowness, the smallness, the exclusivity evident in *The Boys in the Band*. It would be possible, of course, to describe *The Boys in the Band* as a text that aspires to inclusion—as Kantrowitz observes, the film's characters "pose as a complete spectrum of male homosexual behavior." This echoes Pauline Kael's apt (if homophobically inflected) description of the play: "It was like 'The Women,' but with a forties-movie bomber-crew cast: a Catholic, a Jew, a Negro, a butch faggot, a Nellie faggot, a hustler, and so on, and, in place of the bomber crew's possible homosexual, a possible heterosexual."[15] As I have argued elsewhere about the principle of inclusion that prevails in queer studies, a text that touts the differences it seems so capaciously to contain should be met with skepticism; such an effortful show, even as it works to produce a fantasy of absolute inclusion, is likely an attempt to mask the necessary exclusions that any text must make.[16] In this respect, Kantrowitz is correct: *The Boys in the Band*, despite the differences among its characters, does not represent the full spectrum of queer personhood or experience. My disagreement with Kantrowitz comes in contemplating the possibility or desirability of representing such a complete spectrum. Kantrowitz clearly considers such representation both possible and desirable, while *The Boys in the Band* invites two competing claims: not only that such representation is impossible but also that a fully inclusive work of fiction (which can only be a fantasy, the vanishing point of fictional representation) would no longer convey the mark of social division, whether conceived as stigma or rebellion, that the term *queer* signifies.

Indeed, *The Boys in the Band* calls those of us who are committed to queer politics to take a skeptical look at any politics of representation founded on a wish for comprehensive inclusion. As *The Boys in the Band* should help us to observe, the "negative" portrayal and the great particularity of the population represented can be both politically purposeful and aesthetically admirable. A film about the experience of a specific subset of queers, set in the late 1960s, does its best both politically and aesthetically not by offering a sunny or even sympathetic vision of human experience and not by attempting to show what all queer persons experience; it offers a more galvanizing political and aesthetic vision by unsettling the spectator, by being willing to concentrate on a very particular set of persons and circumstances, and by registering the nearly intolerable social experience it depicts in a nearly intolerable cinematic form. Since the moment of New Queer Cinema in the early 1990s, many important films have appeared that help to make the case. Other films that would fail the criteria proposed by both Kameny and Kantrowitz include a variety of marvelous, specifically imagined, and politically significant films, such as *Paris Is Burning* (dir. Jennie Livingston, 1991), *Heavenly Creatures* (dir. Peter Jackson, 1994), *Boys Don't Cry* (dir. Kimberly Peirce, 1999), *Southern Comfort* (dir. Kate Davis, 2001), *Mulholland Dr.* (dir. David Lynch, 2001), *Bad Education* (dir. Pedro Almodóvar, 2004), *Tropical Malady* (dir. Apichatpong Weerasethakul, 2004), *Blue Is the Warmest Color* (dir. Abdellatif Kechiche, 2013), and *Carol* (dir. Todd Haynes, 2015).

*The Boys in the Band* should be valued precisely because of its refusal to supply an easy, affirmative vision of queer life, precisely because it offers a highly particularized vision of the specific characters who inhabit it, and precisely for its unique visual style. Indeed, it deserves recognition as an example of "New Queer Cinema" *avant la lettre*. Some currents in the most recent queer discourse, of course, would prompt the kinds of objections to *The Boys in the Band* voiced by observers like Kantrowitz, but those currents are worth challenging. Part of what makes queer discourse internally contradictory and even incoherent is its tendency to confound affirmative LGBT activist language and the trenchant contemplations of exclusion in queer theory. Though the present book project is deliberately aligned more with the legacy of queer theory than with a populist version of LGBT activism, the distinction between the two can be difficult to maintain. Even in some of the earliest formulations of queer theory, especially those founded on feminist thought, a tension exists between, on the one hand, considerations of the inevitability and power of linguistic exclusion and, on the other, insistence on the political and ethical principles of diversity and inclusion. One way to read the history of queer theory is to understand it as the recursive working-out of this tension, which appears, for example, in foundational work by Teresa de Lauretis and Judith Butler.[17] Now, especially in an academic climate that often prizes the virtues of inclusion, social justice, and civic responsibility, *The Boys in the Band* is bound to be met warily, both within and beyond queer theoretical contexts. In this climate, not only does the principle of multiculturalism flourish, but also the demand for positive images has attained new life; in the era of the It Gets Better Project, which seeks to assure queer youth of a bright future life, *The Boys in the Band* may promise an intolerably dim vision of queer adulthood. One of the regrettable limitations of reassuring prescriptions for a better queer life is their inability to countenance singularly important artifacts of the queer past, however painful or unsettling the encounter with those artifacts may be. A better, queer-theoretical model for the kind of work that this collection of essays performs is one that several of its contributors cite, Heather Love's 2007 book *Feeling Backward: Loss and the Politics of Queer History*.[18] The title of Love's book speaks simultaneously of a subjective queer experience of stigma and of an academic determination to grapple with the materials of the queer past. Contending with *The Boys in the Band* offers no guarantee of comfort or safety, no vision of the unequivocally good gay person, no representation of comprehensive inclusiveness. Contending with *The Boys in the Band* means not only observing the limits of such aesthetic and political values but also formulating alternative, highly nuanced aesthetic and political values.

The next two sections that follow in this introduction lay out in greater depth how existing accounts of *The Boys in the Band* have not simply neglected the film but in fact worked actively to prevent both audiences and scholars from seeing its most extraordinary qualities. The first of these sections conducts a more diachronic reception history of the film, describing in the process how the film has been recurrently positioned as an outmoded relic of a now-overcome past; the second takes a more synchronic look at the critical reception of the film in 1970, which, in my reading, effectively set the limits for appreciating Friedkin's film. In looking to the film's reception, my objective is to suggest how much has remained to be said about this film.

## Period Piece

Over time and in a variety of works—in gay liberation writing, in critical academic treatments, in works of history, and even in more recent reevaluations—*The Boys in the Band* has been simplified and reviled, when not simply neglected. Though various critics, historians, and film scholars over the years have offered cursory acknowledgment of the film's importance, more substantive research and analysis have been woefully lacking. Evidence of *The Boys in the Band*'s significance for its contemporary world abounds in anecdotal mentions of it. The play and, more often, the film versions of *The Boys in the Band* served as common points of reference for many gay writers of the late 1960s and 1970s. A good example of this is *The Best Little Boy in the World*, the memoir Andrew Tobias published under the pseudonym John Reid in 1973.[19] In that book, *The Boys in the Band* receives repeated mention among the gay men the author encounters as he begins to come out of the closet. On the basis of this personal account, at least, it appears that *The Boys in the Band* in the early 1970s functioned as a shared object of interest among gay men.

The limited range of more substantial examinations of *The Boys in the Band* has likely resulted less from benign neglect than from the film's entrenched status as a favored target of criticism from gay liberation writers. Gay liberationists of the 1970s and 1980s actively repudiated the film, constructing an enduring bad reputation for it; sometimes, even now, the very title *The Boys in the Band* has served as shorthand for a preliberated gay male consciousness characterized by self-loathing, insularity, and narcissism. The characterization of its tortured protagonist, Michael, led advocates of the new gay sensibility to reject the film altogether. *The Boys in the Band* nonetheless has occupied an important, even determining role in gay liberation writing; perhaps most crucially, it sometimes figures in gay liberation as a call that gay liberation answered. These gay liberation texts typically repudiate the play or the film, effectively producing *The Boys in the Band* as the negative foundation for liberation. Dennis Altman's 1971 book-length manifesto *Homosexual: Oppression and Liberation* uses Mart Crowley's play throughout as an example of a nonliberated homosexuality, referring to its "stereotype of the guilt-ridden, unhappy homosexual."[20] Writing in the *New York Times* in early 1969—before Stonewall, it is worth noting—Donn Teal (under the pseudonym Ronald Forsythe) included *The Boys in the Band* in his lengthy complaint about the treatment of gay people in mainstream films and plays; his article bore the title "Why Can't 'We' Live Happily Ever After, Too?"[21] These rhetorical uses of *The Boys in the Band* in early gay liberation writing, like Arnie Kantrowitz's, positioned it strategically as the past that the new movement would overcome; these writers sought to replace the unhappiness of the homosexual past with a happier future. The gay liberationist activism of the period participated in this insistent production of an outmoded past. According to John Loughery, at a Los Angeles gay liberation protest against the film version of *The Boys in the Band*, one of the activists carried a sign reading, "*The Boys in the Band*: Best Gay Movie of 1947."[22]

In *The Celluloid Closet* (1981, rev. 1987), first published about a decade after the first wave of the gay liberation movement, Vito Russo supplies a somewhat more favorable account of Friedkin's film, recognizing more directly its complex involvement in gay liberation. Like most liberation histories, Russo's book tells a story of triumph as he traces the lineage of homosexual representation in the movies from the silent era to the 1980s. In his substantial attention to the film, though he calls it a "period piece," he also suggests that it served as a catalyst for gay activism.[23] For Russo, *The Boys in the Band* has functioned as a necessary step toward progress: "[Crowley's] characters were losers or borderline survivors at best, but they paved the way for winners."[24] Unlike Altman and Teal, therefore, Russo sees the film as pivotal for the evolution of gay representation, in part because, he asserts, its characters triggered real responses: "It was the gays in the audiences of 1970 who would eventually form a rebuttal to the [film's] homosexual party guests, and their voices would grow louder with each passing year."[25] In prompting negative reactions in audiences, Russo suggests, *The Boys in the Band* may be understood not simply as a commonly repudiated target in gay liberation but as one of the movement's causes. Though a more balanced approach to the film, Russo's nevertheless treats it as a superseded past, its characters so many prehistoric homosexuals trapped in amber.

This reception among gay-identified writers has influenced the film's treatment among academic writers from the early 1970s to the present. The disdainful treatment that Arnie Kantrowitz gave to *The Boys in the Band* in his article in *College Literature* represents the confluence of academic and activist responses to the film. Meanwhile, a couple of early academic articles looked on *The Boys in the Band* more approvingly: one, by Norine Dresser, appeared in the journal *Western Folklore* in 1974; the other, by Allison Graham, appeared in *Film Criticism* in 1980.[26] This pair of articles indicates, in contrast to Kantrowitz's article, that a somewhat deeper academic treatment was possible at the time. Among scholars in film and literary studies, nonetheless, *The Boys in the Band* lay dormant as an object of critical attention over the next fifteen years, until some academic writers began to address it again in the mid-1990s. Since this period, a small number of significant articles and book chapters by scholars including Joe Carrithers, Philip Brian Harper, Rodger Streitmatter, and Pamela Robertson Wojcik have examined the film and/or the play.[27] Meanwhile, the film typically appears in texts that survey queer cinema, such as Harry M. Benshoff and Sean Griffin's *Queer Images*.[28] Two noteworthy books devoted to the career of William Friedkin feature some attention to *The Boys in the Band*, both composed by writers with careers in the entertainment industry: Nat Segaloff's *Hurricane Billy: The Stormy Life and Films of William Friedkin* (1990) and Thomas D. Clagett's *William Friedkin: Films of Aberration, Obsession, and Reality* (1990, 2nd ed. 2003).[29]

A few histories of gay lives and gay political movements, mostly mass-marketed, have also addressed *The Boys in the Band*. Two that have devoted sustained attention to the play and the film are Charles Kaiser's *The Gay Metropolis: The Landmark History of Gay Life in America since World War II* (1997) and John Loughery's *The Other Side of Silence: Men's Lives and Gay Identities: A Twentieth-Century History* (1998). While these two books both consider the play and the film rather even-handedly, they bear the imprint of conventional thought about *The Boys in the Band* among gay writers like Vito Russo. Both Kaiser and Loughery focus primarily on the play rather than the film. Kaiser's book ultimately observes that by the time the film was released, "many of [Crowley's] words seemed dated."[30] Loughery more directly repeats Russo's gesture, suggesting that the character of Emory, himself representative of all of the film's characters, personified a type of gay personhood that would, in a historical inevitability, "give way to the New Homosexual" of the 1970s.[31] Other works of history treat *The Boys in the Band* minimally and negatively. In *Gay Power: An American Revolution* (2006), David Eisenbach discusses both the play and the film, using it as an example of how works of popular culture "tended to reinforce the old stereotypes."[32] Describing a gay male commune in New York City in 1968, David Carter's book *Stonewall: The Riots That Sparked the Gay Revolution* (2004) notes that the commune's members would quote the "happy homosexual-corpse" line from Crowley's play as evidence that "gay men suffered from self-hatred."[33] Dudley Clendinen and Adam Nagourney's monumental *Out for Good: The Struggle to Build a Gay Rights Movement in America* (1999) discusses only the play, and it does so dismissively in reference to the same line: the play "suggested that it might be better to be dead than gay."[34] Lillian Faderman and Stuart Timmons's *Gay L.A.: A History of Sexual Outlaws, Power Politics, and Lipstick Lesbians* (2006) affords the briefest mention to the film in a discussion of Hollywood representations of gay people, stating that it "offered a host of gay stereotypes, each of them miserable."[35] Still other significant histories of gay liberation ignore *The Boys in the Band* altogether.[36] Taken as a group, most existing political and social histories grant *The Boys in the Band* some place in history, generally invoking it to stand for a pre-Stonewall sensibility that the new era would overcome.

Brief accounts in popular periodicals have reinforced the histories' treatment. The title of *Time*'s online 2015 article on *The Boys in the Band* speaks to the role it has come to occupy in public discourse: "How One Movie Changed LGBT History." Accounts that thus fold a discussion of the film into a tale of social struggle risk obscuring its potentially enduring power; if it is regarded solely as a marker of circumstances now past, it may fail to offer vital information or energy today. The effect of this simplifying form of historicism appears in Vito Russo's claim that the film was a "period piece," and as recently as 2015, J. Hoberman echoed Russo's assessment in his review of the film's release on Blu-ray for the *New York Times*, calling it "once groundbreaking, now a period piece."[37] The aura that hovers around the film in the twenty-first century can make it seem merely a relic of an outmoded world, as when a writer in *Variety* described the film in 2008 as a "camp curio."[38] Also in 2008, upon the film's release on DVD, a writer for the *Advocate* quoted one new viewer of the film as saying, "The movie is like what you'd see in a diorama at Mary's Natural History Museum."[39]

To the extent that these assessments position the film as a relic from a prior moment, they participate in the original wishes of certain gay liberationists to assert that *The Boys in the Band* was already, upon the release of the film, an outmoded representation. Of course, the writers and activists of the gay liberation movement were eager to assert a break with the past—to mark the Stonewall Riots as a definitive rupture with a past of oppression and self-loathing. But this gesture of renouncing *The Boys in the Band* for its datedness can only be historically naïve. It seeks to make the history of the gay political movement the kind of account that Eve Kosofsky Sedgwick called "a unidirectional narrative of supersession," one that proposes absolute breaks between historical moments.[40] Several contributors to the present volume argue convincingly that *The Boys in the Band* was much more actively involved in the politics and historical circumstances of its period than existing treatments of Crowley's play and Friedkin's film have allowed.

One aspect of the film's mise-en-scène, never verbalized in the dialogue, suggests the film's intricate involvement in historical events—and its self-awareness about that involvement. When commentators abjure the film for its being a "period piece," they do so in the mode of condescension, as if they know now what the film could not have known about itself. In a rather queer historiographic gesture that seems to answer these commentators in advance, however, the film acknowledges its historically specific location, suggesting that the film already knows about its datedness. Shown several times in the film prior to the thunderstorm, a chalk drawing on the wall outside Michael's apartment, ornamented with flowers that echo the half dozen red roses Michael has purchased for this occasion, dates and locates the film's action: "Summer NYC 1968." A suggestive backdrop for the film's queer assembly, this inscription silently insists that the film has something important to say about its time and place.

Later in this volume, Ramzi Fawaz offers a valuable reading of how the chalk drawing signifies its historical moment. In the present context, what is striking is the filmmakers' decision—during production in the summer of 1969 for a film to be released in 1970—to call attention to its setting in the past. Underlying certain critical assessments of the film has been an assumption that it means to represent gay people once and for all, but this figure asserts instead the subject matter's historical and geographical contingency. Filmed in 1969, right at the moment of upheaval called Stonewall, *The Boys in the Band* already knows its action belongs to the past, and this highly conspicuous signification of that fact should prompt a slightly different reading from the one that disparages the film for being outdated.

A queer past, dated in chalk.

Among other things, because it is written in chalk, this dating of the film emphasizes its own transitory status. Midway through the film, the storm may have washed the chalk drawing away—the camera never shows the wall afterward—and in this way the film allegorizes a radical historical rupture that might wash away the past and give way to a different future. The figure and its disappearance invite the viewer to imagine that Michael and the other guests might go on to other pursuits in the summer of 1969.

As we will see in the following section, the critical, academic, and historical construction that has for so long represented *The Boys in the Band* as an artifact from the past is not the only discursive maneuver that has prevented audiences of all kinds from reading it accurately or taking it seriously. Indeed, that construction was in many ways shaped by the earliest reviews of the film in 1970, in which the available ways of understanding the film were already highly regulated and, to use the term in its psychoanalytic sense, repressed.

## "Perverse Interest"

*The Boys in the Band* came out in 1970. By this, I mean, of course, that William Friedkin's film of that title enjoyed its world premiere on March 17, 1970, in New York City, followed over the next two weeks by debuts in major North American markets including San Francisco, Washington,

DC, Boston, Philadelphia, Toronto, Los Angeles, and Montreal. Reading the contemporary coverage of the film's release in the popular press produces a host of impressions that, taken together, surely warrant the use of a cliché to summarize the film's immediate reception: it *caused a sensation*. Greeted with fascination, excitement, and no small degree of anxiety, *The Boys in the Band* in fact appears to have brought about a remarkable range of sensations, and it is true that the reviews that appeared in the popular press upon its release were mixed. Adopting the tacit physics of their time, one might readily graph the critical appraisals along a spectrum of aesthetic estimation, with such hostile treatments as Pauline Kael's and Stanley Kauffmann's at one extreme, such virtually unequivocal commendations as Judith Crist's and Leo Lerman's at the other, and the majority of assessments falling somewhere in between. Certain critics found the film's witty dialogue, passionate performances, intensely cloistered mise-en-scène, and frank presentation of a formerly unrepresented gay minority worthy of high praise; but, and sometimes in the very same reviews, the contemporary critics often objected to such aspects of the film as its too-well-made script, excessive use of close-ups, and governing tone of sentimentality. While my remarks in this section offer elements of the sort of reception history that would expand on these topics, my objective is neither to quantify these general appraisals of its worth nor to trace how the critics judged each particular component of the film's content and form.

By studying the small, historically isolated canon of contemporary reviews, I aim to show how they constructed a durable template that has effectively shaped the terms for discussing *The Boys in the Band* since its release. Before reading these critical assessments today, we might expect to find in them ample evidence that the dominant discourse of the time was poorly prepared to engage with such subjects as male homosexuality and camp style, in contrast to our own, more expansive liberalism, vocabulary, and taste; we might expect, in short, to find confirmation that we occupy a superior vantage point from which to observe the content of *The Boys in the Band*. From *Variety* to the *Village Voice*, and from the *Christian Century* to *Cosmopolitan*, the reviews that appeared in mainstream venues show, however, that the dominant discourse of the time not only was capable of considering at length an urban gay male population with a distinctive manner of speech but also had the capacity to include genuinely sophisticated discussions about stereotypical characterization and the psychological consequences of living in or out of the closet—discussions that have persisted around this film over the succeeding decades. While these reviews surely indulge outmoded attitudes about homosexuality—humanist sympathy and disdain prevail, often in strange combination—they nonetheless exhibit serious-minded critical respect for the movie's technique, setting, story line, and persons. A selection of reviews written between March and May of 1970 gives a strong sense that the ideological and aesthetic principles that were articulable in popular U.S. newspapers and magazines at that time are not as far removed from our own as we might wish to imagine. What benefit might a film historian, cultural critic, or theorist of gender and sexuality gain, then, by taking a closer look at this group of early notices? They illustrate not only how far we have not come in our understanding of the film but also how customary responses to it have inherited a set of self-protective critical reflexes that prevent the film from achieving what might otherwise be the revelatory jolt of surprise. Close examination of the contemporary reviews can both take stock of the writing techniques that have protected against surprise and offer alternative possibilities for engaging with the film. Three recurrent rhetorical patterns appear in these reviews: the performance of familiarity with the film's subject matter, the vocal imitation of its characters, and the partial repression of the sexual curiosity it inspires. Together, these patterns demonstrate, often against the stated aims of the reviewers, not that we already know all we need to know about *The Boys in the Band* but how much it has yet to disclose to us.

In other words, and to recast the sentence with which this section began, in the following reading, I address the coming-out of *The Boys in the Band* in 1970 more figuratively than literally. Imagine gathering around you all the intimates whose love and respect you hold most dear to tell them a secret that might radically alter or sever your relationship; now imagine that those people include Andrew Sarris, Gene Siskel, Vincent Canby, and Pauline Kael. The responses to *The Boys in the Band* of these and other critics evoke nothing so well as the available forms for reacting to a declaration of sexual deviance, with certain predictable results. Reading the early encounter between *The Boys in the Band* and its critics as a coming-out allegory entails admitting certain caveats—in a mass market, the relationship between film and reviewer involves very different stakes than those that obtain between, say, a child and a parent—but this reading strategy helps to account for the mixture of stated indifference, verbal parody, and muffled longing for sexual knowledge expressed in the reviews.

The first of these reactions may best explain the enduring tendency today to treat *The Boys in the Band* as a text long exhausted of meaning. To take certain of the critics at their word, perhaps most prominent among the "sensations" caused in the film's earliest screenings was the sensation of boredom. Stanley Kauffmann—who four years earlier had called for undisguised representations of gay men in theater—expresses this response most directly in his review in the *New Republic*, and the knowing tone prevails in notices that appeared in the *New York Times* (Canby), *Variety*, the *New Yorker* (Kael), and *Newsweek* (Morgenstern).[41] These notices adopt a posture of familiarity with the film's population, language, and politics. Their familiarity is not without some objective truth: most of the critics inform their readership that they saw Mart Crowley's 1968 play *The Boys in the Band* prior to seeing Friedkin's adaptation, and many of them devote significant space to comparing the work's success in the two media. Most clearly prefer the play to the film, though Judith Crist in *New York* magazine and John Gruen in *Vogue* find the film superior.[42] But the previous experience of seeing the play does not truly account for this posture of familiarity. Kauffmann, for example, tellingly frames his lack of surprise upon seeing the film not as the effect of having the prior experience of seeing the play but as a response to the text of the play itself: "The insights in this play are as banal as its structure. What is the homosexual's secret? Loneliness, says Crowley. Some news."[43] In sarcastically dismissing the possibility that the film might inform him of something that he does not already know about "the homosexual's secret," Kauffmann's review exemplifies one typical reaction that follows from "the scene of gay coming out," as Sedgwick calls it in *Epistemology of the Closet*.[44] Kauffmann's reaction is to profess no reaction at all: since he knows in advance the banal content of the homosexual's secret, the film can supply no perceptible stimulus that might prompt a reaction. His response to the coming-out of *The Boys in the Band* is, *Tell me something I don't already know*. This nonreaction simultaneously denies the film any original content concerning the homosexual's secret and accomplishes an analeptic sleight of hand: Kauffmann asserts now that he has for some time known all that it would tell him, arrogating for the critic the authority that dispenses information that otherwise would originate in the film. While the person who comes out may be attempting to convey the disruptive force of sexual desire or a unique lived experience of secrecy, the recipient of the news is liable to deflect that attempt by smug reference to a prior, universalizing structure: *I've already known what you're about, and what you're about is neither new nor unique*. In Sedgwick's words, "The position of those who think they *know something about one that one may not know oneself* is an excited and empowered one—whether what they think one doesn't know is that one somehow *is* homosexual, or merely that one's supposed secret is known to them."[45] In the context of *The Boys in the Band*, Kauffmann's claim of familiarity with the homosexual's secret is not reducible to a statement of fact but should be recognized for its performative effects, including identifying the critic with comprehensive knowledge that precludes the very possibility of the film's coming-out. This identification between critic and knowledge of the homosexual's secret is an effort to contain the film's potential to yield wild, unpredictable meanings; Kauffmann's cool assertion of familiarity disavows the possibility that the film might have some unfamiliar or indeed defamiliarizing content.

And what better way is there to exhibit familiarity with *The Boys in the Band* than to show expertise in its language? Surely prompted by the perspective of the film itself, several reviewers adopt the persona of the amateur anthropologist to assess the characters. For example, Vincent Canby calls the film in the title of his review in the *New York Times* a "study of male homosexuality," and his review goes on to describe how the film photographs the characters "in their natural habitats."[46] Especially interesting to the reviewer-anthropologist's ear is Mart Crowley's script, which several critics identify as the truly distinctive aspect of the film; the unsigned review in *Time* magazine remarks favorably on Crowley's talent for "recording" "homosexual patter," and Richard Schickel's one significant note of praise for the film is that it "captures nicely the peculiar patois of the urban homosexual."[47] It is small wonder, then, that some of the critics, perhaps unconsciously, take the time-worn step of going native. Words that belong to the vocabulary spoken by the characters in the film, such as "queen" and "camp," abound in the reviews without the distancing help of quotation marks, as if the reviewer has appropriated the vernacular he or she picked up while in the field. The pose of familiarity in response to the coming-out of *The Boys in the Band* thus extends to the quality that should sound most unfamiliar; the play's witty dialogue, what might seem most original or "inimitable," is the very thing most imitated. The adoption of the voice of the homosexual in these reviews surely has its share of homophobic aggression, a fact equally true in negative and positive notices. Pauline Kael's is the most vicious toward the film and its characters; her free-flowing, repeated use of the word "faggot" seems designed to keep the characters at the farthest possible remove from herself. When Kael criticizes the film's excessive seriousness, though, the distance between her voice and that of the boys abruptly closes. Describing Friedkin's anguished close-ups, she writes, "Every blink and lick of the lips has its rigidly scheduled meaning, and it's all so solemn—like Joan Crawford when she's thinking."[48] This line might have come from the mouth of the film's greatest wit, Harold; coming as it does from a writer who elsewhere seems anxious to disidentify with her faggot subjects, Kael's line invites its reader to consider the implications of what I would call its gay male voice. In this respect, the "negative" review is in fact the mirror image of its "positive" counterpart. Gene Siskel's enthusiastic appraisal of *The Boys in the Band* begins by stating that the film is "incredibly funny," and shortly thereafter he goes on to make a joke of his own, describing the film's main character, Michael, as "the host who changes cashmere sweaters faster than you can say 'Jack Robinthon.'"[49] The joke would smack of mere everyday homophobia, but—coming as it does in a "positive" review—it might more usefully be understood as a poor attempt to imitate the gay male voice. Kael's and Siskel's imitations are not simply examples of mockery—like the ironic discourse employed by characters like Michael and Emory, these imitations, while they may ridicule, more importantly seem to claim a share of the wit that makes the dialogue spoken by these characters so "incredibly funny."[50]

This adoption of the gay male voice represents another version of the performance of familiarity in response to the coming-out of *The Boys in the Band*, but in attempting to show fluency in the native tongue of the urban homosexual, the performance of familiarity in this case, unlike Stanley Kauffmann's, is more recognizable as a fascinated, even desiring one. It comes closer to acknowledging the play of excitement, anxiety, and rivalry at work in "the scene of gay coming out," and for the student of *The Boys in the Band*, it makes possible the imagination of ways in which the film may yet surprise us with what it has to say. For one thing, the unpredictable quality of the desires that the gay male voice voices may be the cause of many critics' displays of familiarity; the insistent repetition of the claim, from 1970 to the present, that the coming-out of *The Boys in the Band* has no news to tell may in fact be an effort to silence the film's still-unexpressed capacity to surprise or to reorient its viewer. Sedgwick tells us that the coming-out statement may make an extraordinary claim on its listener: "the erotic identity of the person who receives the disclosure is apt to be implicated in, hence perturbed by it."[51] The scene of gay coming-out does not necessarily make the listener sexually identical to the speaker, but it insists on altering the relation between the two; to treat the coming-out of *The Boys in the Band* as a subject already known means refusing to hear the claims it might make on its audience, whether that audience is composed of film critics in 1970 or twenty-first-century scholars of film and queer studies.

One subject the early reviews of *The Boys in the Band* avoid in the film is that of gay male sexual behavior. As much as the reviewers profess an easy familiarity with the term *homosexuality* and as much as they can parrot the voices of its homosexuals, they do not explicitly engage with the notion of homosexual practices. But this studied avoidance of sexual specificity itself invites consideration of the sexual dynamics in both the film and the coming-out allegory of its early reception. Consider the conflicted, deeply invested review of *The Boys in the Band* that appeared on March 18 in *Variety*. In one sentence, the writer condenses the posture of familiarity and the imitation of the gay voice that we have observed elsewhere: "the too literately faithful adaptation of Mart Crowley's off-Broadway swish-set piece has enough bitchy, back-biting humor, fascinating character studies, melodrama, and, most of all, perverse interest to draw and hold substantial audiences."[52] The sentence articulates something besides familiarity with and imitation of the homosexual, going so far as to suggest that this thing may matter above all else in evaluating the film's significance for film audiences. According to the writer in *Variety*, what *The Boys in the Band* has, *most of all*, is "perverse interest." What does it mean to say that *The Boys in the Band* has "perverse interest"? What is the content of the thought so suggestively encrypted in the phrase? Of course, this is a textbook example of projection, through which the viewer has attributed to the film what must in fact be his own (homo)sexual curiosity; but the phrase is so generalized, so lacking in explicit content, that it might make room for all sorts of ways of thinking about *The Boys in the Band*. The coming-out of *The Boys in the Band* makes a kind of sexual claim on the reviewer, and the phrase "perverse interest" represents the beginning of a response to that claim. Indeed, the very degree to which the erotic curiosity about the film is successfully repressed in the reviews may give us an idea of how much *The Boys in the Band* may yet disclose. Instead of taking up what this film has yet to show us, the combined effect of existing accounts of *The Boys in the Band*—from the earliest reviews of the film to the most recent works of history and journalism—has been to construct a verdict, spoken as if with one voice, that scorns the film's characterization and regards the film altogether as a relic of a superseded past.

But what would happen if we were to consider the question of the film's "perverse interest" with a more attentive eye and ear? If the reviewers of 1970 were unable to convey directly their wish for access to the homosexual's disclosure—put another way, their repressed wish to occupy the place of the homosexual—we may be better equipped now to appreciate *The Boys in the Band* if we set aside the received ideas about it and observe it anew.

A reading of sexual practices in the film might begin by noting their invisibility: as many commentators have noted, we do not quite see gay sex in the film, and the one romantic kiss Friedkin filmed between Larry and Hank was cut.[53] Yet other ways of thinking about homosexuality are available everywhere in the film: in the kisses that remain (for example, the kisses Cowboy plants on Michael and Harold); in the dialogue's references to tearooms, tricks, baths, ménages à trois, rimming, and blowjobs; in the camera's readiness to survey the men's bodies (as they bathe, dance, sweat); in the erotic expectancy that charges Alan's presence throughout. A more thorough analysis of homosexuality would take up Emory's question "Who do you have to fuck to get a drink around here?" by considering how it might not merely be rhetorical. Indeed, after all that has preceded it, when Michael taunts Alan late in the film with the question "What do you imagine Hank and Larry are doing up there?" both Alan and the audience are well equipped to supply a detailed answer. In light of these observations, all of the stated boredom with which the film was greeted covers over a truly complex and astonishing representation of gay sex.

I comment on the largely unremarked sexuality of the film because it is just one of several potential disclosures to which the early reviews have taught us to shut our ears and our eyes. The film would also surely reward sustained close reading on any of a variety of subjects: the handling of race and ethnicity, evocatively conceptualized together because African American Bernard and Jewish Harold exist on a racial continuum by virtue of a feature they share, "tight black curly hair"; or the discourse about gender, which involves both the men's camp imitation of women and their transgender identification with them; or the subtle tension between a stable, distinctly gay male identity and other, less clearly defined social roles occupied by the very same persons, such as "queer" and "freak." Today, we are equipped with a variety of critical methods for answering questions that have not yet been asked of *The Boys in the Band*. How does this film affect our understanding of William Friedkin's body of work, which we are now poised historically to assess? How might queer theory, with its impulse to unsettle categories of sexual identity, prompt us to reconsider a film that has been simply positioned as a depiction of gay men? How might a deeper engagement with the topic of camp or an application of recent thinking in queer studies about affect help us to hear differently the claims that *The Boys in the Band* makes on us? Pursuing questions like these means setting aside our inherited assumption of familiarity with this film so that we might be available to be surprised by it.

## Band Introductions

The historical distance from *The Boys in the Band*'s turbulent early reception has enabled this volume's contributors to see the film with fresh eyes, and the sheer variety of their approaches testifies to its significance for a host of academic fields today. The very form of this edited collection implies a claim that runs counter to the univocal renunciation of the film: if the textual and sociopolitical dynamics of *The Boys in the Band* are to be understood, then they require multiple, even conflicting framings. The essays' shared concentration on a single cultural artifact not only results in the inclusion of competing arguments about the primary text at this book's center but also enables its chapters to represent at a secondary level a spectrum of available methods in contemporary queer and film studies. Some long-standing critical approaches, such as considerations of film genre and of the auteur, acquire a new vitality when used to examine a film that has a mercurial relation to genre and a director whose signature style is elusive. Moreover, this collection benefits from the emergence of newer methods, perhaps especially those that have followed the gay and lesbian studies of the 1980s and the queer theory of the 1990s. Some of the essays take up the arguments around "positive/negative images" in the tradition of identity politics; some work with a critical vocabulary about such subjects as temporality and affect that are expressive of the most recent debates in queer thought. In different combinations and intensities, perspectives including historicism, empiricism, Marxism, formalism, gender theory, poststructuralism, and critical race theory all make appearances across the contributors' essays, and the contributors themselves come from the disciplines of film and media studies, literary studies, history, theater, and sociology. While the volume does not pretend to survey all possible modes of asking and answering questions about this film, the divergent projects it contains suggest the complex array of motivations and methods available to scholars in the twenty-first century.

This book project began in the rather humble form of a workshop at the 2012 Society for Cinema and Media Studies Conference called "*The Boys in the Band*: The Queer Life of a Gay Film," a workshop prompted by the film's still-recent DVD transfer and by Crayton Robey's documentary feature *Making the Boys*.[54] Like the rest of the session's speakers, I prepared a short talk for the occasion, expecting that this brief foray into a consideration of Friedkin's film would amount to the beginning and end of my work on it. Among the surprises that this book project has afforded me, the first and most motivating was the intensity of that workshop: the scholars who delivered prepared remarks offered a vision of the brilliant and varying products that examination of this film could yield, and the audience members who filled the room were clearly eager to discuss this film at much greater length than the session allowed. The prospect of an edited collection devoted to this film, at first a peculiar whim, slowly and surely became easier to imagine as successful and worthwhile. The existence of other edited collections on individual films made it possible to imagine this one, even as the nonexistence of such a collection in queer studies made the project look necessary.[55] Rather than proceeding with a schematic list of topics to assign to individual contributors, the project developed as I made contact with individual queer-studies scholars across a range of disciplines; in each case, I began by identifying a researcher whose previous work suggested a potentially exciting point of contact with *The Boys in the Band*, but in all cases, I invited the contributors to envision their chapters freely and independently. The outcome of this method is a book that shows the academic value of the "narrowness" of subject matter to which Arnie Kantrowitz objected.

These chapters are organized in three sections, each of which corresponds to one of the terms in the book's subtitle: *cinema, history,* and *queer politics*. The distinctions among these sections are important—it is true that the groups of chapters look intensively into these three domains—but they are also somewhat artificial. Every chapter here has resonance for cinema, history, and queer politics, even as their emphases fall more squarely in one area than in another. In the first section, "Cinematic Transitions," the scholars conduct readings of *The Boys in the Band* in relation to existing appraisals of the film and to its cinematic contexts. Steven Cohan explicates the film by reference to the discourse of camp both in and around the film; in his estimation, the impulse to repudiate the film has stemmed from identifying the film as a whole with its tortured protagonist, Michael, when the film itself provides opportunities to regard the action from the skeptical, ironic perspectives of the camp characters around him. Taking up the affective transformation in Michael that Harold calls "turning," Joe Wlodarz positions Friedkin's film in relation to contemporary cinematic treatments of alcoholism, and his exposition of *The Boys in the Band* makes a splendid case for the politics of Michael's anguish. In a discussion of space and lighting in the film, Ryan Powell demonstrates how this film adopts certain techniques of gothic cinema to evoke a present experience haunted by an oppressive past. Nick Davis examines *The Boys in the Band* in the context of William Friedkin's body of work, and in doing so, he shows how focusing on this film's claustrophobic visual style enables a reframing of Friedkin's career.

The three chapters that make up the second section, "Historical Thresholds," scrutinize *The Boys in the Band* to represent American culture in the throes of transformation. James Wilson traces the history of theatrical productions of *The Boys in the Band*, explaining the galvanic effect that the original production had and then showing how the evolving reputation of the play and film has informed and forced the reconceptualization of stagings from 1968 to 2010. Focusing on the aura of "fun" and "fear" that clung to New York City in the 1970s, David A. Gerstner argues that Friedkin's three New York films of that decade—*The Boys*, *The French Connection*, and *Cruising*—should be understood to register the historical tension between pleasure and anxiety in the form of a cinematic flash. Stephen Vider studies the fascinating but underexamined career of Leonard Frey, the actor who played Harold both Off-Broadway and in the film; Frey's negotiation of the entertainment industry's emergent "Jew Wave" and of the new demands of gay visibility provides a highly compelling case study of the politics of identity from the late 1960s to the 1980s.

The final four essays in this collection are grouped under the heading "Queer-Political Crises," and each one reflects on the political import of *The Boys in the Band* in 1970 and for our contemporary queer discourse. In an act of fabulous critical imagination, Ramzi Fawaz argues that the very elements of *The Boys in the Band* that have been reviled over time—the hostility and bitchiness voiced by the characters—are best understood by reference to the model of late-1960s consciousness-raising. Matthew Tinkcom uses contemporary queer Marxist theory to examine the film's thinking about consumption, showing how the reified objects that make up so much of the film's mise-en-scène express deeply rooted conflicts, including homophobic oppression and class consciousness. J. Todd Ormsbee's chapter places the film in the context of a late-1960s discourse on the possibility and specificity of "gay love," and in doing so, he sheds light on our contemporary discourse about same-sex marriage. Finally, Amy Villarejo considers the allegorical suggestiveness of the film's climactic "telephone game," noting how Michael's apartment functions as a kind of sociopolitical acoustic chamber, tapped by external forces and still resonant today.

*The American Heritage Dictionary* defines the term *flashpoint* first by reference to its literal conceptual meaning in thermodynamics: a flashpoint is "the lowest temperature at which the vapor of a combustible liquid can be made to ignite momentarily in air." A flashpoint represents a threshold, a point past which a certain reaction or event has the potential to take place. The essays collected in this volume explore a cinematic world, a culture, and a set of political ideas all on the brink of radical change. For some chapters, it would be right to call that change an explosion or a revolution; for some others, it would make more sense to think of the change as the slow burn of nearly imperceptible social transformation; for others still, that change means a kind of burst of illumination, or a joyful exuberance that I would not be the first to call *flaming*. What these assembled scholars share is a common awareness that *The Boys in the Band* presents them with an exceptional opportunity to expand our collective knowledge about the intersection of cinematic form, cultural history, and queer political discourse.

## Notes

1. The events popularly known as the Stonewall Riots began as a spontaneous, violent resistance to the police raid of a gay bar in Greenwich Village called the Stonewall Inn in the early morning hours of Saturday, June 28, 1969. That first incident was followed by crowd gatherings and protests on the succeeding two nights, which abated for a couple of days and then resumed on Wednesday and through the following Fourth of July holiday weekend. The best account of the riots is David Carter's *Stonewall: The Riots That Sparked the Gay Revolution* (New York: St. Martin's, 2004). Details about the film's production schedule appear in several sources. One that appears to verify the simultaneity of the film's production with the Stonewall Riots is a Cinema Center press release, which notes that *The Boys in the Band* "went before the cameras in New York in late June 1969." "Production Notes: Mart Crowley's 'The Boys in the Band,'" press release, n.d., Cinema Center Films, Film Study Center, Museum of Modern Art, New York City, 9. See also Katie Kelly, "The 'Boys' Are Having a Bit of a Party Again," *New York Times*, July 13, 1969. Curiously, director William Friedkin misremembers this history, stating in a 2015 interview, "About a year before we started, the Stonewall riots occurred." Matthew Hays, "Back to the *Boys*: An Interview with William Friedkin," *Cineaste* 40, no. 4 (2015): 15.

2. Mart Crowley's play divides the action into two acts with an intermission. In the play, Harold arrives at the end of act 1, and all of the following action takes up the longer second act. See Mart Crowley, *The Boys in the Band* (New York: Samuel French, 1968).

3. Stanley Kauffmann, "Homosexual Drama and Its Disguises," *New York Times*, January 23, 1966. In a 1993 interview, Crowley stated that Kauffmann's article had prompted his writing of the play. See Richard Kramer, "A Play of

Words about a Play," *New York Times*, October 31, 1993. See also Charles Kaiser, *The Gay Metropolis: The Landmark History of Gay Life in America since World War II* (New York: Harcourt Brace, 1997), 185–86.

4. Mart Crowley, "The Author of 'The Boys in the Band' Tells How He Wrote Controversial Work," press release, n.d., Cinema Center Films, Film Study Center, Museum of Modern Art, New York City, 7.

5. The film retains the direct verbal references to Williams and Inge, and though it does not mention Albee by name, its general naturalism, alcohol-fueled intensity, and climactic telephone game all recall elements of that playwright's *Who's Afraid of Virginia Woolf?* (1962).

6. These details about the film adaptation come from "Production Notes," 5–6; Crowley, "Author," 10–11; and Crayton Robey's documentary *Making the Boys* (New York: First Run Features, 2010), DVD. Notably, the film's use of two recordings of Cole Porter's song "Anything Goes" during its opening montage represents a break with Crowley's stipulation about music.

7. Charles Kaiser, *The Gay Metropolis: The Landmark History of Gay Life in America since World War II* (Boston: Houghton Mifflin, 1997), 190. As Kaiser points out in a note, the phrasing in Kameny's letter is subtle: Kameny probably was not even aware of *The Boys in the Band* when he coined the slogan (369). Even so, it is notable that Kameny went on to understand *The Boys in the Band* as the purveyor of an oppression that his own discourse opposed.

8. Arnie Kantrowitz, "Homosexuals and Literature," *College Literature* 36, no. 3 (1974): 326. Kantrowitz adds that his course benefited from an appearance by his friend Vito Russo, who presented a compilation of film clips to represent the depiction of homosexuals in film history (327). Of course, this work became the basis for Russo's widely influential book *The Celluloid Closet: Homosexuality in the Movies*, rev. ed. (New York: Harper and Row, 1987). I return later in this introduction to Russo's account of Friedkin's film.

9. *The Boys in the Band* (1970), directed by William Friedkin (Hollywood, CA: CBS, 2008–15), DVD/Blu-ray.

10. William Friedkin, "Silences," in *The Friedkin Connection: A Memoir* (New York: HarperCollins, 2013), 122–38.

11. Sascha Cohen, "How One Movie Changed LGBT History," *Time.com*, March 17, 2015, http://time.com/3742951/boys-in-the-band/. See Hays, "Back to the *Boys*"; and Travis Crawford, "William Friedkin and *The Boys*," Fandor, August 3, 2015, www.fandor.com/keyframe/william-friedkin.

12. John Loughery, *The Other Side of Silence: Men's Lives and Gay Identities: A Twentieth-Century History* (New York: Holt, 1998), 298.

13. For a very fine account of *Brokeback Mountain*'s popular appeal, see D. A. Miller, "On the Universality of *Brokeback Mountain*," *Film Quarterly* 60, no. 3 (2007): 50–60.

14. Examples of American psychiatric writing that paints the homosexual in pathological shades include Edmund Bergler, *Homosexuality: Disease or Way of Life?* (New York: Hill and Wang, 1956); and Irving Bieber et al., *Homosexuality: A Psychoanalytic Study of Male Homosexuals* (New York: Basic Books, 1962). By way of criticizing Lee Edelman's book *No Future: Queer Theory and the Death Drive*, Jack Halberstam (writing under the name Judith) finds fault with the book's "narrow vision of an archive of negativity" and goes on to connect it to the "excessively small" "gay male archive" that is "bound by a particular range of affective responses." Judith Halberstam, "The Politics of Negativity in Recent Queer Theory," *PMLA* 121, no. 3 (2006): 824.

15. Pauline Kael, "The Current Cinema," *New Yorker*, March 21, 1970, 166.

16. Matt Bell, "When Harry Met Harry," in *Shakesqueer: A Queer Companion to the Complete Works of Shakespeare*, ed. Madhavi Menon (Durham, NC: Duke University Press, 2011), 106–13.

17. See Teresa de Lauretis, "*Queer Theory: Lesbian and Gay Sexualities*: An Introduction," *differences* 3, no. 2 (1991): iii–xviii; and Judith Butler, *Bodies That Matter: On the Discursive Limits of "Sex"* (New York: Routledge, 1993). These influential texts theorize queerness as the mark of exclusion, and both suggest that the project of queer theory should serve the democratic aim of representing formerly marginalized queer figures. De Lauretis, in an essay that includes a critique of "the model of contemporary North American pluralism," insists nevertheless that "racial as well as gender differences are a crucial area of concern for queer theory" (iii, xi). A passage in Butler's book illustrates well the tension between a goal of multicultural inclusion and a recognition of the powerful political forces activated through the inevitable exclusions of discourse: "it is important to resist that theoretical gesture of pathos in which exclusions are simply affirmed as sad necessities of signification. The task is to refigure this necessary 'outside' as a future horizon, one in which the violence of exclusion is perpetually in the process of being overcome. But of equal importance is the preservation of the outside, the site where discourse meets its limits, where the opacity of what is not included in a given regime of truth acts as a disruptive site of linguistic impropriety and unrepresentability, illuminating the violent and contingent boundaries of that normative regime precisely through the inability of that regime to represent that which might pose a fundamental threat to its continuity. In this sense, radical and inclusive representability is not precisely the goal: to include, to speak as, to bring in every marginal and excluded position within a given discourse is to claim that a singular discourse meets its limits nowhere, that it can and will domesticate all signs of discourse" (53).

18. Heather Love, *Feeling Backward: Loss and the Politics of Queer History* (Durham, NC: Duke University Press, 2007).

19. John Reid, *The Best Little Boy in the World* (1976; repr., New York: Ballantine Books, 1993).

20. Dennis Altman, *Homosexual: Oppression and Liberation* (1972; repr., New York: NYU Press, 1993), 178.

21. Donn Teal, "Why Can't 'We' Live Happily Ever After, Too?," *New York Times*, February 23, 1969, published under the pen name Ronald Forsythe and reprinted as appendix A in Teal, *The Gay Militants: How Gay Liberation Began in America, 1969–1971* (New York: St. Martin's, 1995), 335–42.

22. Loughery, *Other Side of Silence*, 297.

23. Vito Russo, *The Celluloid Closet: Homosexuality in the Movies*, rev. ed. (New York: Harper and Row, 1987), 176, 177.

24. Ibid., 175.

25. Ibid., 177.

26. Norine Dresser, "'The Boys in the Band Is Not Another Musical': Male Homosexuals and Their Folklore," *Western Folklore* 33, no. 3 (1974): 205–18; Allison Graham, "'Outrageous!' and 'The Boys in the Band': The Possibilities and Limitations of Coming Out," *Film Criticism*, September 1, 1980, 36–42.

27. See Joe Carrithers, "The Audiences of *The Boys in the Band*," *Journal of Popular Film and Television* 23, no. 2 (1995): 64–70; Philip Brian Harper, "Walk-On Parts and Speaking Subjects: Screen Representations of Black Gay Men," *Callaloo* 18, no. 2 (1995): 390–94; Rodger Streitmatter, "*The Boys in the Band*: Homosexuality Comes to the Big Screen," in *From "Perverts" to "Fab Five": The Media's Changing Depiction of Gay Men and Lesbians* (New York: Routledge, 2009), 26–37; and Pamela Robertson Wojcik, "'We Like Our Apartment': The Playboy Indoors," in *The Apartment Plot: Urban Living in American Film and Popular Culture, 1945 to 1975* (Durham, NC: Duke University Press, 2010), 88–138. Other academic treatments include the following: David Román, "Theater Journals: Dance Liberation," *Theater Journal* 55, no. 3 (2003): vii–xxiv; Timothy Scheie, "Acting Gay in the Age of Queer: Pondering the Revival of *The Boys in the Band*," *Modern Drama* 42, no. 1 (1999): 1–15; William Scroggie, "Producing Identity: From *The Boys in the Band* to Gay Liberation," in *The Queer Sixties*, ed. Patricia Juliana Smith (New York: Routledge, 1999), 237–54; and Ashis Sengupta, "'Coming Out of the Closet': Re-reading *The Boys in the Band* and *On a Muggy Night in Mumbai*," *Journal of American Drama and Theater* 22, no. 1 (2010): 33–49.

28. Harry M. Benshoff and Sean Griffin, *Queer Images: A History of Gay and Lesbian Film in America* (Lanham, MD: Rowman and Littlefield, 2006).

29. Nat Segaloff, *Hurricane Billy: The Stormy Life and Films of William Friedkin* (New York: William Morrow, 1990); Thomas D. Clagett, *William Friedkin: Films of Aberration, Obsession, and Reality*, 2nd ed. (Los Angeles: Silman-James, 2003).

30. Kaiser, *Gay Metropolis*, 190.

31. Loughery, *Other Side of Silence*, 302.

32. David Eisenbach, *Gay Power: An American Revolution* (New York: Carroll and Graf, 2006), 81.

33. Carter, *Stonewall*, 113.

34. Dudley Clendinen and Adam Nagourney, *Out for Good: The Struggle to Build a Gay Rights Movement in America* (New York: Simon and Schuster, 1999), 16.

35. Lillian Faderman and Stuart Timmons, *Gay L.A.: A History of Sexual Outlaws, Power Politics, and Lipstick Lesbians* (New York: Basic Books, 2006), 268.

36. Examples include Linda Hirshman, *Victory: The Triumphant Gay Revolution* (New York: HarperCollins, 2012); Marc Stein, *Rethinking the Gay and Lesbian Movement* (New York: Routledge, 2012); and Lillian Faderman, *The Gay Revolution: The Story of the Struggle* (New York: Simon and Schuster, 2015).

37. J. Hoberman, "Wisecracks in Drag and Blackface in 'Eddie Cantor 4-Film Collection,'" *New York Times*, July 12, 2015.

38. David Mermelstein, "Review: 'The Boys in the Band,'" *Variety*, November 12, 2008.

39. Dave White, "Where the Boys Were," *Advocate*, November 18, 2008, 56.

40. Eve Kosofsky Sedgwick, *Epistemology of the Closet* (Berkeley: University of California Press, 1990), 46.

41. Stanley Kauffmann, "*Women in Love / The Boys in the Band*," *New Republic*, April 18, 1970, 20; Vincent Canby, "Screen: 'Boys in the Band': Crowley Study of Male Homosexuality Opens," *New York Times*, March 18, 1970; Kael, "Current Cinema," 161–67; Joseph Morgenstern, "Eight Desperate Men," *Newsweek*, March 30, 1970, 91.

42. Judith Crist, "Memoir of Greatness Past," *New York*, April 13, 1970, 46–47; John Gruen, "The Boys in the Band, 'Explosive,'" *Vogue*, May 1970, 152.

43. Kauffmann, "*Women in Love / The Boys in the Band*," 28.

44. Sedgwick, *Epistemology*, 81.

45. Ibid., 80.

46. Canby, "Screen: 'Boys in the Band.'"

47. "Shades of Lavender," *Time*, March 30, 1970, 100; Richard Schickel, "Now Playing: The Four-Letter Word," *Life*, April 10, 1970, 12.

48. Kael, "Current Cinema," 167.

49. Gene Siskel, "Movie Review: 'The Boys in the Band,'" *Chicago Tribune*, March 20, 1970, B17.

50. Interest in something called "gay voice" continues, for example, in David Thorpe's 2014 film *Do I Sound Gay?*

51. Sedgwick, *Epistemology*, 81.

52. "The Boys in the Band," *Variety*, March 18, 1970, 18.

53. Friedkin explains the decision to cut the shot, but he adds, "In retrospect, I think we should have kept it" (*Friedkin Connection*, 137).

54. David Gerstner and Joe McElhaney organized and led the workshop, and the other speakers were Paula Massood, Matthew Tinkcom, Crayton Robey, and I.

55. Edited collections devoted to single films include Bruce H. Sklarew, Bonnie S. Kaufman, Ellen Handler Spitz, and Diane Borden, eds., *Bertolucci's "The Last Emperor": Multiple Takes* (Detroit: Wayne State University Press, 1998); Arthur M. Eckstein and Peter Lehman, eds., *"The Searchers": Essays and Reflections on John Ford's Classic Western* (Detroit: Wayne State University Press, 2004); David Slocum, ed., *"Rebel without a Cause": Approaches to a Maverick Masterwork* (Albany: State University of New York Press, 2005); and Yannis Tzioumakis and Siân Lincoln, eds., *The Time of Our Lives: "Dirty Dancing" and Popular Culture* (Detroit: Wayne State University Press, 2013). Pioneering edited collections devoted to queer theory and cinema include Bad Object-Choices, ed., *How Do I Look? Queer Film and Video* (Seattle: Bay, 1991); and Ellis Hanson, ed., *Out Takes: Essays on Queer Theory and Film* (Durham, NC: Duke University Press, 1999). Short, single-authored volumes about individual queer films have more recently appeared, including John Coldstream, *Victim* (London: Palgrave Macmillan, 2011); John Gill, *Far from Heaven* (London: Palgrave Macmillan, 2011); and Lucas Hildebrand, *"Paris Is Burning": A Queer Film Classic* (Vancouver: Arsenal Pulp Press, 2013).

# CINEMATIC TRANSITIONS

# 1

# Let's Hear a Round of Applause for the Camps in the Band

## STEVEN COHAN

*The Boys in the Band* (1970) could not withstand the proverbial test of time before its time had even passed. Upon its release in March 1970, the film was already being perceived as re-creating with seeming historical indifference the Off-Broadway play's antiquated representation of a pre-Stonewall milieu where gays were either sad, self-hating men or flamboyant queens; where homosexual desire was understood by gay men themselves as a poor imitation of heterosexuality; and where camp equaled the closet and therefore should now be repudiated as politically incorrect by gay activists and "straight-acting" gay men alike (despite how camp would later well serve activist campaigns like ACT-UP).[1] At this time, as far as mainstream films were concerned, a gay man had to be neutered, as in the personae of sissy comedians like Paul Lynde in movies or Charles Nelson Reilly on television, or made a figure of abjection, as in the characters Marlon Brando and Rod Steiger played in *Reflections in a Golden Eye* (1967) and *The Sergeant* (1968), respectively. Otherwise, mainstream audiences and most reviewers generally found queer representations offensive or unintelligible—as made evident by the even more hostile critical reception of *Myra Breckinridge* (1970), which opened just a few months after *The Boys in the Band*.[2]

By now, and with reference to both the play and its film version, the reputation of *The Boys in the Band* seems irrevocably bound to that unsympathetic critique. As David W. Dunlop recalled in the *New York Times* about the original stage production as prompted by the play's 1996 revival,

At its opening in 1968, Mart Crowley's Off Broadway play was hailed as a breakthrough, a close-up of gay life more candid than theatergoers had ever witnessed. Audiences were electrified by its frank depiction of eight explicitly homosexual characters stumbling and clawing their way through a most unhappy birthday party.

Halfway through its run, however, "The Boys in the Band" was overtaken by political history and entombed in popular opinion as a homophobic screed.

The proximate cause was the Stonewall uprising in 1969, when patrons of the Stonewall Inn in Greenwich Village battled police officers who were trying to close the gay bar. Their resistance is often cited as the birth of the modern gay-rights movement.

After Stonewall, the play was increasingly dismissed as synonymous with a culture that gay leaders were eager to disavow: closeted, catty, campy, narcissistic, alcoholic and, above all, self-loathing. To underscore their contempt, members of the Gay Liberation Front staged a protest at the Los Angeles premiere of the 1970 movie which was directed by William Friedkin and used the original cast.

Having broken a taboo, "The Boys in the Band" had become taboo itself.[3]

Truth to tell, *The Boys in the Band* had always acknowledged that type of hostile response to its late-1960s portrait of gay male culture through its token straight character, Alan (Peter White). The nonstop camp chatter and repartee of Emory (Cliff Gorman) disgust Alan to the point of violence. "I just can't stand that kind of talk. It just grates on me," he tells Michael (Kenneth Nelson), who asks with feigned innocence, "What kind of talk, Alan?" The straight man replies, "Oh, you know. His brand of humor, I guess." By contrast, Alan is much taken with the more athletic, pipe-smoking, straight-acting demeanor of Hank (Laurence Luckinbill). The undisguised antagonism to Emory's "talk" validates Alan as a "normal" outsider and hence privileged observer of the "unhappy" homosexuals at the party who, to return to Dunlop's account, consequently seem "closeted, catty, campy, narcissistic, alcoholic and, above all, self-loathing." Alan, in short, marks out a viewing position for straight audiences in 1970 that defines itself through an open antagonism to camp ("*that* kind of talk" and "*his* brand of humor") and thus to the queer social milieu still identified by the gay characters' camp.

Such unsympathetic responses to the film still occur, the result, I think, of viewers and critics aligning their responses too closely with Michael, the self-hating leading character and Mart Crowley surrogate, in concert with his heterosexual college roommate, Alan—although, to be sure, in terms of formal and narrative conventions, the film, like the play, does appear to encourage, even structure such a close, if not entirely sympathetic, identification. According to conventional wisdom criticizing the film, together these two tormented characters motivate an audience's distance from all the other gay characters.

Writing in 1995, for example, Joe Carrithers argues that the film version takes obvious pains to enable "a 'comfortable' experience for straight viewers." He points out that "the only successful or happy men in the film" are the couple Hank and Larry (Keith Prentice), whose relationship Carrithers believes most closely resembles a heterosexual marriage, and Alan, the party's observer and crasher and the ostensibly straight spectator's representative, who returns to his wife and children. "None of the other characters in the play or film," Carrithers claims, "elicits sympathy in the audience for gay men and their lives, a criticism that has been made for more than 20 years."[4] Carrithers goes on to locate the emotional isolation of the gay partygoers in the film's camera work and editing, which he believes dwell on lonely faces in close-up as a means of formally distancing straight viewers from the characters, thereby actively preventing audience empathy with their homosexuality. "The screen often shows only one man," Carrithers explains, "suggesting that he is not part of a community but alone. Each time the camera focuses on a group of men (or entire party), it soon changes back to close-ups."[5] However, why cannot one presume the reverse of what Carrithers observes? For is it not just as easy to conclude, while watching *The Boys in the Band*, that every time the camera moves in for a histrionic close-up, the editing changes back to some or all of the characters configured in a group (or as the entire party), registering again the force of their gay communal viewpoints as alternatives to Michael's and Alan's?[6]

Twenty-first-century viewers of *The Boys in the Band* may perhaps be better able to appreciate the greater sexual openness of the partygoers despite the seemingly unsympathetic viewpoint inscribed by Michael and Alan. In a 1999 article, Timothy Scheie points out how history has irrevocably altered one's sense of the play and by implication the film adaptation too. "It is the most outrageously effeminate character," he writes about the play's revival, "the lisping interior decorator Emory, who emerges as the hero of the group when he defiantly stands up to the boorish insults of the drunk Alan and, at the risk of physical injury, dares to exhibit his sexuality while all the others attempt to pass as well as they can."[7]

Scheie is not referring to Emory's camp bravado but to the moment when he verbally lashes back at Alan, who physically attacks him in retaliation, bloodying Emory's face and his sweater. So what the critic has in mind are some dramatic social changes determining what Emory's empowered effeminacy may now signify for gay culture, which has altered the value attributed to his refusing to efface his homosexuality in front of a hostile straight man who presumes his own normality and demands deference to the authority that comes with it. Indeed, from this perspective, Emory now seems more like he could be one of the drag queens at the Stonewall Inn when they finally declared that enough was enough. But even as that implicit sense of retroactive historical heroism gets attached to Emory, it is worth noting that, while I am unaware if the revival's Emory lisped, in the film, although Cliff Gorman purses his lips and speaks breathlessly in a voice like Marilyn Monroe's, he does not lisp. I mention this detail because Scheie's appreciation, it seems to me, is also recuperating what had formerly been the reason for repudiating the film when it premiered, namely that, much as Michael's character invites one to believe, the homosexuals on display here are those sixties stereotypes promulgated by Hollywood, either tormented and self-hating or effeminate and campy to the point of being stereotypical queens—hence the critic's shorthand when referring to Emory as "the lisping interior decorator."

This "new" millennial sense of *The Boys in the Band*, then, does not amount to a radical revision of the material. For the most vocal camp figures—not only Emory but also Harold (Leonard Frey) and to a lesser extent Donald (Frederick Combs)—have always worked to historicize the late-1960s moment of gay culture represented by this film. Their verbal and spatial presence at the birthday party expressively reframes Michael's role as thematic spokesman and author surrogate, creating distance from his perspective by widening the film's queer perspective on the party. Emory's camp motivates his bravery in standing up to Alan, and it also implicitly accounts for why he can later show the same man some unexpected generosity, which Michael mocks derisively. It is the case that Michael himself enters the film expressing a knowing camp wit and sense of camp community, and later, he *thinks* he is being astute and clever in his camp put-downs of his guests until *he* breaks down after most of them leave; but as the evening progresses and he assumes an increasingly smug, superior tone, Michael's camp viewpoint falters, for his friends cease responding to what he says *as* camp. Rather, as he becomes more emotionally isolated from everyone present, Michael's repartee become increasingly hostile and aggressive; furthermore, as his desire to humiliate his friends moves the drama forward toward the requisite confessions in the film's third act, Michael's distance from the party's camaraderie dramatically registers how the camp ethos pervading *The Boys in the Band* reverses the kind of straight viewer disengagement that Carrithers proposes. Far from privileging heterosexual disgust toward homosexuals or degrading the manliness of the gay characters, I argue, the camp humor conveys the communality of the party, characterizes it as gay in both senses of the word rather than just sad, and most of all underscores how an engaged queer camp spectatorship like Emory's or Harold's yields more value and insight than either the alienated straight viewpoint personified by Alan or the self-hating one personified by Michael.

Taking issue with a gay or straight hostile reading of *The Boys in the Band*, this chapter therefore seeks to look beyond Michael and Alan's twinned viewpoint, and, with Carrithers's critique in mind, it will briefly return to the use of background and group shots in relation to close-ups. I intend to reconsider the enduring assessment of *The Boys in the Band* as having been and remaining "always already dated" because of the camp in its characterizations, humor, and outlooks on homosexuality and on the private worlds of gay male culture in sixties Manhattan.

## How to Be Camp

"Camp," as Richard Dyer memorably wrote in an essay first published in 1975, "is not masculine. By definition, camping about is not butch. So camping is a way of being human, witty and vital (for the whole camp stance is full of vitality), without conforming to the drabness and rigidity of the hetero male role."[8] That is not to say, however, that camp feminizes gay men; rather, its strategies of self-representation and subcultural tastes have knowingly worked to distance gay men from the oppressive confinement of the dominant culture's production of heterosexual masculinity as well as femininity. Camp was a phenomenon of passing in the era of closeted homosexuality, to be sure. But while providing a coded discourse for covertly expressing one's homosexuality and reading someone else's, camp was always more than just a means of cruising in public before the blind eyes of straights: as the argot of gay urban culture, camp viewed and reframed the social order from the margins, which is why it defined a queer style of living deliberately set in tension with perceived standards of ordinariness.

Elsewhere, in my book on the MGM musical, I have called camp "the queer eye for a straight guise" because, as a subcultural response to the enforced invisibility of homosexuality in the first half of the twentieth century, camp is best understood as "the ironic, self-reflective style of gay men passing as straight, who kept a 'straight face' so as not to let outsiders in on the joke, while simultaneously winking at the initiated in shared acknowledgement of it."[9] Queer camp (itself, to my mind, always a redundant phrasing) needs to be remembered as a historical social practice responsive to the closeted lives of gay men who inhabited an otherwise straight culture; it was significantly different in tone, complexity, nuance, and irony from its subsequent appropriation in the sixties by pop art and mass camp viewership of old films and film stars. *The Boys in the Band*, both in its representation of gay culture and as a cultural object in its own right, appeared in theaters at the historical moment when camp, in effect, came out of that closet—which goes a long way toward explaining why the film may have seemed so instantly dated to the point of being retrograde, a product *of* the closet. But the timing of its release also accounts for the film's own historical immediacy in capturing when the cultural and sexual politics of camp were made more visible, although, as *The Boys in the Band* shows, the impact was equal parts laughter and discomfort.

In the recent book *How to Be Gay*, David Halperin cites Emory's "camping about" with his birthday present for Harold, the cowboy hustler (Robert La Tourneaux), to illustrate the mapping of gay culture around the dualism of camp queens and butch trade. Halperin refers specifically to the moment when the hustler explains how he hurt his back during a workout: "I lost my grip doing my chin-ups and I fell on my heels and twisted my back." Emory snaps, "You shouldn't wear heels when you do chin-ups." Quoting this exchange, Halperin asks why *The Boys in the Band* even needs to include the young, pretty, and dumb hustler in its representation of a gay party. As he specifically puts the question, "Why is it that, in order for a party composed of gay men to be truly successful, there has to be at least one each of two different species of gay men present: the beauty and the camp? What makes each essential?"[10]

Halperin's aim in this chapter of *How to Be Gay* is to show why gay culture and queer sensibility, epitomized in camp, are always divided from a homosexual desire for male "beauty," which is itself still "[borrowing] from the opposition between masculine and feminine in the dominant, heteronormative gender system."[11] According to Halperin, camping at a gay male social gathering without a virile object of homosexual desire also present would bond the guests together in what he calls "the sisterhood," just as a party guest list of assorted virile young men without campy observers

The Camp and the Beauty. Emory tells Cowboy he shouldn't wear heels when he does chin-ups.

would incite "one-upmanship," turning the party into "an endless display of humorless butch theatrics."[12] In this account, camp (the discourse of gay culture) and male beauty (the impersonal object of gay desire) are situated in opposition to each other, so the binarized terms are understood to be antagonistic. Camp, according to Halperin, is "best understood when it is seen in this *relational* context—as gay male culture's way of trying to disintoxicate itself from its own erotic and aesthetic passion for masculine beauty."[13] As opposites, the beauty and the camp must be paired because the presence of each is necessary to effect the counterbalancing of opposites that provides the gay male gathering (and, by implication, the wider social milieu of gay male passions) with its social coherence—which is also to say that, for Halperin, the camp and the beauty do not coexist as a single person. Each "species of gay men" is "different," he insists, so one is either a camp *or* a beauty.

I well understand that Halperin is trying to account for gay culture's tendency to disaggregate companionship and camaraderie, on one hand, from sexual desiring and homosexual desirability, on the other. "The polarity of queer sensibility and sexual desire," he argues, "reminds those who participate in gay male culture of their inescapable implication in gendered values, erotic dichotomies, and other social meanings." As a result, he concludes, "the world gay men inhabit constantly reminds them of their lack of exemption from the brute realities of sexual stratification, cultural signification, and social power."[14] That statement seems indisputable, to be sure, as *The Boys in* the Band reveals. Never leaving Michael's apartment once the party begins, *The Boys in the Band* visualizes the men's marginalized position according to "the brute realities" of midcentury America, as evident in the opening montage of the characters going about their lives with varying degrees of (in)visibility as gay men in an otherwise straight Manhattan. It follows as well from subsequent remarks of characters about the "outside" world that the privacy of coming together in another gay man's apartment offers relief from the realities of an oppressive heteronormative order, and here in the film, it does so through the queer camaraderie at the birthday party.[15]

As far as concerns the immersion of *The Boys in the Band* in its historical moment, I am therefore not convinced that a tension between the camp and the beauty is what gives that party and its camaraderie their queer coherence as a gathering of gay males. Consider again Cowboy, the supposed "beauty." He may be objectified as one of the birthday gifts, but after his entrance, he is not sexualized by the guests, who make quips that go over his head, insult him to his face, ignore him to the point that he dozes off, or silence him, as Michael does during the game. Harold comments that Cowboy "has unnatural natural beauty" but then asks sarcastically, "How can his beauty ever compare with my soul?" which his mother's rabbi assures him "is a knockout." When Emory asks Harold how he likes his surprise present, Harold replies with ironic understatement: "Oh, I suppose he has an interesting face and body—but it turns me right off because he can't talk intelligently about art." After Emory and Harold banter a bit more, Emory concludes, "She may be dumb, but she's all yours!" Their camp exchange turns the superficial, if "gorgeous," Cowboy into a "she," which effectively makes the two camp observers the "men" in this exchange. Reinforcing Emory and Harold's treatment of the hustler, Donald and Larry, who cruise as actively as the more "effeminate" Emory and Harold, pay no heed to, let alone compete for, Cowboy's physical charms, as one might expect they might do after reading Halperin on the dynamics of a gay male party.

Cowboy not only is an easy target for every camp put-down he receives but also shows little interest himself in promoting his sexual allure at the party, since he is actually hoping to shortchange Emory by still making it to the bars and then getting to bed early to rest his injured back. There are moments when the camera eroticizes Cowboy by dwelling on his body, to be sure, as when Emory cruises him along with two other hustlers in the opening montage or when, stoned on Harold's pot, the hustler later slow dances with the floating red cellophane gift wrapping. Nonetheless, on his own "merits" and lacking the supplementary mediation of the party guests' erotic gazing, the muscular but vacant Cowboy is not an independent figuration of male beauty; on the contrary, he is *already* a camp refraction of male beauty before he arrives at Michael's, being at once the dumb blond and the parody of a sexualized masculinity modeled on "looking straight," the midnight cowboy. Emory, after all, is the one who gives him the cowboy costume, as evident by the cowboy hat in the shopping bag Emory carries when he purchases the hustler's services in the film's opening montage. Cowboy is no intellectual match for anyone at the party. He is eroticized only by virtue of his being given "in trade" as a birthday present, and whatever sexual value he has as the epitome of male "beauty" is thus openly and effectively negated by a camp appropriation that makes him a cartoonish and unthreatening version of the "hetero male role" that, as Dyer noted not too long after *The Boys in the Band*'s release, is drab and rigid—not to say vacuous and boring—and readily available for camp irony at the party.

Because Cowboy is a cartoonish reduction of male beauty, he personifies the commodified stereotype of straight virility, the Marlboro Man turned into seedy hustler in the gay imaginary of the sixties. For this reason and from the perspective of his merely impersonating male "beauty," Cowboy cannot compete with either Larry or Hank, whose more virile masculinity, already apparent in the opening montage, is neither treated with any perceived camp irony by other guests nor subject to Michael's mockery. Indeed, if there is a full-blooded "beauty" in attendance at the party, it ought to be Larry, given his liberal attitudes about sexual desire and promiscuity. In a slight change from the play, in which he is described as a commercial artist, Larry is now represented as a fashion photographer but one without erotic interest in his female models, so his profession links his homosexuality to his deviance from heterosexual virility and desire. Larry's robust homosexuality is never set in any kind of tension with camp wit (which he enjoys) or the camps (who are his friends and for whom he shows affection). Similarly, the body of Larry's partner, the more conservative-appearing and monogamous Hank, is at times featured visually as a potential object for a viewer's homoerotic gaze, as when Hank's open, rain-soaked shirt reveals his hairy chest throughout the film's third act. Further, Hank appears to excite Alan's suppressed homoerotic interest, yet Alan is straight and therefore out of the gay circuit of sexual/camp exchange that Halperin examines. For all Hank's distance from the party's gay argot and energy, he, like his partner, Larry, is also not situated in dialectical opposition to the camps.

Instead of the beauty-camp dialectic stressed by Halperin, then, what I see giving this party its queer coherence—and its biting wit—as an expression of homosexual community is the ability of camp exchanges like Emory and Harold's to disaggregate gay culture not necessarily from gay sexual passion, as Halperin claims (since the camp characters do cruise and go to the baths), but from a heteronormative society that views homosexuality and homosexual culture as simply and perversely "bad" imitations of straight desires and behaviors. The whole point of this birthday party, whether on film or onstage, is that it definitely and defiantly does *not* resemble a social gathering of straight men. That entrée into a milieu otherwise located behind closed doors, as far as straight audiences were concerned, is what electrified them when the play premiered in 1968, as Dunlap recalls, and what the film likewise provides.

## Are You Sure It's Not a Musical?

Halperin's references to "the camp" as "the beauty's" opposite derives from the anthropologist Esther Newton's ethnographic study of gay culture *Mother Camp*, based on field interviews conducted in Chicago and Kansas City in the 1960s and published in 1972. Newton found that, like the drag queen, the camp was a distinctive social position within the queer circles in which she conducted her interviews. It is therefore important to note that, far from setting the camp in opposition to the beauty, as Halperin does, Newton saw the camp linked to drag culture but distinctive from drag queens insofar as the camp did not do drag; rather, the camp functioned socially as "a homosexual wit and clown; his campy productions and performances are a continuous creative strategy for dealing with the homosexual situation, and, in the process, defining a positive homosexual identity."[16] Far from being overly feminized, the camp articulated camp attitudes through his satiric wit and theatrical posturing; functioning as a social commentator speaking for and to his social circle, the camp's knowingness about how straight and gay were each incongruously performative and in dialectic rapport secured his position as an ironic observer queerly distanced from straight tastes, desires, and gendered norms.

*The Boys in the Band* is thoroughly informed by that kind of "positive homosexual identity" as made visible through the camp partygoers. To be sure, reviewers and commentators have always noted the camp humor of Mart Crowley's script, whether with reference to the original play or the subsequent screenplay. Beyond the dialogue, the very title of *The Boys in the Band* already carries with it a recognizable camp valence. It alludes to Judy

Garland in the 1954 version of *A Star Is Born*. In *A Star Is Born*, as Garland's Esther Blodgett nervously gets up to leave for her screen test, James Mason's Norman Maine calms her down by telling her, "It's three o'clock in the morning at the Downbeat Club, and you're singing for yourself and for the boys in the band"—a reference to his earlier witnessing of her singing "The Man That Got Away" in a jam session with band members in an otherwise empty nightclub.

Crowley denies consciously thinking of Garland and her film for his title, stating that he had in mind the more innocuous phrase used when a forties Big Band conductor asked an audience to applaud the musicians backing up a lead singer ("Let's hear a round of applause for the boys in the band"). However, the phrase still resonates with knowledge of the Garland film, as Crowley also begrudgingly admits.[17] After all, in that sequence of *A Star Is Born*, Garland is a band singer, so Mason's reference to the musicians accompanying her as "the boys in the band" is in keeping with the way a band's membership was described, just as Crowley states.

The evocative presence of Garland resonates elsewhere in *The Boys in the Band*, too. Early on, before Michael begins drinking, he mimics Garland's "Get Happy" number from *Summer Stock* (1950) and then imitates the famous "big fat close-up" moment from *A Star Is Born*. "What's more boring than a queen doing a Judy Garland imitation?" Michael asks with a self-deprecating tone, to which Donald replies, "A queen doing a Bette Davis imitation." This moment is not the film's only explicit and timely camp reference to old movie stars. Michael declares to Donald, "The only thing 'mature' means to me is Victor Mature," and his friend comments, "Thanks to the silver screen your neurosis has got style." Nor is Michael the only character with such a camp sensibility based on old movie stars. Emory keeps up with him in offering similar one-liners and references to gay icons of lesser renown, such as Maria Montez and Vera Hruba Ralston; and we see Harold skimming through pages of Michael's glossy coffee-table book *The Films of Joan Crawford*. The art direction likewise reflects the camp decor of Michael's apartment: for instance, a framed poster with a line drawing of Marlene Dietrich, advertising art for her one-woman show on Broadway hangs prominently in his kitchen, and elsewhere we can see a large framed drawing of Gloria Swanson in her Norma Desmond guise.

The cultural significance for gay culture of older icons such as Garland, Davis, Dietrich, and Swanson, not to mention Montez and Ralston, is ephemeral, so they are by now historical figures, easily forgotten by a younger generation of viewers—and of actors too, as it turns out. Since the cast

Michael does Judy.

of the 1996 revival of the play, raised on Bette Midler, apparently had no idea that the second *e* in Davis's first name must be pronounced, the *Eloise* illustrator Hilary Knight, a friend of Crowley's, put together two "training films" to instruct the actors in the play's lost cultural references, one with clips of the iconic stars and B cult figures mentioned by the characters and a second one with the scene from *A Star Is Born* when Mason tells Garland to think of "the boys in the band."[18]

Even if Crowley did not have the allusion to Garland and her boys in the band consciously in mind, then, it has since become firmly attached to his title, especially since the playwright has Michael mime the iconic "big fat close-up" gesture from *A Star Is Born*. More so than references to Davis and others, the Garland association gives the title a gloss that explains just why this group of gay men at the birthday party can be so well described as "the boys in the band"—and it is not through their identification with the star as a gay icon of abjection. The title is an indirect nod as well to the musical numbers that Garland did on film for MGM and onstage at the Palace Theater when she was backed up by a troupe of chorus boys and, in effect, acted as the camp performer around whom they bonded.[19]

Matthew Tinkcom was perhaps the first to note, in conjunction with the star's camp appeal, the longtime filmic association of Garland with "the men who surround her," ranging from her three companions in *The Wizard of Oz* (1939) to the numbers in which she is backed by the chorus boys in *Ziegfeld Follies* (1946), *Summer Stock*, and *A Star Is Born*.[20] To this list, one can add her numbers supported by men in *Ziegfeld Girl* (1941) and *The Pirate* (1948). As Tinkcom comments about her one number in *Ziegfeld Follies*, "The dance ensemble depicts an important relation of queers to the figure of Judy Garland, because the young men in this number seem to adore her as fans, but not necessarily as straight men interested in making a sexual score."[21] In *A Star Is Born*, when Mason tells Garland to get over her nervousness by imagining that she will be singing for the boys in the band, he evokes the same type of nonsexual "support" for her. The phrase "the boys in the band" thus connotes the Big Band era *and* the male chorus boys who both performed with Garland and enacted their adoration of her in her numbers. Hence, through this resonance, Crowley's title almost immediately signifies the sense of queer bonding among gay men, through camp performance and camaraderie, that describes the social world of Michael and his friends.

The Garland allusions are not the only times *The Boys in the Band*, pointedly advertised as *not* being a musical, references this genre's gay camp following. At two key points, the film almost breaks into full-fledged musical numbers with a camp flair: in the opening montage introducing the gay characters as they move about New York City, which is set to Harpers Bizarre's cover of Cole Porter's "Anything Goes," and near the halfway point when partygoers dance together like boys in the chorus to Martha and the Vandellas' "(Love Is Like a) Heat Wave" on the back patio. These "numbers" hint at an alternative way to see queer social formations of gay men of the

Line dancing to "(Love Is Like a) Heat Wave."

sort that Tinkcom evokes—the boys in the chorus or the band who do not necessarily need the female star as their reason (or cover) for bonding together. This "musical" implication of the party's early going sets up a tonal contrast with the more disturbing conclusion of Michael's game, itself no doubt inspired by the dramaturgical examples of more ostensibly "straight" plays of the 1960s by Crowley's contemporaries, notably Edward Albee's *Who's Afraid of Virginia Woolf?* But as much to my point, these "numbers" configure a communality among the men that does not subordinate them to a star "performer," the position Michael unsuccessfully tries to claim as he gets meaner and more controlling following Harold's arrival. Forsaking the excuse of bonding around a female star and so bringing out "the boys" from the shadows of the bandstand to the footlights of center stage, these "numbers" visualize *within* the cinematic frame what Hollywood had formerly suppressed and coded so that it only implicitly existed *outside* the frame.

Those two musical "numbers" are both ensemble pieces, reminding us again how Crowley's choice of a title directs attention to *all* the men attending the birthday party, not just to the author's protagonist and surrogate, Michael, who, as the partygoers get drunker and he gets nastier, tries to be the top camp headliner, the "star" with "the boys in the band" orbiting around him. But Michael lacks the penetrating, if still cruel, insight of Harold, the flamboyant yet sassy wit of Emory, and the ironic distance affected by Donald's menial job in the 'burbs and his weekly appointment with his psychiatrist. Their sarcastic asides and caustic direct address to Michael undercut his arrogance and narcissism, exacerbating his self-hatred and motivating his decision to humiliate his friends at the point when Alan makes a halfhearted attempt to leave. Additionally, as the only two men in a coupled relation, Hank and Larry not only fail to conform to a heterosexual norm, given Larry's "old-fashioned" promiscuity, and disappear to have make-up sex in Michael's bedroom, but at times they visibly appreciate Emory's camp humor, functioning as his amused "butch" audience. (To be fair, at points Hank shrinks from Emory's verbal flamboyance too.) Even the more subdued and marginalized Bernard, the African American bookstore clerk who covertly loans books to Donald, gives a camp gift to Harold—the red, bejeweled, monogrammed knee pads—that causes the birthday boy to break up in raucous laughter. "Bernard, you are such a camp!" Emory applauds his best friend. Michael then tries to top that and steal attention with his punning reference to "Rosemary DeCamp," but the witticism fails to get the response from others that the knee pads have provoked.

The film's camp texture originates in its theatrical source, but it is also evident in William Friedkin's direction, starting with that opening montage structured by Cole Porter's song about breaking social norms and boundaries and extending to Friedkin's use of point-of-view shots to keep the men in view during most scenes. These shots frame Michael critically with a camp's awareness, one that enables us to know exactly what he is doing as he descends into drunken self-loathing, barely suppressed envy of and possible desire for his straight friend Alan, and mean-spirited indifference to his guests' feelings. The camp wit flying about in various forms throughout the evening progressively makes Michael the hostile outsider at his own party, with editing often emphasizing his position on the second-floor landing, in the kitchen, or in a corner silently looking at and thus excluded from the friends congregated in his living room.

For this reason, as noted earlier, I think Carrithers misreads the editing. Each time the camera focuses on a single character, it soon changes back to a small grouping of the men (or to the entire party). Even when quoting the established Hollywood convention for filming a character's soulful confession during the few self-revelatory, self-degrading moments of the game, Friedkin rarely sustains the close-up for very long. Instead he cuts to group shots or reverse shots of others looking and listening or shows at least one other partygoer in frame along with the character delivering a speech, visualizing the community of gay men from which Michael feels excluded. Michael, in fact, seems most relaxed in his bedroom with Donald *before* anyone else arrives. Alan's first phone call then makes Michael anxious since it would result in his coming-out, although his friend already seems to know or else to disavow his knowing. As the party progresses, Michael becomes more disengaged from the exuberant party spirit that Hank, Larry, and Emory bring into his flat when they arrive. A short while later, when Emory, who refuses to conceal his gayness, goads Alan into attacking him, Michael stands frozen and helpless as everyone else rushes to Emory's defense.

Until Michael begins his game, in short, he is mostly an observer of the party, not a participant; but nor is he watching it from the camp's perspective. His nervous viewing of the action, emphasized by edits that cut to him looking at the guests gathered outside on his terrace or in the living room, contrasts with Harold's vantage point as a camp observer, which Friedkin's camera and editing likewise mark, whether when Harold ravenously eats Emory's lasagna or when he removes himself afterward to sit at Michael's desk as an explicit observer of the party. Harold watches what Michael is doing with scorn and irony, calling his friend a "hateful sow" and matching

Michael's isolation from the party.

Michael's attacks on him with parries of his own that knowingly hit the right nerve.

The game Michael drunkenly forces on his guests is his vicious retaliation, his attempt to strip them of the dignity they achieve in no small way through their camp. Given his love of movies, one might say that Michael forcibly turns the camp esprit of a musical's "boys in the band," which initially characterizes the tone of the party, into the pathos of a melodrama, which drives the conventionality of the confessions arising from the party game he forces his guests to play. Moreover, Michael's hysterical sobbing after the party concludes makes all too clear how that mean-spirited effort to drive his guests to abjection has merely highlighted his own self-hatred, which the other boys in this band do not share. It is not surprising that Donald, a Saturday-night regular it appears as the film opens, now refuses to stay the night as Michael heads off to Mass in the final moments of the film. Frankly, I would not want to stay either.

## The Camp That Got Away

My point in this chapter, as I indicated when starting, has been to look past the way *The Boys in the Band* has been critiqued for being "always already" out of date. To be sure, a more sympathetic viewpoint for reframing the film may seem more available today than in 1970, as critics like Scheie noted after the 1996 theatrical revival. No doubt history has altered how contemporary viewers, gay or straight, now locate their sympathies with respect to a character like Emory, who bravely stands up to the homophobic Alan, later generously worries if Alan has eaten, and gently accepts the man's apology. I suggest, however, that this sympathetic viewpoint was already available to audiences through the film's camp figures, even if that viewpoint was not readily taken up in 1970—or for many years afterward. Camp, after all, was a cultural practice before Stonewall, and its political aim was not only to deconstruct heteronormative protocols of gender and sexuality but also to make one's queerness visible to other gay men in spite of and indeed through their culturally enforced invisibility: that was the whole point of pronoun shifting, as evident in Emory's exchange with Harold about Cowboy.

My attention to the camps in *The Boys in the Band* thus means to have bearing on how we continue to understand the historicity of camp. Its historical dimensions as a queer social practice and subversive mode of reception may account for why mainstream and younger gay audiences during the past decades have had trouble locating more positive value in this film's representation of camping gay men. The camps in *The Band* no doubt spoke loudly and humorously to an older gay demographic itself well versed in the code and custom of the closet, while those more involved in the movement probably saw only the urgent need to liberate gay identity from Michael's self-loathing (and Michael's desire to be straight, as Harold persuasively infers). This historicity accounts for shifting attitudes toward camp, which has and has not mattered to gay men culturally, socially, and politically since the sixties; that historicity also records the relative ease with which, starting at that same time when camp was "outed" by Susan Sontag, mass-culture productions and the media were able to appropriate and tame camp, neutering it as any sort of nonqueer guilty pleasure found in nostalgically recoded and parodied objects like old Hollywood movies. The import of *The Boys in the Band*, then, arises from how, as Dunlop's column recalls, the film's very presence as middlebrow entertainment in 1970 confirmed that fault lines were dividing what had only recently been the stable signifying ground of camp for gay men.

This is finally why the camp voiced by the partygoers in *The Boys in the Band* registers a fraught and discomforting ambivalence about what by 1970 was already a dominant politics of sexual visibility but a visibility predicated either on assimilation or on male "beauty" alone, the gay clone look that dominated bar culture in the disco era. The film version of *The Boys in the Band* already seemed dated at that time because it resisted what was becoming the repudiation of camp as the rhetoric defining gay identity historically. Thus, in 1970, Emory seemed too nelly, Harold too neurotic, Donald too alcoholic, and Michael too self-loathing. No one seemed to notice that, except for Michael, who lives beyond his means and racks up debts, the gay characters have jobs, apartments, and friends and at least give the impression in the opening of having satisfying lives.

I myself still recall that what stood out at that time most prominently in journalistic and anecdotal accounts of the film were Michael's speeches after the party concludes and he becomes hysterical. "If we could just not hate ourselves so much," he sobs, his plea appearing to be on behalf of all his homosexual friends and not just himself. Following his anxiety attack, he then asks Donald, "Who was it who always used to say, 'You show me a happy homosexual and I'll show you a gay corpse'?" Donald simply replies, "I don't know," and repeats the question as the two of them laugh. Like Michael's entreaty to end "our" self-hatred, his question, but not Donald's nonanswer, was repeated as the declarative statement summarizing the whole of *The Boys in the Band*. The men's happiness or sadness as homosexuals, however, was never really the point of this party, though their camp camaraderie was. It distinguished their gay culture through its vivid differences from the straight culture surrounding them.

It is therefore safe to say, I think, that the film version of *The Boys in the Band* prompted such hostile responses from so many different quarters in 1970 and afterward because it defied the emerging identity politics that was predicated on distancing itself from the gay history inscribed in camp. That distance is implied by the ease with which so many viewers, even those writing over two decades later, like Carrithers, simply assumed without question that Michael and Alan supplied a united and hostile viewpoint of disidentification from the other boys in the band. But what that alienated viewpoint does not take into account is that, at the end of the film when Michael goes to an early-morning church service, Donald finishes his bottle of brandy, Emory may be thinking about his upcoming trip to San Francisco and that city's baths, Harold is enjoying his birthday present, and Hank and Larry are still upstairs in Michael's bedroom, sexually affirming that their union will not simply mirror the dominant culture's notion of heterosexual monogamy or butch/femme gay male roles. And as the film dissolves to the title cards identifying the cast by name, the soundtrack plays Burt Bacharach's "The Look of Love."

## Notes

1. See Joe Carrithers, "The Audiences of 'The Boys in the Band,'" *Journal of Popular Film & Television* 23, no. 2 (1995): 65, 69–70. See also how the play and its subsequent film version are contextualized in the opening chapters of *Making the Boys: The Story behind "The Boys in the Band,"* dir. Crayton Robey (First Run Features, 2010), DVD.

2. On the reception of *Myra Breckinridge*, see David Scott Diffrient, "'Hard to Handle': Camp Criticism, Trash-Film Reception, and the Transgressive Pleasures of *Myra Breckinridge*," *Cinema Journal* 52, no. 2 (2013): 46–70. Harry M. Benshoff looks at why a small group of films from 1970, including *Myra Breckinridge*, were reviled by critics as "loathsome," though, interestingly, *The Boys in the Band* was exempted from this criticism, mainly because its style was not as excessive and its actors not as well known. See Benshoff, "Beyond the Valley of the Classical Hollywood Cinema: Rethinking the 'Loathsome Film' of 1970," in

*The Shifting Definitions of Genre: Essays on Labeling Films, Television Shows, and Media*, ed. Lincoln Geraghty and Mark Jancovich (Jefferson, NC: McFarland, 2008), 92–109.

3. David W. Dunlap, "Theatre: In a Revival, Echoes of a Gay War of Words," *New York Times*, June 9, 1996, H4.

4. Carrithers, "Audiences," 64–65.

5. Ibid., 65.

6. In fact, it is worth pointing out that those cuts to close-ups are not only overly conventional but also not necessarily convincing of the intimacy or even possible alienation that they may mean to portray. In a respectful but critical review of the film following its Los Angeles premiere, Charles Champlin found the close-ups to be "counter-productive," an artifice of cinematic convention "turning the script into *italics* or ALL CAPITALS," and thus draining the drama from "the claustrophobic seal around the apartment." Champlin, "Motion Picture Review: 'The Boys in the Band,'" *Los Angeles Times*, March 29, 1970, O14.

7. Timothy Scheie, "Acting Gay in the Age of Queer: Pondering the Revival of *The Boys in the Band*," *Modern Drama* 42, no. 1 (1999): 7.

8. Richard Dyer, "It's Being So Camp as Keeps Us Going," in *Camp: Queer Aesthetics and the Performing Subject: A Reader*, ed. Fabio Cleto (Ann Arbor: University of Michigan Press, 1999), 110–11.

9. Steven Cohan, *Incongruous Entertainment: Camp, Cultural Value, and the MGM Musical* (Durham, NC: Duke University Press, 2005), 1. On that same page, I define camp as "the ensemble of strategies used to enact a queer recognition of the incongruities arising from the cultural regulation of gender and sexuality." In fact, the scholarship on camp is by now substantive and quite varied in approach, and space limitations prevent me from going into greater depth on the topic. Thus, for further discussion of camp in both its complexity and historicity as a queer style and taste as well as a cultural practice during the era of the closet, see my introduction to *Incongruous Entertainment* (1–40).

10. David M. Halperin, *How to Be Gay* (Cambridge, MA: Harvard University Press, 2012), 203.

11. Ibid., 208.

12. Ibid., 203.

13. Ibid., 208. This way of thinking, and Halperin is by no means alone in taking this view, considers camp an expression of gay male femininity, the antithesis of virility, straight or otherwise, which is understandable given the long and popular association of camp with female stars and with drag performances. Camp can nonetheless be an expression of queer masculinity too, as I argue about Gene Kelly's dancing in chapter 3 of *Incongruous Entertainment*, 149–99.

14. Halperin, *How to Be Gay*, 217.

15. Pamela Robertson Wojcik offers a smart commentary on the "public privacy" of the apartment in *The Boys in the Band*, including the (in)visibility of the gay characters during the opening montage, in *The Apartment Plot: Urban Living in American Film and Popular Culture* (Durham, NC: Duke University Press, 2010), 133–38. "In a sense," Wojcik comments, "the apartment provides a mirror into which they can enact their ideal gay self, a self that cannot exist as fully or openly in the outside world. At the same time, they acknowledge their varying degrees of difficulty and discomfort with their gay identities" (135). Throughout this chapter, I am arguing, in effect, that the practice, rhetoric, style, and affect of camp enabled it to express both perspectives, often simultaneously.

16. Esther Newton, *Mother Camp: Female Impersonators in America* (Chicago: University of Chicago Press, 1979), 110.

17. "I suppose it could have seeped in," Crowley states about his possible unconscious reference to *A Star Is Born* after disavowing it as his title's source and offering the Big Band explanation instead. "Act 1: The Play—Featurette," supplement on *The Boys in the Band* Kino-Lorber Blu-ray disc (2015). Crowley's account of his title is his standard answer, one he also offered in an interview with London's *Gay Times* in 1993, when he added that he wanted the reference to connote "a slightly outlaw quality; a band as a band of thieves." Quoted in John Rickard, "*The Boys in the Band*, 30 Years Later," *Gay & Lesbian Review* 8, no. 2 (2001): 11.

18. Dunlap, "Theatre," 28. Citing Dunlap's article, Michael R. Schiavi points out how that historical gap poses a pedagogical problem for the play and film: "Teaching the Boys: Mart Crowley in the Millennial Classroom," *Modern Language Studies* 31, no. 2 (2001): 75–90.

19. I discuss at great length how Garland and other female stars in MGM musicals perform as camps for the boys in the chorus in the second chapter of *Incongruous Entertainment*, 88–148.

20. Matthew Tinkcom, *Working Like a Homosexual: Camp, Capital, Cinema* (Durham, NC: Duke University Press, 2002), 201n38. See also 58–59.

21. Ibid., 58.

# 2

## "Turning"

### Alcohol and Affect in *The Boys in the Band*

**JOE WLODARZ**

> Who was it who always used to say, "You show me a happy homosexual, and I'll show you a gay corpse"?
> —Michael in *The Boys in the Band*

The characters in *The Boys in the Band* (dir. William Friedkin, 1970) drink a lot. They also regularly talk about the enabling and disabling effects of alcohol. Cocktail glasses and a drink cart play central roles in the mise-en-scène of the film, and both the expression and repression of queerness in *Boys* are intimately tied to the drinking ritual. Moreover, the key visual and tonal shifts of the film are structurally aligned with the emotional arc of Michael (Kenneth Nelson) as he dramatically falls off the wagon. Harold (Leonard Frey) keeps a wary eye on the drinking of his best friend and repeatedly accuses Michael of "turning." His comment not only calls out the increasingly hostile behavior of Michael but also captures the culturally and politically *transitional* quality of *Boys* itself.[1]

Gay liberationists famously derided the film and the play for their apparent inability to envision gay pride and "happy homosexuals," and this reading of the film was enhanced by the pathologizing tone of much of the mainstream reception of the play. For the *Washington Post*, Crowley's play was "a savage, anguished manifesto of what it means to be a homosexual," while the *Boston Globe* emphasized the boys' "gay community of sorrow."

Gay film scholar Robin Wood recalled seeing the film with his then-wife and whispering to her, "Look what you saved me from." By 1973, gay activist Arthur Bell, protesting the persistence of sissy stereotypes in mainstream film, demanded that Hollywood simply "let the boys in the band die."[2] To signal the specific goals of this chapter, however, I quote from *Time* magazine's review of the play: "Beneath the bitchy, lancing wit of the verbal byplay, playwright Mart Crowley keeps a dead-level eye on the desolating aspects of homosexual life. He records the loveless, brief encounters, the guilt-ridden, blackout reliance on alcohol, the endless courtship rat race of the gay bars with its inevitable quota of rejection, humiliation, and loneliness. Crowley underscores the fact that while the homosexual may pose as a bacchanal of nonconformist pagan delights, he frequently drinks a hemlock-bitter cup of despair."[3]

In examining the representation of drinking as well as alcohol's ties to the expression of both queer sexuality and queer feeling in *The Boys in the Band*, I want to complicate the frequent imposition of a notion of despair and unhappiness onto both the text (particularly the film) *and* pre-Stonewall homosexuality. For drinking, in fact, also facilitates the many moments of laughter, pleasure, and camaraderie that make *Boys* an often-joyous film.

At the same time, I want to use Sara Ahmed's notion of the (hetero)normative burden of "happiness" to grapple with the queer potential of *Boys'* persistent status as an "unhappy archive."[4] Ahmed, for example, points to the ironically enabling quality of the "unhappy ending" in postwar queer fiction as it expanded, rather than diminished, forms of queer visibility.[5] Vito Russo's queer necrology of Hollywood's "celluloid closet" clarifies a similar phenomenon on-screen in the years leading up to Stonewall, and while the boys in the band do manage to survive the film's final reel, criticism of them has typically depended on their affiliation with pre-Stonewall stereotypes of gay men as "closeted, catty, campy, narcissistic, alcoholic, and . . . self-loathing."[6] And yet the critical and affective power of *Boys*, I argue, stems from its refusal (or perhaps historical inability) to separate the pleasures of gay culture and community from queer feelings of rage, despair, shame, and unhappiness. My approach to the film thus builds on Heather Love's nuanced examination of the affective complexity and historiographic value of "feeling backward," particularly in relation to "dark, ambivalent texts" from the queer past that contend with the "painful negotiation of the coming of modern homosexuality."[7] As Love suggests, "Although there are crucial differences between life before gay liberation and life after, feelings of shame, secrecy, and self-hatred are still with us. Rather than disavowing such feelings as the sign of some personal failing, we need to understand them as indications of material and structural continuities between these two eras."[8] Positioned on the cusp of liberation but never quite on the gay side of Stonewall, *Boys* represents a particularly resonant, disturbing, and volatile archive of feelings that nevertheless captures the precariousness of queer expression and identity in a homophobic society.[9] If *Boys* is crucially never *just* an unhappy archive of queer despair, it remains significant for the often-contradictory ways that it situates the "sadness" of gay male life in relation to psychological and sociopolitical notions of homosexuality as well as to the use and abuse of alcohol.

My analysis focuses on Michael, typically seen as the saddest and nastiest figure in *Boys*, to examine the film's fraught negotiation of queer pleasure and pain, happiness and unhappiness.[10] Although he drinks no more than many of his comrades, Michael is singled out as the boy in the band with a notable drinking problem. As such, his representation can appear to collapse alcoholism and homosexuality as equivalent, even causally related, *conditions* rather than social behaviors or roles. In addition to emphasizing the film's resistance to such pathologization, however, I also use Harold's richly ambiguous notion of "turning" to capture the queer affective charge of Michael's disturbing rants in the film, particularly the manner in which they ambivalently stage a form of protest. For if Michael's alcoholism could be viewed metaphorically—aligning homosexuality with disease and vice— his "turning" also functions as a protoliberationist expression of rage targeting heterosexual privilege and internalized homophobia.

Furthermore, in redeploying the oft-maligned stereotype of the "screaming queen," I emphasize ways that Michael's alcohol-fueled rants suggest the *proximity* of an activist-style anger to the "sad" gay men of the pre-Stonewall era.[11] In addition to directly signaling the disinhibition of Michael as he drinks, my use of "turning" is meant to convey the affective and political complexity of the Stonewall era for gay men, particularly aging gay men, as well as the complex feelings that Michael incites in both his party guests and in audiences for the film. Rather than dismiss Michael as a self-loathing, mean drunk, I argue that the rawness, unpredictability, even cruelty of his "turning" effectively captures the affective complexity of straddling the line between pre- and post-Stonewall.[12] Aimed at both friend and foe as well as fueled by a potent combination of booze, trauma, weariness, and wariness, Michael's protestations are far from politically coherent or progressive. And yet the ambivalence of Michael's vocal dissent also foregrounds the manner in which *The Boys in the Band* simultaneously enacts, impedes, *and contests* the presumed happiness of gay liberation.

## "Christ, Was I Drunk Last Night": Alcohol and Repressed Homosexuality

Early in the film, Emory (Cliff Gorman) flings open an upstairs window and shouts, "Who do you have to fuck to get a drink around here?" In addition to kick-starting the drinking ritual, Emory's alignment of sex and booze complements the men's discussion of alcohol's key role in lowering inhibitions, enabling gay sex, and providing an alibi for that very activity: "Christ, was I drunk last night." As Michael explains his experience of guilt and denial after having had gay sex in college, he moves toward the drink cart, reaches for a bottle, and then pulls himself away from it. An earlier scene between Michael and his former lover Donald (Frederick Combs) has established Michael's five-week sobriety and included an extended discussion of Michael's dread of the "icks," the guilt- and anxiety-ridden hangover that always follows a night of heavy drinking: "From that split second when your eyes pop open and you say, 'My God, what did I do last night?' And then suddenly zap, total recall." While Michael's sobriety sets up the familiar narrative device of his relapse, an ambiguous connection is simultaneously drawn between the discomfort of the "icks" and homosexual shame.

Michael resists pouring himself a drink.

The alignment of alcohol abuse with homosexuality has a long history in psychological and sociological literature, and given the film's release before the official depathologization of homosexuality by the American Psychiatric Association (APA) in late 1973, it is hardly surprising that traces of this conflation persist in both the film and its mainstream reception. A 1908 study by the psychiatrist Karl Abraham (translated into English during the Prohibition era) first posited a connection between alcoholism and latent homosexuality. While noting the association of drinking prowess with masculinity, Abraham suggested that alcohol suspends the normal sublimation of homosexual feelings and encourages both physical and emotional intimacy between men.[13] Despite disagreements in the field about Abraham's conclusions, the latency theory lingered well into the postwar period and was intensified by the mainstreaming of Freudian psychoanalysis.[14] In a cultural history of alcoholism in America, Lori Rotskoff notes, "By the 1940s the pathologization of both alcoholism and homosexuality had altered doctors' views of excessive homosocial drinking. Unlike earlier observers of manly saloon rituals, midcentury psychoanalysts were likely to find a latent homosexual hidden behind the face of the 'hard-drinking he-man.'"[15] Donald Cory's 1951 study *The Homosexual in America* rejected the notion that all homosexuals were alcoholics, but he nevertheless supported the theory of alcoholism as a symptom of repressed homosexuality.[16] Both the latency theory and the pathologizing conflation of homosexuality and alcoholism (as shared signs of weakness, failure, oral fixation, excess) also persisted in what Jennifer Terry dubs the "backlash, pulp non-fiction" studies of homosexuality in the early 1960s, including Jess Stearn's *The Sixth Man* (1962).[17]

Cinema of the postwar era both deployed and masked these connections in films such as *The Lost Weekend* (dir. Billy Wilder, 1945), *Come Back, Little Sheba* (dir. Daniel Mann, 1952), *Written on the Wind* (dir. Douglas Sirk, 1956), and *Cat on a Hot Tin Roof* (dir. Richard Brooks, 1958).[18] Charles Jackson's 1944 novel *The Lost Weekend* and its film version helped to popularize a key shift in postwar conceptions of alcoholism, from a Prohibition-era, temperance-movement understanding of alcohol abuse as a moral failing or sin to a medicalized perspective of problem drinking as illness and the alcoholic as "a new category of subjective identity."[19] Billy Wilder's film adaptation, however, famously substituted writer's block for homosexual panic in framing causal factors for the hero's alcoholism.[20] Although the expansion of cocktail culture in the postwar era posited social drinking as an acceptably domesticated form of recreation for middle-class Americans, alcoholism increasingly signaled crises of both gender and sexual identity.[21]

From the impotence and infantilism of Kyle (Robert Stack) in *Written on the Wind* to the sexual and professional failures of Brick (Paul Newman) in *Cat on a Hot Tin Roof*, the male alcoholic in film was marked by an inability to fulfill the normative breadwinner role.

Successful cinematic adaptations of the alcoholism-themed work of gay (or closeted) playwrights such as Tennessee Williams, William Inge, and Edward Albee also invited queer reading strategies that countered the Hollywood Production Code's restrictions on homosexual representation. Searching for an appropriate explanation for Brick's alcoholism in *Cat*, for example, the *New York Times* critic Bosley Crowther openly questioned the film's substitution of "hero-worship" for the play's "strong suggestion of homosexuality."[22] Although the alcoholism film typically worked to reinforce social norms—often through an alignment with the reform-based strategies of Alcoholics Anonymous—its hybridization of the social problem genre with the family melodrama also threatened to undermine suburban ideology and to interrogate the limitations of gender normativity. Alcoholism on film could thus function, Rotskoff suggests, "as a cultural marker of domestic containment and the dissatisfactions it engendered."[23]

In line with the film's historical and sociopolitical liminality, *The Boys in the Band* is ambiguously situated between the era of the social problem film, which attempted to solve the problem of alcoholic deviance, and Hollywood Renaissance films that featured countercultural experimentation with drugs (*Easy Rider* [dir. Dennis Hopper, 1969]; *Midnight Cowboy* [dir. John Schlesinger, 1969]).[24] Michael's drinking is certainly figured as a problem in *Boys*—tied to both social and psychological factors—but the film resists a clear solution to the problem. Moreover, if the drinking and pot smoking of the other characters is at times explicitly presented as a psychological crutch or coping strategy (e.g., Harold's famous, self-deprecating greeting to Michael), it is also pleasurably framed as a social convention that heightens forms of queer expression. Given the primary role of the bar in the history of gay culture and identity, the sociologist Thomas S. Weinberg has suggested that "full participation in gay social life in American society means that one is surrounded by alcohol."[25] *Boys*, in fact, sets itself apart from many of its contemporaries, including *Advise and Consent* (dir. Otto Preminger, 1962) and *The Detective* (dir. Gordon Douglas, 1968), by presenting the space of the gay bar as a fun, inviting, semipublic space for drinking, cruising, and general camaraderie. Shot inside the West Village's legendary bar Julius', site of the Mattachine Society's groundbreaking "Sip-in" protest in 1966, the bar scene in *Boys* anticipates the queer pleasures soon to be found at Michael's

Gay male revelry at New York's legendary bar Julius'.

cocktail party just as it also provides a counterpoint to his own alcoholic temperament.[26]

Beginning with the scene at Julius', *Boys* maintains a consistent visual and thematic focus on the act of drinking as either a communal pleasure or a potential individual vice. Thomas Elsaesser has argued that the ubiquity of alcoholism in film can at times limit its analytic potential, but he also notes that "drink does become interesting in movies where its dynamic significance is developed and its qualities as a visual metaphor recognized: wherever characters are seen swallowing and gulping their drinks as if they were swallowing their humiliations along with their pride, vitality and the life force have become palpably destructive, and a phony libido has turned into real anxiety."[27] Even though the expansive bar at Julius' is reduced to a drink cart in Michael's apartment, the camera, like Michael himself, is repeatedly drawn to it throughout the film. Strategically positioned in a variety of shots, the bar cart is virtually another character in *Boys*. We also see roughly twenty-five separate shots of a character pouring a fresh drink, which can seem indulgent over the course of a two-hour film, even for a queer party of nine. Liquor bottles line the kitchen table, wine glasses make an expected appearance on the terrace during dinner, and countering Michael's initial abstinence, Donald smacks his lips after taking his first sip of a gin and tonic and exhales, "Oh, Christ, is that good." Drink preferences also hint at the gender and class associations of the partygoers: Michael clings to vodka after falling off the wagon, straitlaced Alan (Peter White) sticks to scotch, and Emory whips up a fruity blue whale in the blender

The drink cart as the central focus of the frame.

after scolding Hank (Laurence Luckinbill) for having a "truck driver's" preference for beer. In combining such associations with the recurrent shots of characters holding and drinking cocktails, the film seems to enhance Clive Barnes's succinct description of the play as simply about "a long, bloody, and alcoholic party."[28] As such, the omnipresence of alcohol in the film frame amplifies its dramatic and thematic function in *Boys*.

## Screaming Queens and Queer Euphoria

In Edmund White's recent memoir of New York in the 1970s, *City Boy*, he describes a memorable pair of dinner parties that he spent with Christopher Isherwood, Virgil Thomson, and other friends. As he recalls of the first, "we were all big drinkers in those days and we were soon screaming with merriment." The following evening, White had the group over to his apartment and cooked a notoriously difficult Julia Child recipe. "It was a triumph," he remembers, "and we all screamed with laughter till dawn. Now that I no longer drink, I wonder if I'm capable of such fierce, joyful abandon, such total immersion in the high tides of laughter and forgetting."[29] In an early scene in *Boys* that neatly establishes the casual intimacy between the two men, Michael grumbles to Donald that he is not looking forward to "five screaming queens singing happy birthday" at the party. Then, after Michael refers to the guests as "tired fairies," Donald asks if he is being considered a "screaming queen" or a "tired fairy." Michael playfully snaps back, "I beg your pardon, there will be six tired screaming fairy queens and one anxious queer!" In but one of the many instances in the film in which the stigmatizing terms used to shame queers become terms of endearment, Michael both mocks the screaming queen *and* proclaims his own status as one. Although "screaming queen" was deployed as a slur in the mainstream reception of *Boys*, the film is actually quite attentive to the ecstatic vocal excesses produced by gay men as they drink.[30] As Richard Dyer notes, "it might be inaccurate of straight movies and television to make out that all gay men are screaming queens and that that is something frightful to be, but plenty of men do enjoy a good scream."[31] Granted, not all of the boys in the band are screamers, and Michael, Emory, and Harold scream in a variety of ways over the course of the film; but I nevertheless want to use this frequently despised category to capture the unique, often-pleasurable ways that queer feelings and subjectivities are expressed as well as stifled in the film.

As Michael frantically unlocks his apartment door at the beginning of the film to answer the phone, the hallway is filled with the sound of a screaming baby, which Michael quickly blocks out by shutting the door. Upon the arrival of his guests, however, notably Emory, the screaming returns in queer form, this time within the apartment. Until the arrival of Alan, in fact, Michael's apartment is a safe space to scream, and the shrieks and cries of gay revelry increasingly fill its rooms. Even when Alan's disruption seems imminent, and Michael demands that Emory stop "camping," Emory and Donald's exaggerated performance of low-register sports banter quickly breaks into ecstatic cackling. But as Pamela Robertson Wojcik has

Emory releases an ecstatic wail.

argued in her study of the urban apartment in cinema, "if the bachelor pad partially functions as a closet in which one can try on, secrete, or disclose one's identity, it is nonetheless a permeable space . . . always vulnerable to intrusion."[32] This potential silencing of the euphoric pleasure of the screaming queen becomes particularly evident in the film's iconic "Heat Wave" dance scene.

As the Martha and the Vandellas track begins to play, Larry (Keith Prentice) asks Bernard (Reuben Greene) if he remembers the dance they used to do on Fire Island. Without missing a beat, Emory downs his fruity cocktail, leaps up, and leads the boys in the dance. After Michael jokingly refers to his friends as the "geriatrics Rockettes," he quickly joins the dance line as Donald looks on. The boys' colorful tops—red, blue, yellow, and violet—complement their raucous laughter, and the drink cart remains visible in the energetic cutting of the scene from a variety of angles. With or without a buzz from the booze, these sure look like happy homosexuals to me. The Fire Island reference also connects this exuberant gay revelry to one or more similarly joyous moments in the past. After grabbing Emory's ass, Larry lets out a rhapsodic roar, and the men's laughter then escalates into high-pitched screams. Michael's participation matters; if he is steadily distanced from the boisterous play of his fellow bandmates over the course of the film, he is fully present here. He throws his arms out and his head back in delight as Emory lets out another wail. His own euphoric cry, however, is notably stifled by the piercing whine of the doorbell.

The discordant clash between the buzzer and the boys amplifies the transgressive quality of their gaiety; these screaming queens are making too much noise, and Alan's consequent stare abruptly silences them. By barging into this "heat wave," he stops the party cold. The life drains out of Michael at the sight of his college chum, and he immediately apologizes for the queer spectacle, insisting, "We were just acting *silly*." Emory, however, cannot keep quiet, and after a delicate curtsy, his camp quips resist the straightening of this space until Michael finally drags him into the kitchen. We then see Emory's muffled cries through the kitchen window, as straight talk among Alan, Hank, and Michael takes over on the terrace. The men casually chat about women, sports, and kids, but when Alan mentions that his wife dated Michael in college, Larry, mixing a drink at the cart, cuts through this hetero façade with a perfectly timed drop of a drink stirrer.

After moving to the bedroom for a private chat with Michael, Alan confesses that he finds Hank to be "a very attractive fellow" in nearly the same breath as he scorns Emory for being a "goddamned little pansy." He also tellingly decries Emory's camp banter: "I just can't stand that kind of talk—it grates on me." Critics of both the play and the film frequently mirrored Alan's contempt for this particular "brand of humor"; indeed, mainstream accounts of *Boys* arguably alleviated the "grating" quality of its camp banter by amplifying notions of queer despair. While some critics acknowledged camp's potential as both weapon and armor in a homophobic society, they also tended to frame the cutting quality of camp as *self-directed*.[33] More frequently, when camp was recognized as being aimed elsewhere—at norms of gender and sexuality, for example—it was often reduced to a confirmation of queer unhappiness. For the *Boston Globe*, the "lonely" and "dissatisfied" boys in the film were "cruel because they [were] jealous of men having normal relationships with wives and children."[34] In a negative review of the filmic translation, Charles Champlin likewise praised the play for providing "at least a glimpse of the self-disgust and loneliness behind the strutting façade of superior sensibilities."[35]

Camp in *Boys* is clearly multifaceted, and it can incite a wide variety of audience responses; but the defensive tenor of the mainstream reception denies both camp's critical power *and* its affective quality as a manifestation of queer communal pleasure.[36] Alan, after all, is the only character in the film who finds Emory's camp consistently grating—even Hank is shown chuckling at Emory's wisecracks from time to time. If many of Harold's classic lines—"give me librium or give me meth"—suggest a theatrical quality that projects outward to the audience, Emory's camp is both more physical and more focused on the amusement of his friends. He keeps Larry and Bernard giggling as he repeatedly challenges Alan in his distinctively swish manner. Emory is significantly the *loudest* member of the band—at least until Michael turns—and yet as the film's most stereotypical screaming queen, he is also the site and source of many of its happiest moments.[37] Reflecting on the apparent comfort of Emory with his queer sexuality, Mart Crowley argued that "he uses it as a tool, as his defiance. . . . He probably went on to Stonewall."[38]

Without losing sight of Stonewall as a privileged historical moment in which the screaming queen became a political action and identity, I prefer to situate Emory's camp histrionics in the pre-Stonewall era, before the political embrace of the term *gay* seemed to demand homosexual happiness. The Stonewall era is a particularly rich period to explore the distinction that Sara Ahmed suggests between being "happily queer" and being a "happy queer," between celebrating *moments* of happiness rather than insisting on a more normative *state* of happiness.[39] With regard to *Boys*, I am particularly interested in Ahmed's discussion of "silliness" as an oft-maligned, momentary form of "superficial" or "worthless" happiness whose queer value lies in both its degraded reputation *and* its defiance of a goal-oriented trajectory of happiness.[40] Moreover, as Ahmed argues, "unhappiness with and rage about injustice may even be on a continuum with good feelings that are read as careless and silly. To embrace silliness is to embrace affects that would not ordinarily participate in an affirmative or happiness ethics."[41] Recall that Michael's immediate response to Alan's interruption of the screamingly queer Fire Island dance is to dismiss it as a moment of "acting silly." And yet try as he may to mask it, the queer resonance of "silly" lingers, particularly given that this is a group of adult men. Whether or not Alan has homosexual desires, he is a far cry from silly—"square city," as Michael describes him.

Although Emory's screaming immediately stops, his giggle-inducing remarks when faced with Alan's heteronormative presence crucially blend this alcohol-fueled silliness with the critical edge of camp. This is, after all, how Emory fights, and it does not take long before Alan responds in a more normative manner, namely, homophobic taunts and physical violence. Before Michael begins spewing venom, Alan's violence and his hysterical cries of "freak" and "faggot" anticipate and significantly *incite* Michael's aggressive turning shortly thereafter. Although the stakes are clearly different for Alan than they are for Michael—and his violence more direct—his outburst nonetheless represents a moment of emotional excess fueled by the experience of gay sexuality (and culture) in transition. During the short brawl, Michael is frozen stiff; his dread of mixing his straight past with his gay present has proved prescient. Alan's attack also transforms Emory's joyously queer scream into one of terrified vulnerability—a contrast emphasized by the return of the piercing door buzzer. But if this is indeed the screaming queen Alan desires, one who whimpers rather than grates, his is a hollow victory. For not only do Alan's rabid shrieks of "faggot" come perilously close to the vocal excess he so loathes in Emory, but Emory's camp sensibility quickly incites a scream of a different kind in Harold, who reads Emory's birthday note—attached to the wrist of his male hustler "present"—and lets out a loud, lengthy cackle. In between Emory's/Alan's hysterical wails and Harold's cackle, Michael darts to the bar and downs a glass of vodka. It's now his time to turn.

### Altered States and Alcoholic Rants: Two Types of "Turning"

Although Alan soon flees to the upstairs bathroom to be sick, eliciting another frightened scream from Emory, Harold's arrival signals a fresh form of conflict for Michael. Longtime, intimate friends, Harold and Michael know each other perhaps too well, and they spend much of the remainder of the party sparring. Harold makes quick note of Michael's slip off the wagon, and he warns Michael about his inevitable "icks." He also cautions the guests, "Beware the hostile fag. When he's sober, he's dangerous; when he drinks, he's lethal." Harold pours himself bourbon when he arrives and has wine with dinner, but he is more closely associated with marijuana in the film. Harold arrives to the party stoned, and his burning joint is shown to us before we see even his face. He brusquely explains this coping strategy to Michael: "If I smoke a little grass before I get up the nerve to show my face to the world, it's nobody's goddamn business but my own."

Shortly after Alan retreats, Harold strikes a match against the wall, lights another joint, and announces, "Turning on!"[42] His slow, deliberate line delivery matches his more languid bodily carriage in the film, and while his quips sting, he never raises his voice in anger. Harold is also unashamed about finding the hustler's youthful, muscular body a turn-on, and his affinity for both marijuana and midnight cowboys conveys a proximity to the counterculture that Michael clearly lacks. Harold's rose-tinted glasses likewise suggest an alternative perspective on the social and sexual conflicts that greet him upon arrival. Harold, in fact, presents the queerest approach to the enigma of Alan's sexuality by simply asking, "Who is she? Who was she? Who does she hope to be?"

Michael, on the other hand, finds Alan's ambiguous presence at the party far more unsettling, and Alan's violent outburst triggers both Michael's drinking and his hostility. Clinging to his cocktail glass, Michael refuses Harold's offer of a hit from his joint and instead begins shooting barbs at his guests. Ever attentive to Michael's behavior, Harold pointedly notes, "I'm turning on, and you're just turning." Michael, however, proceeds to lash out at the hustler Cowboy (Robert La Tourneaux) for his ignorance, to pick at Harold's insecurities, and to snap at Emory for calling out Michael's lingering Catholic moralism ("Gilda Guilt"). Harold's sharp retort to two of these insults is simply, "Turning."

The richness of turning as a thematic trope in *Boys* lies in its capturing the affective qualities of gay culture and identity in transition. In addition to marking a more general affective disinhibition, Michael's turning, for Harold, specifically signals an emotional shift from communal affection to antagonism as he begins to turn *against* his own friends. It also exemplifies Michael's apparent reluctance to embrace change, ambiguity, and the possibility of individual and social transformation; he turns in circles rather

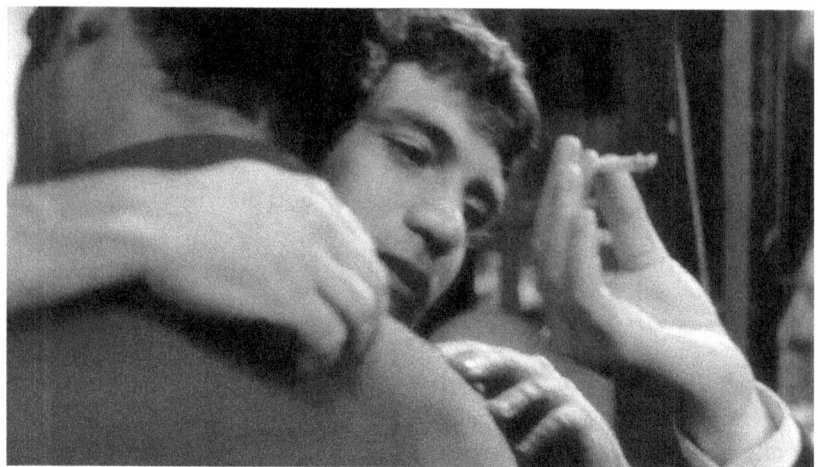
Harold passes a joint as Emory and Bernard slow dance.

than turning on in a countercultural sense. If there remains an ambivalent quality of protest to Michael's rage, his turning nevertheless often redirects personal shame into public acts of shaming. In a more literal sense, Michael frequently turns *away* from the party and its guests as the evening progresses, just as Harold turns away from Michael during some of his nastiest rants. The clock is also turning for these "boys": Harold is now thirty-two, and both he and Michael are accused of performing daily "surgery" on their faces to counter the effects of aging. Despite a shared sense of themselves as "tired old fairies," the difference in their choice of mind-altering substances significantly positions them in opposite directions in relation to the culture of the late 1960s.

In a 1969 *Esquire* article, Tom Burke specifically used the theatrical version of *The Boys in the Band* to mark a cultural shift between an "old" and a "new homosexuality." Months before the screaming queens of *Boys* made their cinematic debut, Burke had already announced their passing. "Pity," he noted, "just when Middle America finally discovered the homosexual, he died."[43] According to Burke, the new homosexual was "indistinguishable from the heterosexual hippie," and as one of his informants explained, while the old homosexual was defined by a "syndrome of drink, guilt, and camp," the new homosexual embraced "dope, freedom, . . . rock, and soul, and the humor of the head."[44] Although for Burke, "the psychedelic life-style was giving [new homosexuality] a form,"[45] sociologist Laud Humphreys remained skeptical of the full-scale transformation that Burke declared. The counterculture had spawned a youthful, nonparodic "virility" among gay men, Humphreys argued, but such figures continued "to coexist with the effete martini sippers of the traditional gay world."[46]

Following dinner and the opening of his birthday gifts, Harold again turns on as *The Boys in the Band* chills out to the soft jazz of Burt Bacharach's "The Look of Love." Michael cues the scene by requesting some music, but when Larry sidles up to him and asks him to dance, Michael insists that he "only leads." A clear precursor to the gay macho type—with a deep voice, hairy chest, implied sexual versatility, *and* camp sensibility—Larry has no qualms about following, but Michael coldly states that he would prefer to "*sip* this one out." He then positions himself in the corner of the terrace with his cocktail glass and cigarette and turns away from the party. Harold, in contrast, uses the passing of the joint to bring the men together, and the fluid slow dancing of Bernard and Emory provides another blissful, if temporary, tonal shift in the film. Friedkin's camera amplifies the psychedelic quality of the scene by filming Cowboy peering through a red cellophane wrapper and colored glass eggs, while separate cuts to Michael foreground his distance from this atypically silent revelry. Far from mellowing out, the vodka has made him edgier. For Ahmed, "happiness involves a way of being aligned with others, *of facing the right way*," but Michael here appears to resist turning toward the counterculture and implicitly moving closer to gay liberation.[47]

After a thunderstorm soaks the pot party, Alan's return sparks Michael's hostility and unleashes the most vicious screaming queen of the film. Michael defiantly blocks Alan's exit, setting him up for the imminent truth

Michael turns away and "sips this one out."

game, as Harold simply notes, "Revolution complete." Messiness and unpredictability shade Michael's rage throughout this sequence, due in part—if only in part—to his drinking. Brutally turning *against* both friend and foe, Michael does not simply revolt but also at times becomes revolting. He nearly provokes a second brawl in the film (with Bernard) after performing a hideously racist shuffling routine that moves Harold to close his eyes and turn away. Michael's volatility likewise enhances the ambivalence of turning as a queer affective experience. He thus comes to embody Ahmed's notion of the "unhappy queer" as among the types of person she calls "affect aliens": "those who are alienated by virtue of how they are affected by the world or how they affect others in the world."[48]

The primary goal of Michael's party game—the humiliating exposure of Alan's homosexuality—depends in part on the persistence of abject queerness. Michael thus stages a spectacle of queer abasement, and his truth game, in which the guests are required to call up the person they have loved most and confess their unrequited love, proves to be a dramatic, if unpredictable, manifestation of his aggression. He baits Alan by insisting that the game is "like watching an accident—you can't look at it, you can't look away." He also thrusts the phone into his guests' faces, hovers in the frame as they make their calls, and belligerently demands that they follow the rules. To some degree, Michael perversely desires this tragic narrative arc; he is ill suited and unprepared for any happy ending that gay liberation might provide.

Throughout the game, Michael repeatedly projects a self-loathing, drunken weakness onto his queer friends. After Emory, for example, delivers

Under the glare of the spotlights, Michael berates Emory.

a heartfelt confession of adolescent love for an older dentist to his friends, he insists on making his call, rips the phone out of Larry's hands, and then crashes to the floor. Michael, shot from a low angle in the glare of the corner spotlights, furiously screams at Emory to "hit that iceberg," for he wants a "smash of a finale." Although Emory smiles and admits, "God, I'm drunk," Michael demands more shame. He lashes out, calling Emory a "falling-down-drunk-nellie-queen." Like many critics and shrinks of the period, Michael conflates queerness and drunkenness in his verbal attack. He also revealingly figures his own alcoholism (and homosexuality) as a matter of *visibility*. In stark contrast to Donald and Emory, who have no qualms proclaiming, even celebrating, their inebriated state, Michael vehemently denies his own drunkenness by insisting, "You cannot *tell* that I am drunk!" The camera, however, presents a different story. For not only does Michael drink during this rant, but in a later scene he is actually *reduced to* a cocktail at the margin of the frame. In this visual collapse of Michael and cocktail glass, his alcoholism potentially slips from the realm of behavior to that of identity. Contrary to his protestations, the camera suggests that we can indeed tell that he is both drunk and *a drunk*.

Michael is nothing if not obsessed with his appearance, but his anxiety about being exposed as both a drunk and a queer points to a deeper conflict that plays into the oft-noted perception of him as "self-loathing." This aspect of the film is typically given a psychological spin, most notably by Harold in his verbal takedown of Michael, but social factors are also at play. Michael clings to the closet not simply because he doesn't want to *be*

Michael is reduced to a cocktail at the edge of the frame.

The telephone taunts Michael.

a homosexual but because he doesn't want to lose privilege as a result of being *seen* as homosexual. Gay liberation will demand a degree of visibility, even happiness, that could disturb his understanding and negotiation of queerness and the closet; he therefore turns away from some of its signs in the film, including nonmonogamy, sexual fluidity, and turning on. At the same time, given that he and his friends have repeatedly been burned by homophobia, most recently through Alan's violent attack, Michael is also determined to deny Alan the privileges of both heterosexuality and the closet. Consequently, when Michael is faced with an alternative outcome to the party game, specifically one that confounds his staging of queer abjection, he resists. During Larry's declaration of nonmonogamous love to Hank, in fact, Michael appears taunted by the presence of the phone in the frame and haunted by his own destructive game.

Dissatisfied with Larry's victory, Michael instead promises a "climactic revelation" and turns his attention to the outing of Alan. By this point in the film, he has actually stopped drinking, and yet the signs and effects of alcohol clearly linger. He shoves Emory and sneers at Harold even as his rage remains primarily directed at Alan. While Michael's battle with Alan is clearly personal, it is never *only* personal. Through his embittered rants, Michael also enacts a critique of both society and self, but seldom in a neat, clean, or progressive manner.

Michael's final confrontation with Alan gains critical and affective force through his fervent interrogation of homophobia as well as the film's *reframing* of the spectacle of queer shame. Even as Michael remains fixated on the exposure of Alan's homosexuality, he also repeatedly assails both Alan's homophobia and the internalized homophobia of gay men.[49] When Alan apologizes to Emory, for example, Michael will have none of it. Keenly aware that Alan's regret does nothing to disturb his own heterosexual privilege, Michael roars, "You can decorate his house for him, Emory, and he can get you out of jail the next time you're arrested on a morals charge." After Hank and Larry retire to the upstairs bedroom, Michael also taunts Alan with the possibility that gay sex is happening there. He then begins shouting a litany of homophobic terms, including ones like "freak" and "pansy" that Alan had earlier used, before at last accusing Alan of being a closet queen. Dripping with sweat, Michael finally hits his peak moment as an angry, screaming queen.

As much as Michael has struggled to put the queer shame of others onstage during the game, he himself becomes the film's primary spectacle of abject queerness as he strains to elicit Alan's confession of love for their college friend Justin. Building on the earlier scene in which Michael's disavowal of his drunkenness was framed from a low angle, the camera tilts up at this instant to position him under the spotlights again. Despite the fact that Michael directs his anger at Alan, the framing and camerawork of the scene ultimately emphasize his own vulnerability, his enactment of queer pain in the face of homophobia. If there is a pre-Stonewall quality to Michael's affinity for the closet, this moment of profound unhappiness clarifies the damage that has also been done. Rather than calling forth a confession of homosexuality, Michael's indignant screaming instead bears

Michael turns his attention to the outing of Alan.

witness to the trauma experienced by Justin, himself, and the many other "boys in the band" of the era. Michael's shouts also crucially grow louder and more intense immediately after Alan refers to "sickness" and "pity" in framing his response to Justin's coming-out. Alan may have apologized to Emory, but he has hardly budged in his association of homosexuality with stigma and illness. Speaking not only for Justin, and blaming not only Alan, Michael viscerally protests, "To this day, he remembers the treatment, the scars he got from *you!*" When Michael finally hits peak volume with his scream—"Call him!"—Donald's noticeable wince clarifies that even if Alan is deaf to it, Michael's pain has in fact been registered (and felt) by at least some of his guests.

### "Absinthial Tragedy": Unhappy Queers and the "Icks"

An unsettling, even moralizing tone charges the moments immediately following Michael's angry scream in *Boys*, including Alan's revelatory phone call to his wife and Harold's consequent attack on Michael for his ostensible self-loathing. However closely aligned with Michael's own hostile staging of queer abasement, these brief scenes have always struck me as unnecessarily cruel on the heels of Michael's emotionally raw self-exposure. Harold fairly reproaches Michael for the "fervor with which [he] annihilate[s]," but Harold's insistence that Michael simply accept his homosexuality does little to counter the persistence of homophobia and heterosexual privilege. If there were indeed political value in figuring homosexuality as unchanging or essential to one's identity in the years before the APA's depathologization, Harold's insistence that Michael will "always" be homosexual nevertheless tends to counter the complexity suggested by the provocative questions that he had earlier posed in relation to Alan. In stark contrast, Michael's extreme unhappiness at this climactic moment of turning, however amplified by the depressive effects of his binge drinking, functions simultaneously as critique, resistance, and expression of trauma. It complicates calls for "happy homosexuals" in films by questioning that narrative, political, and affective trajectory.

Following the humiliating exposure of the truth game and Harold's merciless critique of him, Michael, who has again turned away from the party, lets out a final shattering scream as he desperately calls for Donald's help. "Hitting that iceberg" himself, Michael releases several agonized cries of regret and falls to the floor in trembling, helpless sorrow. Michael's turn from rage to abject despair at the end of the film has long been the moment that "grates" for queer audiences, particularly gay liberationists. As Allen Young argued in his 1971 "A Gay Manifesto," "[The film's] homosexuals are so pitiful that it hardly serves as affirmation for someone trying to come out."[50] While it is fair to say that *Boys* never adopts the affirmative politics of gay pride, I would argue that the often-reductive readings of *Boys* posited by liberationists were heavily shaped by the mainstream reception of the play and film. Perhaps taking a cue from Michael, the liberationists imagined that what *Boys* actually depicted mattered less than how it was ultimately seen. And given some of the responses, who could blame them? In a review of the play, for example, *Life* magazine callously suggested that "the theatrical self-pity of minorities simply slaps paint on their real wretchedness."[51]

Reviews from the period, both mainstream and liberationist, tend to conflate Michael's arc in the film with all homosexuals. It is a mistake that Michael himself even makes when, through a veil of tears, he longs for a different reality: "if *we* could just learn not to hate ourselves quite so very much." Often missed, however, is Donald's immediate response: "*You* used to be a lot worse than *you* are now." The significance of Donald's comment stems not only from its shift from a universalizing "we" to an individualizing "you" but also from the fact that it causes Michael to transition immediately from tears to laughter. Michael's oft-quoted line—"you show me a happy homosexual, and I'll show you a gay corpse"—was read straight by some critics, both heterosexual and homosexual. And yet in the film, the line is immediately followed by a fit of laughter and tellingly framed as

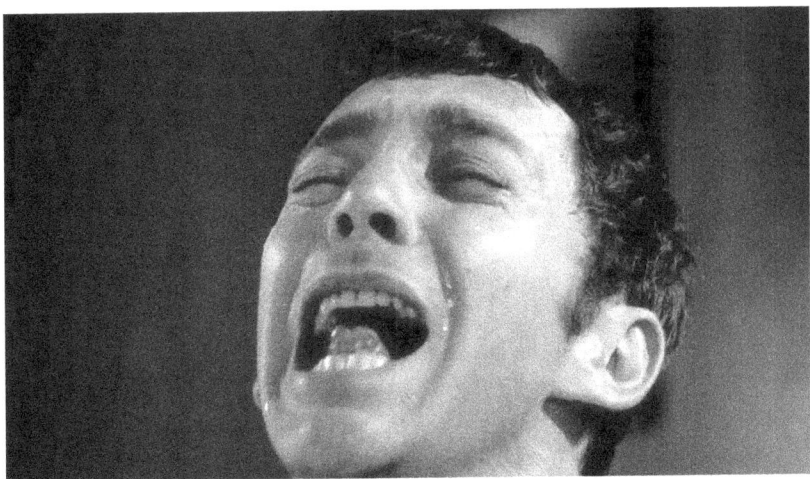

Michael screams out desperately for Donald's help.

The drink cart on display just before Michael's breakdown.

both a joke and as something someone "*used* to say."⁵² Far from figuring the unhappy homosexual as an artifact of the past, however, Michael's laughter instead betrays a knowing skepticism about the possibility of achieving a consistent state of happiness in a virulently homophobic culture. As he calms down with the help of Donald and a Valium, Michael's shift from sorrow to silliness also captures the transitory quality of the experience of both happiness and unhappiness for queers. Michael's spectacular anguish in this scene is difficult to watch and casts a particularly long shadow, but it remains a *moment* of extreme unhappiness rather than confirmation of an afflicted, "pitiful" state. Moreover, the emotional excess and extravagance of Michael's breakdown also suggests other causal factors.

Although Michael's apoplectic rant is surely fueled by more than his inebriated state, his tragic, tear-filled collapse could be somewhat less a consequence of any inherent self-loathing than it is a signal of the depressive turn after a drinking binge. If critics have underestimated the social critique manifested in the scene prior, they have arguably overestimated the meaning of Michael's wailing despair. In one of the few critical responses that at least acknowledged this connection, gay activist Donn Teal—in a 1969 *New York Times* article that asked, "How anguished are homosexuals?"— described the play's ending as "a finale of absinthial tragedy."⁵³ By the end of *Boys*, Michael has surely got the "icks," and the film again visually foregrounds alcohol during his breakdown. When Michael turns away from the party and faces the terrace after Alan's phone call, he is standing directly behind the drink cart. Then, just before he screams out Donald's name, we are shown an unsteady, blurred point of view that telegraphs his drunken state. Finally, when Michael falls to the floor, wailing about the oncoming "anxiety," the cart again takes a prominent position in the frame. As Michael clings to Donald's arms and weeps into his chest, the drink cart seems to bear down on him, amplifying his "icks" and yet also partially explaining his acute despair.

Michael is a messy drunk, and he is also at this point a particularly unhappy queer; but to reduce either him *or* homosexuality to an essential, unwavering "wretchedness" is to overlook the influence of alcohol. Such an approach not only plays into the long-standing association of homosexuality and alcoholism as related afflictions but also conveniently sidesteps the issue of social factors that might drive one to drink. As I have suggested, alcohol's prominent role in Michael's anguished crash intensifies, rather than erases, the pain and trauma expressed through his rant against Alan (and entrenched homophobia). Michael has been adamant about this lingering trauma; he has insisted that Justin "remembered" the treatment and scars he received from Alan. And as he noted earlier about the dreaded "icks," a fleeting moment of disorienting uncertainty is quickly followed by "total recall." In addition to his memory of past injustices, Michael is also significantly reminded of the more immediate suffering that he has inflicted on his guests, leading him to shout, "What have I done?" Michael's breakdown is actually cued by the exit of Emory and Bernard, in which a stumbling drunk Bernard yet again mumbles, "I shouldn't have called." Bernard is still traumatized by the exposure of old wounds, and his

The drink cart bears down on Michael as he weeps.

statement refuses to exonerate Michael in his own moment of agony just as it also suggests a continuum of queer suffering. It hints at ways that racism complicates the trauma of homophobia, a complexity to which Michael is frequently blind.

Given that *Boys* pays particular attention to the damage done both to and by Michael, it is easy to forget that his often-disturbing emotional instability is a characteristic that Alan also shares. Michael, after all, is not the first character in *Boys* to have either an emotional breakdown or a fit of rage; Alan is. Alan is also the character who expresses remorse about his emotional excesses with near-suicidal tendencies: "I could shoot myself for letting myself act that way." But if Michael clearly has a long history of homophobia to blame for his woes, what is Alan's excuse? And why for that matter does Alan's hysterical behavior not lead critics to lament the essential unhappiness of heterosexuality? The answer is clear, but what is significant is that neither the play nor the film lets this matter go. For as Donald—who, unlike Michael, can clearly hold his liquor—finishes off a bottle of brandy, he brings up the issue of Alan's crying spell and wonders why Alan might have left his wife. Michael, by this point, is finished with the truth game, and he closes the film by quoting his father on the unknowable quality of life in general. Donald's reintroduction of Alan's sexual (and emotional) ambiguity, however, once again suggests that Michael's aggressive interrogation of Alan was not solely motivated by his own self-loathing. It also casts the net of unhappiness far and wide; despite Alan's declaration of love to his wife, he hardly leaves the party as a figure of heterosexual happiness.

In addition to pointing out the relative absence of films about alcoholism in the 1970s, Richard Dyer has noted that films on the topic typically lead us to expect "a tale of either sordid decline or of inspiring redemption."[54] Although Michael's prominent unhappiness in the film—as well as disease-based notions of homosexuality—led many critics to read the film in terms of a "sordid decline," *Boys* significantly resists both narrative trajectories. As such, it is very much a film of the late sixties and early seventies, a period in American cinema when ambivalence and incoherence often tested the limits of the Hollywood happy ending, when the silver screen regularly screamed and stung.[55] Even the major films of 1970—*Love Story, Airport, Five Easy Pieces, Joe, Patton*—convey a skepticism about the possibility of happiness. Michael's pronounced anger *and* sadness in the film are hardly anomalous in this cultural and cinematic context and thus figure a certain dissatisfaction with the status quo. As Deborah Gould has suggested in her work on emotion and AIDS activism, "By signaling that something is awry, that things could be and perhaps should be different, affective states can inspire challenges to the social order."⁵⁶ Film critic Stuart Byron recalls being on a panel at the Gay Activist Alliance (GAA) Firehouse in 1971, in which *Boys* was denounced, and simply asking, "If homosexuals weren't like that, what was the need for Gay Liberation?" "No one could answer that question," he added.⁵⁷ Actor David Drake provided a somewhat-different spin on *Boys* at the time of its 1996 revival by suggesting that it actually "has a happy ending" because it led him to realize, "Oh God, they're only a year away from a greater sense of freedom. I know there's a light at the end of this tunnel."⁵⁸

Keeping in mind that Michael's final words to Donald in the play and film are to "turn the lights *out*" when he leaves, it is important to remain aware that Michael's varied enactments of the screaming queen do not necessarily pave the way to a postliberation happy homosexual. What might gay liberation *fail* to provide for Michael, particularly as a middle-aged gay man with a drinking problem? Is he really just a year away from "gay pride"? Are his friends? Is the nation? In using Harold's notion of turning to capture the unsettling queer affective experience of the Stonewall era, I thus want to maintain its ambivalent quality, its potential to signal the uncertain space between affirmation and desolation, intimacy and hostility, liberation and the closet. For not AA, the GAA, or the APA can effectively guarantee a remedy for Michael's malaise. Indeed the facial expressions of *all* of the actors/characters in the film's credit sequence, backed by a reprise of Bacharach's "The Look of Love," aptly convey this sense of ambivalence.

Michael's wary gaze as the liberation era beckons.

However filled with ecstatic emotional highs and devastating lows, *Boys* leaves both its characters and its audiences without a clear political direction or a privileged emotional state. For Ahmed, "feelings may be perverse because they don't always have a point"; their queerness may thus depend on the ways in which they both disturb teleological narratives and continue to *feel* disturbing.[59] As the *Los Angeles Times* noted of the play, "you leave the theater with a dull ache."[60] At the same time, the film's unpredictable affective qualities—its ability to humor, haunt, soothe, and shock—figure both the anguish and the appeal of queerness before liberation. Through Michael in particular, *Boys* conveys wariness about the terms and stakes of happy homosexuality—of the imperative of *gay* itself—even before the first beer bottles are thrown in Sheridan Square. "We can turn shame into pride," Heather Love reminds us, "but we cannot do so once and for all: shame lives on in pride, and pride can easily turn back into shame."[61]

*The Boys in the Band*, like many other Stonewall-era texts, readily traffics in the images and emotions of queer abjection while also encouraging viewers to consider the source and value of deviant feelings as well as the limitations of liberation. The power of pre-Stonewall visions of homosexuality indeed stems from their potential to irritate, unnerve, even offend contemporary sensibilities, while also revealing both social and sexual alternatives to homonormativity. Such fraught queer visions tell us not only what we have been but crucially what we might still be or could one day become. Following Ahmed and Love, my analysis of Michael's volatile turning in *Boys* thus argues for the critical and cultural significance of texts that either refuse or fail to resolve the anguish and unhappiness of preliberation queerness. In addition to charting the complex ways that historical texts continue to hurt, however, an affective queer historiography must also regularly tend to queer culture's proficiency at turning pain into pleasure. For just as the alcohol-fueled laughter, dancing, and euphoric cries of these queer boys remain in productive tension with the film's critical status as an "unhappy archive," they also enhance *Boys*' groundbreaking vision of gay male camaraderie and sexuality. Much like its own loud, bitchy, scarred, sexy, and silly characters, *The Boys in the Band* fully acknowledges and explores the trauma of homophobia—that "hemlock-bitter cup of despair"—while defiantly insisting on the communal pleasures found in a stiff drink and a good scream.

## Notes

1. The *Los Angeles Times*, for example, noted, "The Boys in the Band is at once ahead of its time and behind it." Gregg Kilday, "'Boys in Band' at Two Sites," *Los Angeles Times*, August 20, 1971, F13.

2. Michael Kernan, "Long Search for the 'Boys,'" *Washington Post–Times Herald*, July 6, 1969, G1; Kevin Kelly, "'Boys in the Band' Blends Waspish Wit, Loneliness and Need," *Boston Globe*, May 5, 1969, 20; Robin Wood, quoted in Al LaValley, "Deep Focus: Out of the Closet and on to the Screen," *American Film* 7, no. 10 (1982): 61; Arthur Bell, "Let the Boys in the Band Die," *New York Times*, April 8, 1973, D15.

3. "New Plays: The Boys in the Band," *Time*, April 26, 1968, 97.

4. Sara Ahmed, *The Promise of Happiness* (Durham, NC: Duke University Press, 2010), 17.

5. Ibid., 89.

6. Vito Russo, *The Celluloid Closet: Homosexuality in the Movies*, rev. ed. (New York: Harper and Row, 1987); David W. Dunlap, "In a Revival, Echoes of a Gay War of Words," *New York Times*, June 9, 1996, H4.

7. Heather Love, *Feeling Backward: Loss and the Politics of Queer History* (Durham, NC: Duke University Press, 2007), 4.

8. Ibid., 20–21.

9. On the relationship of affect to queer histories of trauma, see Ann Cvetkovich, *An Archive of Feelings: Trauma, Sexuality, and Lesbian Public Cultures* (Durham, NC: Duke University Press, 2003).

10. As Mart Crowley explained, "All the negative things in the play are represented by Michael, and because he's the leading character, it was his message that a very square American public wanted to receive." Quoted in Russo, *Celluloid Closet*, 177.

11. See Richard Dyer, "Coming Out as Going In: The Image of the Homosexual as a Sad Young Man," in *The Matter of Images: Essays on Representations* (London: Routledge, 1993), 73–92.

12. Turning may be considered a complex "structure of feeling" given its "in-process" quality during a transformative cultural moment. See Raymond Williams, *Marxism and Literature* (Oxford: Oxford University Press, 1977), 128–35.

13. Karl Abraham, "The Psychological Relations between Sexuality and Alcoholism (1908)," in *Selected Papers of Karl Abraham, M.D.*, ed. Ernest Jones, trans. Douglas Bryan and Alix Strachey (London: Hogarth, 1927), 82–83. According to Lori Rotskoff, the English translation of Abraham's article was "the first instance in which 'alcoholism' was used in scientific literature to refer not

simply to the physical effects of drinking but to habitual drinking behavior itself." Lori Rotskoff, *Love on the Rocks: Men, Women, and Alcohol in Post–World War II America* (Chapel Hill: University of North Carolina Press, 2002), 69.

14. See Thomas S. Weinberg, *Gay Men, Drinking, and Alcoholism* (Carbondale: Southern Illinois University Press, 1994), 1–4; John W. Crowley, *The White Logic: Alcoholism and Gender in American Modernist Fiction* (Amherst: University of Massachusetts Press, 1994), 149–50; Edward J. Small Jr. and Barry Leach, "Counseling Homosexual Alcoholics: Ten Case Histories," *Journal of Studies on Alcohol* 38, no. 11 (1977): 2077–80; and Rotskoff, *Love on the Rocks*, 78–81.

15. Rotskoff, *Love on the Rocks*, 79.

16. Donald Webster Cory, *The Homosexual in America: A Subjective Approach* (New York: Greenberg, 1951), 97.

17. Jennifer Terry, *An American Obsession: Science, Medicine, and Homosexuality in Modern Society* (Chicago: University of Chicago Press, 1999), 362–65; Jess Stearn, *The Sixth Man* (London: W. H. Allen, 1962).

18. Key studies of alcoholism in postwar American film include Rotskoff, *Love on the Rocks*; Jim Cook and Mike Lewington, eds., *Images of Alcoholism* (London: BFI, 1979); Norman K. Denzin, *Hollywood Shot by Shot: Alcoholism in American Cinema* (New York: Aldine de Gruyter, 1991); Denise Herd, "Ideology, Melodrama, and the Changing Role of Alcohol Problems in American Films," *Contemporary Drug Problems* 13 (Summer 1986): 213–47; Robin Room, "Alcoholism and Alcoholics Anonymous in U.S. Films, 1945–1962: The Party Ends for the 'Wet Generations,'" *Journal of Studies on Alcohol* 50, no. 4 (1989): 368–81.

19. Rotskoff, *Love on the Rocks*, 64.

20. Russo, *Celluloid Closet*, 96–97.

21. As Rotskoff notes, "in formulating new ideas about alcoholism, a pathology of consumption that could never be domesticated, Americans not only drew boundaries between normal and problem drinking; they also reinscribed divisions between healthy and pathological gender identity" (*Love on the Rocks*, 68). For an analysis of postwar cocktail culture, see ibid., 194–211.

22. Bosley Crowther, "The Fur Flies in 'Cat on a Hot Tin Roof,'" *New York Times*, September 19, 1958, 24. See also Chon Noriega, "'Something's Missing Here!': Homosexuality and Film Reviews during the Production Code Era, 1934–1962," *Cinema Journal* 30, no. 1 (1990): 20–41.

23. Rotskoff, *Love on the Rocks*, 217.

24. Although *Boys* is not included in Denzin's overview of alcoholism in American film, it combines characteristics of films from 1960 to 1966, in which problem drinking is connected to a broader social or psychological problem, and 1966 to 1976, in which drinking and drug use are presented as

"unproblematic, carefree activities, which carry few, if any negative consequences for the drinker/user and his or her associates" (*Hollywood*, 132).

25. Weinberg, *Gay Men*, 149.

26. For an overview of the Julius' bar "Sip-in," see David Carter, *Stonewall: The Riots That Sparked the Gay Revolution* (New York: St. Martin's Griffin, 2004), 47–54.

27. Thomas Elsaesser, "Tales of Sound and Fury: Observations on the Family Melodrama," in *Film Genre Reader III*, ed. Barry Keith Grant (Austin: University of Texas Press, 2003), 390–91.

28. Clive Barnes, "Theater: 'Boys in the Band' Opens Off Broadway," *New York Times*, April 15, 1968, 48.

29. Edmund White, *City Boy: My Life in New York during the 1960s and '70s* (New York: Bloomsbury, 2009), 250–51.

30. Barnes also refers to the play as "screamingly fag" in his review ("Theater," 48). For the use of "screaming queen" in the reception of *Boys*, see John Simon, "'The Boys in the Band' as Object Lesson," *New York*, August 5, 1968, 48; and Judy Klemesrud, "You Don't Have to Be One to Play One," *New York Times*, September 29, 1968, D1.

31. Richard Dyer, "Believing in Fairies: The Author and the Homosexual," in *Inside/Out: Lesbian Theories, Gay Theories*, ed. Diana Fuss (New York: Routledge, 1991), 199.

32. Pamela Robertson Wojcik, *The Apartment Plot: Urban Living in American Film and Popular Culture, 1945–1975* (Durham, NC: Duke University Press, 2010), 133.

33. "Humor, bitchy, bitter, self-deprecatory, becomes the armor of the individual. 'If I can laugh at myself, no one else can laugh at me' sums up the philosophy." Richard L. Coe, "'The Boys in the Band,'" *Washington Post–Herald Tribune*, May 17, 1968, C8.

34. Marjory Adams, "'The Boys in the Band' Is No Musical," *Boston Globe*, March 18, 1970, 14.

35. Charles Champlin, "Motion Picture Review: 'The Boys in the Band,'" *Los Angeles Times*, March 29, 1970, O1. See also Walter Kerr, "'Boys' Mixes Anguish, Antic," *Chicago Tribune*, April 28, 1968, A5.

36. As Steven Cohan argues, "camp also needs to be understood as the formation of a queer *affect*: of taking pleasure in perceiving if not causing category dissonance, whether in representations of heterosexual normality, the values that reiterate it, or the commodities that derive from it." Steven Cohan, *Incongruous Entertainment: Camp, Cultural Value, and the MGM Musical* (Durham, NC: Duke University Press, 2005), 18.

37. In a 1968 profile of the actor Cliff Gorman, one of many that rigorously emphasized his heterosexuality, the *New York Times* labeled Emory "The Definitive Screaming Queen." Klemesrud, "You Don't Have to Be One," D1.

38. Quoted in Dunlap, "In a Revival," H28.

39. Ahmed, *Promise*, 117.

40. Ibid., 220–23.

41. Ibid., 222.

42. A slang phrase for getting high on pot, acid, or other hallucinogens, "turning on" was widely associated with the countercultural icon Timothy Leary, who promoted the slogan "Turn on, Tune in, Drop out" in 1966 and viewed drugs as crucial to the expansion of one's consciousness. Timothy Leary, *Flashbacks: An Autobiography* (New York: G. P. Putnam's Sons, 1990), 248–57.

43. Tom Burke, "The New Homosexuality," *Esquire* 72 (December 1969): 178.

44. Ibid., 306.

45. Ibid., 308.

46. Laud Humphreys, "New Styles in Homosexual Manliness," *Trans-Action* 8, nos. 5–6 (1971): 41.

47. Ahmed, *Promise*, 45, my emphasis.

48. Ibid., 164.

49. William Scroggie has likewise noted a degree of politicization in Michael over the course of the play as he "moves from a rather conciliatory stance vis-à-vis straight society to a much more challenging position." William Scroggie, "Producing Identity: From *The Boys in the Band* to Gay Liberation," in *The Queer Sixties*, ed. Patricia Juliana Smith (London: Routledge, 1999), 247.

50. Allen Young, "A Gay Manifesto," *Ramparts*, November 1971, 55.

51. Wilfrid Sheed, "Gay Life Gets a Sharp Going Over," *Life*, May 24, 1968, 18.

52. *Time* magazine's 1969 cover story on homosexuality, for example, argued that "for the time being at least, there is a savage ring of truth to the now famous line from The Boys in the Band: 'Show me a happy homosexual, and I'll show you a gay corpse." Richard Foster, "The Homosexual: Newly Visible, Newly Understood," *Time*, October 31, 1969, 64.

53. Donn Teal, "How Anguished Are Homosexuals?," *New York Times*, June 1, 1969, D23.

54. Richard Dyer, "The Role of Stereotypes," in Cook and Lewington, *Images*, 18, 20.

55. See Robin Wood, *Hollywood from Vietnam to Reagan* (New York: Columbia University Press, 1986); Thomas Elsaesser, Alexander Horwath, and Noel King, eds., *The Last Great American Picture Show: New Hollywood Cinema in the 1970s* (Amsterdam: Amsterdam University Press, 2004).

56. Deborah B. Gould, *Moving Politics: Emotion and ACT UP's Fight against AIDS* (Chicago: University of Chicago Press, 2009), 26.
57. Stuart Byron, quoted in LaValley, "Deep Focus," 62.
58. David Drake, quoted in Dunlap, "In a Revival," H28.
59. Ahmed, *Promise*, 177.
60. Cecil Smith, "'Boys' Playing Off-Broadway," *Los Angeles Times*, November 12, 1968, C16.
61. Love, *Feeling Backward*, 28.

# 3

## Gothic Spatiality and the Limits of Gay Visibility in *The Boys in the Band*

RYAN POWELL

The 1970 film adaptation of Mart Crowley's *The Boys in the Band* occupies a very specific moment in the history of gay cinema. Released just as the gay liberation movement of the late 1960s and early 1970s coalesced, the film holds an important place within a larger cycle of films that articulate an emergent paradigm of gay visibility. Other such films include *Some of My Best Friends Are . . .* (dir. Mervyn Nelson, 1971), *A Very Natural Thing* (dir. Christopher Larkin, 1974), and *Saturday Night at the Baths* (dir. David Buckley, 1975). At the same time, as a play first performed in 1968—more than a year before the first gay liberation groups began to form in the months following the highly publicized riots that began at New York's Stonewall Inn on June 28, 1969—its characterization of social life among its male-desiring protagonists is unmistakably more informed by older norms of postwar queer life, showcasing a kind of witty, camp negativity that was becoming rarer in film projects conceived during the gay liberation era.

Over the two years that *The Boys in the Band* moved from stage to screen, subjects deemed non-normative in their desire and/or style of self-presentation—trans and bisexual people, male-desiring men and female-desiring women—began actively to engage public attention through direct political action, from riots, protests, and marches to happenings and gay-ins. As a result, the film exhibits a complex historical layering. On the one hand, few changes were made to the play's dialogue when adapting it for film, leaving its narrative focus on pre-gay-liberation social life fully intact; on the other, its appearance on film necessarily takes part in the visibility politics mobilized in the intervening years.

This combination of elements marked by different paradigms of identity is manifest in a tension in many moments during which dialogue runs counter to a gay-affirmative visual syntax. This results in an "incoherent text," to use a phrase coined by Robin Wood: a "work... that [does] not know what [it wants] to say," riddled with "difficulty, accumulated strains, tensions and contradictions."[1] However, the result is not only an incongruent mess of inextricable contradictions. Instead, the filmmakers' visual organization of the story within a gothic framework accentuates the very divergence of paradigms engendered in the split between the dialogue and the formal cinematic technique. Thus, intended or not, the film's simultaneous production and management of its own incoherence foregrounds how coeval yet seemingly contradictory political and ontological paradigms may operate—and be experienced—through layered relations to one another. To put it another way, instead of illustrating a collision of divergent or seemingly incompatible historical moments or the displacement or subordination of one narrative by another, the film's gothic refraction of historical change invites us to consider how various historical modes often construed as distinct may overlap, intermingle, and exist alongside one another in ways often obscured by dominant, teleological models of historical narrative.

*The Boys in the Band*'s deployment of gothic strategies can best be understood through reference to the work of Misha Kavka. As Kavka notes, the screen gothic has a capacity beyond the gothic novel to elaborate gothic ideas and aesthetics through cinematically rendered space: "the effect of fear is produced through transformations, extensions, and misalignments of size and distance that are possible only in three-dimensional space."[2] Cinema may artfully use all of the formal possibilities of filmic elaboration to signal and to allude to things that might otherwise be difficult to represent. *The Boys in the Band* employs a host of gothic techniques to construct a sense of unease that gains in ominous effect by moving beyond direct forms of representational elucidation, from the use of shadows and ominous lighting to disorientingly blurred backgrounds and alarming shifts in the pacing and rhythm of editing and shot distances.

Importantly, however, these techniques work affectively to shape and to accent the film's complex relationship to historical possibility. The film turns on a standard gothic structure in which the viewer is introduced to a stable and rational present, only to watch as that present is violently undermined by the hostile return of mores, conventions, and beliefs characteristic of an earlier, apparently outmoded, period. Typically in the gothic, Enlightenment values such as reason, clarity, individualism, and liberty from authoritarianism are subsumed by atavistic pre-Enlightenment states of being, driven by emotion, superstition, and subjection to unseen, unknown forces. Working from this gothic template, *Boys* is structured neatly in two halves. In the first half, group sociality among male-desiring men is framed positively through a visual rhetoric of affirmative gay action, only to be subsumed by "older" forms of queer sociality cinematically elaborated as dark, threatening, and confining.

In exploring how this bifurcated structure is worked through in *The Boys in the Band*, this chapter looks first at how the film sets up gay visibility as a rationalist enterprise before moving on to look at how it places this within a vengeful dualism; finally, it considers some of the critical inquiries raised by the film's gothic treatment of historical relations between different modes and models of gender and socio-sexual practice. Through this close reading of *Boys* as a screen gothic, I consider how the film challenges viewers to question the possible routes that a social existence organized around male-male desire might take. How do "older" models of queer sociality premised more strongly on gender nonconformity perhaps offer different kinds of liberatory experience than those privileged through the seemingly pragmatic demands of gay visibility? How might the film illustrate some of what is at stake in this historical transition or even invite viewers to reject or think of other ways of constructing these two models in relation to each other? If "gay is good," as the popular slogan posited, then what bad aspects of pregay life might come to haunt it?

## Queer Sociality and the Goodness of Gay

In order to understand the tensions the film mobilizes through the gothic, it is first helpful to look at the two major social paradigms at play in the film: what I call *queer sociality* versus the newer forms of social and political action and interaction being privileged within gay liberation rhetoric and practice, particularly those premised on the demand of producing gay people as visually articulated subjects. One of the most salient differences between preliberation and postliberation social modalities is the way in which each is differently oriented around a "positive" or "negative" outlook.

These different orientations contributed to differently constituted social formations in each case. The earlier queer sociality corresponds with the kinds of queer culture Richard Dyer has identified as typifying "the age of queerness," a rough historical descriptor for the century between the mid- to late 1860s and the late 1960s. Dyer argues that during this period, queerness designated a "notion of sexual attraction . . . that went along with other non-sexual qualities and was humanly (morally, medically, socially) problematic."[3] Queer sociality during this time took up these negative elaborations of queer identity as tools for culture making and social cohesion, most prevalently in urban subcultures. Explaining the "negativity of queer," Dyer notes, "These were defiant assertions of male-male sexuality, refusals of pathology, enthusiastic embracings of difference."[4]

George Chauncey has noted another important development in mid-twentieth-century queer life: the relationship between sexual and nonsexual aspects of queerness began to stratify. He explains,

> Earlier terms—*fairy, queer* and *trade* most commonly—had distinguished various *types* of homosexually active men: effeminate homosexuals, more conventional homosexuals, and masculine heterosexuals who would accept homosexual advances. Gay tended to group all these types together, to de-emphasize their difference by emphasizing the similarity in character they had presumably demonstrated by their choice of sexual partners. A dichotomous system of classification, based now on sexual object choice rather than gender status, had begun to supersede the old.[5]

This shift, away from a multifarious queer negativity and toward a model of gay similarity that more reductively signals sexual object choice, marks the changing narrative investments of preliberation and postliberation film. In fact, like *Boys*, a handful of postwar queer films took up gothic effects as a means of elucidating a critically queer perspective that reveled in images of queer monstrosity, expressing the way that oppression both shaped the lives of queer subjects and could in turn be explored and utilized as material for pleasure (at the levels of both making and viewing). Examples of such films run the gamut from the vampiric drag-queen orgy that stands as the central spectacle of Jack Smith's *Flaming Creatures* (1963) to the street-scene segment of James Bidgood's *Pink Narcissus* (1971), which constructs a fictional Times Square at night, a studio-built demimonde of perverts, dandies, hustlers, drag queens, seminude construction workers, and athletes.

While some strands of gay liberation theory sought to sustain and build on the pleasures and potentials of collectivizing, gender-nonconformist performances of deviance, several prominent strands sought to advance a revisionist historicization that scapegoated gender-nonconforming men, repositioning them as pathological by-products of a bygone era. As the liberationist Craig Alfred Hanson wrote, in a particularly scathing piece titled "The Fairy Princess Exposed," "Because they cannot rationalize why they are gay (except in the context of sin or sickness), gay traditionalists tend to believe that mysterious forces quite beyond their immediate control rule and guide their lives. The centuries of persecution and discrimination by the Christian church and other forces of social control have mesmerized them into believing that they are thoroughly rotten sex degenerates, a class of perverted half-men doomed to live a living hell beyond the scope of humanity. They are unable to imagine that gay is good."[6] Hanson's sentiment demonstrates how certain strands of gay liberation theory worked to situate gay liberation as a corrective to pre-Stonewall queer life. Emblematizing pre-gay-liberation life through the vision of pathologically ignorant and self-destructive queens and perverts allows Hanson to fashion a new, enlightened world of intelligence and goodness, rendered vivid through contrast. One need only return to any number of postwar cultural products (the films listed earlier but also the films of Andy Warhol, Curt McDowell, and George Kuchar, among others; books by writers such as Richard Amory and Parker Tyler; the anthropology of Esther Newton; etc.) to see how queer negativity, even when informed by stereotype and pathology, consistently and inventively translated and repurposed this negativity as a socializing force of cultural critique that had the power to bring people together.

### The Layering of Gay Visibility

In a challenge to Hanson's blunt historical polarization of forces, *Boys* offers a rare instance in which queer sociality and gay visibility are not only formulated alongside each other but layered over each other. I now consider how this operates through the film's engagement with what I call the technology of gay visibility. Gay visibility was not only a rhetorical tool but also a technology. Liberationists, in coming out as gay, produced and manufactured themselves anew. To assert one's position as gay in visual terms meant to employ coming out as a transformative narrative technology that resituated the subject as part of the wider public sphere. Popular forms mediating gay subjects as visibly marked users of public space included the donning of buttons that exclaimed, "Gay Is Good"; T-shirts and placards for marches and rallies with slogans such as "Gay Power"; filmmaking (documentary and fiction) meant to "capture" gay life on film; and, arguably most importantly, the rise of a gay press that circulated photographs and pamphlets that rhetorically "pictured" outness for readers.

Many of the first wave of gay-produced films screening in theaters, following the recent loosening of censorship laws (and indeed playing a central part in that loosening) in the mid- to late '60s themselves helped to develop the mechanics of gay visibility. Films such as *Mondo Rocco* (dir. Pat Rocco, 1970) and *Daydreams from a Cross-Town Bus* (dir. Peter de Rome, 1972) made a virtue of showing gay men moving easily between private, semiprivate, and discernibly public spaces. Gay hardcore porn was no different in this regard: one of the most popular gay porn films of the period, *The Boys in the Sand* (dir. Wakefield Poole, 1971), used its punning title to emphasize gay action as part of the outdoor space of the beach.

In short, these films asserted gay visibility, first and foremost, through visualizing the pedestrian movement of male-desiring men who are socially linked through a combination of montage (cutting between men to establish a sense of similarity and relationality), costuming rich in gay signification, and cuts between shots of gay social interaction in apartments, parties, and bars and shots of participants moving through city streets, whether in civil rights demonstrations or as everyday city dwellers. To show gay people as part of everyday pedestrian locales was to refashion those locales in progressively oriented teleological terms; images of gay people in the city worked as part of a greater cinematic manufacturing of outness that implicitly narrativized a gay transformation through Enlightenment values. Through the use of bright lighting, outdoor locations, and editing that emphasized a sense of easy movement through space, these films foregrounded gay people as an undisruptive element in a coherent, easily graspable, and rational world.

While it is perhaps unsurprising to see lesbians and gay men occupy public space on-screen today, it is important to remember that at the time of *The Boys in the Band*, such representations were still nearly nonexistent in mass-distributed film. In this regard, the first half of the film now provides an opportunity for thinking through how gay existence itself was being actively constructed and modeled through the technology of visibility. How does *The Boys in the Band* work to produce characters as gay, and how does this production work to advance images of gay mobility and freedom that the film will later counter through its gothic treatment?

In order to consider these questions, I look at three locations the film uses in its first half—the street, the bar, and the apartment—all of which work as spaces for constructing gay visibility. I also explore how these moments are interspersed with brief glimpses of a certain gothic expressionism each time the film cuts to the character of Alan, thus introducing a slowly cumulative sense of uncertainty and unease that will come to fruition in the second half of the film.

Extending a version of gay visibility that works to establish gay men as an ethnographic "fact of life," the opening sequence introduces us to the streets of New York via a medium tracking shot that follows Michael as he makes his way through a busy pedestrian thoroughfare. As with the protagonists in similar sequences in several blaxploitation pictures from this period, such as *Shaft* (dir. Gordon Parks, 1971) and *Black Caesar* (dir. Larry Cohen, 1973), Michael is established as both an individual and part of the larger public.[7] From here, the film cuts between vignettes of the ensemble cast similarly going about their lives in the city: Donald drives his car through midday traffic, Emory closes up shop at the fine antiques shop at which he works and rushes off to jump in a cab, Hank plays basketball in a local gym, Larry photographs models in the studio, Alan steps off a plane, Cowboy hustles on the street, Emory walks down a busy avenue with his poodle, Michael shops in a clothing store, and Donald exchanges packages with Bernard, seen working as a clerk at Doubleday bookstore. In short, gay

Peopling the world with gay men. A tracking shot places Michael in everyday space.

Gay patrons at ease. A shot of Hank through the window of Julius' challenges popular imagery that presented gay bar life as cloistered.

men exist. Gay men, like everyone else, are busy participating in the normal activities of everyday American life: working, driving, shopping, exercising. As each shot tracks its subject through his afternoon, the sequence comes together to imply a demographic vastness beyond these specific iterations, a gay life so expansively peopled that it is easy to imagine the segment rolling on ad infinitum. Enhancing this effect is the nondiegetic scoring, which sonically binds the montage together through a modern rendition of the classic show tune "Anything Goes." The layering of all-male voices, combined with the song's whimsical instrumentation, elaborates a social world in which these men, even when shown alone, exist together in relations characterized by lightness and ease.

In the film's first half, interior space is presented as markedly open and uncloseted, with the locations of the gay bar Julius' and Michael's apartment both defined by permeable spatial relations with clear sight lines producing a sense of unfettered movement. In the case of the bar, a shot of Hank looking in through the window frames it as a busy, bright space visible from the street. This shot and the subsequent scene offer a counterpoint to the figuration of gay bars as dark, recessed, tucked-away spaces, out of the sight of everyday life, not only in postwar films such as *Narcissus* (dir. Ben Moore and Willard Maas, 1956) and *Advise and Consent* (dir. Otto Preminger, 1962) but also in more contemporary films such as *Some of My Best Friends Are . . .* and *Saturday Night at the Baths*. Here, instead, is a strong sense of continuity between pedestrian space and the space of the bar. As Hank enters and makes his way through the bar, the film, refusing a voyeuristic or slumming gaze, cuts to a shaky point-of-view shot. We see men of many ages, dressed in suits, ties, and button-down shirts, laughing, smiling, and talking in intimate social clusters. As with the street scene that opens the film, male-desiring men are shown as confident citizens, as at ease in their movements through the city as they are in their close bodily relations with one another.

The apartment is actually little different from the bar in this regard and can be understood as an extension of a city space framed through a syntax of gay visibility. As Richard Meyer has noted in his work on the use of still photography in gay liberation media, it is important to "[keep] in mind the idea of the camera as an active participant, rather than a neutral recorder, of gay liberation."[8] In the case of moving-image production, it is essential to consider how the participatory function of formal cinematic means builds images of gay liberation and imbues them with certain qualities and functions. Like the permeability of outside and inside that defines the bar space, shot type, camera movement, and mise-en-scène are coordinated in the apartment segment to further elaborate spatial permeability, with shots that reinforce a sense of openness and ease of movement between the rooftop patio (positioned in full view of the numerous surrounding apartment buildings and towers), the bedroom, the bathroom, the kitchen, and the living-room area, which functions as a combined entryway, study, bar, and sitting area. Pamela Robertson Wojcik describes this kind of apartment space as one of "public privacy." Arguing that this is constitutive of a kind of "closet in which one can try on, secrete, or disclose one's identity," she notes, "Rather than a simple container, the closet is a space meant to be opened and closed, but is often left open, to communicate with other rooms."[9]

Michael's porous apartment is one of the central areas in which the historical layers that make up *The Boys in the Band* are evident, presenting us with a view of the queer sociality of closet space mediated through the protocols of gay visibility. This results in a number of moments that are exceptional for their invigorating mix of conversational relay, non-normative enactments of gesture, comportment, and bodily relationality, all of which are inflected and indeed celebrated through the film's cinematic construction of gay space. The film foregrounds an entwined set of relations between space and gesture that has a particular resonance with what the architect Aaron Betsky has described as queer space. He explains, "Gesture exaggerates the body, extending it into space, breaking through the mute boundaries of the skin to create a deformed image of the self in a social relationship. Gesture allows for freedom, because it can form an unspoken code that escapes notice and thus control.... Queers are masters of the hidden gesture, the theatrical walk, the creation of close physical connections through the most fleeting motions of the body.... Gesture finds its most physical points in buildings that refuse to sit still, obey orders, or tell a simple story of order."[10] For example, as the men arrive for the party, a sense of fluid, easy, intimate socializing is sustained through the film's mediation of space. The film makes use of medium and medium-long shots that allow for a full view of the apartment as a series of interconnected spaces that the men move around with ease, sitting, leaning, or standing while conversing and dancing with one another. The relatively sparse use of two-shots and close-ups (they are brief and tend to give way quickly to medium shots), combined with the high ceilings and large open doorways and windows (a kitchen window even functions as another door to the patio), sustains the sense of the apartment as an open, expansive extension of the city space established in the opening segment of the film. Here closet sociality appears less ghettoized and entrapped, instead seeming to foster forms of looseness and mobility not possible elsewhere, where the rigidity of more orderly, heteronormative, and masculinist spatial dictates is cast aside in favor of forms of use, movement, and gesture more associated with the feminine.

These mediations of space recalibrate representations that might otherwise feel like little more than brute stereotypes through an actively engaged cinematography that not only supports but elaborates the togetherness created through non-normative gender performance, even for the more masculine members of the group. This is nowhere more evident than in the "Heat Wave" segment, when the group of men come together to reenact a Rockettes-style dance number they developed years ago on Fire Island. Whereas a more distant or stable camera might have presented this scene as a spectacle, a group of men queering out for a heterosexual viewership, the fast-paced editing, guided by the music, and the spontaneity evoked by the montage of multiple shot types and by the combination of fluid and frenzied camera movements amplify a dynamic sense of liberatory movement.

Beginning with a medium shot of Bernard, Emory, and Hank relaxing on the porch together, the camera gently tracks from left to right, refusing to settle on any individual or way of seeing this group formation, visually tracing the sense of bondedness that exists among the men: Bernard leaning back, smoking and thinking about the good old days at Fire Island,

Larry waving the Martha and the Vandellas record jacket in the air, Emory jumping up to dance. Even the men in the background can be seen moving about in a way that echoes the dance, with Michael, in particular, visible on the right-hand side of the frame through an open kitchen window, moving to the window with excitement at what he sees taking form on the patio. As if pulled in by the infectious socializing energy of the dance, the camera rises with Bernard as he gets up from his seat to join in, followed by a cut to Donald and Michael, similarly enthusiastic, as they approach the lineup from behind, with Michael ultimately jumping over a short rooftop wall that separates the kitchen area from the patio to join the men in a synchronized yet adorably haphazard dance.

The "Heat Wave" sequence. The Boys moving into an irresistible social formation.

Cutting from a medium-long shot to a medium shot, the film suggests a vector of forward motion: a single shot of Bernard's arm connecting to Emory's shoulder, linking again from Emory's arm to Larry's shoulder. A sudden cut back to a medium shot from the front of the group catches Larry slapping Emory's ass and then Emory returning the favor, both men cracking up in response to each other's shared transgression of the norms of gender and sexuality that mark the protocols of male friendship. The camera begins to swing and sway forward and backward while following the dance, as if the camera itself is moved by the force of the jubilant dance. Brief deep-focus shots offer us generous views of the patio space before the men and the apartment interior behind, all the way back into the kitchen and the living room.

Rather than simply presenting these fleeting gestures, the camera work and editing here replicate these contours of movement, highlighting gestures that would otherwise be difficult to see: a hand reaching up to touch a shoulder, and male legs moving together and kicking out in ways that might be described as "effeminist," to invoke the title of a liberationist magazine of the time. Through framing, we come to see this dance as a constituent part of the larger spaces of the apartment, the building, and the city, a succession of ever-larger spaces that inhabitants may move through, unregulated, to create impromptu sites of social coalescence.

## Alan's Arrival

This liberationist ethos of visibility marks the first half of the film; however, even early on, contrasting images of shadowy containment and muted, blurred backgrounds begin gothically snaking their way into the film. Forecasting the change in social dynamics that will come with Alan's arrival, his phone calls to Michael at the apartment position him as part of an entirely different visual scheme. In direct contrast to the fluid uses of space and impromptu performance of gesture that define the queer life of the apartment, Alan is situated as a subject of masculine convention, containment, and limited movement.

In short, Alan appears as a figure of an anxious closeted life. Two sequences establish this: in the first, a medium shot of the lively and brightly lit gay bar in the opening sequence cuts to a medium close-up that shows Alan peering out a window at the city below—with the gay life that has just been shown as a constituent part of it—before cutting again to a longer

Alan's isolation in a dreary hotel room is the counterimage to the brighter, open spaces foregrounded to this point in the film.

shot that reveals him within the confines of a dim, drab, and boxy hotel room; in the second, a medium close-up shows him calling Michael from a phone booth, surrounded by dark, busy city streets that, through the use of shallow focus that directly counters the deep-focus aesthetic generally utilized so far, leaves the background a distorted abstraction. Connecting the two city spaces, a honking car horn sounds across a cut from the phone booth to Michael in the apartment, establishing that these spaces are part of the same urban geography yet introducing a highly contrasted register of darkness and distortion to signal each character's different affective relation to that geography.

The gothic traditionally presents a stable, seemingly transparent and rational world and then undermines that world through a slow, intermittent, yet unmistakable process; it establishes a good space where the bad comes creeping in. *Boys* constructs this inside/outside dialectic by bringing the clear and transparently figured space of gay visibility into a tense interplay with a shadowy past that troubles and undermines the certainty of the space. These gradual transitions are often structured to intensify as the plot progresses, light eventually giving way to dark.

This gothic tipping point is reached with Alan's arrival at and interruption of the party at Michael's. Upon his arrival, the dance immediately ceases when the boys execute a twirl only to find this new presence behind them. The boys break out of group formation, and all parties look at each other with discomfort and unease: the boys have been caught or, perhaps more accurately, found out. As the men all sit down, now conversing in a low, serious tone about topics such as work and family life—with the more masculine-presenting Hank taking the lead with Alan—the sudden and dramatic switch in register from camp sociality to earnestness emphasizes the flatness of certain kinds of male social interaction that would be taken for granted as natural, even invisible, in almost any other movie of the period.

Departing from the group, Alan and Michael head upstairs to discuss the mysterious problem that brought Alan to Michael's in the first place, leaving the other boys to return to their camp antics. At this point, both the mise-en-scène and framing are used to establish a sense of division between the (now endangered) heteronormative dynamic of Alan and Michael's friendship and the liberated gay sociality of the boys. In contrast to the warm glow of the paper lamps hanging outside and the boys laughing below, the scene cuts to the now-somber environment of Michael's bedroom, full of shadows and darkness produced by dim spotlighting that creates a chiaroscuro effect. Angled from above, a shot shows Michael closing the window and shutting out the sight and sound of the men on the porch below. Despite now having complete privacy, Alan chooses not to disclose the problem that moved him to get in touch with Michael but instead fixates on his distaste for Emory's "kind of talk." After Michael again inquires as to what brought Alan here, Alan is shown sitting silent and unresponsive, a shroud of shadow now obscuring his face. As Alan continues to evade the question—despite Michael's repeated and increasingly insistent demand for an answer—the film leaves these narrative possibilities of the closet open and hanging over the film, reinforced by Michael's reentering the party and Alan's slipping into the narrative background; no longer visible but still present, he remains confined to the bedroom. Even out of frame, however, Alan's presence as a source of uncertainty hangs over the space of the apartment.

This transitional scene initiates a new phase in the film. Fast-paced dialogue and the intermingling of bodies begin to give way to silence and separation as the film assigns Alan, Michael, and the rest of the group particular places within a closet paradigm. This is managed not only in visual but also in affective terms. As noted by Eve Kosofsky Sedgwick, "'Closetedness' itself is a performance initiated . . . by the speech act of a silence—not a particular silence, but a silence that accrues particularity by fits and starts, in relation to the discourse that surrounds and differentially constitutes it."[11] In getting across the implicit tension—the discomfort created from snowballing questions and ensuing silences—the film's formal techniques construct this silence so that Alan's failure to reply, accruing shadows, becomes evidence of something more terrible than failure, perhaps some kind of inability to speak. This silence is how he, in effect, comes into the terms of the closet. That is, without these elements, Alan is perhaps little more than a man refusing to divulge facts for any number of reasons; however, through these gothicizing visual elements, these silences come to elaborate an evolving context of uncertainty and unreliability that increasingly invites the viewer's speculation.

## The Spatio-temporality of the Queer Surround

The second hour of the film works as a gothic in a wide variety of ways: not only its characteristic iconography but also its structuring of relations between past and present. In relation to the former, Harry Benshoff notes that, in *Boys*, "the iconography of the horror film creeps in: thunder and lightning, Expressionist shadows, ominous musical cues, and hysterical moments of formal excess are used to characterize homosexuals' lives."[12] Parker Tyler notes that the addition of the "intervening storm" marks a division in the film: wreaking havoc on the patio, it forces the men inside, "properly emphasiz[ing] the haphazard, confused frailty of some of the homosexual relations shown."[13]

In order to further understand how the gothic is employed to negotiate the spatio-temporal dynamics set up early on in the story, it is useful to look at how the film works in relation to other gothic films of the postwar years: most notably, the Roger Corman cycle of Edgar Allan Poe adaptations, to which the film bears some striking similarities. Like *The Boys in the Band*, these adaptations took full advantage of the possibilities afforded by the more tightly controlled and affectively malleable aspects of cinematic technique. Unlike the novel or play, film is able to offer more programmatically organized ways of establishing relationships between character and space through placing formal elements in closely coordinated dynamic relations to one another. Through such means, heavily stylized spatial representations may be regularly used to elaborate psychological conditions and states of mind. As Kavka observes, looking across Corman's several Poe adaptations that turn on using the B-movie star Vincent Price as a monstrous antagonist, "Price plays an aesthete of a frozen historical age, an aristocrat isolated from the external world and tied to his class, by the possession of—what else?—a grand labyrinthine house replete with towers, staircases, hidden passageways and dungeons. The spatialization of the frustrated, repressed psyche could not be made more clear, since in these films the house . . . serves as the master's seat and, hence, metaphorically, as the projection of his psyche."[14] Like Corman's Poe-cycle films such as *The Fall of the House of Usher* (1960) and *The Pit and the Pendulum* (1961), *The Boys in the Band* employs a narrative structure in which guests, arriving at the master's residence, unwittingly become subject to a dynamically disturbing destabilization of the space that symbolically echoes his deranged psyche. Following this formula, the film's second half leaves behind a vision of gay collectivity, shifting the film's focalization through the perspective of Michael's precarious psychological state—a state defined by an affectively explosive cocktail of shame, doubt, and paranoia.

This process of symbolically transmuting psychology into spatial terms is nowhere more evident than in the phone game, in which Michael coerces each member of the group to call the one person he has loved the most and to confess his love. The relationship between the spoken and unspoken and the visible and the invisible becomes affectively activated though the screen gothic. The living room is reconfigured into a gothic chamber, replete with shadow-strewn faces, blurred backgrounds, and patches of extreme darkness that render the previously clear contours of the room unclear. Silences continue to grow longer here, signaling an increasing inability for language to bear the weight of articulating the complex emotions being prodded and unearthed. Likewise, the game brings into full force a tense interplay between the said and the seen, as we wonder when the call recipient will put two and two together and match the voice on the other end of the line with the image of the confessor. As Wojcik notes, "the aim of the game is to force a match between image and sound, to reveal oneself to the other person on the line."[15]

On a narrative level, the game reformulates the relative equality among the group in the first half of the film into a new system in which—as with the still-operative yet fading aristocracy of the Price character who acts as an imperial force over the inhabitants of the house—the men become subject to a set of values organized around Michael's propensity for negation. In particular, Michael appears propelled by a desire to reveal both the pleasure of queer sociality and the sanctity of hetero-masculine identity as equally false, or, to use Tyler's words, as positions of "confused frailty." In order to do so, he initiates a game that closely resembles the act of coming out. As coming out changed meaning in the months following Stonewall, from a term designating coming out into gay subculture to a notion of coming out of the closet and revealing oneself as gay within the world at large, it brought with it the expectation to take up this new model. As Samuel Delany has noted, "A good number of people—myself included—who were under the impression we had come out ages ago, now realized we were expected to come out all over again in this wholly new sense."[16] By the time of the film's release in 1970, Michael's gothically elaborated version of coming out resonated with liberationist rhetoric and practice. From a post-gay-liberation-era perspective, the phone game redirects the mechanism and purpose of coming out, a perverse misuse of the new technology that allows Michael to turn his sharp, queer-inflected passion for deviance against the people around him. Through this maneuver, the values and ways of being that were rapidly being positioned by liberationists as part of an outmoded, preliberated past hold sway over the group, so that queer practices of defiance, critique, and camp mockery—filtered through screen gothic effect—come to appear as dangerous manifestations of "the age of queerness."

The phone game reformulates coming out as an opening into one's past, a past that exerts an irrational pull. This negative pull does not affect each character in an identical way; in effect, it breaks characters into a two-tiered class system. Formally, isolating close-ups, extreme contrasts in focus within single frames, and mise-en-scène all work to divide the group visually. Less gender-conforming characters such as Emory and Bernard are established as weak and victimized, whereas Hank, Larry, and Alan, who sport contrastingly naturalizing and masculinist gender presentations, all score highly in the game and emerge with their choices and self-presentations reinforced. The gender non-normativity accommodated by queer sociality now appears to generate a debilitating form of negativity; by contrast, a more masculinist image of gay health is represented as the natural consequence of an identity fashioned around same-sex orientation.

For Bernard and Emory—among the most comfortable of the men with enacting traditionally feminine styles of behavior and performance—their participation in the phone game brings them into extreme fields of isolation. Framing their calls through a gothic temporalization, when each character dials up a past love from his youth, the film cuts to a series of telescoping close-ups that show the men alone and engulfed by a surrounding darkness. As if overtaken by the weight of queer longings that have been denied in the pursuit of a new form of gay stability and self-imposed confidence, the men appear plunged into trances. In the case of Bernard, a medium close-up shows Michael bearing down on him as a sort of tyrannical master, forcing him to make the call. With Bernard brightly lit in the

Gothic Spatiality and the Limits of Gay Visibility in *The Boys in the Band* • 105

The phone game. Michael and the darkness bear down on Bernard.

The phone game. Emory is transfixed by the lost love of a preliberated past.

foreground and Michael slightly out of focus just behind, the image takes on an extreme sense of depth, creating the feeling that with each slow turn of the rotary dial Bernard makes, Michael pushes him further into his past. After Bernard fails to reach his past love, we see him crouched on the steps, shrouded in darkness and completely despondent.

As Emory tells the story of his high school love, a medium shot transforms to a close-up as the camera zooms in, tightly framing his transfixed face. Drained of his usual energy, he mutters in a monotone voice that those who teased him at school about the object of his crush would never know that Emory would "go on loving him years after they'd all forgotten [his] funny secret." Creating an interplay of psychological and spatial exposition, as the camera zooms in, the background grows out of focus. Just as we learn how much weight Emory's past still holds over him—a past that cannot be washed away through the "liberated" imposition of pride—the background becomes, like his past, a space of indefinite proportions appearing outside the bounds of rationality or reason.

These preliberated selves have a counterpoint in Larry, Hank, and Alan and where the phone game takes them. In contrast to Emory and Bernard, who are cast aside under the weight of their own queer longings, each of these men pursues some version or other of a hetero-masculinist telos that brings him in line with normative conventions of manhood: Hank reveals his desire to build a committed, monogamous life with Larry; Larry reveals his desire for notch-on-the-headboard-style independence; and Alan, when pressed to come out as gay by Michael, comes out instead as straight by calling his wife and proclaiming his love to her. This counterpoint is also elaborated visually, with each man styled in relation to heterosexual conventions and, in the case of Hank and Larry, costumed in business-casual attire that bespeaks an air of authentic, unkempt masculinity. Unlike Emory and Bernard, who are floored and weakened by the eruption of past lives coming to haunt the present, Hank and Larry appear alert and punchily disheveled, as if, just out of a boxing ring, they are ready to get on with their

Hank and Larry's business-casual masculinism.

evening, a spirit further advanced as the men successfully escape this chamber of queer horrors and retreat to the bedroom upstairs together.

Through a sort of contra-outing, Michael's dark game reconstructs Emory and Bernard within the rational/irrational dichotomy that marks the gothic, so that the previously admirable sense of outness and confidence of these characters is now revealed to have a festering queer underneath. As figures who long to simply love who they feel love for, they appear locked in a queer purgatory from which liberatory gay sexuality cannot rescue them. Through this process, they become queer objects of fear—a thorn in the side of a gay liberation premised on a firm division of boundaries that (even if it seeks to erode these boundaries) recapitulates the distinction between gay and straight. In terms of both gender presentation and race, Emory's and Bernard's dejection and, ultimately, ejection from the social circumference of the game (for the remainder of the play, we see them cast aside, Emory underneath a pillow on the couch and Bernard collapsed on the steps) works to situate queer sociality as a threat that can be located in men who do not or cannot rise to the occasion of a gay life premised on the sanctity of healthy, white, masculinist, active men in pursuit of a better future for themselves as individuals. It is telling that, while Alan, Hank, Larry, and Donald all pursue the rhetoric of "a better future," neither Emory nor Bernard makes even the slightest foray into aspirational thinking.

The polarization between a negative, non-normative queerness and a masculinist vision of what might (in today's parlance) be called gay health is brought to its apex in the figure of Donald, once all other characters have left the frame and Michael has his climactic breakdown. We might take Michael's repeated crying out of the words "I won't make it" as an indication of his inability to align with the project of a masculinist, future-oriented telos toward a new vision of gay health (condensed in the equation he voices in his later line, "you show me a happy homosexual, and I'll show you a gay corpse"). In contrast to Michael's queer collectivist terms, expressed in his wish, "If *we* could just learn not to hate ourselves quite so very much," Donald's suggestion that "with more work," he believes Michael may be able to "get better" encapsulates his aspirational, self-oriented rhetoric. Echoing the kind of models of gay health that proliferated following the declining efforts of many gay liberationists to destabilize gender norms in the early 1970s, Donald functions to bring an assertive sense of order in an effort to drive out the anxiety that Michael will never be a well-functioning gay man with some good old-fashioned pull-yourself-up-by-the-bootstraps talk. This polarization is reinforced by Donald's and Michael's costuming

Donald as gay health, Michael as queer collapse.

and comportment: Michael in his formal violet cashmere sweater clasping on to Donald, the owner of a casually rumpled, authentic, effortless masculinity, whose blue oxford's shirt sleeves are turned up to reveal his muscles as he reassures Michael.

A rhetoric of gay health, figured in the image of a strong, independent man, developed with the rise of a pop-psychology and self-improvement industry that, from the late 1960s on, became a major source of business for a new breed of psychological practitioner—psychologists, counselors, social workers—working as part of what Sam Binkley has identified as the "caring professions," an area that he argues was undergoing a massive expansion in the 1970s due, in part, to New Age culture.[17] Taking the cue from a slate of books that became immensely popular in the mid-to-late sixties, such as *I'm O.K., You're O.K.* (Thomas Anthony Harris, 1969) and *Games People Play* (Eric Berne, 1964), popular psychology provided a field for generating models of self-improvement and self-development through mental health paradigms.[18] Donald is an excellent example of how the project of self-improvement may, first, work to displace older models of queer sociality with a drive toward personal authenticity incompatible with counterpublic forms of sociality and, second, be premised on certain forms of access (to therapists, books, time for self-reflection) and thus prove highly uneven in availability across populations.

At the film's close, Donald comes to act as the representative for a kind of healthy outness that has since become a dominant form for configuring coming out in pop psychology. For instance, a chart offered by the psychologist Joe Kort expands on the "Cass Model of Gay and Lesbian Identity Formation" developed in the late '70s.[19] In Kort's update, coming out and identity development are collapsed into a single six-stage schematic charting the route to a healthy gay selfhood that coming out will facilitate. In the final stage, titled "Identity Synthesis," the subject achieves three goals: the integration of gay/lesbian identity with "other aspects," the recognition of "supportive heterosexual others," and the sustaining of a position where "sexual identity is still important but not a primary factor in relationships with others." None of these goals mentions gender. Tellingly, all three work to map a trajectory that is defined in contradistinction to forms of difference long associated with queer social life, most notably support through coalitions that form around nonnormativity and the "primacy" of sexual practices that are denied, prohibited, or punished within society at large as an important social and collectivizing adhesive. These relationships should now ostensibly inhere in the apparently wider support systems of dominant heterocentric culture. This model suggests a fantasy world in which multiple forms of oppression can be reconciled through the attainment of a healthy self that no longer reads heterosexual norms as incompatible with or inhospitable to gay or queer life.

## Conclusion: The Persistence of Harold

Despite the fact that since the 1970s gay male life has become increasingly centered on masculinist notions of gay health, the characteristics of male femininity, critical negativity, and camp performance that marked so much of the social terrain of pre-Stonewall queer life have persisted, contrary to the predictions of many liberationists. As long as heteronormativity provides the dominant behavioral template, such characteristics will continue to provide male-desiring men, in the words of David Halperin, "a means by which gay men can assert a particular, non-standard, anti-social way of being, feeling, and behaving."[20] Halperin adds, "the post-Stonewall victory of gay identity over the dykes and queens of an earlier era now appears less like the dawn of liberation than like just another strategy of domination—the long final chapter in the long history of transgender oppression from which, only now, we are starting thankfully to emerge."[21]

Of all the characters in *The Boys in the Band*, none more strongly embodies this "non-standard, anti-social way of being, feeling, and behaving" than Harold. His particular form of queerness hangs over the film. While he is almost entirely absent through the first half of the film, his absence is nonetheless a determinedly marked presence rendered through a gothic temporality of inevitable returns—gorgeously handled through the first shot of the film, as the camera pans across an opulent array of beauty products tilting down to show Harold lathering his legs in the bathtub. Defined through the traditionally feminine pleasures of self-care and self-presentation, Harold, his face obscured, appears first and foremost as a queer body taken up with its own leisure. The film contrasts this queer traditionalism with a modern gay cosmopolitanism through editing. As the film cuts to Michael moving hurriedly through the streets of New York, the Cole Porter version of "Anything Goes" is replaced by an updated pop cover of the song. As if lost in the opulence of his tub through the entire exposition of gay visibility in the film's first half, Harold's "official" arrival, rather late in the film, at his birthday party positions him as an unreconstructed relic of the negative queer past, pointedly rendered in shadows and darkness. His presentation is that of queer monster, a status formally elaborated through some of the most stock gothic elements in the film. A self-described "pock-marked Jew fairy," wearing sunglasses at night and dressed like an undertaker in a black suit that buttons high up around the neck, Harold spends much of the film in the shadowy periphery of the room, chiming in with camp epithets and perceptive comments, haunting the men (particularly Michael) with a clearer vision of who they are and will likely remain despite their aspirations.

Harold's arrival as queer monster.

A future that secures the rights of manhood appears to mean little to Harold. In contrast to Larry, Hank, and Donald, Harold cultivates a deeply antitherapeutic refusal of catharsis that works against rhetorics of gay health that posit a telos of "getting better" as a remedy to the effects of oppression; he refuses even to participate in Michael's game, the mechanism via which catharsis is offered. He and Cowboy, leaving together at the end of the film, are the very archetypes of fairy and trade, unaffected by the psychological crises that have challenged other characters. Instead of learning to *manage a life* living as queer in a straight world, Harold lives queer.

Importantly, however, Harold is emblematic of the way in which queer negativity, even antisociality, may, ironically, contribute to a form of queer social coalescence that finds vitality in the shared deflation of heteromasculinist norms through gender nonconformity: it is his birthday, after all, that brings the men together. Even more, Harold's gothicism is part of the larger structure of the film and the attendant dialectic it establishes between the visible and the invisible or obscure. The only character not to appear within the rhetoric of outness that visually defines the first half of the film, clad in sunglasses and dark clothes, he seems part of a peripheral world almost indigestible to visibility rhetoric.

From a present-day perspective, in which a healthy gay identity formation has become not just a goal but also a right that subjects are entitled to, Harold becomes a critical reminder of how visibility operates through an economy of cultural, social, and monetary privilege. In an age when gay health—informed by the AIDS crisis and the many phobias that have proliferated in its wake—has become the dominant model of gay life, the gothic figuration of Harold becomes a potent antidote to the rhetoric of personal achievement and self-satisfaction that has gained such incredible traction. *Not* full of agency and action, *not* a beautiful individual, and *not* a paragon of physical health contributing to a body culture that reads rigorous body work as a sign of inner vitality and life, Harold is still as invisible today as he would have been in 1970, if not more so. Lurking in a queer surround in which he refuses to "get better," Harold exists as an assertion that there is always something beyond visibility capable of taking hold.

## Notes

1. Robin Wood, *From Vietnam to Reagan* (New York: Columbia University Press, 1986), 46–47.

2. Misha Kavka, "The Gothic on Screen," in *The Cambridge Companion to Gothic Fiction*, ed. Jerrold E. Hogle (Cambridge: Cambridge University Press, 2002), 210.

3. Richard Dyer, *The Culture of Queers* (London: Routledge, 2002), 1.

4. Ibid., 7.

5. George Chauncey, *Gay New York: Gender, Urban Culture, and the Making of the Gay Male World, 1890–1940* (New York: Basic Books, 1994), 20–21.

6. Craig Alfred Hanson, "The Fairy Princess Exposed," in *Out of the Closets: Voices of Gay Liberation*, ed. Karla Jay and Allen Young (New York: Pyramid Books, 1972), 267. Originally published in *Gay Sunshine*, no. 10 (January 10, 1972).

7. Richard Dyer discusses the blaxploitation "street sequence" in "Music and Presence in Blaxploitation Cinema," in *In the Space of a Song: The Uses of Song in Film* (London: Routledge, 2012), 156–74.

8. Richard Meyer, "*Gay Power* circa 1970: Visual Strategies for Sexual Revolution," *GLQ: A Journal of Lesbian and Gay Studies* 12, no. 3 (2006): 447.

9. Pamela Robertson Wojcik, *The Apartment Plot* (Durham, NC: Duke University Press, 2010), 133.

10. Aaron Betsky, *Queer Space: Architecture and Same-Sex Desire* (New York: William Morrow, 1997), 22.

11. Eve Kosofsky Sedgwick, *Epistemology of the Closet* (Berkeley: University of California Press, 1990), 3.

12. Harry M. Benshoff, *Monsters in the Closet: Homosexuality in the Horror Film* (Manchester: Manchester University Press, 1997), 177.

13. Parker Tyler, *Screening the Sexes: Homosexuality and the Movies* (New York: Holt, Reinhart and Winston, 1972), 47.

14. Kavka, "Gothic," 224.

15. Wojcik, *Apartment Plot*, 137.

16. Samuel R. Delany, *Shorter Views: Queer Thoughts & The Politics of the Paraliterary* (Hanover, NH: Wesleyan University Press, 1999), 89.

17. Sam Binkley, *Getting Loose: Lifestyle Consumption in the 1970s* (Durham, NC: Duke University Press, 2007), 79.

18. Thomas Anthony Harris, *I'm O.K., You're O.K.* (New York: Harper and Row, 1969); Thomas Eric Berne, *Games People Play* (New York: Grove, 1964).

19. Joe Kort, "Cass Model of Gay & Lesbian Identity Formation," Joe Kort's website, www.joekort.com/var/joekort2/storage/original/application/818ebb03 27e1c88f4e29200224679ebd.pdf (accessed June 27, 2015).

20. David M. Halperin, *How to Be Gay* (Cambridge, MA: Harvard University Press, 2012), 319.

21. Ibid., 329.

# 4

## Closet Dramas

### Masculinity and Claustrophobia in William Friedkin's Films

NICK DAVIS

**Billy the Comeback Kid**

It is, apparently, okay to like William Friedkin again.[1] The recent revival in film-cultural enthusiasm for this straight son of blue-collar Chicago, who improbably adapted *The Boys in the Band* to film in 1970, follows an early, Icarus-like trajectory that was stark even by Hollywood standards. After establishing himself in television and documentaries in the 1960s, he started inauspiciously in film with the Sonny and Cher frivolity *Good Times* (1967) and a vaudevillian period comedy called *The Night They Raided Minsky's* (1968) that even he disliked. Friedkin preferred his third feature, a transfer of Harold Pinter's *The Birthday Party* (1968) that impressed *Boys* author Mart Crowley, but it faded quickly from theaters. *Boys*, too, garnered less attention than its makers had hoped. Having eluded the public radar after four tries, Friedkin was as surprised as anyone when his fifth film branded him a wunderkind. At thirty-six, he won a Best Director Oscar for *The French Connection* (1971), then followed that gritty, amoral *policier* with *The Exorcist* (1973), a zeitgeist supernova that persists among the top ten ticket sellers in movie history.[2] During the *Exorcist* shoot, the owner of Paramount Pictures recruited Friedkin into an elite auxiliary called the Directors Company, along with Peter Bogdanovich, still hot from *The Last Picture Show* (1971), and Francis Ford Coppola, on the heels of *The Godfather*

(1972). Each could develop and produce any project he wanted, so long as budgets stayed under $3 million. Adjusting for inflation, any of them could make the equivalents of a *Birdman*, *Blue Jasmine*, or *12 Years a Slave* without any fund-raising, executive approval process, or studio oversight.³

Within this two-year window of opportunity, Bogdanovich generated the Oscar-winning *Paper Moon* (1973), and Coppola yielded the Cannes champ *The Conversation* (1974). Friedkin, though, produced nothing. His next film, *Sorcerer* (1977), reimagined the classic French thriller *The Wages of Fear* in a Latin American context of oil plunder and global chaos. Its troubled production, hubristic scale, and financial failure cost Friedkin a new home at Universal, which had lured him away from Paramount after the Directors Company dissolved. Plagued early on by stories of profligate spending, unsafe sets, and volatile conduct—he has copped to slapping actors and even documentary subjects to spark greater emotion for the camera—Friedkin made headlines one more time, when LGBT activists protested *Cruising* (1980), his gruesome murder-mystery set within the gay S&M and leather communities of New York City. Gay writers like the *Village Voice*'s Arthur Bell finagled copies of the movie's script, which pins at least some of the killings on a psychotic homosexual and suggests the straight undercover cop played by Al Pacino may have been driven homicidal by his sojourn in this Stygian underworld. Bell's reports prompted West Village denizens to raise noisy commotions around *Cruising*'s set, rendering recorded sounds unusable, and to hurl objects and epithets at the cast and crew.⁴

Foiled by overreach and assailed on political grounds, Friedkin faced quieter humiliations over the next thirty years: a plagiarism lawsuit, after *Miami Vice*'s Michael Mann alleged that Friedkin's *To Live and Die in L.A.* (1985) ripped off his TV series; a finished feature, the serial-killer drama *Rampage* (1987), that went unreleased in the United States; box-office disasters like *Jade* (1995), which stalled hot careers for its lead actors, David Caruso and Linda Fiorentino; and turkeys like *Deal of the Century* (1983) and *The Guardian* (1990) that Friedkin omits from his memoir. Even relative successes were ill fated. His adaptation of Tracy Letts's play *Bug* (2006) won a prize at Cannes but, upon its U.S. commercial debut, became only the fourth film in thirty years to earn an average grade of "F" from first-night audiences, according to the market-research firm CinemaScore.⁵ *Killer Joe* (2011), derived from another Letts play, debuted in competition at Venice but elicited an NC-17 rating from the Motion Picture Association of America, curtailing the film's advertising, bookings, and grosses. However cursed in the marketplace, these later films stoked a Friedkin resurgence among cinephiles. In 2013, two years after premiering *Killer Joe*, the Venice Film Festival granted Friedkin a Golden Lion for Lifetime Achievement and showcased a digital restoration of the infamous *Sorcerer*, adulated by modern reviewers and soon reissued in theaters. The same year encompassed a retrospective of Friedkin's work at the Brooklyn Academy of Music and the publication of *The Friedkin Connection*, an autobiography as candid about professional ups and downs as it is cagey about private details. (His first three marriages, including one to Jeanne Moreau, merit one sentence more than four hundred pages into the book, which also skips the births of his two sons.)

Friedkin's rotations on the wheel of critical and popular fortune echo those of Crowley's play, indicated by an Off-Broadway revival in 2010 and the theatrical release of *Making the Boys* in 2011. In my experience, the reputation of *The Boys in the Band* always precedes it, as a historical milestone, a horror from an unmissed past, or both. It attracts few casual fans: people either know the whole text cold (Connie Casseroles) or retain the vaguest of memories, save the part where they ran screaming in another direction, as I did at nineteen years old. Content, moreover, is king: nobody has invoked the film's formal properties in any conversation I have ever had about it. Such circumstances foster skewed legacies. Until recently, I recalled *Boys* as gay Guignol, a hijacking narrative in which one Bette Davis locks eight Joan Crawfords inside a Manhattan apartment, serving up barely internalized homophobia like a boiled rat on a platter. But that notion of the film induces lingering astigmatisms. In fact, tonally and visually, the scenes expand well beyond stifling antagonism; the narrative problem is harder to name than "internalized homophobia"; and such formal considerations as the framing of shots are seminal to the film's ideas, echoing but also complicating ideas in the script.

Resolving these oversights entails rejecting a further misimpression that *The Boys in the Band* is marginal or inexplicable within Friedkin's body of work. *The Friedkin Connection* devotes only six pages to *Boys*, concluding a section called "Part I: First Impressions," which all too typically frames *The French Connection* as the effective launch of his career. Most critical analyses assign primary authorship to Crowley's screenplay and to the troupe of actors, seizing rare opportunities to reprise famous stage roles. Even Friedkin, while attesting that *Boys* is now "generally regarded as a landmark film," immediately stipulates, "I believe its power lies in Mart's script and the brilliant performances by the entire cast, which went virtually unrecognized at the time."[6] *Cruising* is the one Friedkin title that prompts coeval analyses with *Boys*, which tend to sideline aesthetics and emphasize instead their controversial representations of gay milieus at two pivotal moments, just after Stonewall and just before AIDS.

If writers seldom frame Friedkin's sensibility as a key factor in how *The Boys in the Band* unfolds on-screen—much less view *Boys* as I do, as a culmination of prior Friedkin tendencies and a premonition of later ones—this reluctance may stem from the generic eclecticism of Friedkin's career and its seeming lack of stylistic continuity. An unusual auteur with an oeuvre encompassing an activist documentary, a pop-music revue, and several stage-to-screen adaptations alongside his higher-grossing crime thrillers, Friedkin suggests more uniting concerns in his work than graphic violence and monomania.[7] Furthermore, recurrent habits of camera work, editing, sound mixing, and storytelling across his outwardly dissimilar projects are often quite subtle—maybe even surprisingly so, for a filmmaker typically associated with car chases and supernatural scares.

This chapter elucidates four interwoven through lines across Friedkin's rangy portfolio, all of them manifest in *Boys* and affording fresh views on the movie and its director. These patterns take different shapes in each project but still afford coherent interpretive frames. First, in a male-dominated filmography inclined toward masculine-coded genres like the action thriller, Friedkin regularly exposes male identities and communities as precarious. Indeed, gayness has been so fixed as *The Boys in the Band*'s primary discursive referent that its general thesis on masculinity may escape notice, thus reducing gay men to sexual or subcultural specificity within a category of maleness that stubbornly presumes heterosexuality as its generic coefficient. Hardly isolated, though, from Friedkin's portraits of haunted cops, embattled alpha males, and slippery doppelgängers, *Boys* emblematizes his recurrent scrutiny of male instability. Second, such scrutiny often accompanies a process by which individual characters coalesce into peculiar collectives, or what Leo Bersani and Ulysse Dutoit have called "forms of being": more complex than simple groups and, in Friedkin's cases, often bedeviled by whatever principle, obligation, or inchoate force also binds them together.[8]

Third, especially in the theatrical adaptations, Friedkin makes careful use of framing, sound, and montage to evoke an unusual and layered affect I call claustrophobia, linked but emphatically not limited to those close quarters that his uneasy ensembles often inhabit. This species of claustrophobia extends to how Friedkin taunts his protagonists with aggressive incursions of the physical world, even as they retreat into private thoughts, and to how characters suffer each other's penetrating gazes and knowledges, no matter how much insulation they attempt. Finally, these intimate aggressions often transpire inside doubly cloistered spaces within already-cramped milieus. This "closeting" motif merits reading from queer standpoints, and not just in gay texts like *Boys*. It overlaps, too, with a purgative impulse in many of Friedkin's films, which vociferously expose secrets or mandate the banishments of people, ideas, or abstract presences deemed intolerable to the collective. Michael's zeal in "outing" his possibly straight friend Alan typifies how desires to expose or expunge often take on lives of their own in Friedkin's films or chase dubious targets. Michael's similar ardor in convening friends, only to upset and disperse them through caustic conjurations of gay shame, captures how threats and remedies in Friedkin are often barely distinguishable and how sources of conflict are flushed but never fully exorcised.

## *Boys* to Men

*The French Connection*'s racist, relentless narcotics cop Jimmy "Popeye" Doyle, played with Oscar-winning bluster by Gene Hackman, remains the most famous male lead in a Friedkin movie, laying a loose template for later, swaggering antiheroes like the four mercenaries in *Sorcerer*, Nick Nolte's hotheaded basketball coach in *Blue Chips* (1994), the smooth-talking assassin "Killer Joe" Cooper, and the plethora of policemen and military officers in half a dozen other features. Popeye's lineage also stretches backward to Friedkin's apprentice years. His first Hollywood job was directing the TV series *The Bold Men* (1965), chronicling such alpha-male exploits as NFL football practices, lion taming, and skydiving sans parachute. Still, Popeye's comparable "boldness," bullying informants and chasing down moving trains in stolen sedans, does not tell his whole story. We first meet him sporting a Santa Claus costume during a stakeout. Even when he and his partner assume less theatrical guises, their flannels, houndstooth coats, and porkpie hats are calculated effects, styled for blending into backgrounds and trailing targets. During these pursuits, dealers and goons ogle and outwit the cops as often as the reverse; the camera alternates points of view, such that wielders of the gaze soon become its abashed objects. The police eventually corner the titular cartel, but "Frog One," Fernando Rey's ghostlike villain—Popeye's foil and double, an archetype of Old World elegance, slipping onto subways and out of warehouses and through everybody's fingers—evaporates as if he were never there.

Friedkin's men, then, are often performing even when they appear gruffly natural. They strive to project muscular personas, built on the implied male privileges of action and invulnerable oversight. They also frequently shadowbox with other avatars of masculinity that are as much unreachable figments as they are flesh-and-blood allies or opponents. *Sorcerer*, sweatier and more strenuous than *The French Connection*, with men and machines alike emitting bestial groans, also imbues masculinity with pyrrhic qualities, even as it doubles down on virile displays. The main reason four exiled criminals accept an impossible mission of transporting live nitroglycerine through the Amazon, aside from money, is to secure documents that will stabilize and notarize their mercurial identities. Despite divergences of genre, style, and political context, *Sorcerer* echoes *Boys'* structure, devoting one hour to forging an all-male cohort and another to sundering it, as members team up and assess each other's Achilles heels, all recognizing that nobody is necessarily who or what he says.

Key films across all periods of Friedkin's career, whatever their other disparities, sustain this interrogation of masculine self-presentation and ostensible self-evidence.[9] Even *Good Times*, based on a script he cowrote without credit, centers on Sonny Bono's crisis of masculine bona fides while toiling on a screenplay for himself and Cher. In seeking a manly archetype he can plausibly inhabit (sheriff? Tarzan? Sam Spade?), he meets pathetic ends in each incarnation. Sonny's frailty contrasts starkly with Cher's utter, indolent self-confidence and the hauteur of George Sanders, formidable as ever as the impatient studio mogul—early proof that effete masculinities are not necessarily disempowered in Friedkin's films, just as badge-holding, tough-talking, heterosexual guy's-guys cannot presume their inviolability. When Reagan-era studios embraced muscle-bound Stallones and Schwarzeneggers as male paragons, Friedkin swerved the other way, setting a sleek action-thriller within what he called "the unisex style of Los Angeles in the 1980s."[10] *To Live and Die in L.A.* foregrounds counterfeit bills as its master trope and treats maleness itself as dubious tender. Replete with queer puns, lingering on some gender-queer performance art, surveying homosocial spaces of the sauna and the locker room, and ultimately cheering a lesbian duo who dupe all the guys, the movie scrambles gendered and sexual codes, gazing dynamics, and even basic boundaries between characters. Detective Richard Chance (William Petersen), the rare Friedkin man possessing matinee-idol looks, hale in the field and proudly cock-baring in the boudoir, proves eminently castratable: he dies abruptly at the wrong end of a villain's much bigger gun. The film unmasks his ostensibly hardy manhood as a highly reproducible sign system when his surviving partner, John Vukovich (John Pankow), previously so neurotic, emerges in the finale having "become" Richard: sporting his style, driving his truck, appropriating his girlfriend.

Another, more recent action thriller, *The Hunted* (2003), stretches a comparable mutation into a feature-length trajectory, as the federally contracted field tracker L. T. Bonham (Tommy Lee Jones) increasingly adopts the bearing and snarl of Aaron Hallam (Benicio Del Toro), his former protégé and now his pledged enemy. As robust as Aaron is, certain lenses and framings lend him a hallucinatory, two-dimensional aspect. He is often heard but not seen. Trick edits repeatedly suggest that, like *The French Connection*'s Frog One, he has vanished into thin air, more an idea than an opponent. Similar filming strategies accrue to Matthew McConaughey's Killer Joe, an enigmatic revenant who insists on his right to disappear if deals go sour. With his sangfroid, aviator shades, and classic black Stetson, Joe is as much a southwestern imago as an actual person. Like Richard Chance in *To Live and Die in L.A.*, he makes one flagrant show of his naked body, offering his leonine frame as metonymic "proof" of his imputed power, yet he too emerges as a somewhat abject object. He stage-manages a sexual encounter with the protracted precision of the not easily aroused. He wields a fast-food chicken wing as a prosthetic penis, an act of misogynistic torture that also reverberates as one of dephallicizing self-effigy. He ends up begging a gun-wielding woman-child for his life. Even this list of undermined masculinities in Friedkin's filmography is not exhaustive. In *The Birthday Party*, Goldberg and McCann, coolly rapacious men-without-qualities, vaporize the braggadocio of Robert Shaw's Stanley, proving its bases to be as flimsy as Lola's coquettishness or Meg's delusions of grandeur. In *Bug*, Peter's body constitutes a battle zone of schizoid self-presentations, from the outpatient's diffidence to the former soldier's rigidity to the bellicosity of the paranoid schizophrenic—unsoothed, despite Hollywood convention, by the healing aloe of sex with a beautiful woman.

Interspersed among these titles, *The Boys in the Band* and *Cruising* similarly query masculine presentations and ostensible self-evidence, rather than standing wholly apart as gay films. In style, theme, and specific vantages on maleness, each resembles other Friedkin films more than they match each other—proving again that homosexuality, for this director, entails no separate or unilateral representational strategy. *Cruising* presages the fractured masculinities and the motif of imposture in *To Live and Die in L.A.* The psyche of the culprit is wildly split; also, once caught, he does not resemble the man we have seen commit several murders. The pursuer's psyche is equally precarious, especially once he adopts his quarry's habits, visits his hangouts, and pirates his trademarks. Not just whodunit questions but whoisthat riddles persist, unresolved. The film ends with Nancy (Karen Allen), the detective's girlfriend, spotting the discarded accoutrements of a highly coded social world of barely distinct men. She toys with these signs *as signs*—marking masculinity, not just homosexuality, as a risky but alluring circuit into which unexpected actors can enter.

Whereas *Cruising*'s plot and point-of-view shots often enjoin us to attempt distinctions among fields of Pacino look-alikes and men conforming to ritual semiotics (which hanky, which pocket, etc.), *The Boys in the Band* conversely assembles a group of cosmetically and temperamentally dissimilar gay men and goads us to discern areas of overlap. The paucity of extravagant grammar or stylistic ruptures in *Boys* can make it seem artless by comparison to other Friedkin efforts, but lest we take its naturalism for granted, the film lays its title over a crowded vanity of toiletries, Band-Aids, and concealers. Their owner, Harold, will later invoke the labors required for him—like the movie, and like masculinity itself—to look casually presentable. (As Crowley recalls in *Making the Boys*, Friedkin fired a cinematographer and three successive mixers early in production, which hardly bespeaks indifference to style.)

The soundtrack begins with Cole Porter's solo recording of "Anything Goes," which gives way to a modern update by the all-male group Harpers Bizarre. The implied fondness for reinterpreting famous originals and for ensembles over solos governs *Boys* in many ways, if not always so harmonically. Several relationships might have pulled primary focus: Michael's and Donald's mutual solicitude, which opens and closes the piece; the doubly misconstrued reunion of Michael and Alan; or the mounting contest between Michael and Harold. Friedkin, though, gives each its due without foregrounding any as the story's linchpin. He distributes screen time liberally among nine actors and frames them more often in clusters than sequestered close-ups, even during act 2's introspective monologues. The film slips into various characters' points of view, in instants of dramatic import (as Alan confronts his first gay party or Michael yells for Donald amid his climactic breakdown) but also in throwaway moments (as Emory locks eyes with various hustlers while window-shopping for Harold's "gift" or Cowboy surveys the patio through magenta cellophane). The frames composed from these multifarious vantages convene almost every conceivable permutation of cast members together at some point. Sometimes these groups reflect conscious character choices: for example, when Donald, Larry, and Hank mollify the rattled Alan by closing ranks as fellow straight-acting white guys. Elsewhere, joint framings accentuate theme or conflict, as when Hank—whom Alan perceives one way but Michael knows to be otherwise—hovers between their foregrounded profiles amid a tense standoff. Other, seemingly arbitrary coframings construct the group as a fluctuating assemblage, entailing everyone's complicity with everyone else. Hence, laid-back Larry happens to join livid Harold in a shot in which Michael attacks him; Harold occupies the blurry background as Emory recalls painful memories; and Bernard holds down half the frame as Michael announces his cruel game.

In at least two ways, these shots serve as quiet provocations. For one thing, by forsaking solitary close-ups more than other films would, these frames solicit constant comparisons among characters, including less intuitive subsets. These evaluations extend to various comportments of maleness on view at Harold's party, even before Michael transforms it into a *Walpurgisnacht* of livable and unlivable masculinities. All are tested, though few are disqualified outright. Memorably, Bernard's coeval burdens of blackness and queerness produce a logic whereby *he* is shamed for tolerating *others'* fetishism and race-baiting jokes. That charge, along with the fallout from the telephone game, finally devastates his "well-adjusted" geniality. Michael's fussed-over but plainly self-divided persona—queeny but vicious toward queendom, bigoted but ruthless toward bigots, aging but outraged by age—also ends in ruin and retreat. By contrast, Harold's self-described ontology as an "ugly, pockmarked Jew fairy" and Emory's ribald effeminacy prove just as resilient as Donald's mail-order comeliness and exegetical self-study or Larry's open-shirted, lantern-jawed insistence on polyamorous prerogatives. In a 2008 piece in which modern twenty-somethings watch *Boys* with perplexity and horror, their middle-aged host underscores the fortitude in Emory's flamboyance: "'Wildest thing about that actor,' I say, 'is that he was totally straight and known for playing tough guys. Except here. Well, sort of here too, now that I think about it. Queens like that were made of titanium.'"[11] As usual in Friedkin's work, no one regimen of maleness, however macho or not, guarantees survival. All become legible *as* scripted regimens, partly through shared frames that invite us to compare them.

Second, these visual strategies register the fact that *The Boys in the Band* grasps its characters neither as a hierarchy nor as a loose klatch of singles and pairs who remain discrete as such. The film constructs the collective in fluid but bonded terms, positing its members as subjects *and* objects, symbiotically joined for better and worse. It marshals them into rotating combos as well as some panoramic group shots, and it telegraphs manifold dynamics among them. Even minus the virtuoso authorial flourishes of a Godard, Almodóvar, or Malick, Friedkin thereby structures (gay) male sociality as what Leo Bersani and Ulysse Dutoit call a "form of being": a specific logic of interrelation and/or nonrelation, dependent on the camera but not fully transparent to it, reconcilable neither with individual subjectivity nor with simplistic models of group identity.[12] Unprompted by kinship, however unsentimental (*Killer Joe*), or by pure accident (*Bug*) or by appointed tasks either civic (*12 Angry Men*) or spiritual (*The Exorcist*) or secretive (*The Birthday Party*), this band of brothers predates the film, given the script's many gestures to prior contacts among them, social and sexual, distant and recent. It will outlast the screenplay's events, too, as few Friedkin collectives do, given Donald's pledge to return next weekend and Harold's promise to phone tomorrow, which "must provoke a 'Please don't!' or a 'WHY?' in the minds of the audience."[13] We watch *The Boys in the Band*, then, not just to track a scenario or to predict an outcome but to enter, however provisionally, a particular group economy. We participate in the characters' mutual witnessing from different points of view, traverse intramural and unstable factions, study surfaces and utterances, and grapple with the paradox whereby repudiation and excoriation appear endemic to this group's makeup as such. By these processes, rendered through specifically cinematic means, we temporarily join the group, whether or not we personally "identify."

In applying a subdued but resonant style to a male collective greater than or different from the sum of its parts, the closest analogue to *The Boys in the Band* in Friedkin's work may be his cable-television remake of *12 Angry Men* (1997). In that film, Friedkin and cinematographer Fred Schuler typically frame each speaker around the deliberation table in long or medium shots, folding one or two auditors into the image, wholly or partly, even when another speaker's face or voice is clearly privileged. While tighter close-ups might have offered a more customary means of conveying these men's failure to "reach" each other, as well as their oppressive closeness within a locked room, Friedkin avoids depicting any actor purely by himself for a full half hour of *12 Angry Men* and for most of the remaining film. Compositions in depth keep multiple characters visible in foregrounds and backgrounds, without sacrificing a sense of their proximity. Even tighter shots of individual jurors typically include another man's blurry shoulder, elbow, or ear. One effect of this pattern is to impede any sense of characters holding forth in a vacuum. Populating the frames with multiple characters underscores that every speech matters as much for who delivers it as for who hears it, and how. Moreover, by visual implication, none of these men remains fully autonomous once a court reconstitutes them as a jurisprudential body—different in kind, and bound to different protocols and ethical challenges, than if the same dozen citizens were to meet under other terms. This form of being gets itchy, especially as tempers flare and windows get shut against a rainstorm. Still, as in *Boys*, physical overcloseness induces less friction among the jurors than each man's intimate confrontation with the others' dissimilar styles and values—a key instance of that spatial, mental, ethical, and audiovisual umbrella concept in Friedkin that I am naming as *claustrophobia*. The same framing strategies allow for direct comparisons among a dozen different comportments of masculinity, including some that shiver into pieces by the end of the story and others that hold fast.

## Close Quarters

Again, what I call claustrophobic *effects* in Friedkin's work attach but do not equate to claustrophobic *spaces*. I am stretching this word to encompass how practical environments in his films accrue unusual audiovisual potency, communicating a world where bodies are subject to mental and material dangers encircling them, to include the imposing strength of other people's viewpoints. As jurists, fugitives, tenants, clerics, cops, enemies, and friends, Friedkin characters depend on people who also give them pause, and are tasked to resolve their relations to them—pressures they often experience as aggressive, even stifling. Eerie camera behaviors, volatile sound mixes, and other aspects of style thus yield thick, heavy ambiences in Friedkin's films, strongly felt but tricky to name, enervating Friedkin's audience as well as his dramatis personae. *Claustrophobia* can thus describe an evaporation of any space for relaxed contemplation (ours or the characters'), the lack of any reprieve from communal hails, and the absence of any green zone for innocuous experience, insulated from physical threat or epistemic challenge.

Friedkin's five theatrical adaptations, all derived from single-location plays, furnish apt showcases for these nuanced effects, partly because their premises entail physical constraint. Only once, for *Killer Joe*, has Friedkin gone the usual Hollywood route of opening up a single-set play into more locations. More important, though, is how each film *differentiates* between literal close quarters and the more layered, conceptually complex claustrophobias I have outlined. The other four films in this group, *The Birthday Party*, *The Boys in the Band*, *12 Angry Men*, and *Bug*, rarely stress the literal crowdedness that Ben Brantley observed in the 2010 Off-Broadway revival of *Boys*, which swamped an already-narrow set with furniture and bric-a-brac, fostering an environment where characters could scarcely move, much less avoid each other.[14] As we have noted, even *12 Angry Men*, the most conventionally styled of these movies, set almost entirely within one chamber, avoids a subliminal constricting of the set or an oppressively close camera that might evoke "claustrophobia" in more conventional terms.[15]

The same is true of *Bug*, a story of demented codependency that otherwise departs from *12 Angry Men*'s more quotidian realism. It offers the flashiest case of Friedkin achieving a claustrophobic scenario and atmosphere through idiosyncratic techniques. As *Bug* proceeds, it increasingly cuts to loud, ambiguously motivated images of maggots, mantises, and blood vessels, even during a pivotal sex scene between the protagonists. These macabre edits proliferate as Michael Shannon's Peter steadily draws Ashley Judd's Aggie into psychotic paranoias about weaponized aphids, paramilitary surveillance, and tracking devices embedded in their flesh. Many films would communicate Peter's escalating hold over Aggie by amplifying the two characters' cramped and crazy-making isolation inside a tiny cabin, but *Bug* unfolds differently. The hotel room, glowing under neon bulbs, cocooned in foil by its deranged denizens and thus deprived of orienting features, gets harder to parse in scale and structure toward the finale—despite camera angles wide enough that we should be able to read where we are. The images seem ever more asphyxiated with portentous implications, even as Friedkin keeps suffocating close-ups or crowded compositions to a minimum.

The most striking aspect of *Bug* is the friction but also the porosity between material and psychological experience, whereby each incurs abruptly on the other. For instance, Aggie's boozy tranquility in *Bug*'s earliest shots is disrupted by unusually loud sounds and quick-cut inserts of the phone blaring, the air conditioner rattling, or the ceiling fan whirring. Objects thus feel close, demanding attention, even when they are visually distant from Aggie in the frame; they effectively pull her (and us) back "into" the hotel room even as her mind wanders. Conversely, the film's equally sudden, equally loud cuts to chattering insects or flowing arteries pull us back "out" of the room just as we begin acclimating to its weird rhythms and rules. Both tendencies prohibit our settling into either a realistic terrain or a fully fantastical milieu. *Bug* and its characters thus inhabit a narrow chasm or a precarious knife-edge between objective and subjective orientations, or between diegetic and nondiegetic coordinates—an even smaller space *conceptually* than it is *physically*, as we draw closer to the characters' fiery demise.

I have stressed edits in *Bug* that shunt us between spectacles that register initially as clearly real or clearly not, making any "space" between those zones feel like no space at all. Just as often, and ever more steadily through the film, *Bug* stages key story beats (a gruesome tooth pulling, a shady doctor's visit) with the stylized lensing and audiovisual intensity that have equally characterized its depictions of objective reality *and* subjective conceit. Resisting either classification, such scenes further dismantle familiar dichotomies like real/imagined or objective/subjective. They instead manifest a version of what Gilles Deleuze calls "free indirect cinema." He even uses a spatial metaphor, mirroring my notion of claustrophobia in Friedkin's work, to describe a type of cinema in which "we no longer know what is imaginary or real, physical or mental, in the situation, not because they are confused, but because we do not have to know and there is *no longer even a place* from which to ask."[16] By that logic, *Bug* evokes not Peter's or Aggie's first-person "subjective" headspace or any "objectively" corroborated experience they share but what Deleuze calls a *virtual* plane of events and impressions, conflating those that actually happen with others that could happen or also happen or feel as if they are happening. As *Bug* amasses more shocking sonic and visual stimuli, the shots grow even denser—in the argot of this chapter, more claustrophobic—with all the ways they could be read and all the possible trajectories and incompatible planes of reality they might imply.

*Bug* pushes this vision of overlapping worlds and indecipherable virtualities to stark, scary extremes, leaving "no place from which to ask" how or why Peter and Aggie slip so quickly and disastrously into their unsustainable form of being. So pronounced in its claustrophobia and its stylistic language, *Bug* might imply that Friedkin only rarely or only recently attempted such "free indirect" filmmaking and that such ventures stand diametrically opposed to, say, the simpler realism of movies like *12 Angry Men*. However, some of Friedkin's first movies—especially but not only his theatrical adaptations—blur objective and subjective orientations, marshaling a free indirect perspective to variously claustrophobic ends. None of these films, including *The Boys in the Band*, are as formally modest as *12 Angry Men* or as florid as *Bug*, but they all vex or reduce the "space" between observable realities and subjective impressions, drenching that space with inchoate, unsettling questions and affects.

These tenets arise as early as Friedkin's documentary *The People vs. Paul Crump* (1962), the project that launched his career, though in this case the director's interest in restrictive environments has nothing to do with theater. Profiling a death-row inmate whose own warden believed he was innocent, and "consciously designed as a polemic to save Crump's life," the film combines standard nonfiction aesthetics with visceral stagings of the alleged crime, semisubjective projections of characters' thoughts, and other New Journalistic flourishes.[17] Centered in one man's long detention within an eight-by-eight-foot cell, *Paul Crump* forgoes many devices by which prison films often literalize spatial constraint: no overhead shots of narrow living quarters, no circumscribed pacing, no pounding of walls or rattling of bars. If anything, as with later Friedkin characters, Paul's headspace comes to feel more crowded and suffocating than his physical barracks. The first postcredits shot is an extreme close-up of Paul's eye between two bars. This image, emphasizing his gaze as well as his bodily captivity, implies that the ensuing movie will chronicle the outward facts of Paul's incarceration but also the memories and terrors informing his perspective on imprisonment, without always differentiating among them. This admixture produces another free indirect experience, profuse with ambiguous spectacles, as sensorially intense in moments of reportage as in speculative embellishments. These images crowd the film with questions about guilt or innocence, reprieve or implacable fate, but proffer "no place from which to ask" what truths they impart or what fates they foretell.

*Paul Crump* often films big spaces as if they are small, and more confined ones with surprising openness or fluidity, constructing claustrophobic atmospheres (and associated themes and characterizations) in nuanced, unexpected ways. Camera angles often make scenes from Paul's earlier life look cramped, however disparate in tone: the barbecue joint where black bon vivants dance in narrow aisles; the bedroom where Paul and Fay insist they made love during the time of the imputed robbery; the modest South Side homes where Paul is arrested twice; the interrogation room where Chicago police coerce a confession; and the room where the *Sun-Times* reporter John Justin Smith solicits Paul's testimonies, which inspire these reenactments. Shots taken through fire escapes, iron railings, and chain-link elevators brand the scene of Paul's alleged crime with a jail-bar motif, tying the past to a future it foretells. Such patterns suggest that life as a working-class black man always felt constricted or that these pre-jail scenes, bearing visual traces of Paul's current milieu, are retroactively filtered through that standpoint.

The film's most bravura depiction of claustrophobia as a mental *and* bodily experience arises during a midfilm montage while a voice-over recounts Paul's roundelay of appeals, denials, and stays of execution. During that narration, documentary images portray the Cook County Jail as a disjointed maze of barred hallways and sterile rooms, indistinguishable from each other, lacking clear spatial relations even when vistas are relatively broad. *Crump* thus molds our view of the jail into a free indirect visual metaphor for the byzantine reprosecutions of Paul's legal case, emphasizing circuitousness even more than confinement and conjuring how *stuck* Paul remains not through tight, static close-ups but via a heavily edited scene in which the camera has room to move. Later, the climactic shots of a possessed electric chair—arm and leg restraints fastening of their own accord, cushioned seat depressed by some invisible occupant—evoke the panicky feeling of being tied down, even amid wide angles on an empty space. They crystallize as well our sense of documentary fact and speculative fiction converging. "It's always there, like the bars that surround you," Paul says about the certainty of his own death, scheduled and postponed fourteen times already by the time the movie starts. Alone or in company, across locations and time frames, grafting real events with reveries and reconstructions, and emanating always a deep and breath-catching agitation, this claustrophobic fact perseveres.

The affect congesting *The Birthday Party*, the closest and most obvious influence on *The Boys in the Band* in Friedkin's oeuvre, is harder to name than the certainty of death. Still, these two films echo earlier and later ones by deploying ambiguous and rotating perspectives, sudden audiovisual assaults, and other formal means of complicating their vantages and enervating their ambiences. Lacking one clear focalizer like Paul, these male-dominated ensemble films suggest masculine rivalry and other ambivalent affinities—some more transparent than others—as the foundations for murky forms of being, uneasily uniting their characters. *The Birthday Party* concerns the arrival of two strangers at a seaside inn, harboring malign intents toward a third guest, all dragooned by their hostess into a falsely mirthful soirée. *Boys* flips that script, as six invitees and two surprise visitors at a birthday bash are lured by Michael into vicious games and reproaches. After early peeks at a dusky English boardwalk and at New York's urban jungle, respectively, each film settles into a primary location that is literally claustrophobic at times, at others more complexly inhospitable, and volatile in its audiovisual textures.

In *The Birthday Party*, disquiet plumes like an odorless gas, seeping from tangible sources in the set or soundtrack, from characters' erratic moods, and from stranger mannerisms in the filmmaking. The script entails a slow, classically Pinteresque escalation of cryptic conflict, tied to mounting intimations that the inn's newest guests, Goldberg and McCann, have crossed paths before with a longer-term resident named Stanley. They evidently intend some act of retributive violence. Even before their arrival, though, scenes emit some of that spooky audiovisual vibrancy that renders other Friedkin sets unnerving, like *Bug*'s hotel room or *The Exorcist*'s town house. The harsh sound of ripping paper disturbs *The Birthday Party*'s otherwise sedate establishing shots of an English town, framed from the perspective of an undisclosed driver; we wonder whose point of view or what imminent action might prompt such a discordant effect. Once inside Meg and Petey's pension, the locking of doors, the emptying of a teapot, and the pouring of cereal inspire tight, handheld close-ups and unusually loud sound cues. These shots feel literally claustrophobic, as does the boxy frame around Meg and Petey seated at table, sometimes filmed through a sliding hatch in the kitchen wall to narrow the image further. Following this prologue, however, rather than maintain this overtly oppressive aesthetic, the camera retreats from the actors for a spell, even as narrative omens accumulate. If anything, Friedkin endows benign-looking encounters with nerve-jangling overtones, while treating darker turns with relative serenity. Thus, a kiss Meg extracts from Stanley after gifting him a drum catalyzes a nervous pan, an eerily quiet close-up, jagged cuts, piercing sounds, and queasy point-of-view shots, as Stanley circles his hostess and pounds away at his toy. By contrast, the arrival of those likely malefactors Goldberg and McCann yields roomy and tranquil full shots, while they pass off nosy questions and bizarre non sequiturs as casual badinage.

Within a generally faithful adaptation of Pinter's play, Friedkin places three stamps on the material, heralding his later take on *The Boys in the Band*. First, his formal choices preserve the piece not as a duel between defined "sides" (say, the men versus the women or the hosts versus their guests) but as a Gordian knot of shuffled affinities, implied by the camera even when invisible to the characters. Why do Goldberg's speeches often corral the whole group into shared shots, despite his divisive presence and opaque motives? Why would McCann's and Meg's solipsistic reminiscences—neither aimed at nor heard by the other—be rendered for so long in one static two-shot? As in *The Boys in the Band* and *12 Angry Men*, albeit more runically, Friedkin's framings suggest disparate and shifting links among the characters, begging to be teased out. Second, *The Birthday Party*'s camera oscillates between seemingly neutral recordings of events and some more alien vantage, as if the inn exerts a motile, free indirect gaze of its own. As in *Bug*, these moments differ from others when the film adopts first-person camera work, like the blurred images after Stanley loses his glasses or the traveling point-of-view shot from over Meg's head, arms outstretched at the bottom of the frame, while she plays blindman's bluff. Such capacities for first-person perspective do not explain odder shots in which the camera cranes down from an exaggeratedly high corner of the dining room and crouches suddenly at table level, while Stanley tells Meg about recent job offers to play piano around the world—again, treating casual moments as sinister ones. Other crane shots and undermotivated pans, tracks, and zooms pose similar riddles of tone and perspective throughout, unlinked to any first-person viewpoint but too strange and conspicuous to pass as dispassionate third person.

*The Birthday Party*, then, evokes actual and virtual purviews on elliptical events in a dramatic idiom less generically hybrid than *The People vs. Paul Crump*'s and less heightened in its effects than *Bug*'s. Amplified sound elements and peculiar framings foster an overclose, cooped-up, frayed-nerve atmosphere for the viewer, approximating or exceeding what the characters experience without bluntly compressing the space. Moreover, the camera's prowling and orbiting movements feel averse to conventional realism. Friedkin thus insinuates an unruly energy inside this obscurely threatened abode, later evoked through even more aggressive devices, such as blackouts, distorted close-ups, high-exposure and high-contrast monochrome, and brief spumes of Brakhage-esque abstraction. Having let these genies of macabre implication out of their bottles, Friedkin makes a third intervention by corking them back up, rendering the crisis-climax-conclusion sequence of the play's three acts even more circular than Pinter does. That is, the late "return to normalcy" feels haunted by the atmospheric unease implied through audiovisual means in prior images of the same spaces. The morning-after finale of *The Birthday Party* reiterates some of the film's earliest shots (a boardwalk, six beach chairs) and the same rituals that inaugurated the previous day (cornflake breakfast, tea, Meg and Petey at table). These reversions feel reassuring yet suspicious, especially once Stanley appears at Goldberg and McCann's side, dazed, blandly suited, and stripped of his truculence.

Who these attachés are and what has prompted Stanley's extradition, justly or unjustly, remain loose ends in Pinter's play. What Friedkin adds is a summoning of violent, ineffable ambience, pervading the characters' interactions, linked but not reducible to Stanley's potential misdeeds and his pursuers' unspecified vengeance. Those gaps in *The Birthday Party*'s story echo the unruly anomalies of its style, which make too strong an impression for us to forget them, even once the film and its characters have settled back into old habits. They also exceed the encounters among Stanley, McCann, and Goldberg, suggesting a disturbing ecology that encompasses the unwitting hosts and their home environment, prior to their disruptive guests' arrival. We are left to wonder what, if anything, has been purged from the boardinghouse as the visitors abscond with their captive or whether the indigenous unrest within the inn—manifest in that slithery camera-consciousness and excitable soundtrack even before the main conflicts arose—has truly been eradicated.

### The Power of Michael Compels You

*The Boys in the Band* sustains all of Friedkin's themes and styles foregrounded thus far, stressing masculine self-performance, mercurial male archetypes, rivalries and scrutinies among men as a form of being, and complex claustrophobias. Beyond the habit of joint framing, which invites viewers to evaluate competing styles of maleness—conferring on these men a feminizing "to-be-looked-at-ness" even while they serve as agents of thought or action—*Boys* blurs subject-object distinctions in other ways. Almost every character steals a moment to primp in a mirror, bolstering his objective appeal, just as almost everyone subjectively dictates the camera's look at some point. Even Cowboy, recruited as a blank avatar of desirability, proud of selling for the high price of twenty dollars, enjoys subjective vantage in some point-of-view shots. Harold, as famously ugly as Cowboy is beautiful, exerts his own objectifying fascination. He arrives into the film via compartmentalized close-ups of his pricy shoes, pinky ring, and improbably rose-colored glasses. As semiotically overdetermined as *The French Connection*'s louchely European villain, the exotic-indigenous warrior in *The Hunted*, or the Marlboro assassin in *Killer Joe*, Harold serves, like those figures, as a transfixing template and phantasmal foil against whom other men gauge their performances of self. At the same time, his piercing gaze and clairvoyant grasp of unspoken truths endow him with formidable subjectivity.

Those close-ups of Harold as he enters hail from Donald's point of view, accompanied by Emory's screams on the soundtrack. Hence, the most rarefied focus on one man's quintessential traits still betrays traces of other men's vantages and affects—another way Friedkin structures these men collectively, each with viewpoints and identities contingent on the others'. Linking cuts and joint framings continually reabsorb each boy into the band. True, Michael stands somewhat apart as proprietor, scorekeeper, and narrative catalyst; his grape-colored V-neck, clashing with the palette of several scenes, visually underscores his dual status as group emcee and garish misfit. The plot and dialogue, though, recurrently enfold Michael into that group he tries hard to diagnose and disdain. When Harold pronounces, "You may very well one day be able to know a heterosexual life if you want it desperately enough . . . but you will always be homosexual as well," he is not just describing Michael's individual fate but an intransigent collective belonging. This insistence on gayness as a no-exit form of being informed, surely, my errant memory of Michael's apartment as insufferably crowded. In fact, the set is fairly spacious and the camera granted some room to move, qualifying any sense of close-quartered paralysis. Still, the steady gravitation of this party into one room; the way sharp words and shrill screams puncture silences and fill spaces, sometimes abruptly; and the edits and framings that tie each man's soliloquies to other men's images, by comparison or contrast, endow *Boys* with Friedkin-style claustrophobias, even when he refuses to film the set like a jail cell.

A final motif bridging *Boys* and other Friedkin films, especially those that invoke physical claustrophobia only to complicate it, is the pivotal role played by some privileged cloister where tensions culminate, on-screen or off, and where purgative momentums intensify. In *12 Angry Men*, a restroom off the deliberation chamber hosts furtive exchanges that ramify powerfully, nudging more jurors to change their votes. Their final obstacle is the recalcitrance of a twelfth juror, who at last uncorks a geyser of narcissistic projections and patrimonial rage that had blocked any empathy with the accused—an overdue release that is arguably the story's climax. In *Bug*, trips to the bathroom consistently escalate anxieties, as routine evacuations become more elaborate (teeth yanked, skin strip-mined), reaching a cathartic frenzy that only self-annihilation can satisfy. Early shots in *The Birthday Party* orient us to the upstairs lodgings as well as downstairs areas. Only once, though, do we revisit this upper floor where Stanley, McCann, and Goldberg sleep and where their inscrutable animosity apparently comes to a head—an undisclosed event that nonetheless dictates the teleology of the film, prompting the departures of all three men.

*The Exorcist* furnishes a paradigmatic case of this pattern, swamping a huge house and surrounding milieu with maternal guilt, religious doubt, and diabolical menace—three overlaid examples of Friedkin so palpably conjuring invisible affects and occult presences that atmospheres grow denser and spaces feel smaller than they are. All three coalesce in the locked, frigid, upstairs bedroom of Regan McNeil, where subject-object polarities explode into free indirect chaos, two dissimilar men test their different mettles at a shared task, and the purgative act that defines the film finally transpires, albeit with uncertain results. When Father Karras (Jason Miller) invites Pazuzu inside him, then fatally throws himself out a high window, he intends to expunge a pervasive but ineffable threat. Still, questions linger as to whether the devil has fully abandoned the girl, the house, or the movie.

*The Boys in the Band* presages *The Exorcist*, not just because Michael seems possessed, acting as priest *and* demon, forcing multiple bodies to do his bidding while pretending to cure them of something, before exiting himself, manifestly uncured—en route, no less, to a midnight Mass. As in *The Exorcist*, *Boys* devotes its second half to ritualized purgation. Secrets, pasts, and sexual truths are coercively summoned. Guests are sent packing. As bodily fluids start flying, from Emory's blood to Alan's vomit, the men have ever more need to repair to Michael's master suite upstairs, a privileged site throughout for both grooming and abject disarray, for attempts at self-sequester and also, happily or not, collective reabsorption. Here, Michael and Donald first play respective roles of inquiring mind and embodied object (Donald, nude, needs a shower) and of confidant and analysand (Donald, dismayed, has missed therapy), though the finale will reverse those dynamics, with Donald posing questions and Michael at sea. Here, Alan hides from the queer guests—an apparent rejection of gayness that, in the eyes of several characters and viewers, backfires as telltale proof of Alan's own homosexuality. Here, Michael turns against Alan, pledging to unmask him before expelling him from the flat. Here, too, Emory embraces forgiveness, the perpetual butt of jokes turned magnanimous "Flo Nightingale." This space is too private for Harold, who prefers jousting in public, but Hank and Larry retire there, unseen, never to return, to restore a conjugal bond that Michael's game almost severed.[18]

If the downstairs of Michael's apartment becomes the bully pulpit where he preaches his gospel of gay misery, and the patio a space where gluttony, dance, and repartee are indulged, the upstairs facilitates physical and psychic triage: showering, spilling, wound dressing, air spray, hairspray, make-up sex, Oedipal confessions, accusations, changes of mind and heart.[19] As usual in Friedkin, extreme sensations of the body unfold in tandem with shifts in thought and perspective. If this semidiscrete space serves as a de facto clinic, it functions also as a closet, albeit a different type for different men, with dissimilar implications. For Michael, this space closely approximates the specific one Eve Kosofsky Sedgwick defines in *Epistemology of the Closet*'s reading of *Billy Budd*, in which Captain Vere's private quarters, unbreached even by Melville's narrator, plays a multiply decisive role among an all-male maritime collective, ripe with homophile desires and purgative impulses. The closet for Sedgwick, like claustrophobia in Friedkin, is metaphorically a space but really a multidimensional conceptual site for blending embodied and epistemic experience, disciplinary and liberatory. Sedgwick personifies the closet in the dour figure of John Claggart, possessed by an erotic yet vindictive mode she calls "homosexual-homophobic knowing."[20] To an extent, Michael inherits Claggart's example, especially in his resolve to force Alan's queer confession. Mixing obsession and contempt with homosexual-homophobic vigor—hating homosexuality but desperate for Alan *to* be gay—Michael oversteps and winds up exiling not just Alan but himself from his own apartment.

At the same time, in Michael's enthusiasm for public trials, staging himself as the group's most surveillant subject *and* a strenuously self-theatricalizing object, punishing his beloved as a means of rendering him all the more conspicuous, he also reprises Captain Vere's role in Sedgwick's gloss on the closet. He repairs to his master suite to enjoy some undisguised doting (it happens with Donald, too) and to galvanize morbid aggressions. As in *Billy Budd*, Michael's strained public conduct among a collective he leads *and* belongs to stems from ambivalent encounters within this privileged space. Unlike Melville's story, though—and unlike, say, *The Birthday Party*, which keeps its "closet" closeted—*The Boys in the Band* affords access to this space where so many paradoxes play out, stoking hate and love, placing men and their bodies in new relations to each other, informing new verdicts about who must stay or must go.

*Boys* concludes without confirming if Michael's weirdly homophobic homophilia has been dispelled or how contagious it proves among his cohort or how inextricable it finally is from his craving for Alan and for sociality with those fellow queers whom he, after all, keeps convening. Much as *The Birthday Party* ends in the ambiguous aftermath of a mysterious ejection from the inn and *The Exorcist* finishes with guilt and diabolism either solaced or more widely dispersed and *Cruising* ends with at least one killer uncaught (lingering on a murder in one bathroom and a shower in a second), *Boys* resolves without resolving. Sedgwick ends her chapter insisting that homophobic projects can never be fulfilled, with homosexuality's origins unclear and its imprints pervasive in the culture. Friedkin no doubt agrees, since his movies showcase repeatedly how purgative missions—linked to and intensified within closet spaces where contradictory roots of individual and communal behavior become especially visible, when we are allowed access to them—invariably fall short of incoherent goals.

Like *Billy Budd*'s battleship and similarly to Friedkin's other confined environments, Michael's apartment becomes a common ground, a locked room, a performance space, a ritual site, a visual metaphor, and a scene of expulsion, based on tumults eased for some but exacerbated for others within a nested series of sanctums. Crucially, Michael's self-hating brand of homosexual-homophobic knowing emerges as an outlier in the film. Not every boy in this fluidly bonded band experiences these spaces, this tumult, or their collective form of being in the same way. Not everyone ventures upstairs for the same reasons or thinks what Michael thinks or sees what Michael sees, as the film's oscillating vantage points insist. Nor, surely, do Friedkin's viewers, across his disparate films or within the shifting terms of a movie like *Boys*, in which no affect or epistemology holds fast for everyone. Theorizations of the closet, too, have evolved and diversified since Sedgwick, just as cinematic visions of homosexuality have multiplied since *Boys* and as Friedkin's stylistic and thematic range continues expanding. Having so often staged complex claustrophobias on film, revisited slippery masculinities, and assessed their unpredictable productions and incomplete purgations, Friedkin's overall take on closets and on the solo or group identities they foster might align better with more recent studies of the closet. Increasingly, scholars stress the coercions but also the creativities linked to various closets, as well as the improbable collectives that subsisted in different eras and contexts within and outside them or at their thresholds.[21] In a similar spirit, Friedkin's movies are tributes to nothing if not instability, liminality, and variation—even a text like *The Boys in the Band*, misremembered so often as monolithically grim and repressed in its worldview.

At the same time, even a body of work this multifarious betrays marks of consistency. I hope I have demonstrated that within Friedkin's oeuvre,

*The Boys in the Band* is neither anomalous nor anonymous but visibly and coherently informed by its director's stylistic propensities and signature themes. *Boys* does not retreat from the formal precision or the techniques and tropes that predominate in other Friedkin films. It feels guided by some early successes and influential on the shaping of subsequent hits (and misses). The gayness of the film is the furthest thing from incidental. At the same time, the vagaries of masculinity in all its forms, the fraughtness of closets and volatile collectives, and the many varieties of claustrophobic unease and ambivalent release are not particular to gay stories, nor are they unique to Harold's indelible birthday party.

## Notes

1. I have paraphrased the opening of the *New York Times* review of a 1996 Off-Broadway revival of Crowley's play: "It is, apparently, O.K. to like *The Boys in the Band* again." Ben Brantley, "As the Boys Return, the Party Isn't Over," *New York Times*, June 21, 1996, www.nytimes.com/1996/06/21/theater/theater-review-as-the-boys-return-the-party-isn-t-over.html.

2. "All-Time Box Office: Domestic Grosses: Adjusted for Ticket Price Inflation," Box Office Mojo, www.boxofficemojo.com/alltime/adjusted.htm (accessed August 22, 2015).

3. According to the U.S. Bureau of Labor Statistics, a film priced at $3 million in 1972, when the Directors Company was formed, translates to one costing around $17 million in 2014. IMDb pages for these contemporary films specify their studio-reported budgets as falling near that range. Bureau of Labor Statistics, U.S. Department of Labor, "CPI Inflation Calculator," www.bls.gov/data/inflation_calculator.htm (accessed July 4, 2015).

4. An immediate, detailed account of the *Cruising* protests can be found in Edward Guthmann, "The *Cruising* Controversy," *Cineaste* 10, no. 3 (1980): 2–8. Jim Hubbard's short film *Stop the Movie (Cruising)* (1980) furnishes their most famous documentary record.

5. Dustin Rowles, "The 8 Films, All Time, to Receive an 'F' from Cinema-Score," Pajiba, December 2, 2012, www.pajiba.com/box_office_round-ups/the-8-films-all-time-to-receive-an-f-from-cinemascore.php.

6. William Friedkin, *The Friedkin Connection* (New York: HarperCollins, 2013), 138.

7. These frames of reference and correspondingly succinct treatments of *Boys* recur in *The Friedkin Connection* and in two external studies of his career: Thomas D. Clagett, *William Friedkin: Films of Aberration, Obsession and Reality*

136 • NICK DAVIS

(Jefferson, NC: McFarland, 1990); and Nat Segaloff, *Hurricane Billy: The Stormy Life and Films of William Friedkin* (New York: William Morrow, 1990). Clagett devotes a comparable number of pages to *Boys* as to peripheral efforts like *Minsky's* or *The Brink's Job* (1978). Segaloff's book ends its longer, richer chapter on *Boys* with an anecdote in which Howard Hawks advises Friedkin to set aside "social problem" pictures and commit to action and excitement. Segaloff does not treat Hawks's counsel as gospel but favors the films that appear to affirm it, save for his dossier on *Cruising* and its troubles.

8. Leo Bersani and Ulysse Dutoit, *Forms of Being* (London: BFI, 2004).

9. One still-pertinent critical paradigm for these male anxieties in Friedkin's films can be found in Lee Edelman's *Homographesis* (New York: Routledge, 1994). Its titular concept names the quandary by which men struggle to demonstrate and thereby consecrate their "masculine" credentials but, in that very act, flout the cardinal rule by which (straight) maleness must *seem* unperformed, by contrast to the flamboyant semiotics of femininity and homosexuality.

10. Friedkin, *Friedkin Connection*, 384.

11. Dave White, "Where the Boys Were," *Advocate*, no. 1019 (November 18, 2008): 56.

12. In *Forms of Being*, Bersani and Dutoit's case studies include the protracted breakups and encounters with opaque worlds in *Contempt*, the garrulous female confidences that the camera declines to overhear in *All about My Mother*, and the diaphanous intersubjectivity among human and nonhuman forms of life in *The Thin Red Line* (*Forms of Being*).

13. Tony Kushner, introduction to *The Boys in the Band*, by Mart Crowley (New York: Alyson Books, 2008), ix.

14. Ben Brantley, "Broken Hearts, Bleeding Psyches," *New York Times*, February 24, 2010, www.nytimes.com/2010/02/24/theater/reviews/24boys.html.

15. Friedkin declines, for example, to mount the walls of his sets on wheels so they could converge as tensions mounted, as Elia Kazan famously did for *A Streetcar Named Desire* (1951).

16. Gilles Deleuze, *Cinema 2: The Time-Image* (1985), trans. Hugh Tomlinson and Robert Galeta (Minneapolis: University of Minnesota Press, 1989), 7, emphasis added.

17. Friedkin, *Friedkin Connection*, 41.

18. In this and other patterns in *Boys*, Bernard is a troubling nonparticipant, neither welcomed into Michael's closet nor seemingly, as Harold is, expressly positioned against it.

19. For a different reading of how the apartment's layout informs the characters' identities, with debts to Sedgwick but different priorities, see Pamela

Robertson Wojcik, *The Apartment Plot: Urban Living in American Film and Popular Culture, 1945 to 1975* (Durham, NC: Duke University Press, 2010), 133–38.

20. The quoted phrase and ensuing tenets of the closet derive from chapter 2 of Eve Kosofsky Sedgwick, *Epistemology of the Closet* (Berkeley: University of California Press, 1990), 91–130.

21. For just a few examples, see Didier Eribon, *Insult and the Making of the Gay Self* (Durham, NC: Duke University Press, 2004), especially 46–55; Cary Howie, *Claustrophilia: The Erotics of Enclosure in Medieval Literature* (New York: Palgrave, 2007); and Dominic Janes, *Picturing the Closet: Male Secrecy and Homosexual Visibility in Britain* (Oxford: Oxford University Press, 2015), which has much to say about how the closet "in fact offered opportunities for a wide variety of forms of self-fulfillment and expression" (23).

# HISTORICAL THRESHOLDS

# 5

## "Who Does She Hope to Be?"

### Celluloid Ghosts, Queer Utopias, and *The Boys* Onstage

**JAMES WILSON**

*The Boys in the Band* looks like a movie, reads like a movie and plays like a movie. . . . And just to make sure that everybody gets the point that it may some day *be* a movie, *The Boys in the Band* features a supporting cast—never visible but always hovering in quasi-madness in the wings—which includes Barbara Stanwyck, Vera Hruba Ralston, Rosemary DeCamp and Maria Montez. ("What have you got against Maria," lisps one lavender lad, "she was a good woman!")
—Rex Reed, "Breakthrough by 'The Boys in the Band'"

Who is she? Who was she? Who does she hope to be?
—Harold in *The Boys in the Band*

*The Boys in the Band* is, in several senses, a very queer play. Of course, as anyone reading this chapter knows, Mart Crowley's Off-Broadway hit focuses on a group of gay men and one putatively straight invader on the occasion of a birthday party. The queerness comes through as characters celebrate gay film icons, including Judy Garland, Bette Davis, and Barbara Stanwyck (and those are just in the first three pages of the script), and dance together as a group and in pairs. As a result of their over-the-top camp dialogue, the cast has been described as a "pack of youngish middle-aged fairy queens shouting bitchicisms at one another down the long night."[1] On another level, the play queers canonical dramatic literature. *The Boys in the Band* is aligned and makes strange bedfellows with other plays, such as Harold Pinter's menacing masterwork *The Birthday Party* (1957, and adapted for the screen by *Boys*' film director, William Friedkin, in 1968) and Edward Albee's connubial Sturm und Drang *Who's Afraid of Virginia Woolf?* (1962). Crowley has said that his play may have been unconsciously motivated by those previous works, but actually, he was inspired by the murdering gay characters, based on Leopold and Loeb, in Alfred Hitchcock's *Rope* (1948), which takes place in real time and focuses on the game of cat-and-mouse—"But which is the cat and which is the mouse?" one of the killers asks—played by the murderers and their former prep-school housemaster.[2] Indeed, as indicated by Rex Reed's insistence that *Boys* is a play passing as a movie (or is it a movie passing as a play?), a good deal of the dramatic tension comes from the coupling of the theatrical with the cinematic.

The play's production history also defies convention. When it opened Off Broadway in 1968, *Boys* was the critics' darling and broke box-office records. The prevailing wisdom of the time dictated that due to its subject matter, the play would not be successful beyond New York City.[3] In point of fact, *Boys* launched a national touring production and was an international hit. It became the first straight (that is, nonmusical) play to have an extended run in Las Vegas, and it was optioned for film within two months of its opening. Even after it was confirmed that the original company of actors would repeat their roles on-screen, A&M Records released a double LP studio cast recording of the entire play. The play's esteem did not last long, though. By the 1980s, the play was reviled and, as one critic declared it, "as psychologically passé as it is dramatically dated."[4] Particularly with the pervasiveness of the film version, the play's revolutionary standing had diminished due to the presumably hackneyed presentation of "fairy queens shouting bitchicisms." The title alone had become a token of pre-Stonewall oppression and called up associations to blackface minstrelsy. Then a queer thing happened to *The Boys in the Band*: by the 1990s, the play was regarded as a seminal work of LGBT theater, and its period of banishment from the stage had ended.[5]

Productions of *The Boys in the Band* since the original have had to carry the weight of politics and nostalgia, as well as the iconic ghosts of William Friedkin's 1970 film version. Signaling both the fear and ardor (affects often occurring simultaneously) that gay men onstage elicit, responses to the play reflect the ways in which its myriad queer aspects are negotiated locally, nationally, and globally. This chapter offers a comprehensive stage history of the play, examining the accumulation of ghosts in the most archived and well-publicized productions. Ghosts come in many different forms in this play, and one need not have a sixth sense to perceive the ghosts that pervade *The Boys in the Band*. Rex Reed notes the spirits of Barbara Stanwyck, Vera Hruba Ralston, Rosemary DeCamp, and Maria Montez "hovering in the wings," but they have been joined by the ghosts of the original actors (preserved on the 1969 original cast recording and in the 1970 film) who haunt the play at every turn. Consequently, audience members, actors, and directors revisiting the play are compelled both to confront and to embrace the ghosts, thereby opening a portal to what José Muñoz refers to as a "queer utopian memory."[6]

The focus on ghosts, utopias, and *The Boys* onstage may seem a poor fit for an anthology devoted to Friedkin's film, but I argue that the play (originally and in subsequent productions) is as informed by film as the film is informed by the play. Not only is *Boys* saturated with film imagery and modeled on Hitchcock's adaptation of Patrick Hamilton's play *Rope* (1929), but also the afterlife of the original is mediated by Friedkin's readily available film version.[7] Although *Boys* is set in a particular historical moment, the gathering, intermingling, and inter*play* of theatrical and celluloid ghosts provide revelations of queer life past, present, and future. In performance, this phenomenon may allow for queer utopian memory, which Muñoz defines as "a utopia that understands its time as reaching beyond some nostalgic past that perhaps never was or some future whose arrival is continuously belated—a utopia in the present."[8] As *Boys* celebrates long-gone Hollywood camp icons, it painfully reminds us of homophobia within and outside that community, engendering a sense of gay community and pointing to political possibilities.

The importance of *Boys* as a written text, live performance, and film is in its continual reminder of the difficulties LGBT people endure. Heather Love explains, "Paying attention to what was difficult in the past may tell us how far we have come, but that is not all it will tell us; it also makes visible the damage that we live with in the present."[9] As a historical artifact, the play offers up chances for mourning what (and whom) gay male communities have lost and affords opportunities for critiquing what they have become, thereby fueling political action. And as a piece of theater, the immediacy of the performance facilitates a queer utopian memory, mixing a material present with an invented past and a contemplated future. This reflection on gay lives is summed up in Harold's metaphysical quandary,

"Who is she? Who was she? Who does she hope to be?"[10] Examining the play and teasing out the ghosts across generations and geographies provide keys for answering these questions.

## Who Was She?

Before *Boys* was burdened with social significance, it was a big, fat hit play, which had been buoyed by generally excellent reviews when it opened on April 14, 1968, at the 299-seat Theatre Four on Fifty-Fifth Street in Manhattan. The notices helped propel ticket sales, which were already quite substantial from word of mouth. Clive Barnes, the chief critic of the *New York Times*, was a champion of the play throughout its run, reviewing it on three separate occasions. He gave the show one of its boldest pull quotes in an advertisement: "The play . . . is by far the frankest treatment of homosexuality I have ever seen on stage." Barnes found some faults in the writing, commenting on the bald exposition in the play's opening moments, and he thought the humor and camp elements (which he describes as "screamingly funny and screamingly fag") lost their pungency by the end of the evening.[11]

The camp elements, especially in the embracing of Hollywood imagery, contributed to the cinematic filter through which many critics viewed the play. As deconstructionist theorists might say, *The Boys in the Band* was *always already* a movie. Rex Reed identifies the diva imitations, the "42nd Street hustler dressed like a midnight cowboy" (the film of James Leo Herlihy's 1965 novel was released a year after *Boys* opened), "and the best bitchy dialogue since 'All About Eve.'"[12] In addition, several critics, including Barnes, compared the play to Albee's *Virginia Woolf?* (released as a film in 1966) with its acidic language and the climactic game of "get-the-guest," but the play's distinction was its presumably authentic, ethnographic, and filmic documentarian view of gay men and their lifestyle. Ted Kalem in *Time* described the play's context as a "netherworld," and Jack Kroll compared it to a zoological experience: "The hothouse pungency and serrated neurasthenia of a very real milieu is brilliantly caught—the boys in the band have the preening, pecking paroxysmic elegance of bright-feathered fighting cocks."[13] In fact, the exposure of this clandestine underworld was enough to keep some daily newspapers away entirely, including the *New York Daily News*, which maintained a policy throughout the 1960s to embargo reviews of plays containing explicitly gay or lesbian content.[14]

Contributing to a sense of cinematic realism were Robert Moore's direction and his ability to mine rich performances from the nine-person cast. In a review for *Vogue*, Anthony West singled out each member of the "beautifully balanced and astonishingly effective cast": "Kenneth Nelson does wonders in the lead, managing to retain the audience's sympathy and respect even when dissolving into tearful self-pity, and Frederick Combs is quietly distinguished and at times very touching as his loving prop and support. Cliff Gorman, Reuben Greene, and Robert La Tourneaux give performances of a beautifully measured extravagance in the principal comic parts; and Leonard Frey, Laurence Luckinbill, Keith Prentice, and Peter White are all admirable in the very demanding minor roles."[15] With the outstanding reviews, provocative subject matter, and noteworthy cast, *Boys* was poised to stay put at Theatre Four for a long time and make a lot of money for its backers. When *Boys* closed after 1,001 performances in New York, it had become one of the longest running Off-Broadway shows of all time and one of the most lucrative as well. The play cost $20,000 to produce in 1968 (which was in fact lower than the Off-Broadway standard of the time), and by the time it closed on September 6, 1970—figuring in national tour and film revenues—each investor had made 1,450 percent profit on each $400 share.[16]

During the run of the original production, which opened just over fourteen months before the Stonewall Riots and closed just over fourteen months after, there was a noticeable shift in the way in which individuals in the press wrote about the play. Hailed as a breakthrough in 1968, *Boys* was haunted by politically antiquated spirits by 1970 and was already shadowed by apparitions of its former self. For instance, ten months after Clive Barnes wrote his initial review (and still four months before Stonewall), he revisited the play with its new cast and found that it held up generally well. Barnes's description of some of the characters—"Michael, a slightly aging Roman Catholic fag"; "Harold, a slightly aging Jewish fag"; "Bernard, the Negro queer"; and "Emory, the one fairy queen of limp-wristed legend in the play"—would be considered more than just a bit offensive today, but he praised the work as "the best American play for some few seasons."[17] Just over a year later, in April 1970, Barnes reviewed for a final time the original Off-Broadway production, and his attitude shows a seismic shift. He was not as enthusiastic about the current cast members, several of whom had appeared in the touring production, and he felt by and large that they paled by comparison with the ghosts of the original cast. "That first cast was so carefully picked," he explained, "that nothing could possibly match it." More importantly, he felt that the play was the product of a particular moment, long since passed; in short, in just two years, *Boys in the Band* had "become a period piece." He wrote, "The liberating sense of breakthrough is missing. I am also more and more disturbed by the antihomosexual element in the play. I do not believe that all homosexuals are nearly as miserable as Mr. Crowley would have us believe. Some of my best friends are homosexual, and basically neither sadder nor gladder than my heterosexual friends."[18] Perhaps Barnes's homosexual best friends rebuked him, but the character identifications in his review had also lost their colorfully homophobic descriptors. In the latest review, Michael is no longer described as a "Roman Catholic fag" but as "the party giver who plays nasty games on his guests"; Harold is not a "Jewish fag" but "the guest of honor who is celebrating, none too resignedly, his birthday"; Bernard is simply noted for his "puzzled pain"; and only Emory retains his fairy status, earning the designation "the calculated Queen of the May."[19] Once a celebration of queer visibility, the visible queers of *The Boys in the Band* were relics of a different time and place. A group of gay men dancing indoors to the Fire Island Madison, a riff on the popular line dance of the 1960s, seemed quaint compared with the rebellious queers outdoors fighting in the streets and marching in parades.

The film version was still more than a year away, but the *Boys'* circulation in mass culture contributed to the outcry against the play. An anonymous source in *Variety* bemoaned the representations of gay men that sanctioned "the straight image of homosexual life as a living hell, like 'Boys in the Band.'"[20] Donn Teal, a writer for the *New York Times*, was even more direct in condemning the play's perpetuation of gay stereotypes when he wrote about the release of the original cast recording. In an unusual turn, the complete performance of *Boys in the Band* was preserved on vinyl,[21] and as a commodity sold in record stores throughout the country, the play would potentially reach larger and more remote audiences. Teal worried that the sheer availability of the LP would strengthen engrained attitudes about gay men, especially among (in his view) more provincial and less sophisticated individuals listening to the record at home. Speaking on behalf of gay men, he explained,

> The average among us are appalled that the heterosexual (and maladjusted homosexual) may believe our typical soirée founders on—or flourishes by—self-degrading confessions like "The Truth Game"; that we store up barbiturates as Harold does for "the long winter of his death"; that our parents have all been "killer whales"; and that we regularly address each other as "fairy" and "fag." "The Boys" exude selfishness,

self-absorption, and self-indulgence. Worst of all, they not only bespeak, they *proclaim*, guilt feelings through every utterance Crowley has given them. Though we grant that the New York playgoer may not be so blithely duped into accepting the stereotypes of this show, we wonder what will be the thoughts of, say, less up-to-date Kansas Citians when, turntables revolving, they hear Michael's second-act wail: "If we could just learn not to *hate* ourselves so much."[22]

Over the next two and a half decades, *Boys* would be disparaged for trafficking in unsavory gay representations, and the title itself would summon the specter of the self-hating queer.[23] The criticism of the play would even supplant recognition of the tremendous success (and arguably among gay men in particular) it enjoyed in New York, on tour throughout the United States, and internationally.[24]

## At Home and Abroad: The Boys and the Brand

As with many hit shows, *The Boys in the Band* transitioned from a mere New York phenomenon to a national and international brand name. The film rights were sold in May 1968, and while the Off-Broadway production was still selling strong, a national tour and a Las Vegas production launched in 1969.[25] Yet this play was not like other plays, and its difference marked it wherever it went. Clive Barnes claimed in his first review that as an outcome of the meticulous authenticity represented in the characters' world, *Boys* is not simply "a play about homosexuality" but a "*homosexual play*."[26] Assuming a sexual identity for the play rather than a typical genre description ("comedy," "drama," or "play with music," for instance) reflects the ways it was received on its tour of major U.S. cities. The production was shadowed by its designation as a "gay play," and *Boys*' arrival in major cities became a litmus test for the marketability and utopian promises of homosexual liberation in the months immediately before and after the Stonewall Riots in June 1969. Local reactions revealed the conflicted national stances toward gay visibility.

By the end of the 1960s, homosexuality had ostensibly become ubiquitous, and in theaters and cinemas, gay characters and themes had seemingly burst out of the closet doors and threatened cultural dominance. *Variety* reported that Los Angeles might earn the label "the Gay Way" as there would be "four homo-themed plays running concurrently" (the other three being John Herbert's *Fortune and Men's Eyes*, Colin Spencer's *Spitting Image*, and Charles Dyer's *Staircase*).[27] A few weeks later, the same paper declared that Hollywood was capitalizing on lesbian and gay story lines. Declaring "Homo 'n' Lesbo Films at Peak," *Variety* affirmed that the success of *The Fox* (1967), Mark Rydell's adaptation of the D. H. Lawrence novella, had initiated a vogue in "sexual perversion on the screen."[28]

Even as gay-themed plays and films attracted a great deal of attention, cities across the country did not deliver occasions for queer utopia. The reviews for *Boys* were generally favorable in DC, for example, but audience turnout was meager. The show's management blamed this on the political and labor culture in that city. *Variety*, with characteristic scorn, wrote, "Homos, it's pointed out, are subject to instant dismissal from so-called sensitive Government agencies (State, Defense, etc.), so employees in those offices are afraid to be seen in the audience at 'Boys.'"[29] While it had not been uncommon for actors taking roles in the play to be wary of its effects on their professional and personal lives, the situation in DC highlights the fact that some spectators held similar concerns about a presumed homosexuality by association. Similarly, the second national company had a highly touted, open-ended run at Caesars Palace in Las Vegas. The production was notable as "the first legitimate theatrical production ever staged [in Las Vegas] in its entirety."[30] Unfortunately, it did not hit the jackpot and failed to compete with the revues and casino attractions. The Vegas management said the disappointing attendance had nothing to do with the play's subject matter, but *Back Stage* reported differently, claiming, "Several couples walked out before the intermission. Others sat through it but protested later to the Caesars Palace management." The paper interviewed several audience members (all of them presumably heterosexual), who were dismayed by the coarse language. "'We've never heard some of those words on a stage before,' gasped one scandalized spectator between acts, the whirring of slot machines sounding in the background, 'and not all of them off!'"[31]

*Boys* played well in international theater centers, such as in England, France, Denmark, Australia, Japan, and Israel, where it was treated as a socially realistic documentary, and its transnational circulation coincided with the transmission of homophile political culture globally. Homophile activists across the United States and in several countries throughout the world created a network of intellectual and cultural links in the decades following World War II. Distributing pamphlets, organizing conferences, creating travel guides, and publishing narrative accounts were just some of the ways in which these small groups helped raise consciousness about same-sex sexuality. The efforts were intended to reflect the universality and naturalness of homosexuality.[32] Peter Jackson, however, cautions against assuming that gay culture exported from the United States to countries around the world created a monolithic gay identity. While the flow of images, cultural artifacts, activist ideas, and tourist services across national borders generated a form of "global queering," LGBT transnational cultures are formed from local agency, and the effect of foreign capitalism on the histories of these cultures is far more complex than previously thought.[33] While *The Boys in the Band* was deemed a *homosexual play* as it traversed the United States, abroad it was regarded as an *American homosexual play*. In fact, many of the reviewers went to great effort to explain that the characters were distinctively foreign. Local audiences were encouraged to enter into the play's world as if tourists to a strange land and were allowed a privileged view of the customs, behaviors, and rituals of the American aboriginals.

The first international production of the play opened at Wyndham's Theatre in London's West End in February 1969. The show opened with most of the original New York cast (with Tom Aldredge replacing Cliff Gorman), and the reviews were generally favorable. Some of the critics suggested *Boys* presented an authentic, uncontaminated view of (American) male homosexuality, claiming Crowley's characters revealed the true nature "beneath the homosexual mask."[34] A few of the reviewers, insinuating nationalistic superiority, found the play base, tawdry, and amateurish. Benedict Nightingale described it as "a play about homosexuals for homosexuals," and he went on to write that, while members of the audience—"as gay a crowd [he had] seen in years"—apparently appreciated having their own lives depicted onstage, he found the presentation simplistic. England had decriminalized homosexuality in 1967 through an act of Parliament resulting from the Wolfenden Report a decade before. To Nightingale, the play's depiction of homosexuality seemed naïve and provincial: "Perhaps such attitudes are more common among educated Americans than they are here; perhaps the play would have meant more before the Wolfenden reforms."[35]

Other English reviewers commented on the play as if it were an anthropological presentation, haunted by colonialism and offering a peek at gay men in their native habitat. Herbert Kretzmer, a critic for the *Daily Express*, described the performance as a "well-documented Cook's travel guide to the world of the urban male homosexual."[36] Ronald Bryden of the *Observer* also regarded the piece as an exercise in U.S. colonialism, but his description tilted toward the exoticization of the indigenous, comparing the experience to a staged Native American powwow or Wild West show. He said the production "fails to disguise behind whizbang Broadway production a basically cheap and cheapening tourist bus-tour of Faggsville, New York, with the natives wearing their traditional homosexual costumes, dancing their tribal dances and generally camping it up for the visitors."[37] The exotica was surely part of the play's appeal, and it performed quite successfully, running 386 performances and launching a UK national tour. At the time, it was the longest running London production of an Off-Broadway play.[38]

The play was translated and adapted for a number of productions throughout Europe, but it was always treated as a distinctively American (as opposed to universal) creation. The producers of the French version, titled *Les garçons de la bande*, which opened at the Edouard VII theater on September 18, 1969, had toyed with the idea of changing the setting to Paris but in the end decided that Bernard Giquel, the play's adaptor, should retain the original New York locale "to keep it all very remote and foreign." As *Variety* reported, Parisian audiences would more easily tolerate shocking language and behaviors from American characters than from French.[39] Audiences received the play enthusiastically, but some of the critics found it offensive. Jean Dutourd, a critic for *France-Soir*, compared the theatrical experience to "a visit to the zoo's monkey-house."[40] As Ken Nielsen writes about the Danish production of the play, which was translated as *Bøsserne* (The gays), the version that opened in 1969 went to great lengths to show that the characters and situations onstage were not localized but distinctly other.[41] The "problem" of homosexuality is then an American problem, and the hysterical, campy, and grotesque gay creatures are the by-products of U.S. culture, not Danish.

As the controversy surrounding the Melbourne, Australia, production demonstrates, queer utopias are often regulated by homophobic mechanisms of the state but offer sites of possible resistance. Members of the Melbourne Vice Squad attended several performances of *Boys* and charged three actors with "having uttered obscene language." The magistrate hearing the case subsequently saw the show himself and overturned the conviction because he considered the infractions "so trifling."[42] The language of the play remained unchanged, and the production continued to sell out. This was not the end of the story, however. The members of the Vice Squad sought and received "an order for a review" of the original decision. The magistrate was ordered to overturn his ruling and convict the three actors. One of the actors was fined A$10, and the two others were fined A$25. The offending words in the script were substituted with nonoffensive ones.[43] The production quietly played out its run, and by the time the movie was released in March 1970, national and international productions were fewer and farther between.[44]

## And the Band Plays On

By 1996, *The Boys in the Band* was haunted by the original actors, captured for eternity in Friedkin's film. In June of that year, the first New York revival, produced by the WPA Theater company in Chelsea, opened Off Broadway. There was a good deal of press about the show's return, and most sources suggested that New York was ready to welcome with open hearts—if not necessarily open minds—the prodigal play. The first sentence of Ben Brantley's *New York Times* review in June 1996 summed up the cordial reception with which the revival was greeted: "It is, apparently, O.K.," he wrote, "to like 'The Boys in the Band' again."[45] The play had shed much of its weight in identity politics and, thus, could be viewed as a theatrical curio, or at least as a historical and nostalgia-laden artifact. As most of the critics and journalists marking the play's arrival attested, attitudes toward gay men had changed dramatically in the nearly three decades since it first appeared, and gay-themed plays and musicals, including, most notably, *Bent* (1978), *Torch Song Trilogy* (1982), *La cage aux folles* (1983), *The Normal Heart* (1985), *Falsettos* (1992), *Angels in America* (1993), and *Love! Valour! Compassion!* (1995), were standard fare on New York stages. Yet the revival opened as gay communities were still reeling from the devastation of AIDS, and the threat of contagion and the ghostly presence of those who had been lost to the disease haunted Crowley's characters and milieu.

The revival opened at the WPA's theater on Twenty-Third Street in Manhattan, and after concluding a six-week limited run in July 1996, the production reopened at the Off-Broadway Lucille Lortel Theatre in early August and played an additional eighty-eight performances. Directed by Kenneth Elliott, who had helmed Charles Busch's plays in the 1980s and 1990s, the show boasted a number of familiar names from New York's downtown performance scene. For instance, David Drake, whose one-person show *The Night Larry Kramer Kissed Me* (1992) had run for more than a year, played Michael, and he was joined by two other playwrights/solo performers, David Greenspan (Harold) and James Lecesne (Emory). The notices for the revival were generally mixed, and faults were attributed as much to the production, best summed up as "competent," as they were to the play itself.[46] Just as critics in 1968 pointed to the dramaturgical faults, or what Ben Brantley in his 1996 review called "a fairly creaky piece of craftsmanship," the revival reviewers maintained similar qualms.[47] Howard Kissel, the first critic from New York's *Daily News* who actually reviewed a production of the play, however, was more forgiving of the script's perceived flaws. He found the second-act party game "a bit melodramatic but harrowing" and the ensuing revelations of self-hatred "quaint," but he argued that time had not been unkind to Crowley's work: "The star of the evening is the play itself—solidly built, still moving and enormously entertaining."[48] While many of the critics gave the ensemble of actors varying degrees of praise, Barnes compared the current cast with the "extraordinary" original, claiming "the present group bears up to memory's unfair and golden comparison extremely well."[49]

To adopt Jacques Derrida's term alluding to the "absent present," *traces* of the original production and film circulated throughout the 1996 revival.[50] Fragments of dialogue and gestures from *Boys* had entered the queer lexicon in the intervening quarter of a century, and these offered moments of shared history and sense of community. Bitchicisms recorded for the Off-Broadway cast LP and Friedkin's soundtrack had become gay stock phrases, and the intonations of the original voices were part of a collective queer unconscious.[51] Such lines as "Well, one thing you can say for masturbation . . . you certainly don't have to look your best" (13) and "Who do you have to fuck to get a drink around here?" (23) were met with joyous recognition by many in the audiences.[52] These occurrences of queer utopia united LGBT audience members (particularly gay men) across generations through aural snapshots of a common popular culture. At the same time, some of the traces had grown fainter and more obscure in the ensuing years. References that might have collectivized audiences in 1968 had become ancient history. The production team recognized this during rehearsals when some of the actors, several of whom had little or no familiarity with the play or movie and whose own queer histories did not include Hollywood films of the 1930s and '40s, were at sea with the play's cinematic allusions. "Some [of the cast members] were so young they pronounced Bette Davis as if they were talking about Bette Midler," Mart Crowley told the *Times*.[53] Various celluloid ghosts needed to be resuscitated, so Crowley's friend Hilary Knight, a book illustrator and movie buff, created two "training films" for the actors. The videotapes included the scene from *A Star Is Born* in which James Mason gives a pep talk to Judy Garland, prompting her to imagine, in a famous line, that she is singing just for herself "and the boys in the band." The videos also contained movie clips of some of the famous stars and "demi-celebrities" referenced in the script, such as Betty Grable, Bette Davis, Vera Hruba Ralston, Maria Montez, and Barbara Stanwyck.[54] Camp, apparently, has to be carefully taught.

Whereas some of the ripostes evoked instances of shared pleasure in the revival, other bits of dialogue took on new and ominous meanings within the social and political context of 1996. For example, when Donald first enters at the top of the play, Michael asks him why he has arrived so early, and he replies that his psychiatrist has canceled their appointment. "Why'd the prick cancel?" asks Michael. Donald answers, "A virus or something. He looked awful" (11). A few minutes later, Donald claims the analyst stopped the session abruptly, saying, "Donald, I have to cancel tonight—I'm just too sick" (12). While the play very much takes place in the late 1960s and the revival's program notes established the setting as 1968, the shadow of AIDS pervaded the production, and Michael's suggestion of a "gay corpse" (81) took on an even darker connotation. Glimpses of New York City before the AIDS crisis abound in the script, including flippant discussion of drunken one-night stands (24–25), the baths (28–29), hustlers (embodied by Cowboy), and "promiscuous," open relationships (71). In the context of the play, Michael's East Side apartment seems cocooned within a vibrantly queer playground of sexual activity and experimentation. Inside the apartment, gay sex and illicit activities are recalled, joked about, and argued over, but except for the possibility of Hank and Larry getting physically intimate offstage in Michael's bedroom, there is no onstage carnality. Throughout the city that surrounds the world of the play, though, gay sex is profuse, public, and marketable. While this may have titillated (or morally appalled) audiences in 1968, coming off city health measures to combat AIDS in the 1980s and Giuliani's antisex crusades in the 1990s, the environment outside the play (from a 1996 perspective) seems dangerous, illegal, and rife with infection. Contributing to this foreboding atmosphere are the specters of the original cast members. As the media covering the opening of the revival pointed out, by July 1996 five of the nine original cast members and the director had all died of AIDS: Robert La Tourneaux (in 1986, age forty-one), Leonard Frey (in 1988, age forty-nine), Frederick Combs (in 1992, age fifty-seven), Keith Prentice (in 1992, age fifty-two), Kenneth Nelson (in 1993, age sixty-three), and Robert Moore (in 1984, age fifty-seven). The play's ghosts were at variance with the textual free spirits, and gay past, present, and future collided.

Health regulations and new attitudes toward sex redefined what it meant to be gay in the 1990s. Building on and critiquing Douglas Crimp's claim that AIDS health regulations triggered a demise of "a culture of sexual possibility," José Muñoz argues that the pre-HIV/AIDS-epidemic era is signified in the cultural imagination as "a queer sex utopia."[55] He cites Crimp's description of a "historically specific gay male lifeworld," in which "sex was everywhere for us, and everything we wanted to venture: Golden showers and water sports, cocksucking and rimming, fucking and fist fucking."[56] Muñoz reminds us that though utopias are always imagined, they are politically essential. They help us envision alternative social existences and provide a tool for gauging our current realities. *Boys* ends with Michael and Donald hoping for a better future for gay men ("If we could just *learn* not to hate ourselves so very much"; 81) and admitting that there are things they can never know ("As my father said to me when he died in my arms, 'I don't understand any of it. I never did'"; 83). Juxtaposing the relative sexual freedom of the late 1960s and early 1970s, the regulated gay sex of the 1990s, and the characters' hope for happier prospects produces a queer utopian memory. Mourning the deceased, reviving the ghosts, and sharing in the recognition of shared traces offered political and communal sustenance in an AIDS-ravaged New York City.

## Old Ghosts, New Host

The social and political landscape for gays and lesbians had altered dramatically by the time the next major New York revival of *The Boys in the Band* opened in February 2010. For example, while President Bill Clinton endorsed the Defense of Marriage Act in 1996, in 2004 Massachusetts became the first state to legalize same-sex marriage, and by 2010 four more states had passed similar laws. The poll data reflected this notable shift. A Gallup poll in 1996, for instance, showed that 27 percent of all Americans were in favor of legalizing same-sex marriage; in 2010, 44 percent favored legalization.[57] Circumstances around other hot-button LGBT issues reflected similar changes. In 2003, in the case of *Lawrence v. Texas*, the Supreme Court struck down the Texas sodomy law, thereby making same-sex sexual activity legal in every state of the nation. Clinton instituted "Don't Ask, Don't Tell" in 1994, and openly gay men and lesbians were prohibited from serving in the military. But in 2010, 70 percent of Americans polled believed that gay service members should be allowed to serve openly.[58] (The policy was struck down in 2011, and the defeat of the Defense of Marriage Act followed in 2013.) And finally, while the number of known deaths of people with AIDS was 34,947 in 1996,[59] in 2010 this number was less than half, with a reported 15,529 deaths.[60] Audiences would have a very different perspective on the lives of gay men than they would in 1968 or 1996, and the responses to the 2010 revival reflected the new cultural mind-set.

This shift in perspective was augmented by the directorial approach and the scenic design, which placed audience members directly in the world of the play. Perhaps as the film had become even more indelible over the decades, the production team set out to create a living movie of *Boys*. Director Jack Cummings III and his design team, which included Sandra Goldmark (sets), Dane Laffrey (lighting), and Kathryn Rohe (costumes), pushed the sense of realism nearly to the limit in his site-specific production for New York's Transport Group Theater Company.[61] The play was staged in a converted photography studio in a Chelsea penthouse, and the space included an excellent view of the Empire State Building. This was, in other words, prime real estate. As the members of the audience entered, they were immediately inside Michael's apartment. The bar was to the right on crossing the threshold, and the bedroom was against the far wall. A few steps went up to the bedroom, and floor-to-ceiling vertical blinds set the room off from the rest of the space. In the center of the playing area were a couch, divan, beanbag chair, and other pieces of furniture to enable cozy conversation. There was space enough for ninety-nine audience members, who were seated in sections throughout the room, and the action took place throughout the room. This meant no one had a bad seat: at some point, actors might hover near you or right in front of you. This also meant that no one had a very good seat: at some point, actors might perform a crucial moment behind you, or they might be obstructed by a piece of furniture. The play was performed without intermission (and reentrance was not allowed if audience members left during the show), and Crowley had trimmed the text so that it ran a bladder-friendly two hours. Cummings had said that one of his goals of staging the play environmentally was to make the experience of the play closer to watching (and being in) a film. In an interview with an *Out* magazine reporter, he said, "We've had our time looking at these characters from afar in that neat frame of a proscenium. I thought, What would it be like if we physically brought the audience into the apartment? Would it be more filmic where you're seeing extreme close-ups and getting more deep focus?"[62] The staging also contributed to a feeling of entrapment as leaving would entail dodging set pieces and actors. Reticent theatergoers, however, did not need to worry about an interactive experience, a point on which Crowley was very firm. When Cummings told the playwright of the staging intentions, Crowley was adamant that the line between actors and audience was reinforced unlike in other immersive shows he had seen: "I hated 'Cats,' and in 'Hair,' I don't care if Gavin Creel kisses me—I don't want him anywhere near me with that sweaty wig!"[63]

The reviews for the production were generally quite positive, and many critics found that Cummings's approach elucidated the play in a number of interesting ways. The *Advocate*'s Brandon Voss explained, "With the aid of homelike lamp lighting and the fact that the party progresses in real time, you do feel like you're a part of the action—like watching a bitchy gay Avatar."[64] Elizabeth Vincentelli of the *New York Post* pointed to the reflexive emotional and physical reactions that the proximity of the action evoked: "When the fur starts to fly, it could very well hit you in the face. Within seconds, you forget you're watching a show and it's a struggle not to yell 'Don't let Alan in!' or 'Don't pick up the phone!'"[65] And *Variety*'s David Rooney claimed that the staging decisions actually smoothed over the play's oft-cited problematic dramaturgy and the "anachronistic" (presumably he means overly negative) portrayals of gay men represented in the play: "The real accomplishment of the staging by Jack Cummings III, however, is that it physically minimizes the vast cultural distance separating the audience from the landmark 1968 play. Being so close to the well-paced action somehow helps pardon the mechanical methods used to steer the bitchy banter into ugly confrontation. And it serves to distract from the more uneasy anachronisms of this candid pre-Stonewall self-portrait of the gay American male."[66] Ben Brantley of the *New York Times* was one of the few critics to poop out on this party. He called it "unevenly acted, emotionally claustrophobic," and he felt that much of the humor had been minimized. He wrote, "Before the play began I heard a middle-aged man gleefully quoting some of the script's choicer period insults, a reminder that for certain fans 'The Boys in the Band' retains undeniable camp appeal. Yet when those lines were spoken in the show they elicited only half-hearted laughs. Audiences expecting a frolicsome the-way-we-were evening are advised to stay home."[67]

As Brantley's eavesdropping indicates, the ghosts of the 1968 production and Friedkin's film version had taken up residence in the Chelsea loft space. With the availability of the DVD, which had been released in 2008, and with accessibility of the film via Netflix and YouTube, comparisons were frequently cited. Terry Teachout of the *Wall Street Journal* addressed this in his review: "Any revival of 'The Boys in the Band' must contend with memories of

William Friedkin's 1970 film version, which documents the performances of the entire 1968 Off-Broadway cast, one of the finest ensembles ever to appear on an American stage."[68] Traces of the original continued to provide flashes of recognition and conditioned the ways in which some theatergoers saw the play in new productions. Cummings's staging may have allowed for the theatrical equivalent of different camera angles, but the raw footage remained the same. So, for many audience members, *The Boys in the Band* is not a typical theater experience. The play is a repository of replayed vocal intonations, half-remembered queer emotions, and collective LGBT experiences.

Any new production of *The Boys in the Band* is steeped in nostalgia and the accretion of history. Audience members familiar with LGBT issues in the United States cannot help but be reminded of pre-Stonewall oppression, and the play is riddled with the ghostly reminders of AIDS. The play also allows for moments of queer utopia as spectators revel in the social and political progress since 1968. Yet the dissonance caused by the competing hosts and ghosts signifies continuing frustrations and defeats. Utopia is illusive; the struggles are eternal and insinuate that LGBT people have not yet achieved complete social acceptance. Michael may tell Harold that "it's not always like it happens in plays, not all faggots bump themselves off at the end of the story" (55), but in real life gay men do indeed bump themselves off and are bumped off for being so-called faggots. In September 2010, a few months after the revival closed, the media focused its attention on the suicide of Tyler Clementi, who threw himself off the George Washington Bridge after his roommate at Rutgers University used a webcam to broadcast and publicly mock his gay trysts. The case inspired a number of public figures, including Barack Obama, Hillary Clinton, and Ellen DeGeneres, to speak out against gay bullying, and it coincided with Dan Savage and Terry Miller's "It Gets Better" Internet and video project to help kids struggling with issues of identity and harassment. A few weeks later, in October 2010, New York City was rattled by an incident of gay bashing at the Stonewall Inn in the West Village. Two young men from Staten Island shouted homophobic slurs at Benjamin Carver, a thirty-four-year-old man from Washington, DC, and then punched him several times in the face when he refused to hand over twenty dollars.[69] In May 2013, Mark Carson was murdered a few blocks from the Stonewall Inn, also a result of homophobia.[70] These are just a few of the incidents that have occurred since the 2010 revival.

While Ben Brantley is correct when he says a visit to *The Boys in the Band* can be "a frolicsome the-way-we-were evening," the play can additionally, as Brantley notes about the 2010 staging, provide an unsettling evening.

We may laugh as the boys verbally joust with each other, take comfort in the familiarity of film allusions and fading Hollywood icons, and enjoy a degree of hopefulness in the characters' historically elapsed hopelessness. Crowley's unlikely utopic masterwork offers a vision of gay life as it was, as it is, and as it might be.

## Notes

1. Clive Barnes, "Theater: 'Boys in the Band' Opens Off Broadway," *New York Times*, April 15, 1968.

2. Mart Crowley, "A Conversation with Mart Crowley," interview by the author, May 16, 2014, CUNY Graduate Center, New York City.

3. On its prospects for touring, Richard Hummler contended, "'The Boys in the Band' is hardly for kiddie audiences, of course, and it would take a genius to book a tour, but there might be a film in it." Hummler, "Off-B'way Review: *The Boys in the Band*," *Variety*, April 17, 1968.

4. Alvin Klein, "'Boys in the Band' Hits Unhappy Chord," *New York Times*, March 1, 1981.

5. Michael R. Schiavi describes the play as "the linchpin of modern gay drama and, possibly, sensibility." Schiavi, "Teaching the *Boys*: Mart Crowley in the Millennial Classroom," *Modern Language Studies* 31, no. 2 (2001): 76. Many gay writers have noted the bearing it has had on them and their work. See, for instance, Patrick Healy, "'The Band' Helped Writers Find Their Beat," *New York Times*, March 7, 2010. In interviews with Healy, Larry Kramer calls the play "life-changing," and Tony Kushner says the theatricality and politics of *Boys* influenced his own writing of *Angels in America*.

6. José Esteban Muñoz, *Cruising Utopia: The Then and There of Queer Futurity* (New York: NYU Press, 2009), 35.

7. For a discussion of the relationship of film and theater and the ways in which "the proliferation of intermedial performance is one of the hallmarks of contemporary theater," see Martin Harries, "Theater and Media before 'New' Media: Beckett's *Film* and *Play*," *Theater* 42, no. 2 (2012): 6–25.

8. Muñoz, *Cruising Utopia*, 37.

9. Heather Love, *Feeling Backward: Loss and the Politics of Queer History* (Cambridge, MA: Harvard University Press, 2007), 29.

10. Mart Crowley, *The Boys in the Band*, reprinted in *Out Plays: Landmark Gay and Lesbian Plays of the Twentieth Century*, ed. Ben Hodges (New York: Alyson Books, 2008), 43. Subsequent references to the play's text are cited parenthetically in the text.

11. Barnes, "Theater."

12. Rex Reed, "Breakthrough by 'The Boys in the Band,'" *New York Times*, April 15, 1968.

13. Ted Kalem, "New Plays: The Boys in the Band," *Time*, April 26, 1968, 97; Jack Kroll, "'The Boys in the Band': Queer Comedy," *Newsweek*, April 29, 1968, 93–94.

14. "N.Y. News Continues Not to Review Homo Plays," *Variety*, March 5, 1969.

15. Anthony West, "Vogue's Spotlight: Theatre," *Vogue*, August 1, 1968, 64.

16. "'Boys' Has Netted 1,450% Thus Far; Folds This Week," *Variety*, September 2, 1970.

17. Clive Barnes, "'The Boys in the Band' Is Still a Sad Gay Romp," *New York Times*, February 18, 1969.

18. Clive Barnes, "Stage: Birthday for 'Boys in the Band,'" *New York Times*, April 18, 1970.

19. Ibid.

20. Quoted in Richard Hummler, "Figure Homo Play Successes Cater to Sizable Minority of Legit Public," *Variety*, October 29, 1969.

21. Off-Broadway and Broadway musical cast albums were fairly ubiquitous in the 1960s, but very few plays were recorded. *Who's Afraid of Virginia Woolf?* (1963) was a notable exception. *Variety* notes that the *Boys* recording was A&M's first foray into spoken-word records, and because of the subject matter, marketing was kept to a minimum: "Since the play's thematic focus on homosexuality precludes air play, A&M is setting up a special merchandising campaign in the college and 'underground' markets. The cast album will also be advertised on the air, albeit with no illustrative excerpts." "A&M Records Waxes Off-Broadway 'Band,'" *Variety*, January 22, 1969.

22. Donn Teal, "How Anguished Are Homosexuals?," *New York Times*, June 1, 1969.

23. Timothy Scheie says the play was disparaged because images of self-hating homosexuals were "anathema to the new mantra of Gay Pride," which emerged in the 1970s. Doric Wilson's play about the Stonewall Riots, *Street Theater* (1982), for instance, includes the preppy characters of Michael and Donald, who seclude themselves within the comforts of a chic apartment and are dismissive of the rebellious queers on Christopher Street. Scheie writes, "Wilson condemns Crowley's closeted and self-blaming characters for their complicity with the forces that repress them, a tacit alliance that perhaps contributed to the play's success in a mainstream venue." Scheie, "Acting Gay in the Age of Queer: Pondering the Revival of *The Boys in the Band*," *Modern Drama* 42, no. 1 (1999): 5–6.

24. Teal says that "dozens—scores?—of homosexuals have returned to see 'The Boys' twice, even three times" ("How Anguished Are Homosexuals?"),

and Clive Barnes alludes to a common perception at the time that audiences were mostly male, jokingly stating, "I hear 'Boys in the Band' is even considering putting 'Ladies Invited' notices outside the theater." Barnes, "Where Is U.S. Theater? It's Alive Off Broadway," *New York Times*, May 28, 1968.

25. "CBS Films' Unusual Play Buy: Off-B'way Homo Click," *Variety*, May 29, 1968, 1, 62.

26. Barnes, "Theater," emphasis mine.

27. "Four Homo Plays May Convert L.A. into a 'Gay Way,'" *Variety*, January 1, 1969.

28. James R. Parish, "Homo 'n' Lesbo Films at Peak: Deviate Theme Now 'Boxoffice,'" *Variety*, January 15, 1969.

29. "'Boys' Limp in D.C.; Blame Gov't Tabu on Homo Workers," *Variety*, July 23, 1969.

30. Steven V. Roberts, "Las Vegas Greets Legitimate Theater," *New York Times*, August 1, 1969.

31. "Vegas Shocked by 'Boys in the Band,'" *Back Stage*, August 15, 1969, 16.

32. David S. Churchill, "Transnationalism and Homophile Political Culture in the Postwar Decades," *GLQ: A Journal of Lesbian and Gay Studies* 15, no. 1 (2009): 35.

33. Peter A. Jackson, "Capitalism and Global Queering: National Markets, Parallels among Sexual Cultures, and Multiple Queer Modernities," *GLQ: A Journal of Lesbian and Gay Studies* 15, no. 3 (2009): 359.

34. B. A. Young, *Financial Times* critic, quoted in "OK Reviews for 'Boys' in London; Only 2 Negatives," *Variety*, February 19, 1969.

35. Benedict Nightingale, "A Lovely Death, My Lambs," *New Statesman*, February 21, 1969, 267.

36. Quoted in "OK Reviews for 'Boys' in London."

37. Quoted in ibid.

38. "'The Boys' Will Go on Tour," *Stage and Television Today*, December 24, 1969, 12.

39. Herbert R. Lottman, "Paris Tolerates Sex Only When It's from O'seas," *Variety*, January 7, 1970.

40. Thomas Quinn Curtiss, "Parisians Hail Premiere of 'The Boys in the Band,'" *New York Times*, September 20, 1969.

41. Ken Nielsen, "Exporting America: Theatre, Gay Male Identity, and Anti-Americanism in Denmark and West Germany" (Ph.D. diss., CUNY Graduate Center, 2011), 100.

42. "Vice Squad at 'Boys in the Band': No Conviction," *Stage and Television Today*, August 7, 1969, 1, 15.

43. "'Boys in the Band' Actors Fined," *Stage and Television Today*, October 23, 1969, 19.

44. Notably, in 1972 a community theater production in Yorktown Heights, New York, received a good deal of attention. The company of actors was made up of local nonprofessional actors, including a vocational education teacher, a lawyer, an IBM field engineer, and an insurance salesman. Many of the actors claimed, though, that they did not want audiences to mistake them for "real-life" homosexuals. "If every person in the room thinks I'm queer for the two and a half hours I'm onstage," one actor stated, "that's great. But I'm not sure I want them to go out of the theater thinking that." "A Homosexual Drama Enlightens Actors," *New York Times*, December 10, 1972.

45. Ben Brantley, "As the Boys Return, the Party Isn't Over," *New York Times*, June 21, 1996.

46. Jonathan Mandell, "Gay Life in the Bad Old Days of 1968," *New York Newsday*, June 21, 1996.

47. Brantley, "As the Boys Return."

48. Howard Kissel, "And the 'Band' Plays On," *Daily News*, June 21, 1996.

49. Clive Barnes, "'The Boys in the Band' Still Plays Well," *New York Post*, June 21, 1996.

50. Jacques Derrida, *Of Grammatology*, trans. Gayatri Chakravorty Spivak, corrected ed. (Baltimore: Johns Hopkins University Press, 1997), 71.

51. Michael Feingold states in his review of the revival, "The play's half-dozen most famous wisecracks have become gay public property, but hearing the entire script again reminds you sharply that the wisecracks are only the tip of an iceberg of acutely heard, skillfully crafted dialogue." Feingold, "Queerly Beloved," *Village Voice*, July 2, 1996.

52. Clive Barnes claimed that "nowadays one recognizes certain lines as if they were Wilde or Orton" ("'The Boys in the Band' Still Plays Well").

53. David W. Dunlap, "In a Revival, Echoes of a Gay War of Words," *New York Times*, June 9, 1996.

54. Ibid.

55. Muñoz, *Cruising Utopia*, 33–34.

56. Quoted in ibid., 34

57. Jeffrey M. Jones, "Americans' Opposition to Gay Marriage Eases Slightly," Gallup Politics, May 24, 2010, www.gallup.com/poll/128291/americans-opposition-gay-marriage-eases-slightly.aspx.

58. Lymari Morales, "In U.S., Broad, Steady Support for Openly Gay Service Members," Gallup Politics, May 10, 2010, www.gallup.com/poll/127904/Broad-Steady-Support-Openly-Gay-Service-Members.aspx.

59. FACT, "A Brief Timeline of AIDS," www.factlv.org/timeline.htm (accessed August 25, 2014).

60. The Centers for Disease Control and Prevention points out that the figures do not stipulate how the people with AIDS died (that is, from the disease itself or other causes). Centers for Disease Control and Prevention, "HIV in the United States: At a Glance," December 3, 2013, www.cdc.gov/hiv/statistics/basics/ataglance.html.

61. The description is based on production photos and my own experiences on February 15, 2010.

62. Tim Murphy, "The Boys Are Back in Town," *Out*, February 23, 2010, www.out.com/entertainment/2010/02/23/boys-are-back-town.

63. Quoted in David Noh, "The Man behind 'The Boys,'" *Gay City News*, February 18, 2010.

64. "Seat Filler: NYC Theater Guide for February 2010," *Advocate.com*, February 23, 2010, www.advocate.com/arts-entertainment/theater/2010/02/23/seat-filler-advocates-guide-theater.

65. Elizabeth Vincentelli, "Cocktails and Crossfire," *New York Post*, February 22, 2010.

66. David Rooney, "Review: 'The Boys in the Band,'" *Variety*, February 21, 2010.

67. Ben Brantley, "Broken Hearts, Bleeding Psyches," *New York Times*, February 24, 2010.

68. Terry Teachout, "The Boys in the Band Are Back in Town," *Wall Street Journal*, February 26, 2010.

69. T. J. Raphael and Corky Siemaszko, "Gay Bash Victim Benjamin Carver Replays Stonewall Attack on Blog: Writes He 'Never Felt Fear,'" *New York Daily News*, October 5, 2010.

70. Marc Santora and Joseph Goldstein, "In the Shadow of the Stonewall Inn, a Gay Man Is Killed," *New York Times*, May 19, 2013.

# 6

## The Boys in the City

### Disintegration, Transformation, and the Cinematic Flash in William Friedkin's New York City Films (1970–80)

#### DAVID A. GERSTNER

> Go ahead! Bite the Big Apple. Don't mind the maggots.
> —Mick Jagger and Keith Richards, "Shatter"

### Setting the Scene

Mike Davis, author of *City of Quartz: Excavating the Future in Los Angeles*, provides a promotional review for Miriam Greenberg's book *Branding New York: How a City in Crisis Was Sold to the World*. The review describes her study of the way New York City packaged itself during the turmoil of the late 1960s and 1970s as a "cunning, wonderfully dialectical analysis." The most pointed "dialectical analysis" in Greenberg's study, it turns out, is her dramatic posing of one conception of New York City as "Fun City" against another as "Fear City." The dialectical split, played out within approximately ten tense years of each other (1966 and 1975), signals the emotional and psychological atmosphere that defined New York City under Mayors John Lindsay and Abe Beame.

This chapter considers the historical transition from "Fun City" to "Fear City" not as a dialectical negation; instead, it explores "Fun" and "Fear" as co-relational phenomena that combine to create the city's thrilling yet unsettling frisson in William Friedkin's 1970s New York City trilogy.

Specifically, the unnerving, troubling, and pleasurable dimensions of male-to-male relations in *The Boys in the Band* (1970), *The French Connection* (1971), and *Cruising* (1980) commingle "Fun" and "Fear" in such a way that their opposing forces fold into each other, sustaining an uneasy and unyielding tension that operate as defining characteristics of 1970s New York.[1]

To establish this strained urban atmosphere, Friedkin presents what he calls a "gritty macho" mise-en-scène, manufactured with low-key lighting and fast film stock as well as use of dissonant/asynchronous musical soundtracks and a concentrated hand in the editing room.[2] His films are particularly claustrophobic due to the tightly framed sequences that, as Thomas D. Clagett describes them, are highly constructed by cinematic "light, shadow, speed, and movement to tell his story."[3] His cinema from the 1970s, therefore, aesthetically reckons with New York's complex and often-sordid contemporaneous history by confining the city's kinetic energy within a delimited and crumbling mise-en-scène. Within this tautly composed framework, a *cinematic flash* occurs in the films and serves as a temporary release valve from the films' compressed space and time. Not only does Friedkin's cinematic flash involve a heightened use of light and sound through which energies are expended; his flash corresponds to his male characters' dramatically charged dance performances that shed light, as it were, on men's uneasiness with their own masculine identity. For a brief moment—more and more brief by the time we reach *Cruising*—the cinematic frame erupts in a frenzy of light, a shift in soundtrack, and a highly charged masculine body movement. Significantly, the protagonist caught in the flash fails to break out from the city's imprisoned setting, in which men especially find themselves, as Friedkin describes his characters' typical situation, "with their backs to the wall and few alternatives."[4]

If Friedkin's cinema is one invested in what the producer and director Bud Yorkin calls "texture, ambiance, flavor, and feeling," in which his characters have their backs to the wall, it is a cinema that coincides with New York's volatile history.[5] As Friedkin designs it, that history is riddled with entangled gender relations among men and the decomposing places they urgently hope to hold together. His masculinist world fails to hold together. The films' characters disintegrate along with, yet transform precisely because of, the encroaching cinematic and historical world in which they live. Mixing a range of cinematic technique with a long-standing interest in documentary-style filmmaking, Friedkin's cinematic atmosphere facilitates (to borrow from Miriam Hansen's turn on Kracauer's film theory) "the disintegration and transformation of the phenomenal world."[6] Briefly but nonetheless significantly, *The Boys in the Band* launches the disintegrative/transformative aesthetic that crystallizes around Friedkin's cinematic rendering of 1970s New York as a place of "Fun" and "Fear."

## Fun

Although never officially marketed as a slogan, Mayor John Lindsay's booster-spirited epithet "Fun City" was coined just as New York's infrastructure began to crumble, crime rates edged upward, and cracks started to show in the city's coffers. Indeed, first mentioned in a television interview in 1966, his enthusiastic characterization was meant as "an effort to lift people's spirits at the start of the bitter, twelve-day transit strike" that had just beset the already-perturbed city.[7] The anticipated economic windfall that was supposed to accompany Robert Moses's extravagant 1964–65 world's fair never came to pass, and as a result, New Yorkers in 1966 remained annoyed, still reeling from the disappointment. Soon after, they were something more than annoyed when the debilitating fiscal crisis took on full force in the mid-1970s. "Fun City" was already hard to swallow for the working classes and minorities who found it difficult to make ends meet by the late 1960s, well before the major hardships to follow. Workers and minorities were the most crippled demographics when the fiscal crisis reached its zenith in 1975. Nevertheless, private enterprise and corporate leaders embraced Lindsay's joyful overtures as their thoughts turned away from city residents and toward the task of *rebranding* New York as open for business and safe for tourists.[8]

One year after Lindsay claimed New York City—that is, Manhattan—as "Fun City," the magazine *New York* first appeared on newsstands (and later, appositely, on billboards in *The French Connection*). The Manhattan-centric publication introduced "new journalism" that appealed to a narrowly defined, culturally savvy, and ready-to-spend middle class. *New York* quickly became a major platform, at once gritty and stylish, for reviving white, middle-class interest in the city that had grown stale and weary. *New York*'s editors, Milton Glaser and Clay Felker, envisioned "a magazine that will reveal a complete picture of the city, warts and all."[9] Tom Wolfe identified this urban dichotomy in his *New York* columns as uniquely New York; he called the new journalism "radical chic." In the magazine's glossy pages, it explored creative ways for consumers to practice new options for shopping, dining, and other cultural activities in a volatile urban setting. (Not unlike the 1920s, white New Yorkers went "slumming.")

While the culture industry revised the public's imagination about New York City for tourists, the city's elected officials engaged in their own rhetorical strategies, which affected the city's inhabitants. In the name of "civilization," the mayor's commissioner for the New York City Housing and Development Administration (HDA), Roger Starr, proposed a model of urban planning that he termed "Planned Shrinkage." His plan claimed that the city was in need of "urban triage."[10] Ultimately, Starr's plan sought to (and eventually did) eliminate services to the city's "neediest districts" in order to serve better and to sustain specific sectors of Manhattan. While Mayor Beame officially renounced Starr's rhetoric, it was rhetoric backed up by strategic management and future HDA action.[11] In fact, Beame's stated disavowal of "Planned Shrinkage" rings hollow since the mayor took no action against Starr. Hence, Beame implicitly, and in some instances explicitly (as we will see), accepted Starr's racist *and* homophobic designs for the city. It was the City Council that finally forced Starr out of office. A presence or not, officially or unofficially, Starr's initiatives methodically proceeded under future administrations.

If "Fun City" hoped to capture "the idealism and hope of the Lindsay era," it did so under the lengthening shadow of accruing debt and amid the marshaling of public and private funds to protect white corporate interests in Manhattan.[12] With the onset of the 1975–76 fiscal crisis, the city underwent significant retrenchment. Fifty-thousand blue-collar city jobs were in jeopardy. The promise that "Fun City" would lure tourists, foster new business, and supplement jobs lost to manufacturing was revealed to be less optimistic and more cold-blooded than Lindsay's show of bravura had indicated. According to Greenberg, although one "could still argue that the improved city image provided by tourism marketing was beneficial" for promoting tourism, manufacturing, and city services, the "benefits did not make up for the net jobs lost city-wide between 1967 and 1982, which at over 365,000 represented a 10 percent decline."[13] The wedge dividing cultural and economic sectors was thus driven further in by separating the interests of the working classes and the middle classes. Hence, within ten years, Lindsay's "Fun City" and its unequal cuts across class prompted a new slogan: "Fear City."

## Fear

The year 1975 marked a critical moment in New York City politics and labor relations. As the fiscal crisis culminated, city services were drastically cut, and municipal workers across racial divides refused to go down without a fight. In a mode of "counter-branding" (as Greenberg defines it), a coalition of male-dominated union workers formed the Committee for Public Safety and rewrote Lindsay's "Fun City." Engineered by unions that included firefighters and police officers, an alternative media campaign debuted: "Welcome to Fear City." Though loudly announced and vigorously distributed in pamphlets that greeted travelers at New York's airports, the slogan was short-lived. Mayor Beame's office, along with private corporate entities, successfully squashed the unions' campaign through the courts. Nevertheless, national and international media organizations had already widely covered the union campaign before it was shut down. Moreover, tourists' and corporate investors' anxieties were only exacerbated by the spectacles of riots, fires, and blackouts, abundant evidence contradicting the "fun" in "Fun City." As the city burned on live television and Howard Cosell directed his audience to observe the flames just beyond Yankee Stadium, sixty million viewers found little reason to disagree with the unions. "Welcome to Fear City" was not misleading.[14]

"Fun" and "Fear" were thus critical signifiers that framed the idea and experience of 1970s New York, and both the news media and the government connected them to (rather reductively conceived) divisions of race and class. But to what extent did the use of these signifiers in a popular discourse about race and class obscure their no-less-important relations to the politics of gender and sexuality, relations that invariably fold back into class and race? And if television and newspapers facilitated a logic of simple binaries, how did the film industry generally, and individual filmmakers such as Friedkin, respond to the ostensibly mutually dependent campaigns of "Fun" and "Fear"? To what cinematic aesthetic did Friedkin turn to evoke the city's uncomfortable, ambiguous place in the world? Rethinking Barry Keith Grant's claim that "[Stan] Brakhage's four-minute silent 16mm film [*Wonder Ring*, 1955] captures a greater truth about New York than 'realist' narrative movies like *The French Connection*," I suggest that Friedkin's New York trilogy reveals a "a greater truth about New York" because it is a cinema that sensually aestheticizes masculine disintegration.[15]

## Movie-Made New York

In *Branding New York*, Greenberg argues that New York's fiscal trauma was coupled with an "image crisis" from the beginning of the 1960s. Significantly, the institutionalization of the New York film industry in fact coincided with the cultural, economic, and political fracturing that marked the 1960s. In 1966, the year that heralded "Fun City," the famously photogenic Mayor Lindsay also established the Mayor's Office of Film, Theatre, and Broadcasting (MOFTB). Organized to streamline film production and to create new jobs in the city, it further served as a critical tool in shaping the idea of the city. Its purpose was to create "a series of images and feelings, and with them an impression of value."[16] Working with the New York State Department of Commerce (which originally prepared shooting permits), MOFTB was singularly dedicated to facilitating film production, while it cinematically showcased, as Lindsay wrote in an open letter to the public, "our parks and museums, our streets and courthouses, our libraries and monuments, all these things that make New York unique."[17] Yet, for all Lindsay and his supporters' stated enthusiasm for MOFTB, not every resulting representation of the city was a vision of urban uplift, and MOFTB was not always an ideal institution for meeting the film industry's needs.[18] Nonetheless, the challenges and failures were outweighed by its successes.

The city and the local film industry soon realized that any resource that reinforced media production in the city was crucial to bringing New York into the public imagination. If *New York* magazine succeeded in glamorizing New York City in its pages—"warts and all"—the film industry could certainly do the same with the movies. To be sure, whatever criticisms surfaced, the MOFTB during Lindsay's eight-year term ushered "366 movies [into production] . . . or an average of 46 films per year, as compared to only 13 features filmed in New York in 1965."[19] As a result, New York City *was* seen around the world.

Working together, Greenberg argues, city government, MOFTB, and local corporations "devised strategies to recreate, market, and consistently manage the image of New York as a brand." A broad coalition formed between, on the one hand, "city and state government, traditional city boosters based in tourism and real estate," and, on the other, "management consultants, media producers, [and] advertising firms" whose attention to "new fields of psychographics, Pop Art, and creative advertising" generated a new approach to "branding" New York City.[20] Crucial to this mix of creative types and government authorities was New York City's exceptional access to media, especially film. "The rise of live television," Greenberg explains, "and the continued strength of theater also supported the film revival in New York in the late 1950s and 1960s, providing training for technicians and editors, opportunities for would-be Hollywood directors, jobs for social-realist documentarians, and a scene for avant-garde filmmakers. The film and television world also intersected with the growing downtown movement of Pop Art and Film, and by the early 1970s with the underground press and video arts movements."[21] The unexpected results of this media campaign were at once applauded by and worrisome for city branders. While "Pop Art and Film" stimulated creative directors to develop new images for their advertising campaigns, that same aesthetic championed graffiti art, pornography, rock 'n' roll, and gay culture—artistic forms that did not necessarily play well to straitlaced tourists. Given Greenberg's linking of the city's "growing downtown" underground arts movement to New York's feature-film production, she surprisingly overlooks the connection between New York filmmaking and gay culture. Her omission is particularly odd since well-known "Pop Film" titles such as Andy Warhol's *The Chelsea Girls* (1966) received a great deal of press, and a number of people involved in the branding initiative surely saw some of those films. Warhol and his Superstars were extraordinary representatives of what Tom Wolfe famously went on to call "radical chic."[22]

Moreover, given Greenberg's linking of television and theater to the inevitable fortunes of feature-film production, her omission of Mart Crowley's stage play *The Boys in the Band* (1968), adapted to film by Friedkin in 1970, is still more striking. She further excludes Friedkin's film *Cruising*, a film shot in 1979 and critical to the gay movement. Friedkin's two queer films are invaluable texts when considering the highly transformative events for New York City *and* post-Stonewall gay culture during the 1970s. In another and not unrelated register, his films are invaluable when tracing the way straight white men responded to this culture through film. Both of Friedkin's gay-themed films involve straight white men immersed in very gay cultures, and all three of the Friedkin films studied here show New York's male cultures, gay and straight, caught between the pleasures of fun and fear. And while *The French Connection* is noted by Greenberg in her study, *The Boys in the Band* and *Cruising* would have been valuable and obvious additions for the two "New York" film-genre categories she proposes.[23]

Indeed, Lindsay's term "Fun City" was surely interpreted with many different connotations—gay connotations included—about just what "Fun" entailed. Although Lindsay's enthusiasm was characterized as a public-relations boon for drawing to Midtown Manhattan white, heterosexual tourists who longed for theater, shopping, and dining, it is not unthinkable that another demographic—homosexuals—was similarly drawn by Lindsay's good looks and New York's seductive fun. Not incorrectly, however, gay tourists and gay locals had every reason to remain cautious about Lindsay's optimism. While gays and lesbians "read between the lines" of the administration's invitation, queer pleasures in New York were mired in a history of police harassment and cultural prejudice. The Republican mayor, in fact, offered mixed messages when addressing the very pervasive police harassment about which gay men, especially, were concerned. For some New Yorkers and would-be tourists, Lindsay's election was a glimmer of hope for gay men seeking protection from aggressive and homophobic cops. For gay tourists, Lindsay's charm and his glamorous administration suggested that sexual adventures in the big city would not be interfered with by a guerrilla police force.[24]

Undoubtedly, many film viewers and other media-savvy connoisseurs recognized the image of New York culture *as* gay. While many thrilled at the possibility of visiting or living in the city precisely for this reason, others suspected that the city's emergent gay presence represented the first step down the treacherous road to immorality. Nevertheless, if "Pop Art" saliently informed the creative drive behind New York's fashionable marketing techniques, gay and straight art directors who developed the hip new media formats were well aware of—if not active participants in—"Pop Art's" attendant queer culture.

Greenberg's neglect of Friedkin's gay films notwithstanding, her omission coincides, more disconcertingly, with her exclusion of the connection between the gay movement and other political movements in New York. This is particularly unfortunate since the gay movement and Friedkin's films were intimately involved in the class and race dynamics that Greenberg addresses. The Stonewall Riots in 1969, John Wojtowicz's 1972 bank robbery (motivated by the aim of obtaining surgery for his transgender wife), the formation of multiple gay political organizations, the cross-cultural activities in Times Square porn theaters, the resistance to the gay movement by police officers, and the protests against the making of *Cruising* were significant politicized actions that occurred during the economic crises and across racial and class boundaries.[25] Friedkin's films are key signposts from this politically raucous period.

## A Packed Gay Life

For gays (and "straights"), the city's queer underground held much promise for those who sought escape from suburban ideals of domesticity and morality. Robert Atkins recounts his visits to New York as a young gay man in the 1970s, when a "visit to Studio 54 or to the Continental Baths, where non-gay *chanteuse*/gay icon Better Midler performed poolside, more or less placed gay life within reach of hetero America. To dismiss these visits by the non-gay as mere voyeurism or cultural tourism is to grossly oversimplify."[26] Nevertheless, for gay-identified men, there was no denying it: New York was *the* scene for a range of sexual possibilities and experimentation. While politicians, corporations, and unions squabbled over the terms for New York as a place of either "Fun" or "Fear," gay culture developed within the overlapping experiences offered under these terms. It did so unexpectedly, viscerally, and homosexually.[27]

While the interior spaces of the Continental Baths and Studio 54 were popular draws for gay locals and out-of-towners during the 1970s, the city also appealed to those who preferred open-air activities such as "the novelty of outdoor sex to be had in Central or Riverside Parks, on Fire Island, or on the piers or trucks of the Village and Meatpacking Districts."[28] Alternatively, the Anvil, Boots and Saddle, and the Mineshaft—the sites for Friedkin's gay-world settings in *Cruising*—were characterized by "the gritty, smoke-stained paneling and pool table of the levis-'n'-leather bars decorated with posters of the Marlboro Man and mustachioed guys who wanted to look like him."[29] These bars provided pool tables, slings, tubs for watersports, and bondage paraphernalia (props important for *Cruising*); one's sexual appetites were not only satisfied but in fact expanded. More genteel hustler, "standing-and-modeling," and piano bars were also part of the scene. At these locations, one might envision bumping into some of the men portrayed in *The Boys in the Band*. The baths, as the example of Emory (Cliff Gorman) in *The Boys* reminds us, were where any number of these sex-driven scenes crisscrossed one another.[30]

Dancing was a vital component of New York's nightlife. Douglas Crimp's recollection of the period supplements Atkins's notes on the Continental Baths. As Crimp recalls, "the Continental Baths introduced disco in 1970."[31] Dancing at Flamingo and the Saint, gay men indulged simultaneously in drugs, the hard-driving disco beat, and multiple sex partners. Friedkin's films amplify the period's gay experience as they draw on the scenes that Atkins and Crimp conjure.

These gay 1970s pleasures, however, indicate neither the miraculous disappearance of homophobia from New York nor gay culture's protection from the city's dire fiscal situation, with its politically charged implications for race and class relations. During the Lindsay and Beame administrations, gay men, across race and class, were subjected to what amounted to institutionalized homophobia by both the police and the fire department.[32] By the early 1970s, police could cavalierly inform their gay victims that any official complaints made to the city would fall on deaf ears: Arthur Bell recalled that after harassing him on the street, an officer told him, "Call the mayor's office. It won't do any fucking good. We're always on top, and you're always on the bottom."[33] Not unlike the racism that drives many uniformed officers, homophobia was secured with unwritten law in police enforcement.

If police officers sought to assert themselves as "tops" and Roger Starr's institutionalized "Planned Shrinkage" sought to emasculate symbolically nonwhite and nonheterosexual communities, the institutional framing of the city's culture was conceived in rhetoric at once racist and homophobic. For Starr and Beame's dream to cleanse New York City of its unwanted, the significance of the intersection of race, class, and sexuality cannot be underestimated. The perverts and sex workers of Times Square and Manhattan's West Side were high on the administration's list. Samuel R. Delany describes these areas' sexually active porn-film theaters, of which he was fond. Delany tells us,

> The population was incredibly heterogeneous—white, black, Hispanic, Asian, Native American, and a variety of Pacific Islanders. In the Forty-second Street area's sex theaters, specifically, since I started frequenting them in 1975, I've met playwrights, carpenters, opera singers, telephone repair men, stockbrokers, guys on welfare, guys with trust funds, guys on crutches, on walkers, in wheelchairs, teachers, warehouse workers, male nurses, fancy chefs, guys who worked at Dunkin Donuts, guys who gave out flyers on street corners, guys who drove garbage trucks, and guys who washed windows on the Empire State Building.[34]

In summarizing a visit to the Mineshaft on jock-strap night when scouting locations for *Cruising* in 1979, Friedkin similarly notes the gay environment: "Everyone was in a jock strap, some with leather boots and vests, executioner masks or leather jackets. Men of all races, colors, and social status mingled as equals."[35]

The multiracial context in which a broad cross-section of working-class and multiethnic queers concentrated was, it turns out, ground zero for "Planned Shrinkage." To be sure, the link between Beame and Starr's

Haussmann-like plans to do away with the city's undesirables was in play well before the mayor took office. As Delany recalls, Beame, when stumping for votes during his mayoral election campaign, stood outside the Times Square porn theater Show World and declared, "If you elect me, I promise you before my term of office is through, this place will be *gone* from the city."[36]

Whether through ironic play and/or sincere political action, the terms "Fun" and "Fear" were critical components of queers' response to homophobia and "Planned Shrinkage." Institutional homophobia made way for unexpected results, even fostering the pursuit of homosexual activity. For instance, homophobic rhetoric meant to scare gays away from heteronormative spaces had the opposite effect when it unknowingly introduced gays to covert queer delights. The homophobes' thrill in chasing away queers actually encouraged gays to make their way to locations they may otherwise have been unaware of. The risk of being caught only heightened the city's seductive allure. Consider Charles Gaines's 1974 *Pumping Iron: The Art and Sport of Bodybuilding*. When describing how easy it is to find locations to weight train, Gaines offers a word of caution: "Almost every YMCA in America has a weight room, and all of the ones I know about (with a few exceptions, like the big Y on Central Park West where the faggots will track you to the shower with their heads down like they were following a spoor) are wonderful places to train."[37] For a gay audience, Gaines's homophobia pinpointed precisely where they might mix pleasure with danger.

Queer fun and games, however, also took on a combative spirit when gays directly challenged homophobia by linking it to broader political contexts. In "By Way of Introduction: Notes from One Gay Life," John D'Emilio notes such connections when he recounts his journey in becoming politically active as a gay man in New York. Hailing from the Bronx, D'Emilio writes, he "discovered sex—in the subways, in deserted lots, alongside highways in the Bronx. In Grand Central Terminal and Times Square and Bryant Park. In movie theaters in Manhattan. And always without names exchanged. The sex was fast, explosive, and terrifying." And while "to every encounter [he] brought the *fear* of being found out, ... through all of this [he] had *fun*."[38] Navigating uncertain terrain in which "fun" and "fear" registered at every sexual turn, he also discovered a thriving and wide-ranging political current in New York at Columbia University. While studying at Columbia, D'Emilio's homosexuality overlapped with other student movements: "Columbia between 1966 and 1970 was awash with the antiwar and racial politics sweeping over the nation's campuses. Though much of my extracurricular energy focused on crafting a gay life, I was also caught in the political turmoil."[39]

The complex political and cultural circumstances that at once enabled a dynamically defined queer culture and allowed racism and homophobia to fester were the markers of a disintegrative, transforming New York. Institutional homophobia does not disappear overnight. At best, an uneasy rapprochement formed between gays and New York City government during the late 1970s.[40] Nonetheless, as late as 1980 (when *Cruising* appeared on the screen), Richard D. Hongisto, former San Francisco police sheriff (1972–77) and current New York State commissioner of correction, remained unconvinced that enough had been accomplished to abolish institutional homophobia. Hongisto lambasted the International Association of Chiefs of Police (IACP) for reconfirming in 1979 a 1958 statute that established a "no-hire" policy for homosexuals.[41] In the civil rights magazine *Perspective*, Hongisto offered a strongly worded criticism of the IACP's action. He took umbrage at the resolution's claim that gays would be "offensive" to the "manliness quotient" instilled in the "male-dominated" fraternity.[42]

Hongisto thus insightfully exposed how gender relations, sexual identity, and masculine performativity all informed officially sanctioned homophobia. Institutional homophobia during the 1970s was a symptom of social relations—*homosocial* relations—in deep flux. The link between homosociality and homophobia, examined elegantly by Eve Kosofsky Sedgwick, is important for the way we view Friedkin's New York trilogy.[43] Observing the flux of men's movements through clearly defined spaces, Friedkin identifies emotional and psychological shards that cut into hetero-masculinist presumptions about the relationships between masculinity and the places men occupy. Provocatively, the interwoven histories of homophobia, the gay movement, and the fiscal crisis are intimately connected to Friedkin's vision of New York. Mirroring the city's culture, Friedkin reveals a place that afforded multiple pleasures for a gay man's "packed life" while keeping the aura of fear and danger in circulation.[44]

Gay male friendships in *The Boys in the Band*, morally ambiguous male detectives in *The French Connection*, and the intermingled relationship established when these two groups come together in *Cruising* are foregrounded as instrumental elements to New York's unyielding identification as "Fun" and "Fear" City. Friedkin envisions New York as a combination of Fun and Fear, providing a tensely contained yet vibrant mise-en-scène for his cinema of disintegration and transformation.

While the director has made it clear that ambiguity recurrently marks his protagonists' dénouements, I wish to highlight three sequences from the trilogy that occur in three distinct New York spaces—the street, the subway, and the gay bar. Here, Friedkin registers the gender/sexual anxiety that men experienced in 1970s New York. For Friedkin, a cinematic *flash* marks that anxiety as a masculine transformation, in which the ideals of masculinity disintegrate and then disintegrate further, producing an endless cinematic unfolding in which masculinity disintegrates and transforms.

## Cinematic Logics of Disintegration and Transformation

When Peter Dews chastised theorists of "poststructuralism" and "deconstruction" in *Logics of Disintegration*, he concluded that their critical posturing was void—not only politically but also philosophically, libidinally, and culturally.[45] First published in 1987, when perhaps he was unaware of the political possibilities that poststructuralism and deconstruction opened for queers, Dews's book was not open to the value of irony, double moves, and "play" for the way queers think about gender, sexuality, race, and—in provocative ways—class. Siegfried Kracauer's and Miriam Hansen's theories are alluring, as I have suggested earlier in this chapter, because New York's disintegration is inseparable from its transformation. At once, the city's stressed environment generates movements within and across cultural and political spheres that unevenly fold into one another. Friedkin's cinematic evocations of disintegration-transformation anticipates Anselm Haverkamp's reading of New York as "a place in permanent destruction, in continuous decay, as it seems, but more precisely a city in permanent change, in gender trouble and racial controversy. It is here that one gets, now and then, a new sense of the political qua deconstruction."[46]

How might we analyze Friedkin's cinematic atmosphere, which evokes the queer city in disintegration and transformation? What is the sensibility that presides over the cinematic techniques that give shape to Friedkin's New York and associate it with "Fun" and "Fear"? While working in television in Chicago as a young man, Friedkin began to make documentary films, launching the aesthetic-conceptual framework he brought to narrative film. In interviews, Friedkin often refers to documentary style as the aesthetic tool that allowed him to choreograph the twinned relationship of "Fun" and "Fear," along with their correlatives, pleasure and pain. To achieve a style equal to the tension between pleasure and pain, Friedkin collaborated with cinematographers who worked well with natural light and placed the camera *within* a scene. For example, when describing to the cinematographer Owen Roizam the desired look for *The French Connection*, the director emphasized, "Handheld natural light, push the exposures, no big lights at night, no lights at all on the streets during the day, bounce lights off the ceiling on interiors. We're going to shoot practical locations, no sets—police stations, bars, hotel rooms—and shots have to look like they were 'stolen.'"[47] Friedkin's vision for *The French Connection* is recognizable in the cinematic choices we see and hear both in the film's immediate predecessor, *The Boys in the Band* (especially its exteriors), and, later, in *Cruising*. By "stealing" shots, insisting on "no sets" and "handheld natural light," Friedkin's cinematic education via the French New Wave, Italian Neo-Realism, and skills honed in documentary filmmaking made for a complex repertoire of resources from which he could draw to engineer apparently spontaneous events and manufacture raw urban qualities. For Friedkin, as a result, style produces "an impression of the period."[48]

Whether framing his subject in tight close-up as Friedkin does in his early documentary *The People vs. Paul Crump* (1962) or containing characters in claustrophobic spaces that are doubly contained by agitated and dissonant soundtracks, he constructs male characters who are caught within a cinematic friction created when "gritty macho" documentary style meets Hollywood-narrative impulses.[49] The squeezed relationship between body and space, between genre and narrative, emanates with paradoxical affect.[50]

To create the "gritty macho look," Friedkin films low-lit exteriors with a fast film stock—for both day and night—so that street scenes, apartments, subway stations, and police departments all appear equally compressed and grungy yet kinetically charged. The deconstructed and grubby city, which houses uncertain masculine psychological and sociological states, is formally conveyed through highly conceived cinematic expression. The contradictory imbrication of the disturbing comedy-drama permeates the very aesthetic of the films and, as such, blurs the distinction between exterior and interior worlds. Limited to a set of windows and doors in Friedkin's interiors, natural light is a rare commodity in his films; even where natural light does exist, the boundaries between interior and exterior light-scapes is typically unclear. Hence, both the toxic-green fluorescent lighting that fills police stations in *The French Connection* and *Cruising* and the limited distribution of light from the nearly windowless apartment in *The Boys* are intra- and interpenetrative.

Ultimately, Friedkin's thematic center—pleasure/pain—draws his characters into ever-tightened temporal and spatial dimensions in which movement is minimized yet excruciatingly salient. Exteriors are as confining, as *alienating*, as Friedkin's interiors. Fast film stock and "natural" lighting yield the grainy look that Bud Yorkin described as Friedkin's "texture, ambiance, flavor, and feeling." In this way, gritty mise-en-scène encroaches on a character's interior life-world, while also psychologically isolating him. Friedkin's exteriors thus offer limited relief from the narrative tensions playing out in apartments, police stations, and clubs. Troubled and uncertain men move awkwardly through the outside world and into interior spaces, only to draw the people around them into their less-than-stable place in the world.

Friedkin's ambiguous men do transform, despite their cramped situations, but they do so by moving from one mode of disintegration into another. To make the transformation, a flash of theatricalized light and sound technique pops. As a cinematic break, the flash of light, along with an intricately produced soundtrack, signifies the transition of masculine identity. With stunning precision, Friedkin's cinematic flash presents a series of dances for men that are at once freeing and entrapping, cinematic expressions of Fun and Fear.

## Dance, Girl, Dance

The gender-troubled and sexually uncertain men in *The Boys* (Alan, played by Peter White), *The French Connection* (Popeye Doyle, played by Gene Hackman), and *Cruising* (Steve Burns, played by Al Pacino) are inexorably caught between exterior and interior worlds. In *The Boys*, Alan embodies the questioning of sexual identity, and as such, he struggles differently than the gay-identified men in the film do. Notably, we see his struggle play out as his search for a place to occupy finally. While the film's gay men are funneled directly into the apartment of Michael (Kenneth Nelson), Alan's movement in the film is indecisive, caught between inside and outside.

During the first thirty minutes of *The Boys*, we move back and forth between the city streets and Michael's apartment. The well-known montage that introduces the gay men in the film ushers us through crowded Manhattan streets. Donald (Frederick Combs) beats a direct path through the Lincoln Tunnel to join his gay comrades. Skyless Manhattan is nonetheless vibrantly rendered as Michael elegantly gambols across Fifth Avenue with what we will soon learn are most likely unpaid-for packages. Once Emory (Cliff Gorman) turns off the lights in his already-tomb-like interior decoration shop, he exits into the intensely hectic and brighter—albeit tightly framed—streets in search of his birthday present for Harold (Leonard Frey), the hustler "Cowboy" (Robert La Tourneaux).

Alan, however, arrives from outside the city on a plane from Washington, DC. Stepping off the plane, he looks unsure if he wishes to stay or to leave. Arriving from the sky that is about to close in on him, the enigmatic Alan (is he gay? is he "straight"?) serves as the catalyst who draws what remains of the vexed urban setting into the dramas that play out in Michael's overstuffed and gay-buffeted apartment.[51] While other characters nonchalantly maneuver the city's annoyances (such as *restaurateuse* Elaine, who looks disparagingly at Emory and his lasagna) and pleasures (such as the parking attendant with whom Donald flirts), Alan spends his initial scenes moping in his hotel room, where he grapples with whether he should see Michael to discuss what may be his marriage woes.

The final exterior shots we see in the film in fact involve Alan wavering back and forth about what his next move should be. After Alan first telephones Michael from his hotel room, his second call to Michael takes place from a phone booth in Midtown. In this shot, he is compressed within an interior space situated as part of the city's exterior landscape, in which the ambient urban setting seeps into the booth's transparent windows. From the booth's invisible privacy, Alan speaks to Michael while the guests for Harold's birthday party enjoy one another's company. They laugh and dance while party lights surround them and festive cocktails satiate them. Alan apologizes for disrupting Michael's evening and suggests they meet for lunch the next day. Agreeing, Michael returns to his guests. Unpredictable Alan, however, decides to arrive unannounced at the birthday party. This final phone call before arriving at Michael's doorstep is important to describe since it draws attention to Friedkin's cinematic technique, focusing its lens as it does on ambiguous masculine identity.

When Alan rings Michael from the phone booth, we see him tightly framed in the booth. The shot uses a telephoto lens (a fifty-millimeter lens, slightly longer than a normal thirty-five-millimeter lens), with the effect that the background appears to compress the foreground. The booth's overhead fluorescent bulb creates a noxious green halo over Alan that permeates the booth and his figure within it. As the two men converse, the scene cuts between Alan in black tie and Michael in an elegant cravat. Alan apologizes to Michael for burdening him with his problems, while Michael informs

Cinematic flashes dance across the frame, disrupting Alan's heterosexual manhood in *The Boys in the Band*.

Alan that (given the party about which Alan does not know the context) it is better they meet for lunch the next day.

On the cut back to Alan, a changed light pattern presents itself: the saturating fluorescent green light is now dotted by myriad colored lights, suggesting the city's feverish night light-scape. As the variation of colored lights pop on and around Alan, they disconcertingly mimic the party lights we have previously seen hanging on Michael's terrace. In the phone booth, however, the lights appear less mirthful. By the time Alan suggests a place and time to meet for lunch, a single white light hovers over the space between the phone's receiver and Alan's mouth. The lingering and flashing white light anticipates Alan's white lie since, although other arrangements were made, he shows up at Michael's apartment. When Alan finally exits the booth, the city lights are emblazoned. They encircle him as he crosses the street, allowing the camera lens to form a large prismatic light around him. The refracted light assumes the shape of a target, with Alan squarely in its center.

The city's lights—from exterior to interior and back again—lure Alan. Whatever the reasons for Alan's angst, he is drawn to Michael's queer, interior world. Just before Alan arrives, and in a bravura moment, Friedkin directs a multiangled sequence in which the boys, framed with the terrace's party lights, dance to Martha and the Vandellas' "Heat Wave." The group's pleasure is interrupted by Alan's arrival, however, signified by the sound of the door buzzer. Expecting Harold, the boys are surprised to see, from their perspective, the unknown Alan.

Alan's entrance into Michael's interior carries the reminder of the exterior world from which the gay boys have sought refuge. The incursion foregrounds the permeability, perhaps the fragility, of the gay world the boys have manufactured in their apartments and the always-present reality that fun is never far removed from fear. Indeed, in this instance, Friedkin's cinematic flash fuses light, sound, and dance at a crucial narrative moment when homosexual strategies are employed to take on the homophobic world that exists just outside their doorway.

Not the first or the last film to use cinematic lighting and party mise-en-scène to indicate narrative and character transition, *The Boys* follows through on Friedkin's cinematic exploration of homosociality, homo-erotics, and homophobia in Harold Pinter's *The Birthday Party*. As in that film, Friedkin turns to choreographed dance sequences, heightened by theatrical lighting, a mobile camera, and varied camera angles, to mark a male protagonist's transitional place in the world.[52] The New York trilogy prominently engages dance at the moment that coherent male self-perception stumbles. Hence, the "Fun" gay men enjoy while dancing on their New York rooftop is stymied by the specter of "Fear." Other than courageous and flamboyant Emory, the boys adjust their behavior to realign with the expectations of hetero-masculinity that Alan has dragged into their shielded environment. As such, the sequences in which dance occur are transitional grounds on which men assume roles as deceived and deceiver—to themselves and to others.

*The French Connection* is no exception to this pattern. In the film, Popeye performs a pas de deux with the international drug king "Frog One" (Fernando Rey), a dance in which masculine ideals are strained. "Good" and "bad" guy, Popeye and Frog One, move from city streets into an exemplary convergence of exterior and interior: the subway. Marked by their tenuous cultural capital as cop/criminal and drug-lord/bourgeois, Popeye and Frog One step onto the dance floor—the subway platform. Through their dance, law and social decorum commingle with the tawdry and the unsavory. Friedkin's cinematic flash in this instance—a deft negotiation of sound *and* image—disintegrates film genres as their cinematic conventions collide, and the two men dance together on the meeting ground of fun and fear.

As Don Ellis's brilliantly dissonant musical composition drops from the scene, and as we exit Manhattan's streets to enter the Grand Central subway station, the camera energetically follows first Frog One and then, after a cut, Popeye down the subway stairs. With Ellis's city-street motif silenced, the "live" ambient sound from the station takes over the soundtrack. The rapid pitter-patter of hurried passengers' shoes echoes the taps we might hear from a chorus line prior to the principals' entrance. The grainy blue-green winter light associated with the exterior streets blurs with the subway's interior green-yellow, damp and dingy atmosphere. As the men descend and the camera follows, bright neon lights suddenly appear from the fast-food concessions on the platform. Their carnival-like illumination cuts through the subway's fluorescent pallor.

The stage on which this performance takes place could easily be mistaken for a dilapidated MGM soundstage that once housed Vincente Minnelli's *The Band Wagon* (1953). It is not hard to imagine the sly yet debonair movement of Fred Astaire or the virile pirouettes of Gene Kelly ghosting the Popeye–and–Frog One interlude. Hence, the electrifying carnivalesque lights in this derelict musical provide an ironic spin on genre as Friedkin directs the gamesmanship between the bedraggled cop and the internationally suave drug smuggler. Friedkin (re)composes a musical number without music and without the manly Gene Kelly or the sophisticated Fred Astaire. Here, the cinematic flash occurs with our descent into the subway tunnel, where boardwalk-style lights illuminate the otherwise-murky atmosphere. Significantly, Friedkin drops the nondiegetic music we hear prior to entering the tunnel. In this way, *The French Connection* disables and disrupts the generic codes associated with the police-crime thriller *and* the musical.[53] Indeed, the bright lights of the concession stands in *The French Connection* play differently than those in *The Band Wagon*, where the concession stands' lights signify frivolity and work in concert with joyous music. In Friedkin's 1970s New York, the lights are not quite so lustrous, and the music—already far from exuberant beyond the subway's corridors—is evacuated.

Friedkin's pas de deux is filmed and edited as a performance in which the subway platform and its trains are the staging ground for elegant man-to-man combat (think Gene Kelley and Fred Astaire in their competitive and only-filmed duet in *Ziegfeld Follies* [1946]). The camera joins the scene as a mobile participant with the ballet's corps (the passengers). Popeye and Frog One dance in a game of hide-and-seek as they move in and out of subway cars. After the first movement on and off the car, Frog One leads by slipping out onto the platform; Popeye follows. Both men take note of each other. Like Alan in *The Boys*, whose movement between interior and

Friedkin's homosocial pas de deux in *The French Connection*.

exterior announces a transition in identity, Popeye wrestles with exterior demons (Frog One) and interior ones (his own disturbed, white, racist manhood). In the meantime, Frog One casually reads his newspaper and saunters over to the concession stands. The shining marquees advertising cold drinks, candy apples, and custard are juxtaposed with the elegant but nonetheless potentially violent maneuvering taking place on the platform.

As another train arrives, Frog One purposefully and solemnly moves toward the emptying train. Again, passengers' shoes evoke the sound of tap dancing. The pause at the concession stand draws to a close, and the male-to-male dance ensues. Mirroring the characters' movement, the camera glides along the grimy platform while "Pop Art"–like Coca-Cola advertisements burst into the mobile frame. On and off, back and forth, the men navigate their partner's moves between train and platform. Finally—and with an adroit use of an umbrella (the elegance of Astaire combined with a famous metonym for Kelly)—Frog One blocks the subway door and tricks his persistent shadow. In beautifully paced choreography, Frog One remains on the train after his umbrella has held the door open. Like Popeye, we presume he will exit. Popeye thus appears to follow his cue but in fact misses it when stepping onto the platform. The doors close, the train departs. Popeye is now left behind. Frog One bids adieu to the frustrated cop with the wave of his gloved hand, as the train pulls away. Infuriated, Popeye desperately chases the train, trying in vain to pry open its doors. Ellis's discordant soundtrack returns. Equal to the crumbling infrastructure that surrounds him, Popeye is in a state of ethical and moral decomposition. As

Clagett puts it, "He and the streets have become one."⁵⁴ For Friedkin, then, the disintegration of Hollywood genre folds into and simultaneously with the disintegrating masculine bodies that move across the scene. And, yet, Friedkin's aesthetic turn on the decaying cinematic genre—and the men who navigate its decomposing mise-en-scène—is not final word on Hollywood genre/gender. *The French Connection* reveals American cinema and American men in unsettling transformation.

The dance sequence that most explicitly brings together the threads of hetero-masculinity, male homosexuality, and homophobia woven through the New York trilogy appears in *Cruising*. The film wrestles with the fragile lines between homosociality and homosexuality, cop and criminal, homophobia and homosexual desire. *Cruising* confronts the imperceptible moment when sexual desire crosses from abstract recognition into material realization. When Steve Burns finally gets on the dance floor, the transition flashes before his very eyes—and ours.

Like the film's two New York predecessors, *Cruising* fits into Friedkin's narrative concerns about ambiguous identity and its unsettling transformation. From the outset, Burns's identity is multiplied and split. In his role as an undercover cop who has been assigned to track a killer of gay men in leather bars, Burns's sense of his identity becomes more and more fraught. The film leaves us unsure about the meaning of his identity crisis, making him suspect as both potential homosexual and potential murderer. Burns dons leather and moves into New York's gay center, the West Village, and the film follows him as his work makes him cross unforeseen and unconscious boundaries. Burns immerses himself in the world of sadomasochistic pain and pleasure, and his research takes him to the likes of the Mineshaft, with its sweaty sensuality, and to the gothic-lit and densely tree-covered cruising grounds of the Rambles in Central Park. Once again, Friedkin's New York exteriors, like his interiors, provide little or no sense of egress.

Michael Worton describes "cruising" as the particularly gay male activity that brushes against and fragments the hetero-androcentric concept of a unified self. "Our cultural tradition," Worton writes, "consistently and forcefully promotes the belief that fragmentation and the fragmentary are suspect and dangerous, states to be avoided at all costs. This is particularly true of masculinity which . . . has been enclosed in a form of obligatory closedness in order for patriarchy and the phallic order to be preserved."⁵⁵ To cruise "exposes the workings of pleasure and desire"; it is "inhabited by uncertainty and insecurity, and its directness about sex is expressed in a narration that meanders about in labyrinth loops."⁵⁶ Following Worton, if the dance performed on the cruising ground displays (homo)sexual pleasure and identity as fragmented, it is to dance that Friedkin similarly turns.

Given this definition, it is no surprise that Friedkin's film is often critiqued as a plot in search of a cohesive narrative.[57] But to insist on knowing once and for all "who" the murderer is and "who" Steve Burns is would make for a dull cinematic experience about cruising. The intrigue and draw of *Cruising* rest precisely in its cinematic "labyrinth loops." Its "directness" is "about sex" between men, an activity not easily turned into narrative.[58]

"In a memorable scene" in *Cruising*, Joe Wlodarz recounts, Steve Burns cruises a leather bar, where he is cruised by another man, who leads him onto the dance floor. "Burns gets into the music," Wlodarz continues, "after sniffing ether from a soaked hankie. . . . Close-ups of Burns's ever-increasing pleasure and his sweat-soaked body are then intercut with shots of three nearly naked men groping each other, another suspect cruising him, a quick insert of [a] fisting scenario, and an electric American flag."[59] Burns's cruising-dance is heightened not only by the sequence's "frenzied editing," as Wlodarz explains, but also by Friedkin's tightly framed images, which erupt with sudden bursts of light that match Burns's drugged high on the dance floor. As Burns *burns*, American masculinity and sexuality explode into shards on the dance floor. Here, male-to-male erotic encounter reaffirms the ultimate fantasies of institutionalized homophobia because the frenetic desire unleashed is not simply uncontainable; it is *unnarratable*. *Cruising* puts on a cinematic display of the contingent and homosexualized boundaries that only ostensibly separate (homophobic) law and (homosexual) desire.

Masculine disintegration and transformation on the dance floor in *Cruising*.

Whereas Wlodarz sees the "radical possibility of... *pleasure* in such sexual activities and contexts," he finds that "William Friedkin either cannot see [it] or willfully shuts [it] down."[60] I contend that Friedkin sees precisely "the radical pleasure" in the cinematic flash (what Wlodarz terms "the blast"). The cinematic flash—soundtrack and image—tears through the film's more consistent aesthetic that shapes the rest of the film. The pulsing lights, the pounding of very ungay music (not disco), and the intercutting of color and black-and-white film stock squarely situate *Cruising*'s dance number at the moment Steve Burns disintegrates and transforms into a man who no longer holds the capacity to control either his desire or the spaces he occupies.

Because cruising does not lend itself to a totalized experience of identity through a "straight"-forward narrative structure, Friedkin instead foregrounds cruising—the dance—as a display of masculinity and relations between men as nothing less than, nothing more than, "fragmented and fragmentary." If such encounters between men are "suspect and dangerous, states to be avoided at all costs," Friedkin capitalizes on the danger through a cinematic flash, one resonant with the pleasure that is "Fun" and "Fear." Friedkin's boys in the city tremble within the director's "gritty" New York mise-en-scène to the extent that the desire they seek to exercise between one another is challenged by the very movements they must make to navigate within the urban setting that at once contains and makes available that desire.

## Notes

1. *The Night They Raided Minsky's* (1968) and *The Exorcist* (1973) also represent 1970s New York's urban setting. Though *The Exorcist* is based in Washington, DC, its New York City sequences echo the style of the trilogy.

2. I consider Friedkin's filmmaking concepts and practices through the descriptions in his memoir and in Thomas Clagett's book. See William Friedkin, *The Friedkin Connection: A Memoir* (New York: Harper Perennial, 2014); and Thomas D. Clagett, *William Friedkin: Films of Aberration, Obsession, and Reality*, 2nd ed. (Los Angeles: Silman-James, 2003).

3. Clagett, *William Friedkin*, 22.

4. Friedkin, *Friedkin*, 232.

5. Quoted in ibid., 49.

6. Miriam Hansen, *Cinema and Experience: Siegfried Kracauer, Walter Benjamin, and Theodor W. Adorno* (Berkeley: University of California Press,

2012), 38. On Friedkin's devotion to documentary technique, see Friedkin, *Friedkin*, and Clagett, *William Friedkin*.

7. Miriam Greenberg, *Branding New York: How a City in Crisis Was Sold to the World* (New York: Routledge, 2008), 55.

8. Greenberg argues that New York's rebranding was directly targeted to white, middle-class suburbanites, not city dwellers (ibid.).

9. Ibid., 79.

10. Starr stated, the city "can no longer be the place of opportunity.... Our urban system is based on the theory of taking the peasant and turning him into an industrial worker. Now there are no industrial jobs. Why not keep him a peasant?" (quoted in ibid., 141). See "Roger Starr, New York Planning Official, Author and Editorial Writer, Is Dead at 83," *New York Times*, September 11, 2001, www.nytimes.com/2001/09/11/nyregion/roger-starr-new-york-planning-official-author-and-editorial-writer-is-dead-at-83.html. See also Miranda J. Martinez, *Power at the Roots: Gentrification, Community Gardens, and the Puerto Ricans of the Lower East Side* (Plymouth, UK: Lexington Books, 2010), 16; Jule Sze, *Noxious New York: The Racial Politics of Urban Health and Environmental Justice* (Cambridge, MA: MIT Press, 2007), 69–70; and Deborah Wallace and Rodrick Wallace, *A Plague on Your Houses: How New York Was Burned Down and National Public Health Crumbled* (London: Verso, 1998), 21–45.

11. Relevantly, see Fergus Bordewich, "The Future of New York: A Tale of Two Cities," *New York*, July 23, 1979, 32–40. See also Joe Flood, "New York City: The Birthplace of Reaganomics," *New York*, February 18, 2011, http://nymag.com/daily/intelligencer/2011/02/new_york_city_the_birthplace_o.html.

12. Greenberg, *Branding*, 55.

13. Ibid., 133, 218.

14. On "Fear City," see ibid., 133–40; on Cosell, see Joe Flood, *The Fires: How a Computer Formula, Big Ideas, and the Best Intentions Burned Down New York City—and Determined the Future of Cities* (New York: Riverhead Books, 2010), 14.

15. Barry Keith Grant, "Paradise Lost and Found: A Bronx Tale," in *City That Never Sleeps: New York and the Filmic Imagination*, ed. Murray Pomerance (New Brunswick, NJ: Rutgers University Press, 2007), 53.

16. Greenberg, *Branding*, 34.

17. Mayor's Office of Film, Theatre, and Broadcasting, "Office History," www.nyc.gov/html/film/html/about/office-history.shtml (accessed August 30, 2015).

18. Martin Scorcese shot *Mean Streets* (1973), for instance, primarily in Los Angeles because it was "easier to get the permits to shoot with a non-union crew." See Sean Axmaker, "*Mean Streets*," Turner Classic Movies, www.tcm.com/this-month/article/236444%7C0/Mean-Streets.html (accessed December

9, 2015). Friedkin confirms the existence of a film commission when making *The French Connection*, but the mayor's office gave little support (*Friedkin*, 173).

19. Greenberg, *Branding*, 54.

20. Ibid., 34.

21. Ibid., 53.

22. Tom Wolfe, "Radical Chic: That Party at Lenny's," *New York*, June 8, 1970, 26–56.

23. Greenberg's first list is "Asphalt Jungle Films, 1967–1976"; the second is "New York Exploitation Films, 1976–1993" (*Branding*, 156–57). "Asphalt Jungle Films" are morally "complex" (153), while "New York Exploitation Films" are less "artistically sophisticated" (153).

24. Although Lindsay did not directly court homosexuals, Steven A. Rosen writes that he "promised [in his 1966 inauguration speech] to combat terror in the streets" and to eliminate police corruption; his promises fell short. Rosen, "Police Harassment of Homosexual Women and Men in New York City, 1960–1980," *Columbia Human Rights Law Review* 12, no. 159 (1980–81): 168. Nonetheless, Lindsay's charm won the hearts of the Mattachine Society (ibid., 169). See also Jean O'Leary's report to the federal Commission on Civil Rights (delivered December 12–13, 1978): "Statement of Jean O'Leary, Co-Executive Director, National Gay Task Force," in *Police Practices and the Preservation of Civil Rights: A Consultation by the United States Commission on Civil Rights* (Washington, DC: Superintendent of Documents, U.S. Government Printing Office, 1978), 7–12.

25. Wojtowicz's heist is the basis for Sidney Lumet's 1975 *Dog Day Afternoon*. See Alison Berg's documentary *The Dog* (2013). On the intersection of class and homosexuality, see John D'Emilio's *Sexual Politics, Sexual Communities: The Making of a Homosexual Minority in the United States, 1940–1970* (Chicago: University of Chicago Press, 1983). Arthur Bell's writings in the *Village Voice* prompted protests against police homophobia and the filming of *Cruising* in 1979.

26. Robert Atkins, "From Stonewall to Ground Zero," in *New York Calling: From Blackout to Bloomberg*, ed. Marshall Berman and Brian Berger (London: Reaktion Books, 2007), 254.

27. See Annette Pritchard, Nigel J. Morgan, and Diane Sedgley, "Reaching Out to the Gay Tourist: Opportunities and Threats in an Emerging Market Segment," *Tourism Management* 19, no. 3 (1998): 273–82.

28. Atkins, "From Stonewall," 255.

29. Ibid. On preparing locations for *Cruising*, see Friedkin, *Friedkin*, 360–72.

30. See also Emory Lewis, *Cue's New York: A Leisurely Guide to Manhattan* (New York: Van Rees, 1963). Lewis encourages visitors to explore widely the city's "infinite variety," where, for instance, the Savannah Club's "interracial

shows [include a] pretty young lady [who] strips and turns out to be a man" (192). Thanks to Sally Milner for sharing this.

31. Douglas Crimp, "*Disss*-Co (A Fragment): From *Before Pictures*, a Memoir of 1970s New York," *Criticism* 50, no. 1 (2008): 15.

32. In 1972, Michael Maye, the president of the Uniformed Firefighters Association and a former boxing champion, attacked members of the Gay Activists Alliance as they distributed pamphlets outside a dinner that Maye was attending. Despite the police presence, he was not arrested. See Rosen, "Police Harassment," 178.

33. Quoted in ibid., 180. A mayor's staff member confirmed that the mayor had lost control of the police (ibid., 177).

34. Samuel R. Delany, *Times Square Red, Times Square Blue* (New York: NYU Press, 1999), 15.

35. Friedkin, *Friedkin*, 364.

36. Delany, *Times Square*, 104, emphasis in original.

37. Quoted in Crimp, "*Disss*-Co," 18n5.

38. John D'Emilio, "By Way of Introduction: Notes from One Gay Life," in *Making Trouble: Essays on Gay History, Politics, and the University* (New York: Routledge, 1992), xv, emphasis added.

39. Ibid., xxiii. D'Emilio met his lover, Tomás, in 1970 on a subway platform.

40. Finally, in 1978—ironically under Mayor Ed Koch, whose leadership failed miserably when AIDS devastated the same community he claimed to protect in the 1970s—"discrimination based on sexual orientation in all agencies under mayoral control" was officially prohibited. Rosen, "Police Harassment," 186.

41. Richard D. Hongisto, "Why Are There No Gay 'Choir Boys'? Ask Your Friendly Chief of Police," *Perspectives* 12, no. 2 (1980): 39–40.

42. Ibid., 40. When legislation was introduced in the New York City Council to end discrimination against homosexuals, police and firefighter associations strongly argued against the bill "because firefighters work and sleep in close quarters." Rosen, "Police Harassment," 185.

43. Eve Kosofsky Sedgwick, *Between Men: English Literature and Male Homosocial Desire* (New York: Columbia University Press, 1985).

44. The phrase "densely packed gay life" appears in D'Emilio, "By Way of Introduction," xxvii.

45. Peter Dews, *Logics of Disintegration: Post-Structuralist Thought and the Claims of Critical Theory*, 3rd ed. (London: Verso, 2007).

46. Anselm Haverkamp, "Deconstruction Is/As Neopragmatism? Preliminary Remarks on Deconstruction in America," in *Deconstruction Is/In America: A New Sense of the Political*, ed. Anselm Haverkamp (New York: NYU Press, 1995), 11.

47. Friedkin, *Friedkin*, 161.

48. Ibid., 144.

49. The grittiness of Friedkin's exteriors are not exclusive to the New York films, yet he contrasts "the gritty macho look" of the New York films with the "feminine sensibility" of *To Live and Die in L.A.* (1985). Ibid., 384.

50. He was drawn to Harold Pinter's play *The Birthday Party* because it was described as a "comedy of menace." Ibid., 54.

51. Clagett, among others, questions Alan's sexual orientation (*William Friedkin*, 99).

52. A game of blindman's bluff is the dance the guests perform in *The Birthday Party*.

53. Minnelli's *The Band Wagon* had earlier merged the hard-boiled narrative of a Mickey Spillane with the musical, featuring Fred Astaire. On Gene Kelly's masculinist dance style, see David A. Gerstner, "Dancer from the Dance: Gene Kelly, Television, and the Beauty of Movement," *Velvet Light Trap* 49 (Spring 2002): 48–66.

54. Clagett, *William Friedkin*, 123.

55. Michael Worton, "Cruising (through) Encounters," in *Gay Signatures: Gay and Lesbian Theory, Fiction and Film in France, 1945–1995*, ed. Owen Heathcote, Alex Hughes, and James S. Williams (Oxford, UK: Berg, 1998), 29–30.

56. Ibid., 45.

57. Clagett is representative (*William Friedkin*, 258–71).

58. Worton's essay draws on a number of French writings about cruising. See, further, David A. Gerstner, "Choreographing Homosexual Desire in Philippe Vallois's *Johan*," *Camera Obscura* 28, no. 3/84 (2013): 124–57.

59. Joe Wlodarz, "Al Pacino: From the Mob to the Mineshaft," in *Hollywood Reborn: Movie Stars of the 1970s* (New Brunswick, NJ: Rutgers University Press, 2010), 79.

60. Ibid., 79, emphasis in original.

# 7

## "Nobody's Goddamn Business but My Own"

### Leonard Frey and the Politics of Gay and Jewish Visibility in the 1970s

STEPHEN VIDER

When Leonard Frey died in August 1988, at the age of forty-nine, both his *New York Times* and *Los Angeles Times* obituaries were accompanied by a portrait of the actor playing Motel the tailor in the 1971 film *Fiddler on the Roof*.[1] The choice of the portrait aligned Frey with the role of Tevye's son-in-law-to-be—capped, bearded, and bespectacled, wishing only to marry his childhood sweetheart and to purchase a mechanical sewing machine. The part had earned Frey an Oscar nomination, but it was not the role that first made him famous. A year before the release of *Fiddler*, Frey gained nationwide attention, and acclaim, for his role as Harold in the film *The Boys in the Band*. It was, in fact, a portrait of Frey as Harold—his hair curly, his cheeks scarred, his eyes hidden behind sunglasses, and a joint hanging from his lips—that first introduced national audiences to the actor. The poster for the film featured two photographs, one of Harold and the second of the film's Cowboy, captioned, "Today is Harold's birthday. This is his present." The part of Harold was, in many ways, more typical of the roles Frey played in the years to come: deadpan, sardonic, and, in more ways than one, queer. Still, the portrait of the sweet and gangly Motel was the one that these major newspapers' readers saw when they learned Frey had died of AIDS.

The choice to memorialize Frey as Motel rather than Harold undoubtedly reflected many editorial factors—the sway of an Oscar nod, the lasting

Leonard Frey as Harold (1970). (Getty Images)    Leonard Frey as Motel (1972). (Getty Images)

appeal of *Fiddler on the Roof*—but it also hinted at the shifting politics of Jewish and gay visibility in American culture. Throughout the late 1960s and '70s, explicit representations of Jewish life became more and more widely circulated, through novels, stand-up comedy, film, and television, while, at the same time, increasing numbers of artists and celebrities self-consciously embraced their Jewishness.[2] *Fiddler on the Roof* itself helped to fuel this Jewish revival. The musical and film adaptation provided American Ashkenazi Jews a nostalgic keepsake of the world their ancestors left behind at the same time that it affirmed cultural adaptation: "tradition" is both celebrated and confronted. Just as important, the story could be shared and appreciated by Jews and non-Jews alike. The Jewish immigrant story had become an American story.[3]

For gay performers and gay culture, the scene was different: despite the growth and proliferation of LGBT communities, political organizations, and media in the 1970s, by the 1980s the Christian right had fueled a major backlash, contributing to heightened homophobia that was only exacerbated by the emergence of AIDS.[4] And while representation of LGBT characters and story lines on film, television, and theater expanded in the 1970s and '80s, coming out as gay or lesbian, or getting typecast for gay parts, was still seen by most actors and agents as a career killer.[5] Popular ambivalence, if not outward prejudice, toward lesbians and gay men could translate into obituaries, too.[6] Even as the *New York Times* and *Los Angeles Times* tacitly outed Frey, disclosing his death from AIDS, the choice of photograph recast Frey as straight by association. Motel, a poor Russian Jewish tailor in pursuit of a wife, was easy to love and easy to mourn. Harold, a self-proclaimed "thirty-two-year-old, ugly, pockmarked Jew fairy" was more challenging and elusive—more, in fact, like Frey.[7]

This chapter looks at Frey's performances as Harold and Motel, as well as his self-presentation in newspaper interviews and television talk shows, to reconsider the ways representations of Jewishness and queerness circulated in the 1970s and '80s: how Jews and queers were seen and what kinds of "others" they were seen to be. It also provides a case study in the performance of celebrity, examining how one actor, on the edge of stardom, came to navigate competing demands for disclosure and discretion, revelation and obfuscation—Jewish transparency on the one hand, queer opacity on the other.

My reading of Frey's fluctuating visibility draws especially on recent work on opacity in queer studies and performance studies. As Nicholas de Villiers conceptualizes in his 2013 book *Opacity and the Closet*, opacity functions as a discursive strategy that resists calls for confession—where the refusal itself becomes an object of fascination. De Villiers attends particularly to modes of cultural production that promise "truth telling, the revelation of secrets, authenticity, and transparency"—the interview among them.[8] De Villiers's work resonates with Daphne Brooks's conception of "spectacular opacity" in *Bodies in Dissent*. For an array of black performers in the nineteenth century, Brooks argues, the spectacle of opaque performance operated as an emancipatory means of self-invention and resistance, unsettling dominant cultural scripts of black and white, and of male and female, through the body.[9]

This chapter builds on these works to reconsider the history of gay and Jewish visibility politics as they inflected each other in the post–World War II United States. Over the past decade, scholars of American Jewish culture have turned increasingly to questions about social performance and public representation.[10] Still relatively few works in Jewish studies have considered how same-sex sexuality has shaped performances and perceptions of Jewish difference. Queer studies, meanwhile, has tended not to take up Jewishness as a category of difference, even as it has moved to analyze more fully the intersections of sexuality and gender with ethnicity and race.[11]

This omission reflects in part the uncertain place of Jewish studies within ethnic studies: how much can and should Jewish experience and identity be compared with those of other ethnic groups?[12] To frame Jewish culture in terms of ethnic studies seems to privilege the "ethno-racial" character of Jewish identity—an identity dependent not on religious practice but on bloodlines and social affiliation.[13] Even then, the ethnic dimensions of Jewish culture are relatively distinct: historical studies of Jewish identity have shown how Jews came to be regarded, and to present themselves, as white over the course of the twentieth century, enabling access to forms of economic and social privilege that were inaccessible to African Americans, Asian Americans, Latinos, and others.[14] At the same time, reifying Jewishness as whiteness risks oversimplifying the various valences it has carried, and various forms it has taken, in different moments and places. By reading Jewishness as ethnicity, I do not mean to essentialize Jewishness or to equate it with other kinds of ethnic or racial difference. Rather, I hope to interrogate the performance of Jewishness as both different from and intersecting with other forms of group affiliation and oppression.

Looking at Frey's performances moves us away from binaries of visible/invisible, identified/disidentified, acceptance/rejection, normative/queer, to think about performances of affiliation and identity as ongoing negotiations between the performer and the spectator, to think about the ways "identity" manifests itself in everyday life, not as a "self" to which to be true but as a surface to be managed and manipulated. I must also admit that my peculiar fascination with Frey may have something to do with my own queer, effeminate, white, Ashkenazic resemblance to Harold, Motel, and Frey: we have notable noses and curly dark hair, we are anxious and awkward at parties.

Examining Frey's performances of Jewishness and queerness may be particularly generative because of the ways Jews and gay men were historically central to sociological, popular, and political formulations of identity, affiliation, "deviance," and social integration in the 1960s and '70s. In the 1963 book *Stigma: Notes on the Management of Spoiled Identity*, Erving Goffman returns repeatedly to both gay men and Jews as examples of social outsiders who must manipulate how and to whom they present themselves. In one typical section, on "in-group alignments," Goffman argues that the "stigmatized individual" may call attention to his or her "special" contributions and qualities in mixed company and even "flaunt some stereotypical attributes which he could easily cover; thus one finds second generation Jews who aggressively interlard their speech with Jewish idiom and accent, and the militant gay who are patriotically swish in public places."[15] Susan Sontag, writing on camp humor, also compares "Jews and homosexuals" as "the outstanding creative minorities in contemporary urban culture."

Sontag essentializes both groups, but only inasmuch as she believes both groups have essentialized themselves: just as "the Jews pinned their hopes for integrating into modern society on promoting the moral sense," so "homosexuals have pinned their integration into society on promoting the aesthetic sense."[16]

Gay rights activists of the 1950s and '60s frequently compared homosexuals to two groups: African Americans and American Jews, who waged similar battles, they believed, against social prejudice. In a fictional piece from *ONE* magazine titled "Some of My Best Friends Are Jews . . . ," the author imagined an ongoing dialogue with a friend who easily "understands and accepts" the "difference of, say, the Jews," but requires more convincing to believe homosexuals qualify as a minority in need of understanding, too.[17] The homophile leader Frank Kameny, himself raised Jewish, also frequently drew parallels between antigay, anti-Jewish, and antiblack prejudice and discrimination, taking for granted an already long tradition comparing African American and Jewish oppressions. In a 1961 letter to the chairman of the Civil Service Commission protesting employment discrimination, Kameny described homosexuals as "a minority in no slightest way different, as such, from other minority groups, such as the Negroes and the Jews," and therefore, deserving equal treatment.[18]

While such analogies could prove politically effective, they inevitably oversimplified the histories and identities they invoked, and overlooked possible intersections. The same sociologists (many of them Jewish) who conceptualized ethnicity in the 1960s tended to underplay the difference skin color made, presenting Jewish experiences of "assimilation" as the model "American ethnic pattern." This conceptualization of cultural assimilation tended to reify white American culture as the measure, at the same time celebrating Ashkenazi Jews for their success as a "model minority."[19] While the term *assimilation* originated in sociological studies of race and ethnicity, it has also come to be widely used in understanding how gay men might be integrated into American society—both through mainstream adoption of gay culture and through gay men's conformity to heteronormative values—as in the "assimilationist" push for same-sex marriage.[20]

Frey's self-conscious negotiation of his dual identities, both Jewish and gay, challenges such neat sociological analogizing and, with it, the value of assimilation as a framework for understanding how identities are performed. For Frey, Jewishness and queerness were not simply analogous but overlapping. Frey performed his queerness through his Jewishness, his avowed ethnicity doubling as an opaque expression of sexual difference.

## Queer Opacity

In February 1968, Leonard Frey was interviewed on camera by the choreographer Jerome Robbins. The interview was one of many exercises in which Frey took part as a performer in Robbins's short-lived American Theatre Lab. Alongside two other actors, Frey answered questions about his parents' occupations (his father was a wholesale fruit seller, his mother a "housewife"), his suit size (39 regular), major illnesses (appendicitis, intestinal worms, hemorrhoids), awards ("best camper" at Camp Chickagami), and what other career he would like to have if he were not an actor (none). Frey answered all the questions in a deadpan style—his voice barely modulating, his face muscles barely moving.[21] Designed as fodder for future improvisational performance, the session was recorded only a few months before *The Boys in the Band* had its Off-Broadway premiere at Theatre Four on Fifty-Fifth Street, where it ran for over one thousand performances.[22] Frey could not have known it at the time, but it was good practice: in the three years to come, Frey was interviewed repeatedly about his career, his upbringing, and his social and sexual life. He appeared in local and national newspapers and made regular appearances on *The Tonight Show* and *Dick Cavett*. The BBC even filmed a short special titled "Who Is Leonard Frey?"

Frey grew accustomed early on to being an outsider. Born in 1938, he was the younger of two sons of Charles and Henrietta Frey. It was a mixed marriage—Charles was Lutheran, and Henrietta was Jewish—but Leonard was raised predominantly Lutheran. Frey's sister-in-law Sally, who married Frey's older brother, was the daughter of the Lutheran minister whose church Frey's family attended. As Sally told me in a phone interview in April 2015, "The people in our neighborhood were either Catholic or Protestant. And so he wanted to be with the rest of the group. So when his class was getting confirmed in the Protestant church, he asked his mom and dad if he could get confirmed with them. And they said, 'Sure, what the heck.' That's when his mother started going to church." But by the time Frey went to James Madison High School, he was often targeted for being overweight and awkward. One of his legs was also shorter than the other.[23]

Frey made his first appearance on television while still in high school: in 1954, he appeared on the TV game show *Sense and Nonsense* to raise money for the Brooklyn Museum Art School.[24] Two years later, he headed to Cooper Union to train as a painter but found himself drawn to theater. As Frey recalled in one interview, he and a fellow undergraduate, Dolores, would regularly go to the Broadway theater where *The World of Suzie Wong* was playing: "Dolores would sneak into the alley and come out, and then I'd say, 'O, you were wonderful, darling.' We thought theater people were all chic and phony, which they are, and that they called everybody darling, which they do."[25] Soon after, Frey left Cooper Union to study acting at the Neighborhood Playhouse School of Theater and was cast in a series of supporting roles: in the Off-Broadway operetta *Little Mary Sunshine*; in *The Coach with the Six Insides*, Jean Erdman's adaptation of *Finnegans Wake*; and in Adrienne Kennedy's *Funnyhouse of a Negro*.

Frey's biggest break came with *Fiddler on the Roof*. In October 1963, Frey wrote a letter to Jerome Robbins asking to be considered for the musical. Perhaps, Frey suggested, Robbins would remember him from *The Coach with the Six Insides*: "I was the tall, dark haired, large nosed, noisy one." He wrote earnestly, "I'd like to come and see you, Mr. Robbins, about 'Tevye.' Please let me. Ever since I started in the theater, it's been my hope to work with you."[26] Frey was eventually cast in the role of Mendel, the rabbi's son, for the show's premiere on Broadway in September 1964. A year later, in July 1965, he took over the part of Motel, the tailor—the part he reprised several years later in Norman Jewison's film adaptation.[27]

Frey (*left*) in 1962 performance of *The Coach with the Six Insides*. (Museum of the City of New York)

Still, it was the role of Harold in *The Boys in the Band*—the 1970 film in particular—that brought Frey unprecedented attention and acclaim. While reviews of the play had emphasized the strong acting across the cast, reviews of the film regularly singled out Frey in particular. In the *New York Times*, Vincent Canby noted, "In the film, as in the play, the most interesting character—the only one who might have an identity beyond that as a homosexual—is Harold. . . . All of the performances are good, and that of Leonard Frey, as Harold, is much better than good. He's excellent without disturbing the ensemble."[28] In *Saturday Review*'s largely tepid take on the film, the critic Hollis Alpert noted similarly that Frey "all but carries the film on his sagging shoulders."[29] In *Gay* magazine, although Peter Ogren decried the film for trotting out gay stereotypes to the straight masses, he saved a good word for Frey, whom he described as "simply magnificent."[30]

The praise spoke not only to the skill of Frey's performance but also to the canniness of Mart Crowley's writing. As Crowley explained to me in a phone interview in June 2015, most of the characters were based on people he knew. The character of Harold was inspired by the dancer and choreographer Howard Jeffrey (born Schwartz). Crowley first met Jeffrey while working for Natalie Wood, whom he accompanied to the set of *West Side Story*. Jeffrey was working as Jerome Robbins's assistant. Crowley and Jeffrey were never lovers, but they became best friends and for a time lived in the same apartment building in Beverly Hills. Crowley recalled, "Everybody loved Howard. Everybody always thought he was the funniest, the sharpest, the most entertaining."[31]

The influence of Howard Jeffrey on Harold, and the play, can be seen in a cache of Jeffrey's letters to Crowley, archived with Crowley's papers at UCLA. The letters, spanning three decades, reveal Jeffrey's campy, self-deprecating, gossipy wit. He began and ended multiple letters with the phrase "Oh Mary, don't ask"—a line Emory delivers in *The Boys in the Band*.[32] In a letter sent from England, Jeffrey wrote that he missed Crowley and the chance to speak with someone who understood him. "It's just that *Life* is never as good as I want it to be & depression always sits around the corner waiting to come in simply by 'one pimple' or a few pounds over weight or some one who is very very beautiful. Christ I've gone on and on and haven't even gotten to *all* the things I meant to."[33] Back in California, Jeffrey also took Crowley to the birthday party that inspired the film's setting. Crowley eventually dedicated the play to Jeffrey, along with another friend, Doug Murray (the basis for Donald).

But while Harold may have been inspired by Jeffrey, the character also, inevitably, took on a life of his own—especially as developed by Frey. High-camp, high-pitched, and high, Frey's Harold could not be reduced to stereotype: he defied the boundaries of gay representation. The role both drew from and shaped Frey's own deadpan style. In both his performance as Harold and his self-presentation, Frey perfected a style of performance between hypervisibility and invisibility—a mode of embodiment and expression that both resisted and attracted attention, both confessed and hid.

Harold is opaque from the start. The film begins with a long shot that first shows a chair embroidered with a gold crown and the name "Princess Hal" and then pans left to reveal a marble vanity, covered almost completely with a variety of beauty products and remedies, including creams, pills, a bottle of Pepto-Bismol, and a Band-Aid box. The camera then moves up to the mirror, where the reflection reveals someone enjoying a bath, legs covered in white soap bubbles. Only later, or on re-viewing, can the viewer fully put together that it is Harold in the bathtub, that the Band-Aid box on the sink in fact hides his marijuana stash, and that it is his elaborate skin-care and pot-smoking routine that delays his arrival at the party.

That opacity, Harold's hiddenness, runs throughout the film: the doorbell rings twice, but neither time is it Harold (once it is the cake, and once it is Alan, Michael's possibly straight, possibly closeted college friend). When Harold finally does arrive, he is lit dimly and fragmented in three successive close-ups: we first see his patent-leather black shoes as he crosses his feet; next we see his fey left hand, with an amethyst pinky ring, limply holding a

Harold's entrance in *The Boys in the Band* (1970).

lit joint before flicking away its ash; and then we see his expressionless face, lit only from behind and to the left, his eyes hidden by tinted glasses.

Harold's opacity also extends to Frey's vocal styling: he plays Harold as darkly deadpan and nasal, his affect and voice always controlled—even when he bursts into laughter or delivers a sharp retort. When Michael chides him for being late to his own party, Harold offers this famous reply: "What I *am*, Michael, is a thirty-two-year-old, ugly, pock-marked Jew fairy—and if it takes me a little while to pull myself together and if I smoke a little grass before I can get up the nerve to show my face to the world, it's nobody's goddamn business but my own. And how are *you* this evening?" As he speaks the line, he moves slowly toward Michael and the camera, his upper body barely shifting—as restrained as Michael is bitchy. But what is so mesmerizing and memorable about the line is the way it both reveals and repulses: Harold simultaneously unmasks his stigmatized identities and actions and insists that they are "nobody's goddamn business." Harold's identifications and actions are private matters, but they are not exactly secret, either.

This opacity should not be read simply as personal style: it is also a tactical response to competing social demands of "confession" and "authenticity," on the one hand, and "respectability" and "conformity," on the other. When the play first premiered, it was often lauded for its "honesty" in all its humor and despair. *Time* called it "a funny, sad and honest play about a set of mixed-up human beings who happen to be deviates."[34] *Look* called the film "the most touching and honest portrayal of homosexual life ever to come to the screen."[35] But the play is actually divided on whether complete "honesty," with others and with oneself, should or can be achieved. Michael, in particular, seems at once driven by and skeptical of confession—whether in its Catholic or psychoanalytic form. He is endlessly critical of Donald's shrink, but he also initiates the party's final game, in which each guest is asked to telephone the one person he has truly loved. Harold's solution is to sit out the game entirely.

Michael and Harold ultimately represent two different methods of managing information through social performance, of negotiating what Goffman called a "spoiled identity" among both insiders and outsiders. Michael begins the party happily enough, keeping away from alcohol and cigarettes, but begins to unravel when the self-avowed heterosexual Alan arrives unexpectedly, precisely at the moment when Michael and his friends are remembering and reperforming a synchronized dance from Fire Island. Harold refuses to modulate his performance. When he meets Alan, far from covering, Harold camps, "Who is she? Who was she? Who does she hope to be?" At the same time, no one may ever fully know what psychological wounds Harold carries; as Michael reveals, Harold is hoarding pills for a dramatic end. As a strategy for negotiating stigma, Harold's opacity prevents anyone from knowing, at any moment, whether he is self-destructing or laughing on the inside. When Michael scoffs at Harold, "You're *absolutely* paranoid about *absolutely* everything," Harold replies, "Oh, yeah, well, why don't you *not* tell me about it?"

The trouble for Harold, and for *The Boys in the Band*, was that the very strategies of information management and social performance the play captured were fast falling out of fashion: the gay liberation movement that emerged in the late 1960s, like other forms of 1960s radicalism and counterculture, privileged authenticity and self-actualization—rereading as hopeless self-hatred the sorts of covering, masking, and modulation presented and interrogated in *The Boys in the Band*.[36] When Michael accuses Alan of being a "closet queen," of being "in the closet," he does not expect him to "come out" to his wife—only to himself. But the very metaphors of "the closet" and "coming out" shifted in the years to come. The term "coming out" originally emerged within urban gay subcultures to signify one's entrance or initiation in the "gay" world. Only after the emergence of gay liberation did it come to mean a broader, more public act of self-disclosure beyond the boundaries of the gay community.[37] The term *closet queen*, meanwhile, was itself a relatively recent coinage—it did not appear in Gershon Legman's 1941 homosexual lexicon (the closest term was *hidden queen*), but it did appear in Donald Webster Cory and John Leroy's 1963 lexicon, to describe a "male homosexual, usually effeminate, who is shy, retiring, and does not make close relationships with others."[38] By 1970, however, "coming out of the closet" had become a political imperative: as Carl Wittman put it in "A Gay Manifesto," "If we are liberated we are open with our sexuality. Closet queenery must end. *Come out*."[39]

To many gay liberation activists and writers, *The Boys in the Band* looked retrograde and conservative by comparison, providing the wrong kind of publicity and reaffirming stereotypes of gay weakness, effeminacy, and self-hatred. The criticisms were not unknown to the actors. Frey never did interviews with the gay press, but he did do one with *After Dark*, a magazine about entertainment, movies, theater, and dance, with a substantial gay readership, though the magazine never said so outright. Frey admitted reading "a couple of those dirty newspapers they have on the newsstands, you know, the ones that everybody buys that cost much too much money, well anyway, the variety with a fairy flavor to them always have a put-down of *Boys*. They say it isn't realistic." He also recalled attending a discussion of the play in Brooklyn—"full of Brooklyn Heights homosexuals." One audience member stood up and said, "You know there are some happy homosexuals!"[40]

The visibility of the film also presented a challenge for its actors: the risk of typecasting. For casting agents, as well as audiences, it proved difficult to separate the actors from the roles they played. For starters, the publicity tended to blur the line between the actors and the characters they played: a six-page spread in *Look* magazine titled "The Faces of the Boys in the Band," published in December 1969, featured photographs of the cast, all dressed in character. The black-and-white portraits, by Irving Penn, were intimate, carefully lit close-ups with a sense of pensive vulnerability, most of the actors looking away from the camera. The portrait of Frey as Harold occupied a full page, featuring pockmarked makeup, curly hair, long sideburns, and dark glasses resting on his head, with his thumb against his lips. The accompanying text, like that for the other portraits, did not describe the actor but his character, quoting at length from the play. Far from disrupting the "honesty" of the play, the photograph and description of Harold made nearly invisible any real person behind the role he played.[41]

At the same time, few of the actors had had major film or stage roles before *The Boys in the Band*. As a result, Cliff Gorman worked hard to distance himself from his Obie Award–winning performance as the effeminate Emory. Already in 1968, a *New York Times* piece titled "You Don't Have to Be One to Play One" featured a photograph of Gorman holding his wife tightly. A 1970 *Life* article, published on the heels of the film's release, similarly insisted on Gorman's hetero-masculinity. As Gorman explained, "I realized that people think of you as the part you're playing, and it was something I'd have to live down. It was like having eunuch written on your tunic, when you just took the wrong cloak."[42]

Frey engineered a more complex, if still fraught, response, a style of opacity worthy of Harold. After the stage production of *The Boys in the Band*, Frey was offered many more parts in the explicitly gay mold of Harold. Peter Sellers saw Frey in the London production of the play and decided to give him a small part in the madcap 1969 film *The Magic Christian*, as the ship's effete psychiatrist, Lawrence Faggot (pronounced fã-gō′). Frey later recalled, "After I saw the finished picture and my role in it I heartily wished Sellers hadn't bothered to be so generous."[43] Frey also took a similarly small but funny role in Otto Preminger's 1970 film *Tell Me That You Love Me, Junie Moon*, playing Guiles, a queeny fashion photographer who adopts (and, it is suggested, turns gay) Warren, one of the film's main characters, as a child. In a campy flashback, Guiles serves Warren what he calls "tuna fish flambeau," only to die swiftly of food poisoning.[44]

But soon after *The Boys in the Band* was filmed, Frey revealed in later interviews, he began rejecting gay parts for fear of being permanently typecast. In *After Dark*, Frey commented on the frequent assumption that playing a gay role meant you were a gay actor: "There is such a terribly uptight feeling in this business about playing a fairy. You can play muggers, murderers, or a child molester, yet nobody thinks you are a mugger, murderer, or child molester.... When I was in *Fiddler on the Roof* nobody thought that I was helping out the B'nai Brith on my days off. But as soon as you *play* a fairy, you *are* a fairy."[45] Frey was clear that he did not regret taking the role and knew it had been a major boost to his career. But after the release of the film, he found himself increasingly frustrated by the limited range of roles he was offered.[46]

Frey also grew more strategic in discussing—or rather, not discussing—his sexuality. Initially, he could be quite coy. In one of the earliest interviews with the cast, published in *Women's Wear Daily*, Frey had this to say: "Harold is a 32-year-old ugly pockmarked Jew fairy, only a few of which I qualify for, ... one from Column A, two from Column B."[47] But in the years to come, reporters danced more and more around the question of Frey's sexuality. The questioning placed Frey in an uncomfortable position and left him searching for new ways to address the issue. In one interview, with the *Chicago Tribune*, Frey encouraged the reporter Carol Kramer to ask him outright if he was a homosexual. After months of journalists hinting about whether, in Kramer's words, "he was [cough, cough] well, anything like Harold," Frey was proud to have finally come up with a one-liner in response. The problem was, he realized, with a snap of the fingers, the joke only worked if the interviewer was male. "Question: 'Are you a homosexual?' Answer: 'No, but thanks anyway.'"[48]

Frey's emerging celebrity status, in fact, placed him at odds with the emerging visibility politics of gay liberation. Boston activist and writer Michael Bronski later recalled seeing the film version of *The Boys in the Band* with three friends when it premiered. They did not quite identify with the "queens" on-screen, but they did get a thrill from seeing actors they presumed were gay playing gay parts: as Bronski explained, playing a gay role seemed to them as close to "coming out" as any actor would come. But they felt betrayed soon after, when they saw Frey on *The Dick Cavett Show*. When the host asked whether people now assumed Frey was gay because of the film, the actor responded with a joke about oral sex: he gagged when the doctor put even a tongue depressor in his mouth. As Bronski wrote, "No one expected him to admit that he was homosexual, but somehow the illusion that he might be was shattered." Bronski described it as a "non-denial denial."[49]

Yet the binaries of visibility and authenticity inherent in gay liberation's models of "coming out" and "the closet" made it difficult at the time—and make it difficult still—to appreciate the bind that Frey found himself in and the complex ways he negotiated his identifications and self-presentation in the fear, and face, of stigmatization of gay men within Hollywood, the theater, and American society at large. Frey himself was hardly a "closet queen." As Sally Frey recalled, Leonard told his parents he was gay when he was still a teenager. They sent him to a psychiatrist, but the doctor told them, Sally recalled, "He's fine, don't worry about it, he knows exactly what he's doing," and that was the end of that.[50] Frey's nephew Charlie Frey also recalled regularly visiting his uncle at his home in Greenwich Village, where he met Frey's friends and a few male romantic partners. Frey also took his nephew on trips to the Pines on Fire Island, including one in the early '70s when Charlie, at the time around seven years old, walked hand in hand along the beach with Frey's fellow *Boys* cast-mate Robert La Tourneaux.[51] A year after Frey's disappointing *Dick Cavett* appearance, Michael Bronski also saw another side of the actor: a friend sneaked him backstage at Lincoln Center to catch a glimpse of Frey in his dressing room, following a performance of *Beggar on Horseback*. As Bronski wrote, "What most remains vivid in my mind is that from his joking and dishing backstage it was clear that Frey was gay." It was, for Bronski, "a revelation to be savored."[52] Gay liberation had prioritized public avowals of homosexuality, yet for Frey, as for Harold, codes and camp provided queer connection enough. But being gay was not Frey's only mode of identification.

## Jewish Transparency

Frey's performance as Harold was at the same time underlined by a new form of Jewish visibility that emerged in the 1960s and '70s: Jewish ethnicity as spectacle. Jewish American life in the 1950s was shaped, predominantly, by a drive for assimilation: as Jewish families moved from the cities to newly built suburbs, they sought to "fit in" with their Christian neighbors. For many, synagogues and Hebrew schools became a way of demonstrating an "American" attachment to religion (and rebuking fears of Jewish Communism).[53]

In *Catholic, Protestant, Jew*, Will Herberg elevated Judaism as one of three major American religions, part of the country's supposed "Judeo-Christian" heritage, predicting that "religion" would eventually displace ethnicity and race as markers of distinction.[54] But religion was not the only path. In a description of the suburb of Park Forest, the sociologist Herbert Gans also described new Jewish suburbanites hoping to still *feel* Jewish without *appearing* too Jewish. Much as gay men learned to drop and listen for code words (including the word *gay* itself), suburban Jews actively, if anxiously, scanned their blocks for other Jews, hoping to detect a particular mannerism or "look," throwing references to corned beef or Passover into conversation and seeing whether neighbors nodded in recognition. They formed social clubs like the B'nai Brith Lodge and the Council of Jewish Women, even as the majority skipped High Holiday services.[55] Tensions over Jewish visibility were also exposed in Philip Roth's early story "Eli, the Fanatic," in which a group of suburban Jews is threatened by the arrival of a group of black-hatted Hasidic Holocaust survivors. The "old" suburbanites do not deny their Jewishness, but they do not want it made too noticeable either.[56]

That drive to assimilate also led to heightened anxieties about Jewish decline and disappearance: in the pages of *Commentary*, for example, Stanley Hyman wrote, "Some of us now, proud in Jewish cultural identity, have not much more to transmit than a few words of mispronounced Yiddish, a midnight longing for a pastrami sandwich, a sardonic anecdote."[57] In becoming more "American" and distancing themselves from ethnic or religious particularity, Jews became more "white" but risked becoming invisible, even to themselves.

The assimilationist strain in Jewish American culture began to shift, however, in the 1960s, as performers drew on Jewish difference as a source of humor. Jewish vaudeville of the 1910s and '20s had often drawn comedy from the figure of the immigrant "greenhorn," with thick Yiddish accent, but dialect humor had largely fallen out of favor in the 1940s and '50s and was all but unheard on television.[58] Jewish performers of the 1960s, including Mel Brooks, Lenny Bruce, Mike Nichols and Elaine May, and Allan Sherman, however, found new humor in Jewish life, particularly differences across family generations and frequently the comic trope of the suffocating and castrating Jewish mother.[59] Such humor inevitably led to debates about whether this "negative" publicity was necessarily "good for the Jews." Philip Roth, for example, encountered ongoing criticisms from Jewish readers and advocacy groups, who worried his representations of Jewish adulterers and schemers, published in the *New Yorker*, no less, would give Jews a bad name among "the goyim." Roth responded at length in a 1963 essay, "Writing about Jews": "If there are Jews who have begun to find the stories the novelists tell more provocative and pertinent than the sermons of some of the rabbis, perhaps it is because there are regions of feeling and consciousness in them which cannot be reached by the oratory of self-congratulation and self-pity."[60]

Such debates paralleled discussions about Jewish political activism, too: as Michael Staub recounts in *Torn at the Roots*, in 1969 Columbia University's Jewish Advisory Board declined to renew the campus chaplain and "radical rabbi" A. Bruce Goldman after he supported a student strike—this after he had publicly opposed the Vietnam War.[61] As Goldman put it, "The board felt that I was making my Jewishness too visible, too conspicuous, and that this would raise anti-Semitic feelings which would jeopardize future admission of Jews to the university."[62]

Harold's Jewishness must be understood against this ongoing debate about Jewish visibility. Harold is never anything less than forthcoming about his Jewish background, but he is less sure what it means. He is decidedly not religious: in one scene, Harold waxes poetic on the nature of inner and outer beauty. Looking at Cowboy, he reflects, "How can *his* beauty ever compare with *my* soul? And although I've never seen my soul, I understand from my mother's rabbi that it's a knock-out. I, however, cannot seem to locate it for a gander. And if I could, I'd sell it in a flash, for some skin-deep, transitory, meaningless beauty." Harold's evident rejection of religion is a contrast to Michael's ambivalent attachment to Catholicism, as Harold calls it, "that great insurance policy called The Church." Their relationships to religion echo Mart Crowley's and Howard Jeffrey's. As Crowley told me, "We had both been saddled with our religions and tortured by them both, and we decided to dump them both when we discovered psychoanalysis, I think, and never looked back. Howard was much more religion-free than I was. I still think I, even at that time, was still clinging to some wreckage of the Catholic Church—witness Michael going to church at the end of the play."[63]

More than through religion, Harold is marked as Jewish in his body: the stage directions describe Harold as having an "unusual Semitic face," and his hair is described by Emory as "very, very tight, tight, black curly hair," another marker of Jewish bodily difference.[64] The filming of Frey as Harold emphasizes both: the first shot of Harold's face is head-on, with lighting from the back and the left side, emphasizing the outline of his hair. The camera also repeatedly captures Harold/Frey from the side, drawing attention to the shape of his nose. The scene in which Harold trades jibes with

Harold in profile: "It's only in the eye of the beholder."

Michael on the transitory nature of beauty, noting, "it's only in the eye of the beholder," is primarily filmed with Harold/Frey's face in profile. Harold's bodily Jewishness, in fact, intersects and overlaps with his bodily queerness. It was such images of Jewish weakness that gave rise to the counterimage of Jewish hypermasculinity and power in the Zionist imagination. Harold is not the heroic "muscle Jew" or the "sabra" lauded by many observers following Israel's victory and land capture in the Six-Day War. His body is instead marked as "Diasporic": effeminate and queer.[65]

Harold also bore a strong similarity to Alexander Portnoy, the anxiety-ridden antihero of Roth's 1969 novel *Portnoy's Complaint*, who travels to Israel at the novel's end only to find himself figuratively emasculated and literally impotent. For Portnoy, Jewish weakness is only a step away from homosexuality. In one rant, Portnoy wonders how his mother did not turn him into a "fruitcake": "Mother, the beach at Fire Island is strewn with the bodies of nice Jewish boys, in bikinis and Bain de Soleil, . . . who helped mommies set up mah-jongg tiles when the ladies came on Monday night to play."[66]

Harold, however, seems undisturbed by his Jewish "weakness," finding in Jewishness instead a source of humor and distinction. To Michael, Harold says, invoking a Yiddish/German version of Michael's "icks": "You are going to have schmertz tomorrow you wouldn't believe." In the play, Michael replies, "May I kiss the hem of your schmata, Doctor Freud?"[67] In another scene, Harold provides a stand-up-ready "mother" routine: he explains he used to keep his marijuana in an oregano jar in the kitchen and kept "accidentally turning [his] hateful mother on with the salad. . . . No matter what meal she comes over for—even if it's breakfast—she says, 'Let's have a salad!'" Howard Jeffrey, too, could find humor in his Jewishness. In one note, he apologized for abandoning Crowley and heading to the baths, "spatzerin (yiddish for 'promenading around') off to the tubs."[68] He ended a poem to Crowley, on the occasion of his birthday, with the lines, "For everyone today's a joy / Mohammedan or Jew or goy / Today Mart Crowley is a birthday boy!"[69] And while he dropped his family name, Schwartz, he gave the name to his cat.[70] Jeffrey shared his Jewishness as a mode of friendship. But the character of Harold uses his Jewishness to repel, too: at the play's end, Donald promises to see him soon. Harold replies, "Yeah. How about a year from Shavuot?"

Harold's Diasporic Jewishness also functions differently than Motel the tailor's. In the movie version of *Fiddler on the Roof*, filmed on location in Yugoslavia soon after the release of *The Boys in the Band*, Frey plays Motel as far sweeter and more innocent than Harold—and, in the beginning, far less effectual.[71] Harold may need to smoke a joint to show his face, but when he does, he demands to be seen, however opaquely. Motel struggles to be noticed at all. In an early scene, Motel comes to Tevye's home looking for the family's oldest daughter, Tzeitel: he runs toward the house, his arms and *tzitzit* waving at his sides, and then opens the front door just enough to show his face. He finds instead Tevye's wife, Golde, and Yente the matchmaker, making plans for Tzeitel's marriage to Lazar Wolf, the local butcher and also a wealthy widower. Later, Motel confronts Tevye, demanding that he and Tzeitel be allowed to marry instead—they have already pledged themselves to each other. Once again, he must struggle to be seen and heard, and he borrows a line from Tzeitel: "Even a poor tailor is entitled to some happiness!" The story line, closely following Sholem Aleichem's original story, figures Motel's demand not only as a break with tradition but also as an assertion of manhood: as Frey sings in "Wonder of Wonders," "Out of a worthless lump of clay, God has made a man today." The song also figures "the promised land" not as the Land of Israel but as marriage. Motel may never become a "muscle Jew," but he does become, in Golde's words, "a person," an English translation of the Yiddish *mensch*. The ultimate success of *Fiddler on the Roof* derived, in large part, from the transformation of Diasporic Jewishness into a source of pride, at the very moment when Israel ascended in the American Jewish imagination. Jewish traditions could be changed and challenged, and Jewish boys could become men; and they did not need their own land to do so.

Motel's entrance in *Fiddler on the Roof*: "Good afternoon. Is Tzeitel in the house?" (1972).

In the years when *Fiddler* was filmed and released, Frey also seems to have grown more and more identified with his own Jewish heritage, linking him to what J. Hoberman has called Hollywood's "Jew Wave," the rise of self-consciously Jewish celebrities including Lenny Bruce, Barbra Streisand, Woody Allen, Dustin Hoffman, and Elliott Gould.[72] In the same interviews in which Frey dissembled about or avoided discussion of his sexuality, he disclosed his Jewishness as a source of both nostalgia and growing pride. In a 1972 interview with the *Jewish Exponent*, Frey explained, "Though my mother was Jewish, and I grew up in Flatbush, the only Jewish upbringing I had was from the table, you know, latkes and stuff. I know nothing about the rituals of Judaism." While preparing for *Fiddler*, Frey was first exposed to Jewish literature and history: "I read Sholem Aleichem and an anthology about the Jewish shtetl called *Life Is with People*, which Jerome Robbins gave us. I read it four times and became completely hooked on the Jewish religion—it's so tied up with life!" In a later interview, Frey went further (covering over his links to the Lutheran church): "My upbringing was totally Jewish—matzo balls all the way."[73]

Frey's eager avowal of his Jewishness is a striking contrast to his evasions around sexuality. In the 1960s, sociologists and gay activists could easily compare Jewishness and homosexuality as stigmatized identifications. But by the 1970s, Jewishness—Jewish men, in particular—had suddenly become acceptable and "desirable." As the 1978 *Shikse's Guide to Jewish Men* put it, "Throughout recent history, the sexual heroes have been the Clark Gables, Humphrey Bogarts, Gregory Pecks, Robert Redfords. Now, today, the Elliott Goulds, George Segals, Dustin Hoffmans herald the beginning of a new super sex star, the Jewish man. He is in. He is here and he is now."[74] For an actor like Frey, Jewish visibility was a boon, while gay visibility remained a risk.

Frey's performance of his own Jewishness, however, owed less to male stars like Hoffman and Gould than to another icon of 1960s Jewish and popular culture: Barbra Streisand. Like Streisand, Frey frequently drew attention to his Jewish looks, his nose in particular, and to his Brooklyn background. "When I grew up," Frey told one reporter, "all the movie stars were gods and goddesses and had blond hair and little turned up noses."[75] Frey even said he was encouraged to get a nose job but refused, much as Streisand famously had, although Frey did not credit her as an influence.[76] In another interview, Frey described himself as looking like a "kook,"[77] a word, derived from *cuckoo*, most frequently applied to Streisand and other female comic performers of the 1960s and '70s, including Goldie Hawn and Joan Rivers. For Frey, this feminized, Jewish "kookiness"—his charming eccentricity—provided an alibi to make his queerness visible while leaving his sexuality unspoken. It was a new performance with similar effects, drawing in and distancing an audience at once. "When I go into a producer's office," Frey reasoned, "he is apt to think, 'This certainly isn't the man to play the head of United States Steel.' But he'll think a little beyond this and come up with 'He's great as the guy who blows up the plant.'"[78]

In the years following *The Boys in the Band* and *Fiddler*, Frey's kookiness proved more and more central to his appeal: he continued to work on the stage throughout the 1970s, but by the 1980s he was acting primarily on television, in short-lived sitcoms like the Western spoof *Best of the West* (1981), playing an eastern, corrupt, and effete saloon keeper, and *Mr. Smith* (1983), acting opposite an orangutan. He also appeared routinely on game shows like *Hollywood Squares*. Frey's kookiness made for a unique mode of opacity, not covering his otherness but layering one form of difference over the other. Frey exploited the overlap between two stereotypes of male effeminacy—the Diasporic Jew and the homosexual—to smuggle both into the mainstream.

## Notes

Thank you to David S. Byers, Levi Prombaum, Aaron Lecklider, and Matt Bell for their feedback and encouragement in writing and revising, and to Sally Frey, Charlie Frey, and Mart Crowley for their generous interviews with me.

1. Mel Gussow, "Leonard Frey, Actor, Dies at 49; Was in 'Fiddler' and Other Films," *New York Times*, August 25, 1988; "Leonard Frey, Played Motel the Tailor in 'Fiddler,'" *Los Angeles Times*, August 26, 1988.

2. On Jewish involvement and visibility in American media, see J. Hoberman and Jeffrey Shandler, *Entertaining America: Jews, Movies, and Broadcasting* (Princeton, NJ: Princeton University Press, 2003).

3. On the production and reception of *Fiddler on the Roof*, see Seth L. Wolitz, "The Americanization of Tevye or Boarding the Jewish 'Mayflower,'" *American Quarterly* 40, no. 4 (1988): 514–36; and Alisa Solomon, *Wonder of Wonders: A Cultural History of "Fiddler on the Roof"* (New York: Macmillan, 2013).

4. On 1970s gay activism and the conservative backlash, see Michael Bronski's overview in *A Queer History of the United States* (Boston: Beacon, 2011), 205–35.

5. On gay visibility in media and the entertainment industry, see Larry P. Gross, *Up from Invisibility: Lesbians, Gay Men, and the Media in America* (New York: Columbia University Press, 2001); and Stephen Tropiano, *The Prime Time Closet: A History of Gays and Lesbians on TV* (New York: Applause Theater and Cinema, 2002).

6. For an analysis of AIDS obituaries, see Peter Nardi, "AIDS and Obituaries: The Perpetuation of Stigma in the Press," in *Culture and AIDS*, ed. Donald A. Feldman (Westport, CT: Praeger, 1990), 159–68.

7. *The Boys in the Band* (1970), directed by William Friedkin (CBS, 2008), DVD. All *Boys in the Band* quotes are from the film unless otherwise noted.

8. Nicholas de Villiers, *Opacity and the Closet: Queer Tactics in Foucault, Barthes, and Warhol* (Minneapolis: University of Minnesota Press, 2012), 6.

9. Daphne Brooks, *Bodies in Dissent: Spectacular Performances of Race and Freedom, 1850–1910* (Durham, NC: Duke University Press, 2006), 8. See also Shane Vogel, "Lena Horne's Impersona," *Camera Obscura* 23, no. 1/67 (2008): 11–45.

10. See for example Henry Bial, *Acting Jewish: Negotiating Ethnicity on the American Stage and Screen* (Ann Arbor: University of Michigan Press, 2005); David Kaufman, *Jewhooing the Sixties: American Celebrity and Jewish Identity; Sandy Koufax, Lenny Bruce, Bob Dylan, and Barbra Streisand* (Waltham, MA: Brandeis University Press, 2012); Rebecca Rossen, *Dancing Jewish: Jewish Identity in American Modern and Postmodern Dance* (New York: Oxford University Press, 2014); and Lori Harrison-Kahan, *The White Negress: Literature, Minstrelsy, and the Black-Jewish Imaginary* (New Brunswick, NJ: Rutgers University Press, 2011).

11. For important exceptions, see Daniel Boyarin, Daniel Itzkovitz, and Ann Pellegrini, eds., *Queer Theory and the Jewish Question* (New York: Columbia

University Press, 2003); Jonathan C. Friedman, *Rainbow Jews: Jewish and Gay Identity in the Performing Arts* (Lanham, MD: Lexington Books, 2007); and Warren Hoffman, *The Passing Game: Queering Jewish American Culture* (Syracuse, NY: Syracuse University Press, 2009). See also José Esteban Muñoz's discussion of the Yiddish poem in *Carmelita Tropicana* in his *Disidentifications: Queers of Color and the Performance of Politics* (Minneapolis: University of Minnesota Press, 1999), 123–24.

12. On the place of Jewish studies in ethnic studies, see Daniel Boyarin and Jonathan Boyarin, "Introduction: So What's New?," in *Jews and Other Differences: The New Jewish Cultural Studies*, ed. Jonathan Boyarin and Daniel Boyarin (Minneapolis: University of Minnesota Press, 1997); Jennifer Glaser, "Race, Ethnicity, Postcoloniality, and the New Jewish (Trans)cultural Studies," *Literature Compass* 10, no. 3 (2013): 217–23; and essays in "Finding Home: The Future of Jewish American Literary Study," ed. Lori Harrison-Kahan and Josh Lambert, special issue, *MELUS: Multi-Ethnic Literature of the U.S.* 37, no. 2 (2012).

13. See especially Susan A. Glenn, "In the Blood? Consent, Descent, and the Ironies of Jewish Identity," *Jewish Social Studies* 8, no. 2 (2002): 139–52.

14. Karen Brodkin, *How Jews Became White Folks and What That Says about Race in America* (New Brunswick, NJ: Rutgers University Press, 1998); Matthew Frye Jacobson, *Whiteness of a Different Color: European Immigrants and the Alchemy of Race* (Cambridge, MA: Harvard University Press, 1998); and Matthew Frye Jacobson, *Roots Too: White Ethnic Revival in Post–Civil Rights America* (Cambridge, MA: Harvard University Press, 2006).

15. Erving Goffman, *Stigma: Notes on the Management of Spoiled Identity* (Englewood Cliffs, NJ: Prentice Hall, 1963), 113–14. See also Erving Goffman, *The Presentation of Self in Everyday Life* (Garden City, NY: Doubleday, 1959).

16. Susan Sontag, "Notes on 'Camp,'" in *Against Interpretation and Other Essays* (New York: Farrar, Straus and Giroux, 1966), 290. Originally published in *Partisan Review* 31, no. 4 (1964): 515–30. As Robin Bernstein has pointed out to me, Sontag's bifurcation of Jewish and homosexual patterns of integration also represses the existence of Jewish homosexuals.

17. Jay Wallace, "Some of My Best Friends Are Jews . . . ," *ONE*, June 1960, 23–26.

18. Franklin Kameny to John Macy Jr., Civil Service Commission Chairman, June 5, 1961, in *Gay Is Good: The Life and Letters of Gay Rights Pioneer Franklin Kameny*, ed. Michael G. Long (Syracuse, NY: Syracuse University Press 2014), 38. See also, for example, Leo Ebreo, "A Homosexual Ghetto?," *Ladder*, December 1965, 4–8; and Franklin Kameny, "Gay Is Good" (1969), in *We Are Everywhere: A Historical Sourcebook of Gay and Lesbian Politics*, ed. Mark Blasius and Shane Phelan (New York: Routledge, 1997), 366–76.

19. See Lila Corwin Berman's discussion of ethnicity and sociology in *Speaking of Jews: Rabbis, Intellectuals, and the Creation of an American Public Identity* (Berkeley: University of California Press, 2009).

20. On the history of the term *assimilation*, see Russell A. Kazal, "Revisiting Assimilation: The Rise, Fall, and Reappraisal of a Concept in American Ethnic History," *American Historical Review* 100, no. 2 (1995): 437–71. On marriage, heteronormativity, and assimilation, see Michael Warner, *The Trouble with Normal: Sex, Politics, and the Ethics of Queer Life* (New York: Free Press, 1999). See also George Chauncey's discussion of the uses of the term *assimilation* in discussions of same-sex marriage in *Why Marriage? The History Shaping Today's Debate over Gay Equality* (New York: Basic Books, 2004), 122.

21. Jerome Robbins, Barry Primus, Leonard Frey, and J. A. Preston, "Questionnaire Discussion, Part I," February 17, 1968, video recording, Jerome Robbins Collection, New York Public Library for the Performing Arts.

22. Frey did not appear in the earlier Playwrights Unit workshop production, in January 1968, at the Vandam Street Theater in the West Village. See production history in David Allison Crespy, *Richard Barr: The Playwright's Producer* (Carbondale: Southern Illinois University Press, 2013), 151–56.

23. Sally Frey, phone interview by the author, April 14, 2015. For more on Frey's upbringing, see Carol Kramer, "Wry Frey Answers Unasked Questions," *Chicago Tribune*, June 21, 1970; and Johna Blinn, "Leonard Frey's Specialty Is Scotch Eggs," *Atlanta Constitution*, June 4, 1970.

24. *Sense and Nonsense*, episode, 1954, WABD, digitized at https://archive.org/details/senseandnonsense1954 (accessed October 6, 2015).

25. Kramer, "Wry Frey."

26. Frey to Robbins, October 15, 1963, box 5, folder 6, item 334, Jerome Robbins Papers, (S)*MGZMD 130, Jerome Robbins Dance Division, New York Public Library for the Performing Arts.

27. "Fiddler on the Roof: Opening Night Cast," Playbill.com, www.playbill.com/show/detail/cast/6051/fiddler-on-the-roof-at-imperial-theatre (accessed October 6, 2015).

28. Vincent Canby, "Screen: 'Boys in the Band,'" *New York Times*, March 18, 1970.

29. Hollis Alpert, "Harold's Birthday," *Saturday Review*, April 4, 1970, 24.

30. Peter Ogren, "The Bores in the Band," *Gay*, January 4, 1971, 17.

31. Mart Crowley, phone interview by the author, June 4, 2015.

32. For example, see handwritten letter from Jeffrey to Crowley, June 12–13, 1966, from the Westbury in London, box 65, folder 4 (Jeffrey, Howard. 1961–1984/undated), Mart Crowley Papers (Collection PASC 318), UCLA Library Special Collections, Charles E. Young Research Library, UCLA.

33. Jeffrey to Crowley, July 21, 1966, part 3, ibid.
34. "New Plays: The Boys in the Band," *Time*, April 26, 1968, 113.
35. Jack Star, "The Faces of the Boys in the Band," *Look*, December 2, 1969, 63.
36. On the discourse of authenticity in gay liberation, see for example Jeffrey Escoffier, *American Homo: Community and Perversity* (Berkeley: University of California Press, 1998), 15–18, 124–27.
37. On the shifting meaning of "coming out," see John D'Emilio, *Sexual Politics, Sexual Communities: The Making of a Homosexual Minority in the United States, 1940-1970*, 2nd ed. (Chicago: University of Chicago Press, 1998), 235–36; and George Chauncey, *Gay New York: Gender, Urban Culture, and the Making of the Gay Male World, 1890-1940* (New York: Basic Books, 1994), 6–8.
38. Gershon Legman, "The Language of Homosexuality: An American Glossary," in *Sex Variants*, by George W. Henry (New York: Paul B. Hoeber, 1941), vol. 2, appendix 6, 1149–79; Donald Webster Cory and John P. LeRoy, *The Homosexual and His Society: A View from Within* (New York: Citadel, 1963), 262.
39. Carl Wittman, "A Gay Manifesto," in *Out of the Closets: Voices of Gay Liberation*, ed. Karla Jay and Allen Young (1972; repr., New York: Pyramid Books, 1974), 334. Originally appeared as "Refugees from Amerika: A Gay Manifesto," *San Francisco Free Press*, December 22, 1969–January 7, 1970.
40. Craig Zadan, "Leonard Frey: Just One of the 'Boys,'" *After Dark*, February 1970, 26.
41. Star, "Faces of the Boys in the Band," 62–68. Photographs by Irving Penn.
42. Judy Klemesrud, "You Don't Have to Be One to Play One," *New York Times*, September 29, 1968; "The Man from 'The Boys in the Band,'" *Life*, May 8, 1970, 49–50.
43. Marjory Adams, "Happily Chose Stage over Art: Actor Frey Never Needs Job," *Boston Globe*, March 23, 1971.
44. On camp humor and cooking, see Stephen Vider, "'Oh Hell, May, Why Don't You People Have a Cookbook?': Camp Humor and Gay Domesticity," *American Quarterly* 65, no. 4 (2013): 877–904.
45. Zadan, "Leonard Frey," 26.
46. Kurt Lassen, "Young Actor Feels Type Cast," *Times Recorder* (Zanesville, OH), June 15, 1970.
47. Julie Baumgold, "Strike Up the Band, BOYS," *Women's Wear Daily*, May 9, 1968, 4.
48. Kramer, "Wry Frey."
49. Michael Bronski, "Leonard Frey, 1938-1988: An Appreciation," *Gay Community News*, September 4, 1988, 6.
50. Sally Frey, phone interview.

51. Charlie Frey, phone interview by the author, April 14, 2015, and email correspondence, September 7, 2015.

52. Bronski, "Leonard Frey."

53. Edward S. Shapiro, *A Time for Healing: American Jewry since World War II* (Baltimore: Johns Hopkins University Press, 1992).

54. Will Herberg, *Protestant, Catholic, Jew: An Essay in American Religious Sociology* (Garden City, NY: Anchor Books, 1960).

55. Herbert J. Gans, "Park Forest: Birth of a Jewish Community: A Documentary," *Commentary*, April 1951, 330–39.

56. Philip Roth, "Eli, the Fanatic," in *Goodbye, Columbus and Five Short Stories* (Boston: Houghton Mifflin, 1959), 247–98.

57. Stanley Edgar Hyman, "The Two Worlds of David Daiches," *Commentary*, November 1956, 456.

58. On early Jewish dialect humor, see Ted Merwin, *In Their Own Image: New York Jews in Jazz Age Popular Culture* (New Brunswick, NJ: Rutgers University Press, 2006).

59. Kaufman, *Jewhooing the Sixties*, 41–43, 99–155; Joyce Antler, *You Never Call! You Never Write! A History of the Jewish Mother* (New York: Oxford University Press, 2007), 101–47.

60. Philip Roth, "Writing about Jews," *Commentary*, December 1963, 452.

61. Michael E. Staub, *Torn at the Roots: The Crisis of Jewish Liberalism in Postwar America* (New York: Columbia University Press, 2002), 1–4.

62. A. Bruce Goldman to the *Columbia Owl*, April 23, 1969, quoted in Nat Hentoff, "The Warm-Up," *Village Voice*, May 22, 1969.

63. Crowley, phone interview.

64. Mart Crowley, *The Boys in the Band* (New York: Farrar, Straus and Giroux, 1968), 7, 77.

65. On conceptions of Jewish effeminacy, weakness, and illness in nineteenth- and early twentieth-century Europe and Max Nordau's call for "muscular Judaism," see Sander L. Gilman, "Jewish Madness and Gender," in *Freud, Race, and Gender* (Princeton, NJ: Princeton University Press, 1995), 93–168, especially 105–6; and Sander L. Gilman, "Otto Weininger and Sigmund Freud: Race and Gender in the Shaping of Psychoanalysis," in *Jews and Gender: Responses to Otto Weininger*, ed. Nancy Anne Harrowitz and Barbara Hyams (Philadelphia: Temple University Press, 1995), 103–20. On Jewishness, "muscle Jews," and the Six-Day War, see Eric J. Sundquist, *Strangers in the Land: Blacks, Jews, Post-Holocaust America* (Cambridge, MA: Harvard University Press, 2008), 319–22.

66. Philip Roth, *Portnoy's Complaint* (New York: Random House, 1969), 125. See also discussion of the novel in Hoffman, *Passing Game*, 106–23.

67. Crowley, *Boys in the Band*, 99.

68. Undated handwritten letter, beginning, "I really feel terrible and I apologize," box 65, folder 4, Mart Crowley Papers. A more standard transliteration today would be *shpatzirn*.

69. Undated poem, box 65, folder 4, Mart Crowley Papers. Crowley told me the poem was likely from 1966. Email correspondence with the author, September 8, 2015.

70. Jeffrey references his cat Schwartz ("I know he sends his Uncle Mart all his love") in an undated typed letter beginning, "I can't type at all," box 65, folder 4, Mart Crowley Papers.

71. *Fiddler on the Roof*, directed by Norman Jewison (2011), DVD.

72. J. Hoberman, "The Goulden Age," *Village Voice*, April 10, 2007.

73. Jane Biberman, "Leonard Frey on His Trip—Yugoslavia Mud to the Rivoli," *Jewish Exponent*, February 18, 1972; Michael Elkin, "Frey: Well 'Armed' Actor: On the Scene," *Jewish Exponent*, November 24, 1978.

74. Marsha Richman and Katie O'Donnell, *The Shikse's Guide to Jewish Men* (New York: Bantam, 1978), v.

75. Kramer, "Wry Frey."

76. Norton Mockridge, "New York Scene: Must Be the Play's the Thing," *Springfield (MA) Union*, April 30, 1970. As Kauffman notes, Streisand began talking about her refusal to get a nose job as early as 1964 (*Jewhooing the Sixties*, 219–22).

77. Adams, "Happily Chose Stage."

78. Ibid.

# QUEER-POLITICAL CRISES

# 8

## "Beware the Hostile Fag"

### Acidic Intimacies and Gay Male Consciousness-Raising in *The Boys in the Band*

**RAMZI FAWAZ**

> Speak Pains to Recall Pains
>     —the Chinese Revolution
> Tell It Like It Is
>     —the Black Revolution
> Bitch, Sisters, Bitch
>     —the Final Revolution
>         —New York Radical Women
>           meeting poster composed
>           by Kathie Sarachild (1968)

> I need to be together with other gay men. We have not been together—we've not had enough self respect for that.... We need to recognize one another wherever we are, start talking to each other.... We need consciousness-raising groups and communes. Our gay souls have nearly been stomped to death in that desert called America. If we are to bloom, we can only do it together.
>         —Gary Alinder, "My Gay Soul" (1970)

In November 1968, Kathie Sarachild, a founding member of the Redstockings, an early collective of the women's liberation movement, presented an outline for a new form of feminist political practice at the first national Women's Liberation Conference. She dubbed this practice "consciousness-raising" or "CR." Consciousness-raising was a collective practice of publicly speaking personal truth to uncover shared experiences of patriarchal oppression. In Sarachild's words, CR required women to meet in "rap groups" or "bitch sessions," in which they would "recall and share [their] bitter experiences" of sexism.[1] In making those recollections public, consciousness-raising would create a space for "evaluating [women's] feelings" and provide the context for "cross-examination," in which women could interrogate and formulate judgments about their relationship to structures of gendered oppression.[2] Such a practice, it was theorized, would link the personal with the political in the most systematic and immediately visceral way, encouraging women "to look for explanations for each part of [their] history in terms of the social or cultural dynamic created by sexism—rather than in terms of the personal dynamic."[3] Having recently made the radical political decision to cut ties with the New Left and the liberal wing of the National Organization for Women, leaders of women's liberation were keen to develop a mode of internal critique that could provide women with tools to make many more such decisions for their political freedom.[4]

In April 1968, six months before Sarachild's speech, Mart Crowley's explosive play *The Boys in the Band* appeared Off Broadway. Without precedent, the play depicted a group of gay men engaged in a series of fiery debates about the nature of gay desire, identity, and social life that unfold across a single evening at a birthday party gone awry. At a "smartly appointed duplex apartment in the East Fifties" of Midtown Manhattan, a diverse circle of eight gay men—among them a bookstore clerk, a fashion photographer, a public school teacher, and a luxury antiques dealer—convene to celebrate the birthday of their mutual friend Harold.[5] When Alan, a homophobic former college roommate of the host, Michael, crashes the party, his presence brings repressed tensions among the group to the surface. These tensions overwhelm the party atmosphere, resulting in a series of painful revelations about the men's internalized self-hatred, experiences of unrequited love and sexual shame, and their individual forms of resistance to a homophobic society. If Sarachild's speech articulated the form and content of a developing practice of feminist consciousness-raising rooted in collective public dialogues, *The Boys in the Band* appeared to enact an early version of this practice directly in front of theater audiences by presenting one of the longest and most searing public "bitch sessions" ever performed on the American stage.

Just as feminist consciousness-raising centralized the importance of *group process* in the form of a women's conversation circle as a generative site for "pooling" experiences of sexism, the second half of *The Boys in the Band* similarly presents a group of gay men arranged in a circle, passionately sharing experiences of homophobia; whereas feminist consciousness-raising underscored the value of women's feelings as a source of knowledge that might allow them to speak truth to power, so too the members of this gay male group are driven by feelings of rage, bitterness, and sadness to rail against homophobia's power to constrain their social existence; and finally, whereas one of feminist consciousness-raising's central goals was the production of *concepts* for analyzing the logics of male domination that underwrote women's lives, in the bitchy and hilarious witticisms that the gay male characters of *The Boys in the Band* sling at one another and at the heterosexual world that shuns them, they articulate concepts they have developed to identify and frustrate the homophobic logics that underwrote *their* lives.[6]

With the 1970 film adaptation of Crowley's play, *The Boys in the Band* became not only the first explicitly gay movie distributed to a mass audience but also arguably the only Hollywood film to visually represent and model consciousness-raising as it was taken up and adapted by different publics, including urban gay men. By March 1970, the month of the film's release, CR had been a staple of radical feminist practice for more than sixteen months, while CR practices had been introduced to the Gay Liberation Front, the vanguard organization of the gay liberation movement, by the Redstockings member Karla Jay in November of the previous year.[7] When Jay and coeditor Allen Young published *Out of the Closets: Voices of Gay Liberation*, the first U.S. anthology of LGBT political writing, in January 1972, the collection included A Gay Male Group's "Notes on Gay Male Consciousness-Raising," an adaptation of Sarachild's CR program for gay men that, according to the writing of other contributors, was indicative of the forms of CR gay men had been engaging since 1970.[8] If the 1968 theatrical version of *The Boys in the Band* appeared to presage or anticipate the moment of consciousness-raising's ascendancy in feminist practice, the 1970 film appeared on the other side of CR's full institution in both feminist and gay liberationist circles. Far from being out-of-date by the time of its release, the film adaptation of *The Boys in the Band* made its debut at exactly the moment when feminist and gay consciousness-raising began to diffuse into the wider culture; in this context, the film accrued a host of new meanings beyond its theatrical version, now not only depicting the seeming fractiousness of gay men as a group but also documenting gay men's heart-wrenching emotional labor to negotiate newly "liberated" identities and social worlds *despite* the homophobic logics that continued to plague their lives.

This chapter reinterprets the film adaptation of *The Boys in the Band* as a text that indexes the early adoption of radical feminist political practices within the gay male social culture of the late 1960s and early 1970s. In the "truth game" the men play in the film's second half, the characters are positioned in a circle, while engaging in a protracted "bitch session" in which they "recall and share [their] bitter experiences" of unrequited love. These recollections of trauma around same-sex desire, homophobia, and their social consequences enable both the characters in the film and its viewers to take into account a broader range of gay male experience than either institutional homophobia or internalized self-hatred allow for, thereby enacting feminist consciousness-raising's stated conceptual goal of "building a collage of similar experiences ... by pooling description of the forms oppression has taken in each individual's life."[9] In the movie, this practice of "pooling" multiple, often incommensurate lived experiences or perspectives on the world—what the political theorist Hannah Arendt identifies as the foundation of "enlarged" or "representative thinking"—involves members of the group verbally relating their distinctive stories but also the plot's canny visual movement between them, so that we "see" each character both figuratively and literally in a way that provides a kaleidoscopic view of gay male lived experience.[10] It is from this position of "enlarged thinking" that the men inch toward a new set of standards for making critical judgments, ones that equip them to better understand their social and psychic location in an emergent and diverse gay male social culture. The struggle to arrive at those standards is the film's version of consciousness-raising, for it both results in the characters' uneven movement to new locations in relation to their experiences of homophobia (and their responses to it) and the potential solicitation of viewers to formulate their own judgments not only about each character and their conflicted interactions but also about the broader social consequences of homophobia and sexism, that is, to "form an opinion ... by taking account of other views."[11]

This process is depicted in the movie as emotionally (and sometimes physically) violent and extraordinarily intellectually demanding; the breathless pace of barbed speech in the narrative suggests the level of cognitive and verbal skill required to navigate the complexities of gay male affective bonds, variously organized around feelings of smugness and superiority, loneliness and intense desire for community, and love tempered by insecurity and self-doubt. Yet the film's version of CR—impassioned, angry, unpredictable, and uncensored—revealed some of the unexpected volatility that this practice could unleash (a volatility feminists often assumed they could control through the elaborated rules set forth by the Redstockings' original CR manifesto).[12] *The Boys in the Band* underscored the necessity of formulating an equally powerful practice of *critical judgment* within *all* forms of social interaction—not merely the aspects of one's life amenable to politicization—where critical judgment is understood as the ability to distinguish claims motivated by insecurity, unrequited desire, or misdirected blame from claims that accurately identify social injustice. The film allows us to see how political forms like the feminist consciousness-raising program and its imagined circle of interlocutors could provide a powerful analogy for lived social forms like the gay male friendship circle; in turn, the movie's ability to use film form to visualize such overlaps allows it to function as a potential cultural transmitter of consciousness-raising in both its structure and its values. My contention is that this practice, as the film presents it, empowers its participants to develop more effective judgments of one another *and* the systems of power that oppress them, consequently strengthening social bonds between queers, women, and sexual and gender outlaws—bonds that became newly imaginable at the very historical moment when members of the women's and gay liberation movements were abandoning the known worlds of sexism, homophobia, and self-hatred, in search of an uncharted territory of freedom, sexual liberation, and rich sociality.

## Acidic Intimacies

*The Boys in the Band* has been lambasted by critics for its judgmental, bitchy tone and for the vitriol that the characters, particularly Michael, spew at their supposed friends and intimates. As William Scroggie recounts, "In 1971, gay liberationist Dennis Altman called *The Boys in the Band* 'Crowley's portrait of unredeemed misery,'" and "another gay liberationist, Peter Fisher . . . wrote '*The Boys in the Band* . . . presents a stereotypical picture of unhappy people unable to come to terms with themselves.'"[13] The by-now-clichéd criticisms of the film's negativity fail to explain the conceptual power of the movie on three fronts. First, by focusing on the alienation such hostility among the guests implies about late 1960s gay male experience, critics ignore the powerful *intimacy* that underlies the conflicted engagements depicted in the movie. Despite the frustrations the men express about their social and sexual lives, *The Boys in the Band* is a showcase in *acidic intimacies*, or painful but deep-rooted social bonds, rather than an exposé on gay male anomie. These intimacies are *acidic* in the sense that they register the bitterness or sting of bonds cemented through shared knowledge of another gay man's insecurities, manipulations, and character flaws. Early in the film, Michael tries to align himself with Alan's genteel values by piously claiming to his friend and former lover Donald, "Believe it or not, there was a time in my life when I didn't go around *announcing* I was a faggot.... I didn't come out until after college," to which Donald retorts, "It seems to me that the first time we tricked we met in a gay bar on Third Avenue during your *junior* year." "Cunt," Michael responds with a sarcastic smile. These instances of barbed retort, dotting the entire narrative, display the double-edge of shared lived experiences that also make all parties vulnerable to being called out for self-deception and evasion.

Second, critics' condemnation of the film's depiction of regressive gay male stereotypes willfully subordinates both the formal structure of the narrative and the social scene into which the characters are placed, in favor of reading the film as a decontextualized depiction of rigid character types. Across the film, we witness or hear about numerous forms of gay male sociality. In the film's opening sequence, following a kaleidoscopic montage of the characters, the movie displays a panorama of a gay bar packed with men

*Life* portrays the dark interior of a gay leather bar in 1964.

*The Boys in the Band* depicts the lively, upbeat social life of a New York gay bar in 1970.

socializing. This long shot provides visual evidence of a vibrant and diverse gay male social culture in late-1960s and early-1970s New York City. The scene visually echoes and contradicts the famed 1964 *Life* magazine photo spread "Homosexuality in America," which opens with a foreboding image of the darkened interior of a gay leather bar with a group of shadowed faces amid the crowd of "deviants." A far cry from this "sad and sordid world," the bar in *The Boys in the Band* is brightly lit and overflowing with smiling, laughing faces, a site of convivial flirtation.[14]

In the same opening sequence, we see men cruise each other, while throughout the film we hear conversation detailing the social conventions of gay bathhouses, reminiscences about the communal experience of Fire Island, furtive visits to gay bars with closeted college chums, the circulation of shared cultural references between gay friends (from Bette Davis to Tennessee Williams), and globe-trotting sexual adventures; these experiences indicate the expansive range of gay male sociality across differences of race, class, and sexual and cultural taste, rather than isolation or homogeneity. Moreover, the intimacies between the characters are strikingly heterogeneous: we see gay best friends (Michael and Harold), ex-lovers (Michael and Donald), former college roommates (Michael and Alan), former tricks (Donald and Larry), the polyamorous couple and the ménage à trois (Larry and Hank), and of course, the loosely knitted, but surprisingly intimate, gay friendship circle itself. Even as each of these forms of sociality potentially presents a categorical "type" of interaction that has stereotypical features—the stranger sociality of gay men who trick together like Donald and

Larry or the performative intensity of the effeminate "screaming queen" like Emory—the particular ways each character inhabits these types in relation to others become the basis for the film's depiction of a crisis in judgment. In essence, the film asks, how does one form objective opinions, and make definitive claims, about a way of life that has become so extraordinarily expansive, so irreducibly particular, so distinctly diverse?

*The Boys in the Band* responds to this question through a relentlessly dialogic narrative: put simply, the narrative is driven by ceaseless, rapid-fire talk, producing a ballistic experience of constant call and response, witticism and reply, argument and rebuttal. The hatefulness and ridicule expressed by characters are feelings performed in the company of others and felicitous of response in fierce interaction. Acidic speech is repeatedly named as such—as when Harold describes Michael's barbs as "hateful"—and those who speak it are called out for their actions. Some, like Michael, exhibit an almost manic drive *to be held accountable by others*—that is, confronted and forced to respond to criticisms of one's actions—which is understood as a potentially therapeutic outcome of being fairly judged. Michael plays his level of hostility toward the group to Harold's absolute limit, attacking his friend so relentlessly (even after Harold warns, "I know this game you're playing. . . . I can beat you at it. So don't push me.") that it is as though he unconsciously seeks to elicit a response that would refuse, and thereby provide insight about, his bitterness.

No guest leaves Michael's apartment until the very end of their "hostile" dialogue, committing to the psychic and social consequences that might unfold from their sparring. Equally crucial, upon evening's end, Harold's parting words to Michael are "Call you tomorrow," while Donald affirms he will be back next Saturday to "spend the night." Despite what Harold calls the "fervor with which [Michael] annihilate[s]," Michael's antagonism toward his company is strangely *productive* of their social bonds. By the closing shot, we know more about each character, they know more about one another, and they have explained themselves and their experiences with greater depth than ever before; yet knowledge of Alan's "true" sexuality, of whether the evening's events will alter his homophobic views, or whether the men will leave politically enlightened remains open. In this way, the film embraces the power of dialogic engagement in the form of consciousness-raising but presses back against the radical feminist assumption that the political consequences of such a practice could or should be predictably coordinated as a linear movement to political enlightenment.

Third, and finally, critics' willful overlooking of the film's social dimensions has led to a related failure to account for its rebellious, anti-homophobic spirit. In the characters' bombastic refusal to accept the specter of homophobic judgment (either in external sources like the heterosexual superiority of Alan or internal ones like Michael's disgust at his friends' flamboyance), they embody the spirit of radical feminist and gay liberationist politics *affectively*. My reading of the film takes seriously the idea, central to feminist and gay CR, that gay men's *feelings* about their oppression might function as a source of political knowledge; the film argues that we might learn something fundamental about how homophobia functions from these angry "screaming queens" precisely *because* they are willing to scream about its painful consequences. In 1968, Sarachild wrote, "We're saying that when [women] had hysterical fits, when we took things 'too' personally, that we weren't underneath our feelings, but responding with our feelings correctly to a given situation of injustice."[15] Echoing this logic, A Gay Male Group's "Notes on Gay Male Consciousness-Raising" opens by acknowledging that "*Gay males feel pain.*"[16] Both statements recognize that one's emotional responses to sexism and homophobia, rather than being personal or indulgent, are legitimate evidence of the unjust workings of patriarchal power. The text's willingness to represent painful feelings onstage and on-screen has led many critics and viewers to dismiss *The Boys in the Band* as depicting the worst aspects of gay male identity and experience; yet this interpretation colludes with a homophobic and sexist logic that views intense emotionality as immature, denigrating the possibility that negative emotions might be an acute register of homophobic injustice and, consequently, a rebellious act against it.

Consider a scene near the conclusion of the film: after various members of the group have narrated stories of unrequited love, Michael confronts Alan about his cruel shunning of their mutual college friend Justin, a gay man with whom Alan was purportedly in a romantic friendship but whom he cut off when Justin verbalized his gay desires. Michael rages, "You ended the friendship, Alan, because you couldn't face the truth about yourself. You could go along, sleeping with Justin, as long as he lied to himself and you lied to yourself and you both dated girls and labeled yourselves men and called yourselves just fond friends. But Justin finally had to be honest.... You couldn't take it and so you destroyed the friendship.... [To] this day he still remembers the treatment—the scars he got from you.... Call him and apologize." This moment is easily dismissed because of the questionable motives behind Michael's demand and the potential misfire of his assumption that Alan is gay; yet, in the context of gay liberation's bold refusal of "marriage, family, and home that our society holds up as normal," what could possibly be more rebellious than a gay man demanding accountability from a straight man for his homophobic violence against another gay man?[17] Like Sarachild's injunction for women to see their feelings as a guide to a theory of their oppression, Michael takes Justin's emotional "scars" as a legitimate register of homophobic injustice; those scars offer Michael an opening to theorize and call out the heterosexist logics that allow Alan to "label himself a man" and take advantage of the privileges that that identity entails.

This bold representation and legitimation of gay men's feelings was enabled by consciousness-raising practices in both women's and gay liberation that embraced the value of cross-examination, allowed participants to develop a voice within a collectively organized political practice, and worked to deconstruct resistances to consciousness-raising, which, according to the original feminist CR program, included "false identification with the oppressor," "rugged individualism," and "excusing the oppressor."[18] Yet *The Boys in the Band*'s conceptual innovation of feminist CR was to refuse the feminist premise that consciousness-raising must take place in a nonjudgmental space; it understood that for sexism and homophobia to be appropriately judged, those who might best be equipped to lob such a critique would need to work through their own conflicted judgments about themselves and one another. Perhaps most daringly, the film catalyzes this necessary but difficult struggle by materializing the force of homophobia in an actual figure, Michael's former college roommate Alan. Whereas feminist CR imagined patriarchy as an abstracted oppressor a given group would identify, analyze, and finally take action against from an initial location of relative psychic safety, in *The Boys in the Band*, homophobia is embodied in a person who aggressively inhabits the space of the gay gathering, demanding not merely abstract analysis but substantive response in the form of critical judgments about the men's relationships to homophobic privilege and power.

## Performing Judgment

*The Boys in the Band* is a relentlessly judgmental text. From one perspective, the characters' negative exposures of one another's personal failures and inadequacies are directly opposed to the founding feminist CR principle of nonjudgmentalness. As Pamela Allen explained in her description of CR group process in 1969, what is important "is the fact that someone listens and does not ridicule. . . . Unless women are given a non-judgmental space in which to express themselves, we will never have the strength or the perception to deal with the ambivalences which are a part of us all."[19] In *The Boys in the Band*, the men's judgmentalness and ridiculing of one another, the domination of the conversation by a single member of the group (Michael), the use (and abuse) of alcohol and other mood-altering substances, and the interruptions of one another's testimony are all elements that undermine the value of nonjudgment in a "safe" space. Moreover, the baldly misogynistic language used by many of the characters—including such sexist terms as "slut," "cunt," and "bitch"—alongside the deep phobia of effeminacy that Alan, Michael, and Hank exhibit, might seem to immediately undercut the film's performance of feminist practices and ideals. Yet such qualities uncomfortably, but frankly, register the lingering power of internalized homophobia among gay men—captured in the fear of being seen as "incomplete" or "womanly" men—while also suggesting the repurposing and reuse of sexist terms as part of the playful, bitchy, acidic intimacies developed within gay male social life. From this perspective, the stated commitment to nonjudgmentalness in feminist CR implied a naively utopian wish that group process might uncover an essentially conflict-free female experience for women to draw on in achieving their political goals, downplaying the fact that women themselves might also feel the lingering pull of patriarchal demands to uphold true femininity or might simply feel rage, meanness, or insecurity toward other women.

Unsurprisingly, testimonies from practitioners of feminist and gay CR in this period reveal that the lived experience of CR groups rarely achieved their lofty ideals of nonjudgmentalness, often exposing complex emotional conflicts and underscoring deep inequalities between participants. Describing one of the Redstockings' first CR meetings, Karla Jay recounts Kathie Sarachild's overzealous interruptions and judgments of participants' testimony as undermining Sarachild's own CR program injunction to *listen to other women*; in an account of gay male CR practices in the first gay men's living collective in New York City in 1971, John Knoebel explains how jealousies, unacknowledged racism and classism, and conflicting political commitments led to the breakdown of the collective's social bonds despite their consistent engagement in CR group process; and, perhaps most movingly, in a description of participating in a six-month-long CR group in New York City, June Arnold documents an epiphanic moment when disagreements about each woman's view of her sex life led some members to exclaim jubilantly, "'I guess we're not going to get to any conclusions from this session—we're all saying completely different things!' 'Beautiful! Maybe that's what liberation really is.'"[20] These testimonies show how CR unleashed unexpected and messy conflicts in the attempted movement between the personal and the political for women and gay men alike. Feminist CR's negative stance toward *judgmentalness* had the downside of potentially silencing the socially and politically necessary act of *judging*, that is, forming an opinion about and developing substantive responses to an object of collective concern. Consequently, the negative and conflicted aspects of the men's dialogue in *The Boys in the Band* encourage viewers to develop their own critical faculty of judgment, in order to parse different forms of criticism precisely, from the most personal character assassinations to the most generative rebuttals of entrenched thinking.

The film produces a distinction between the cultivated practice of gay male *judgmentalness* (or "bitchiness"), on the one hand, and the faculty of *critical judgment*, on the other. Yet it does not place these categories in a developmental narrative, in which an individual evolves out of the former into a mature, "adult" capacity for objective judgment. Rather, *The Boys in the Band* acknowledges the conceptual power of both judgmentalness *and* judgment in gay male social life, while stressing the importance of *distinguishing* them. In the narrative, judgmentalness ironically functions as a form of gay male community building: it is a highly developed code of verbal sparring that requires common cultural references and the recognition of others' personal characters. When deployed outside the gay male collective, judgmentalness is a useful weapon against homophobia, a cultivated condescension toward straight culture and its banal, normalizing force; within the gay male social milieu, it often functions as a loving form of social antagonism among friends that implies an intimate "knowingness" of one another's flaws. This is exhibited in A Gay Male Group's "Notes on Gay Male Consciousness-Raising," whose lengthy catalog of different forms of "resisting consciousness" (more numerous and specific than those named in Sarachild's original program) admitted a willingness to lodge judgments against gay men's cultivated habits of evasion, including "continual use of drugs and drink during meetings" (think Michael), "coming late to meetings or missing them with no excuse" (think Harold), and "not revealing physical attractions" (think Donald).[21] There is something undeniably bitchy about this catalog of *resisting consciousness* that suggests an insider's knowing side-eye to often unaccounted-for gay male bad behavior; *The Boys in the Band* takes this willingness to express judgmentalness to the extreme, making *accountability*, rather than nonjudgmentalness, its central value.

Early in the film, as Michael readies for his guests, he asks Donald, "What are you so depressed about? Other than the usual *everything*, I mean?" When Donald refuses to answer, Michael sarcastically replies, "Well, if you're not going to tell me, how can we have a conversation *in depth*—a warm, rewarding, meaningful friendship?" Michael bitchily calls out Donald's melancholic tendencies, while couching his barb in genuine care for his friend's anxieties. Even as he pokes fun at social "depth" amid the pervasive superficiality of gay social culture, he lovingly elicits the emotional confession he denigrates: Donald finally divulges his struggles over his gay identity and its potential rootedness in parental disappointment and "a neurotic compulsion not to succeed." Donald's miming of the clichéd narrative of abnormal childhood development, supported by his psychologist (and by a homophobic American culture), enables Michael to subject this story to critique: "Christ, how sick analysts must get of hearing how Mommy and Daddy made their darlin' into a fairy." The exchange presents gay male judgmentalness as an alternative value system that cannily sees behind and deconstructs the clichés of pathologizing definitions of gay male identity, consequently producing more humane intimacies between gay men (while brilliantly turning the accusation of homosexuality's "sickness" back onto the psychotherapists who enforce these stories).

If gay male judgmentalness can produce alternative intimacies outside the gaze of societal and clinical homophobia, *critical judgment* serves as a tool for holding other gay men accountable for their speech and actions. Critical judgment involves the capacity to take in multiple viewpoints on the same circumstances in order to form substantive opinions about them that have qualitative weight—that is, not simply pointing out inadequacies or problems but suggesting what should be done about them.[22] Critical judgment then, is about the production of normative standards of social conduct. If bitchiness brings gay men together, critical judgment allows them to stand apart, to call one another out, to hold others accountable. According to *The Boys in the Band*, both are crucial to the maintenance of heterogeneous community; it is their confusion, or the inability to distinguish between them, the film suggests, that is *destructive* of collective life.

The movie's array of characters presents viewers with a range of perspectives from which to look on the evening's events, yet the film frames this larger set of outlooks within three primary *models* for judging the content of the party, embodied by its three central characters. In the naïve all-American blueblood Alan, the cynical yet emotionally vulnerable Michael, and the self-effacing Harold, the film presents distinct models of judgment that take different founding criteria and have varied consequences for queer social life. These models can be understood respectively as the ideological, the ambivalent, and the judicious. The film typologically reduces each character to these frameworks but sets them in dynamic interaction, with explosive and unpredictable results.

The film presents Alan, Michael's former college roommate and a Washington, DC, patrician, as an allegorical figure for societal homophobia. His judgment against homosexuality precedes his physical presence at the gay male gathering. When Michael explains to Donald his squeamishness about introducing Alan to a group of "screaming queens," he explains that Alan and his "social type" have "certain standards" that "we have to acknowledge." Those standards are aligned with normative heterosexuality, proper gender performance, and discretion regarding sexual impropriety; as Alan later explains to Michael, "I couldn't care less what people do—as long as they don't do it in public—or—try to force their ways on the whole damned world." In his view, "the whole damned world" is a normatively heterosexual one, and the performance of nontraditional masculinity or same-sex desire constitutes that norm's forceful violation.

Alan, then, represents a judgment informed by the belief in universally shared (heterosexual) standards by which all external realities can be measured; these "standards" are so pervasive that, as Michael's declaration confirms, "*we* have to acknowledge them." It is no surprise that Alan experiences a visceral revulsion at Emory's exaggerated femininity, privately explaining to Michael with barely restrained disgust, "he just seems like such a goddamn pansy." The rage that Alan directs at Emory is an outcome of Emory's daring *refusal* to acknowledge the universal value of Alan's heterosexual masculine privilege. Alan repeatedly invokes the universality of his position when he entreats Michael with the phrase "you know" to indicate their presumed shared values regarding the public, flamboyant sexuality Emory represents: "Oh come on man, *you know* me—*you know* how I feel—your private life is your affair" (my italics). Invoking a transparent understanding between "men," Alan rhetorically constitutes the universality of his position by presuming similitude of feelings across personalities and social positions. Though Michael initially presents Alan's position as understandable, even justifiable by certain social standards, their private conversation unhinges his initial alignment with homophobic propriety. Against Alan's repeated invocations of the commonly known and universally shared positions he holds, Michael engages in an act of cross-examination—a central practice of feminist consciousness-raising—that reorients the assumed universality of Alan's worldview toward the *particularity* of his social position. In response to Alan's assumption that Michael knows his viewpoint, Michael coldly replies, "No, I didn't know that about you," and demands to know, "Why are you here?" and "What were you crying about on the telephone?" These requests reduce Alan to the specificity of his own actions.

In Michael's cross-examination, he exhibits a second form of judgment best described as ambivalent. Michael is undoubtedly the most judgmental character in *The Boys in the Band*, bringing down world-rending condemnations against every party guest, including himself. Yet Michael's claims flicker between a biting moralism, exhibited in his bitchy *judgmentalness*, and a righteous quest for justice, exhibited in his *critical judgment* of homophobia. These positions compete as contradictory motives animating Michael's speech and action and are embodied in his concept of "The Christ-was-I-drunk-last-night syndrome." He explains the phrase: "You know, when you made it with some guy in school, and the next day when you faced each other there was always a lot of crap about 'Man, was I drunk last night! Christ, I don't remember a thing!'" Michael uses this phrase to indicate both an immature form of self-loathing instilled in gay men about their sexual desires—one that requires them to pretend that sexual liaisons had never happened—and the lies that straight men use to deny their sexual activities with other men. The phrase captures the element of CR group process that Pamela Allen called "analyzing," in which CR participants respond to their aggregated experiences of sexism by developing concepts that describe and illuminate the social conditions of women's oppression.[23] Yet whereas feminist CR imagined a pure progression from sharing experiences to conceptual analysis that always landed on the side of women as an oppressed class, Michael's concepts for identifying homophobic lies are ambivalently produced in the thick of living life as a gay man in uneven relationship to others who share his sexual identity. A concept like "The Christ-was-I-drunk-last-night syndrome" is ambivalent in the sense that it reveals feelings of bitterness toward *both* the privilege of heteronormative ideology *and* the hypocritical self-deceptions of gay men. Michael seems intent on overcoming his ambivalence by analyzing all parties with concepts he believes will reveal their "true" selves beneath the lies they tell themselves.

Michael's obsessive pursuit of "the facts" in all things leads him to assume that certain truths—for instance, Alan's potential homosexuality—merely need to be uncovered through forceful revelation. This zealous truth seeking reveals Michael's continued commitment to universal values, though perhaps reconstituted ones organized less by heterosexism (like Alan's) than by gay moralism. In one instance, Michael harangues Harold about his self-torturing beauty regimen: "Standing before a bathroom mirror for hours and hours before you can walk out on the street. And looking no different after Christ knows how many . . . ointments and creams. . . . Yes, you've got scars on your face—but they're not that bad and if you'd leave yourself alone you wouldn't have any more than you've already awarded yourself." Michael's ambivalence is apparent in his simultaneous judgmentalness toward his friend's unhealthy vanity and his critical judgment of the pernicious cultural beauty standards that constrain gay men. It is the increasing *inability* to distinguish between these positions—brought on, in part, by the contradictory demands of a homophobic society—that marks Michael as a "hostile fag"; rather than villainize that hostility, *The Boys in the Band* presents it as a dynamic force that can potentially bring into being new forms of consciousness.

Michael's ambivalence is on the cusp of the revolutionary. Throughout the evening, Harold comically calls Michael's frenzied attacks a form of "turning," a figurative centripetal revolution producing enough dynamic tension to spin outward yet remaining tightly coiled; moreover, throughout the first half of the movie, Michael is repeatedly filmed standing before a wall on his patio chalked with the words "Summer 1968," referencing the year of the New Left's political implosion and fracturing into a new spate of radical movements. Michael's figurative "turning" presents him as poised to jettison one set of pernicious universal values but unable to imagine what the world might look like devoid of another set of shared values decoupled from gay moralism (hence his investment in the Catholic church, what Harold calls his "insurance policy" against life's unpredictability). Harold at one point flatly states, "Michael, . . . you don't know what side of the fence you're on. If somebody says something pro-religion, you're against them. If somebody denies God, you're against *them*. One might say you have a problem in that area."

Harold breaks the deadlock of the "problem" of judgment that Michael's ambivalence and Alan's universalism produce. Irreverent and self-deprecating, Harold has no time for truths that do not help a life flourish. His battles with self-hatred have literally scarred him, and his response to both self-inflicted and societally imposed mutilation is, quite literally, to *laugh*. Harold enters the narrative immediately after Alan's violent assault on Emory midway through the party, walking in on a spectacle of

Summer of 1968.

homophobic rage. Instead of reacting negatively to the events, he calmly reads Emory's birthday card—a bitchy injunction to "roll over and play dead" (read: be "banged" by the cowboy hustler whom Emory has purchased as his gift)—and explodes into raucous laughter that undercuts the gravity of Alan's actions. When Michael scolds Harold, "What's so fucking funny?" Harold retorts, "Life. Life's a goddam laugh-riot. You remember life." Harold's willingness to laugh at even the most bitter aspects of gay experience indicates his openness to being amused by "life" and its over-the-top ridiculousness, while also functioning as a critical weapon that equalizes the playing field between gay and straight. By hyperbolically vocalizing his immense pleasure at Emory's gift, an offering that would traditionally be deemed distasteful in more "straight" settings, Harold values Emory's gay sensibilities while debasing Alan's out-of-control behavior, which appears embarrassingly out of step with gay male conviviality and playfulness. Unlike Alan and Michael, Harold is eminently self-critical and disparages the value of exposure, recognizing the social limitations of acts of cruel revelation. When Michael lobs his acidic criticism of Harold's beauty regimen, Harold replies, "You'd really like me to compliment you now, for being so honest, wouldn't you? . . . Slut." In an act of counter-exposure, Harold reveals the ruse of a certain kind of "truth telling" that speaks in the name of authenticity and justice but is in fact self-serving.

Unlike Michael, whose single conceptual move is to expose, Harold wields a form of *judicious* critical judgment that *discerns* between which truths should remain private and which deserve public airing. Harold's discernment is evident in his investment in maintaining a realm of private intimacy among friends, which is the foundation for love in the face of fierce criticism. When Larry asks Harold to tell the group what Michael has engraved on his birthday gift (a photograph of Michael in a silver frame), Harold holds back: "Just . . . something personal." Despite all that Michael has done to air Harold's dirty laundry, Harold remains committed to distinguishing between those known intimacies that need to be made public and those that should be held close to the heart. Harold is never framed as inherently morally superior to Michael. As Harold points out, he and Michael "are a match" because of how well they "play each other's game." Rather, the film suggests that Harold's judicious attitude toward *this* particular evening's events is a consequence of his position relative to Michael's emotional implosion—that is, Harold's capacity for judiciousness emerges *in the context of* a dialogic and combative evening of social engagement. The film argues that judiciousness might be one radical consequence of being forced to take into account multiple viewpoints, which Harold is able to do only by witnessing recognizable aspects of his own identity inhabited and performed by others. In light of the perspective this view affords, it is unsurprising that, when Michael finally holds Alan accountable for his actions by demanding he stay for the truth game, Harold says, "Revolution complete." What Harold initially considers Michael's ceaseless, insular "turning" becomes a revolution both figurative and literal—an act of rebellion against Alan indicating Michael's momentary but decisive jettisoning of his ambivalence—that Harold's judicious viewpoint can discern. The moment signals the completion of a *conceptual* circle of thought that in turn produces the *actual* circle that organizes the game the men play.

## "Revolution Complete"

If Alan, Michael, and Harold embody various models of judgment, the truth game that unfolds over the second half of the film sets them in motion by borrowing a dynamic political form, the consciousness-raising circle. Michael sets up a game in which each group member must call the person he has loved most and confess his love to them; each participant is judged by a scoring system that distributes points based on how close he comes to revealing his true feelings to the object of his love. Though the game seems organized around the mere admission of love, it results in various group members explaining the contexts in which a specific love came into being and the social constraints that prevented its fulfillment. The game's coercive aspect unwittingly produces the conditions under which gay men's feelings are treated as a source of "truth" about lived social relations. Yet this reality is infused with Michael's ambivalence. On the one hand, by publicizing the repeatedly failed trajectory of same-sex desire, Michael seeks to ridicule his friends' naïve hopes for sentimental love in the face of societal homophobia. On the other, by legitimizing the concrete *fact* of gay love, he appears intent on eliciting from Alan a dual confession of closeted homosexuality *and* of repressed love for Justin. Following a classical model of feminist CR, Michael seems to imagine that the game can produce such a powerful sense of universally shared experience of gay male shame that its force will make visible and destroy Alan's hetero-patriarchal edifice. Yet the necessarily dialogic nature of the game Michael sets up means that he is unable to predict the content, delivery, or outcome of the stories that are told in the circle; consequently, the game ends up exposing the truth of gay male *heterogeneity*, rather than essential identity, while also acknowledging the complex and uneven effects of societal homophobia.

This expansive view of gay male heterogeneity models a form of "enlarged thinking" that can respond to conflicted circumstances *in the absence of* universal standards for adjudication. This notion of "enlarged" or "representative thinking" is captured by Arendt when she explains that critical judgment requires that "I form an opinion by considering a given issue from different viewpoints, by making present to my mind the standpoints of those who are absent; that is, I represent them. . . . The more people's standpoints I have present in my mind while I am pondering a given issue, . . . the stronger will be my capacity for representative thinking and the more valid my final conclusions, my opinion."[24] In the truth game's multiplicitous view of who gay men are and how their experiences and desires might alter what counts as "normal," it becomes a living rebuttal to Alan's universalism. It transforms consciousness-raising from a practice striving toward unity into a process that demands substantive responses to heterogeneity, which, according to writers like Jay, Arnold, and Vivian Gornick, was often what the *lived* experience of CR practice was felt to be. Gornick describes the experience: "Coming together, as they do, week after week for many months, the women who are 'in a group' begin to exchange an extraordinary sense of multiple identification. . . . Thus looking at one's history and experience in consciousness-raising sessions is rather like shaking a kaleidoscope and watching all the same pieces rearrange themselves into an altogether other picture [that makes] each piece appear . . . full of unexpected meaning."[25]

This cultivation of "multiple identification" is powerfully captured in the tortured exchange between Larry and Hank, in which they overturn numerous expectations about monogamy, proper masculinity, and intimacy. Larry and Hank are the only romantic couple in the group. As handsome, gainfully employed gay men, they seem to embody an ideal of romantic fulfillment that many of the group members long for. Yet from the moment Hank and Larry are introduced in the movie's opening sequence, their relationship is depicted as strained by jealousies and miscommunication (we first see them together when an irritated Hank shoves his way through a crowded gay bar to pull Larry away from his flirtations). When Michael demands that the two take their turn in the game, they are forced to articulate dramatically different, and potentially incommensurate, outlooks on companionate love.

Hank is attached to monogamy and marriage as expressions of committed love, while Larry believes in polyamory as a release valve that allows long-term relationships to work by granting partners the freedom to explore their sexual relations with others. Rather than opposing these views to each other, the narrative contextualizes each. The script suggests that Hank's attachment to monogamy may be the outcome of multiple circumstances: his insecurities entering a sexually promiscuous gay male social world after living most of his life as a monogamously partnered straight man; his nostalgic memories of marriage; or perhaps simply habit. Alternatively, Larry explains his desire for polyamory as both an expression of his natural sex drive and an extension of his social life among gay men, an alternative site of personal fulfillment from marriage. What is required is not relinquishing either position but the ability to see from each other's perspective to develop substantive responses to different contexts for inhabiting gay desire.

The scene of Hank and Larry's argument accomplishes three key conceptual movements that characterize the truth game more broadly. First, it exposes significant differences among the group members, in this instance differences about what a proper romantic relationship looks like for gay men but in other interactions differences in responses to homophobia, in approaches to racial sensitivity, and in class background. Second, the game publicizes homophobic conditions that prevent the expression of same-sex love. Alan's universal standards of judgment are potentially undone by the collective stories told but especially by Hank's narrative. When Alan vehemently refuses to acknowledge the reality of Hank's homosexuality, calling it "disgusting" and referring to heterosexual affairs as "normal," Hank replies, "It just doesn't always work out that way, Alan." The mere statement that things "don't always work out" in the way of a universally presumed heterosexuality baldly refutes Alan's illusions not only of Hank but of normative heterosexuality as well: to see an effeminate man like Emory claim gay identity is no surprise, but Hank poses an impossible paradox, namely, that a man who appears just like the upright, heterosexual Alan could be gay.

Moreover, the film visually holds characters like Alan to account for their homophobic reactions by relentlessly tracking their expressions of anguish, confusion, and disgust when they seek to disengage from difficult conversations about same-sex desire. In the exchange between Hank and Alan about Hank's homosexuality, Alan abruptly turns away from Hank when Hank admits, "I left my wife for Larry." As Alan turns, he states, "I'm really not interested in hearing about it," to which Michael responds, "Sure you are. Go ahead, Hankela, tell him all about it." When these two lines are spoken, the camera follows Alan's downturned and distressed face but keeps Hank and Michael in view behind him, both refusing to allow him to disconnect from the conversation. This camera work—in which characters' facial expressions and the interlocutors who have elicited them are held together on-screen—doubly formalizes the dialogic work of consciousness-raising that the game is analogous to, not only holding the characters visually accountable to the unfolding dialogue but also reminding viewers that they too are potential participants in the circle.

Finally, the game allows for internal critique among the gay male members of the group, both creating the space for telling stories and allowing each member to hold others accountable for *how* they tell their stories. When Hank tells his sad tale of a failed marriage and a life upended by coming out, Larry refuses Hank's sentimental self-portrait: "Why am I always the goddamned villain in the piece?! If I'm not thought of as a happy-home wrecker, I'm an impossible son of a bitch to live with! . . . It's my right to lead my sex life without answering to anybody. . . . Numerous relations is a part of who I am!" In this powerful moment, Larry refuses the normalizing narrative that reduces gay male promiscuity to a destructive force, instead telling a different story about sexual freedom as an embodied way of relating to others that exceeds any given sexual orientation.

Harold, despite recusing himself from the game, is the character who appears most often in the background of scenes throughout its unfolding. Harold's distanced on-screen presence—underscored by his literal seat outside the circle—alongside his handful of comic interjections to the men's stories, signals his mediated engagement in the game, rather than his complete removal from it. As the political theorist Linda Zerilli states, drawing on Arendt, "Judging involves neither becoming identical with you, nor . . . with myself, but 'thinking in my own identity where actually I am not.' . . . Outsideness suggests that we understand and judge from a position that is neither identical nor incommensurable but . . . at once separate from and related to that which we judge."[26] Harold's decision to position himself in such a way that he is like the participants (a gay man) but unlike them (a nonplayer) is exactly what allows him to absorb the multiple viewpoints articulated throughout the evening and formulate a judgment on the basis of those views, rather than any universally predetermined set of values. As a result of staking out this position, by evening's end, Harold confidently "takes his turn" at the game and renders the following judgment on Michael, one that responds to Michael's violent exposure of other characters' inadequacies but also binds him and the other members of the gay male circle together collectively: "Now it's my turn, Michael. And ready or not, here goes. You're a sad and pathetic man. You're a homosexual and you don't want to be. But there is nothing you can do to change it. Not all your prayers to your God, not all the analysis you can buy in all the years you've got left to live. You may very well one day be able to know a heterosexual life if you want it desperately enough—if you pursue it with the fervor with which you annihilate—but you will always be homosexual as well. Always, Michael. Always. Until the day you die." In this breathtaking speech, Harold delivers a critical judgment born from his careful viewing of the night's events and his willingness to inhabit an "insider-outsider" position that allows him a more impartial, but not fully deracinated, view of the scene. He is keen to make public the shared condition of internalized homophobia that can motivate "hateful" speech like Michael's, while deploying that exposure not to humiliate or destroy but to hold another accountable *and* to reaffirm that other's social belonging. In reminding Michael that he will always be a homosexual, Harold counters Michael's ambivalent desire to belong, but *not* to a category so denigrated and despised as homosexuality. In doing so, Harold is naming Michael "one of us," reminding him that no matter what source he seeks out to define his condition—God or psychotherapist—he will always be part of the circle he has shamed.

At the moment when Harold begins this speech, Michael, in utter abjection after his failed attempt to out Alan, has literally turned away from the scene of emotional carnage he has orchestrated. Once again, the camera refuses to allow Michael his disengaged solitude. We follow Harold's gaze as he walks across the room to confront his friend, until he stands directly beside Michael, speaking at the side of his face. Finally, in the film's most intimate shot, Harold delivers the last two lines of his speech in a tight close-up, Michael's profile silhouetted against Harold's visage. The dramatic image of Michael's profile bisecting Harold's face figuratively suggests the overlapping nature of their psyches, while also distinguishing them, since their actual profiles face different directions. This double movement of comparison and distinction, the oscillation that defines representative thinking, is underscored by the fact that the close-up highlights Harold's pockmarked cheek. This visual feature reminds us of the physical scars that *his* self-hatred have wrought. He and Michael are indeed similar, but the circumstances of the evening, which allowed Harold to step out of his insider position, have also made it possible for him to exercise his newly raised consciousness by making an informed judgment that creates distance for the sake of holding another accountable but simultaneously reasserts the continuity of gay community *amid* difference and disagreement. Hence, even in the "face" of Michael and Harold's clash, Harold's parting words are, "Call you tomorrow." What the content of that conversation might be remains entirely open to possibility.

This chapter has sought to make two claims about *The Boys in the Band* and its continued relevance to the study of gay and feminist social formations

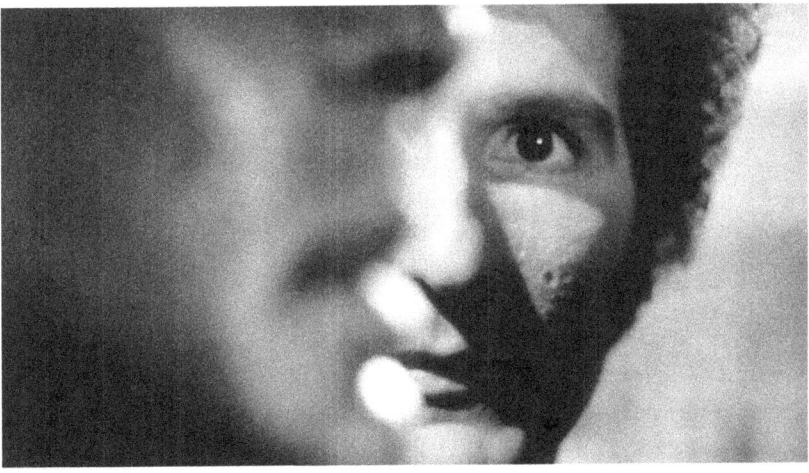

Harold's judgment.

in the twenty-first century. First, *The Boys in the Band*'s depiction of furious collective dialogue between gay men offers one avenue for exploring the rich connections between the social and political conflicts that animated women's and gay liberation: the gay male friendship circle takes the form of a consciousness-raising group; the men's shame about their homosexuality is framed in terms of their failures to live up to traditional gender roles and beauty standards; the hateful speech that dominates the conversation echoes the personal attacks that Jo Freeman would call "trashing" within the women's movement;[27] and the forms of evasion and refusal to account for one's actions that each character enacts echo the forms of "resisting consciousness" that Sarachild detailed in her "Program for Feminist 'Consciousness Raising.'" These and countless other links suggest the need to develop a stronger account of the complex interaction between the social and political valences of women's and gay liberation, one attentive to the role of *culture* as a site where the political innovations of these movements were expressed in creative terms. Reading the film as a formal embodiment of feminist CR practice illuminates how cultural forms might function to transmit *and* test the conceptual limits of political forms by placing them into new and unexpected contexts and imagining a wider range of publics for their use.

Second, in an era when gay male social formations have attained unprecedented political, economic, and cultural power in the modern United States with no formal ties to feminist politics, *The Boys in the Band* remains one of the most compelling refusals of affirmative gay identity politics in twenty-first-century popular culture. Notwithstanding the undeniable continued power of homophobia and the religious right's bolstering of antigay legislation, legal victories for same-sex marriage, the repeal of "Don't Ask, Don't Tell," and gay men's explosive visibility and active participation in the production of American media content have lifted this social group's status to new heights. Out of these perhaps-limited successes, urban gay male culture has jettisoned previous commitments to self-criticism grounded in a feminist political practice of consciousness-raising.

Here I speak as a participant-observer more than a scholar, taking the injunction of feminist CR practice to treat feelings as knowledge by relying on my felt experience of navigating gay male social culture. From this viewpoint, I suggest speculatively that in the wake of increasing public acceptance and accessibility to the privileges of normative American society, middle-class urban gay men have found numerous ways of courting validation from inside and outside their community, responding to decades of homophobia with an ecstatic show of capacity: the ability to maintain beautiful bodies and exceptional creative careers and to flexibly manage the celebrated institutions of marriage, child rearing, and home ownership, *as well as* open relationships, circuit parties, and gay cruises, all the while exhibiting no anger or frustration in the face of societal homophobia. Gay men's feelings, which in the context of gay liberation and AIDS activism were valued for their ability to register the pain and violence of homophobia, are increasingly valued only if they embody the range of *positive* affects that come with demanding and achieving successful middle-class life or mastering the range of sexual liaisons and pleasures that come with having access to money, men, and travel. We may now express indignation only at the denial of civil liberties, while genuine anger or frustration directed toward other gay men for their attachment to pernicious politics and a broader culture of homophobic and racist violence can only be understood as bitterness (i.e., those who rage are simply losers who did not get their share) rather than as a productive registering of inequalities that can and should be addressed.

Perhaps the most powerful way in which such feelings have been made illegitimate is by the deeroticization of anger and rebellion among gay men: it is no longer sexy to dissent, to disagree, to demand something politically from one's interlocutors as it was at the height of gay liberation and AIDS activism, and this seems apparent in everything from the condemnation one might receive for critiquing the narrow political achievement of gay marriage to a simple disagreement of how one chooses to interpret a movie. While writing this chapter I accidentally ran into a man at a San Francisco café who had previously pursued me energetically on an online sex and dating application; when he learned I was revising a chapter on *The Boys in the Band*, he expressed his disdain for the movie's depiction of the most stereotypical aspects of gay male bitchery. Internally I bristled at this clichéd critique—and smelled the whiff of not a little internalized homophobia at his hyperbolic miming of the characters' effeminate affect. But he was cute, and I wanted to know more. I explained my sense of the movie's depiction of rebellious gay men as a powerful political claim, its consciousness-raising, and its critical camp irony as being courageous. He pointed out that camp irony was *not sexy*—it was not possible, that is, to see the men in the movie as sexually desirable because of their flamboyant excess. We concluded our conversation on a friendly note, yet this man who had consistently sought me out for two weeks online never reached out to me again during my travels. The possible reasons for this are, of course, infinite. But questions lingered: Did associating myself with the loud, rebellious, and demanding spirit of this movie desexualize me? Had I bruised his ego by disagreeing with his interpretation of the film, and did a bruised ego mean instantaneous loss of sexual interest? Surely, chemistry alone might have dictated the outcome; but I could not shake the feeling that the contentious experience of disagreeing, even on something as simple as a movie's content, had marked me as "difficult," and hence unsexy—*difficult* in the way the men of *The Boys in the Band* are difficult, and hence dangerous. I wondered if the contemporary meaning of male homosexuality has become a "desire for the same" not only in terms of the presumed gender of one's sexual object-choice but also in terms of political values, so that gay male erotic life requires mind-numbing similitude across every scale of embodied and political life to remain secure in its sexual identity. I wondered too how substantial gay men's participation in the future of American democratic life could be, if gay male culture's litmus test for the social and political significance and legibility of any subject is how erotically desirable he is: in other words, what does it mean to extend care, investment, significance in anyone and anything you do not want to fuck? But these were lofty wonderings. I kept mulling, I met another handsome man for dinner, and then I rewatched *The Boys in the Band*.

Nearly half a century since the cinematic release of *The Boys in the Band*, it continues to provide a compelling alternative to the culture of gay male affirmation; it is, in a sense, a radically "new" narrative in the context of contemporary gay identity politics because it validates those worldviews and feeling states most commonly seen as antithetical to gay upward mobility, social advancement, and affirmation, such as negativity, bitterness, anger, depression, self-loathing, confusion, ambivalence, and frustration. In so doing, it rethinks the rhetorical framework within which critiques of affirmative gay culture and its heteronormative assumptions can only ever be read in the idiom of resentment or failure to live up to the promise of a fully assimilated gay life. The film embraces the *generative* aspects of bitterness, its ability to lay bare formerly suppressed emotions and the unfairness of gay life. It also suggests that other emotions and affective investments might be involved in a critique of gay male culture, including a demand for accountability, ethical standards of conduct, and collective care. Above all, *The Boys in the Band* demands *engagement*. It refuses to dissociate love from critique, intimacy from accountability, and collective life from fractious disagreement. It demands that we keep speaking to one another, keep turning toward each other, until our revolution is complete.

## Notes

The New York Radical Women meeting poster is quoted in Carol Hanisch, "A Women's Liberation Tribute to William Hinton and the Women of Long Bow," speech delivered April 3, 1999, www.carolhanisch.org/Speeches/Hinton Speech/HintonTribSpeech.html; Gary Alinder, "My Gay Soul" (1970), in *Out of the Closets: Voices of Gay Liberation*, ed. Karla Jay and Allen Young (1972; repr., New York: NYU Press, 1992), 283.

1. Kathie Sarachild, "A Program for Feminist 'Consciousness Raising,'" in *Notes from the Second Year: Women's Liberation: Major Writings of the Radical Feminists*, ed. New York Radical Women (New York: Radical Feminism, 1970), 78.

2. Ibid., 79.

3. Vivian Gornick, "Consciousness," in *Radical Feminism: A Documentary Reader*, ed. Barbara Crow (1971; repr., New York: NYU Press, 2000), 288.

4. Deborah Michals, "From 'Consciousness Expansion' to 'Consciousness Raising': Feminism and the Countercultural Politics of the Self," in *Imagine Nation: The American Counterculture of the 1960s and '70s*, ed. Peter Braunstein and Michael William Doyle (New York: Routledge, 2001), 41–68.

5. Mart Crowley, *The Boys in the Band*, 40th anniversary ed. (New York: Alyson Books, 2008), 3. All subsequent citations from the original theatrical production and the film adaptation are, respectively, from this edition of the play and from *The Boys in the Band* (1970), directed by William Friedkin (Paramount Studios, 2008), DVD.

6. Sarachild, "Program," 78–79; Karla Jay, *Tales of the Lavender Menace: A Memoir of Liberation* (New York: Basic Books, 2000), 51; and Pamela Allen, "The Small Group Process," in Crow, *Radical Feminism*, 280–81.

7. Jay, *Lavender Menace*, 94–95; Dennis Altman, *Homosexual: Oppression and Liberation* (1972; repr., St. Lucia, Australia: University of Queensland Press, 2012), 146–49.

8. A Gay Male Group, "Notes on Gay Male Consciousness Raising," in Jay and Young, *Out of the Closets*, 293–301.

9. Allen, "Small Group Process," 279.

10. Hannah Arendt, *Between Past and Future* (1954; repr., New York: Penguin, 2006), 221.

11. Linda Zerilli, "Towards a Feminist Theory of Judgment," *Signs* 34, no. 2 (2009): 18.

12. Jay, *Lavender Menace*, 62.

13. William Scroggie, "Producing Identity: From *The Boys in the Band* to Gay Liberation," in *The Queer Sixties*, ed. Patricia Juliana Smith (London: Routledge, 1999), 238.

14. Paul Welch, "Homosexuality in America," *Life*, June 26, 1964, 66.
15. Sarachild, "Program," 78.
16. A Gay Male Group, "Notes," 293.
17. Altman, *Homosexual*, 25.
18. Sarachild, "Program," 79.
19. Allen, "Small Group Process," 278.

20. Jay, *Lavender Menace*, 52; John Knoebel, "Somewhere in the Right Direction: Testimony of My Experience in a Gay Male Living Collective," in Jay and Young, *Out of the Closets*, 314–15; June Arnold, "Consciousness-Raising," in Crow, *Radical Feminism*, 285.

21. A Gay Male Group, "Notes," 298–99. Sarachild's original "Program" listed only eleven "classic forms of resisting consciousness," by comparison to a Gay Male Group's twenty-point list (which included extensive subentries for four items). Sarachild's list tended to be general, addressing not specific behaviors but broad worldviews or habits of thought including "Anti-womanism," "False identification with the oppressor," and "Self-blame!" (79).

22. Zerilli, "Towards a Feminist Theory," 14.
23. Allen, "Small Group Process," 280–81.
24. Arendt, *Between Past and Future*, 237.
25. Gornick, "Consciousness," 288.
26. Zerilli, "Judgment," 20.
27. Jo Freeman, "Trashing: The Dark Side of Sisterhood," *Ms.*, April 1976, 49–51, 92–98.

# 9

## "A Credit to the Homosexual"

### The Boys in the Band and the Appearances of Queer Debt

**MATTHEW TINKCOM**

What are the operations necessary to deploy male-male desire as the glue rather than as the solvent of a hierarchical male disciplinary order?
—Eve Kosofsky Sedgwick, *Epistemology of the Closet*

To talk or to hear others talk of philosophy always gives me the greatest pleasure, to say nothing of the profit. On the other hand, when I hear certain other kinds of talk, especially for example, that of you rich people and businessmen, I am profoundly depressed, and I pity you who are my companions because you think that you are doing something when in reality you are doing nothing. I imagine that you pity me in return, and think me an unhappy creature, and very probably you think right. But, you see, I *know* of you what you only *think* of me—there is the difference.
—Apollodorus in Plato's *Symposium*

The specter of the commodity—its required labors, its forms of exchange, its hold on the fetishistic imagination—haunts *The Boys in the Band* just as it haunts the queer cultures of the past four decades since Mart Crowley's stage play was adapted for film by the director William Friedkin. In that measure of things, we might look to the film to discover the manner in which it articulates queer affect—both in terms of pleasure and in terms of shame—as it is imbricated with the economic dimensions of the lives of the film's characters. The answer to Eve Sedgwick's question about the operations necessary to hold male-male desire together as the glue of a male hierarchical order can be seen as the operations of labor, consumption, debt, and spending alongside the practices and ideations of sexuality. Sedgwick posed her question for the purpose of understanding how the homophobic imaginary customarily provides the context for modern homophilic expression, and in that regard my reading of her words as an entrée into making sense of *The Boys in the Band* is ironic; in my discussion of the film here, I invert the more typical interpretation of *The Boys in the Band* as the vexed expression of a nascent queer culture emerging in the public culture of cinema, and instead I interpret the film's deployment of economic terms to express a different love that cannot speak its name: the love of clothing, alcohol, food, cigarettes, marijuana, books. Put another way, *The Boys in the Band* signals the ability of queer male desire to appear through a coming-out but not solely that of the male sexual subject; in addition, it is the coming out of the material and economic conditions of these particular queer men's lives: the film displays the emergence of the affective economics of queer male desire in the particular historical moment in which the film debuted. The tropes of appearances—of closets, of coming out—give a new weight to *The Boys in the Band* because of its depictions of male homosexuality and consumerism: little of the former and a lot of the latter. Rather than insist on the untenable separation of these two aspects of queer life, though, we should consider how they are bound up one with the other and how one of the most powerful closets in this narrative is the one that the economic aspect of queer life inhabits.

In this chapter, I argue that *The Boys in the Band* needs to be understood within the dialectic of sexuality and capital, where each of those aspects of contemporary life serves to define the other, and this dialectic plays out in the film's narrative through the reified products that circulate through the film's mise-en-scène. Further, the film's organizing idea of the closet—the metaphor of queer subjectivity in which the secret of the subject's desire is revealed by acts of unclosetting—pertains equally to the status of such reified commodities as it does to the economic lives of the film's queer characters. The central figures of Harold and Michael play this out through the manner in which each man discusses the decisions he makes about his physical appearance as it is shaped by his work, income, debt, and consumption. The film's depiction of various reified goods—especially in the giving of gifts—allows us to understand the subtle and varied meanings of such reifications, the related practice of fetishization, and, ultimately, the central contradiction of reification: it allows the alienating commodity to have reign over the consumer's life, through both psychic investment and monetary debt, *and* it makes possible the manner in which the reified commodity provides the opportunity for new—dare we say it, liberatory—possibilities of social bonds through the commodity's reinvention.

## Not Cashmere but Vicuna: The Closet and Reification

One of the most significant differences between Crowley's stage play and Friedkin's adaptation is the film's addition of an opening sequence that orients the spectator within the world in which the film's narrative takes place, late-1960s Manhattan. The opening shot of the film locates that world in more constrained fashion to a specific locale: the bathroom. Here, the camera pans across a sink cluttered with the working tools of the labor of appearance—soaps, lotions, a tube of toothpaste, nail clippers, a spray bottle—and we discover not the Club Baths of anonymous sexual encounters with others (about which jokes will be made later in the film) but a bath with the different erotic charge of self-regard and self-invention. The opening shot's mobile framing across the debris of the toilette concludes by tilting up to reveal, within the reflection of the bathroom mirror, the body of a man—presumably, we subsequently discern, Harold—as he bathes while the other characters, soon to be discovered in the montage of their daily lives in New York, move across the streets and shops of Manhattan.

The masturbatory possibilities of Harold's bath are held off-screen, and in this regard the film's opening gesture underscores one of the film's most famous jokes (made by Michael: "Well, there's one thing to be said for masturbation: you certainly don't have to look your best"). Looking your best and the best kinds of looking (i.e., what the spectator performs) are conjoined in this image through the disclosure of the most intimate bodily act that the film offers (Harold stroking his soapsudsed feet together in languor), and the association of sexuality and consumption inaugurates the film's queer male metropolitan habitus. *The Boys in the Band* opens by displaying bodily homoerotic depictions in terms of consumption, because Harold's closet is occupied only by himself and his consumer goods. The "coming out" gesture in this first moment of the film, then, is not that of any character—the spectator cannot on first viewing know that this is any specific figure within the film—but the emergence of the commodity and its reification and fetishization within queer life. Furthermore, the closet here is a mess—it is dirty, cluttered, overly full, and despite the subsequent disclosure within the narrative of Harold's interest in his appearance, the closet he shares with all his beauty products is squalid.

I here introduce the critical concept of reification for making sense of all the products—including those in Harold's bathroom—that will appear within *The Boys in the Band*. *Reification* means the process in which a thought is rendered into an object, and the source term in German, *verdinglichung*, is translated variously as "objectification," "concretization," or, most commonly, "reification." For an idea to be reified, it needs to take shape in the world in the materiality of things—that is, it needs to be manufactured—and the shape it takes is a result of social relations among humans. This latter aspect of the concept allows us to understand that no idea can be reified unless it is shared among those who produce it as well as among those who are affected by it. This might seem counterintuitive in that we are tempted to think that the object comes first and then its mental associations are built on it; reification, however, suggests otherwise: that the inaugurating thought of a product (for it is in the products of the capitalist economy that most reification occurs) is both determinative and yet only partial—partial because what the consumer does with the product (including what she or he thinks about it) reshapes its meanings in the specific setting of the consuming subject's daily life.

By way of example, we might think of Michael's invocation of the consumer brand—here, the French marketing name of Hermès—as the reification of a certain set of ideas about, in no particular order of priority, France, luxury, comfort, exclusion, and so on. If we ask ourselves what this particular brand reifies within the queer context of *The Boys in the Band*, we begin to see that the object of the sweater contains within it both more general ideas about what a brand name summons in the mind of the consumer and the specific ideas that the thing conveys for particular subjects. Thus, Hermès means the comparatively rare commodity accessible, by dint of expense, to fewer consumers and thus heralds the idea of social status as social exclusion. Michael's discarding the Hermès sweater on the floor (about which more will be said in a moment) suggests, in the terms that he and Donald share, that the commodity here is acknowledged as one of prestige and exclusion—that the commodity here is acknowledged as one consumption not accessible to all—as well as something that he himself can scorn. This ambivalent status of the branded product—its being desirable and yet also being rejected—encapsulates the experiences of being queer men that Michael and Donald describe in this particular scene.[1]

Understood as the transformation of human social relations into a particular idea about a given commodity—or, more bluntly, endowing the commodity with the human traits of its subject—reification demands that we scrutinize the objects of consumption to observe how they express the social relations that have given rise to such commodities and, in turn, those social relations that commodities facilitate. The figurative power of the queer closet helps to reveal two secrets about the commodity: first, that the commodity does indeed crystallize fantasies about it and, second, that it in fact possesses no such capacity inherently—it is, after all, the object of which the subject insists on maintaining that fantasy. In the first, the consumer would have the commodity be the occasion in which to realize his or her utopian fantasies of individual fulfillment and social solidarity, while in the second, it turns out that no product can bear such ideological weight: the commodity always eventually disappoints because the inflated promises of its gratifications dissipate all too quickly. In this regard, the first (partial) glimpse of Harold in the opening shot depicts the closet-of-the-commodity out of which he will emerge at the party, and this image contrasts with the subsequent title shots of the various partygoers as they migrate to the birthday celebration from their daily lives. Michael shops for the party, Emory closes the boutique in which he works and then shops for Harold's gift, Donald exchanges his borrowed books from Bernard at the shop where Bernard works, and unifying these depictions is the commerce of daily life—all the while that the primping use of the beauty products in Harold's bath forms the terminus of the commodity and its next dialectical moment of coming out within the domain of queer life. For all the sense of the *business* of the images that open the film, Harold's closeting of his commodities and himself defines the larger logic of the film and combines queer lives with consumption and debt. In a positive register, we should note, the reified commodities of Harold's bath hold out the possibility of the queer subject who attempts to fetishize the commodity around an idea of self-determination.

The theme of the bathroom-as-closet—of people and of commodity fetishes—develops immediately in the film when, after the title sequence, the film's first scene repeats the imagery of Harold's bathroom.[2] The scene begins with Michael giving to Donald his own shopping bag of beauty supplies, including a can of hairspray with the brand name Control, which, as Michael rightly notes, has been deracinated from any association with femininity; he remarks that "the words 'For Men' are written about thirty-seven times all over the goddamn can!" and Donald retorts that this product should be called "Butch Assurance." The closet of the bath functions as the place where the coming-out—of queer consumers and queer commodities—begins with dual assurance of nonfemininity/effeminacy and hypermasculinity. Significant about this exchange is the sense that the commodity is itself gendered and, as Donald's comment indicates, is anxious about its gender; the repeated declamation that the product Control is for men crystallizes the manner in which the product expresses the concerns of the consumer more fully than he himself might, and it does so through an assurance: the male consumer who uses Control will maintain control—not only over his hair but over the entire social field in which he appears.

In the subsequent exchange between Michael and Donald, we discover how their biographies and psychologies are captured and played out within the material conditions of their lives, and this takes the form of a conversation that the larger culture sedulously avoids: the intimate discourse between friends about money, debt, and their related forms of affect (here, regret and longing). Donald narrates the sense of his life's failure as made possible by the vicissitudes of family—namely, his parents—and that he now has to "work [his] ass off for forty-five lousy dollars a week scrubbing floors."[3] In response, Michael seeks to console by complaining of the dissatisfaction he feels with his own circumstances, whereupon Donald suggests that Michael's life appears as a success in that "it takes a certain flair to squander one's unemployment check at Pavillon." The dialogue then takes up the question of how one might be an exemplary kind of queer man:

> MICHAEL: What's so snappy about being head over heels in debt? The only thing smart about it is the ingenious ways I dodge the bill collectors.
> DONALD: Come to think of it, you're the type that gives faggots a bad name.
> MICHAEL: And you, Donald, you are a credit to the homosexual. A reliable, hard-working, floor-scrubbing, bill-paying fag who don't owe nothin' to nobody.
> DONALD: I am a model fairy.
> MICHAEL: You think it's just nifty how I've always flitted from Beverly Hills to Rome to Acapulco to Amsterdam, picking up a lot of one-night stands and a lot of custom-made duds along the trail. Well I'm here to

tell you that the only place in all those miles—the only place I've ever been *happy*—was on the goddamn plane.

The detail that animates this exchange between Michael and Donald is a gesture (written as a stage direction in Crowley's play) in which Michael has pulled off the sweater he is wearing and, "letting it land where it may," finds another one in his closet to wear, prompting Donald to ask, "where'd you get that sweater?"[4] Michael responds, "This clever little shop on the right bank called Hermès" and adds that the sweater is not, as Donald presumed, cashmere but vicuna.

Remarkable about this exchange is the efficient way that Michael and Donald's shared dismay over the circumstances of their lives and the manner in which they each live is visually expressed through a dramatic rejection of the branded commodity. This vexed rejection, simultaneously confirming and denying the allure of the luxury commodity as it does, reifies the object, here the Hermès vicuna sweater: it allows the commodity to serve as the occasion in which to express the affect of the characters.

Kevin Floyd discusses the concept of reification as it relates to queer subjectivity by asserting, "Reification refers to a certain misapprehension of capitalist social relations; it identifies the very process of social differentiation within capital as fundamentally and objectively mystifying, as preempting any critical comprehension of the social." Key for my discussion here, he adds that "reification compels an experience of privatization and isolation, an experience of exchange relations as impermeable to human intervention."[5] I am particularly interested here in how Floyd's account provides the theoretical ground for understanding the manner in which these closeted scenes of the bath—of Harold's initial image and of Michael and Donald's conversation—engage with reifications of the more general social exclusion and subjective dislocation within the economic sphere that queers experience as subjects of capital, while, in dialectical fashion, the reified object serves doubly as the object for the queer subject to discover within the economics of common life objects—that is, commodities—and as the object through which to articulate queer subjectivity itself and to comprehend gender and sexuality through economics.

Worth recognizing, though, is that we must take care not to veer toward the reductive assessment of such queer experience as somehow "merely" a misrecognition of the allegedly truer material ground of subjectivity, a path that Floyd's account invites us to understand dialectically in his assertion of the possibility of (and, indeed, necessity for) a queer Marxist philosophy.

While reification might seem like the category through which to understand how alienated subjects fasten on some fragment of the total ensemble of relations in capitalist political economy—the commodity fetish standing most visibly as the most powerful such fragment—it is also true that reification is the particular entrée into critique most powerfully at hand. As Floyd suggests, "to think sexuality in reification's terms is to begin to see the way in which reification refers to a social dynamic that opens up critical vantages on the totality of capital as much as it closes them down."[6]

Michael confesses to Donald in his most poignant and, dare we say it, transgressive movement toward what Floyd identifies as the dialectic of queer reification in a speech given both to Donald and to himself, the latter in the form of the painting of Michael that hangs on his bedroom wall. In that image, we see Michael in the idealized form of the elegant queer man, complete with ascot, who gazes with sangfroid on the figure of the living Michael, who has become indebted—truly *in debt*—to the maintenance of this image of his young beauty. He remarks quietly, "Run, charge, run, buy, borrow, make, spend, run, squander, beg, run, run, run, waste, waste, waste. And why? And why?" After a pause, as if to demonstrate the awkwardness of this dramatic disclosure, he concludes, "Finis. Applause."[7] Donald then embraces Michael as he moves to gaze on himself in the bathroom mirror—the reflection of himself that is *not* the ideal of the portrait—and Michael turns the conversation to playful self-mocking by joking, "There's nothing quite as good as feeling sorry for yourself, is there?"

The oscillation within this conversation between the sexual and the economic, and the recognition and catachrestic misrecognition of one for the other, help us to understand how each is a metaphor for the other: the sense of social exclusion, harassment, and shame visited on these men for their sexuality is compensated through the utopian possibilities that the commodity form and related kinds of consumption herald (here, named Hermès); on the other hand, the depletions of labor find their expression in the alienated sexualities in which other men become solely *reified* others—"a lot of custom-made duds along the trail." The sense in which Michael here speaks both about clothing and sexual encounters as "duds" and their being "custom-made" enforces the sense that each helps to describe the other: that the dud clothing never fully fulfills the expectations placed on it, while the men with whom he makes sexual contact are custom-made for Michael's own sexual fantasies in their ability to disappoint him. And those terms are exchangeable: the custom-made clothing never quite fits, while the men—no matter how appealing—never can equal the erotic longing they instill. Couched in economic terms, there are costs for the subject, in this case Michael, to maintain an idea of liberation through the commodity fetish, all the while that the commodity fetish, even in its most densely reified form, must be revealed, that is, must come out, as unable to meet the fantastic needs of the consumer. The densely entwined forms of self-insight, critique, affect, and affection in this early moment adumbrate the larger narrative of the film itself and form the queer anti-reifying gesture of *The Boys in the Band*.

## On the Closet and the Commodity Fetish

The closet—as figuration of subjectivity, as disciplinary and regulatory mode of sexuality, as "regime of knowing," according to Sedgwick—exhibits strong homologies to the "metaphysical subtleties" of the commodity that Karl Marx asserted.[8] Part of what makes the commodity more subtle than we might suspect is its emergence at the moment of consumption; the consumer, as Marx asserts, brings the commodity to life in the social sphere of subjects. That aspect of the commodity that endows it with the quality of the fetish is in the very cognitive human act of perceiving the commodity as bearing some agency of its own—it simultaneously becomes both reified and vivified, dead and alive. The closet is a feature not only of the lives of *people* but of *things*, as well, things like commodities and fetishes. The closet-of-the-commodity, then, holds in abeyance what the commodity—and, by association, the consumer—can be in the future life that they share together, and the strong erotic charge of the bond between the two forms the central ideation of the commodity in daily life. If the long-standing corporate motto of General Electric, "we bring good things to life," bluntly warns of the animating process of production, then the efforts of the consumer reanimate the consumer product with new meanings in the consumer's world.

Two commentaries on the closet aid in understanding the dual, entwined registers of subjectivity—closeting and consumption—that *The Boys in the Band* stages. As Sedgwick asserts, the closet is a way of knowing the world—an episteme—organized through the binaries of identity (but not subjectivity) as they have developed in the past two centuries. One such binary, I argue, is that of commodity *and* fetish, where the former takes shape as the rationalized, marketed, discernible object of the capitalist production cycle, while the latter emerges *from* the commodity as the irrational, inchoate—in short, the erotic—correspondent to the commodity. This latter element forms the exciting secret from which discourses of the closet, as Sedgwick notes, gain their seemingly undepletable energy; more to the point, when Sedgwick comments that "the gay closet is not a feature only of the lives of gay people,"[9] we might add a variation: the gay closet is a feature not only of gay people but also of gay commodities—or more to the point of this discussion, of those commodities whose consumption is vital to the lives of gay people. Any consumer who has ever had the experience of thinking about a product—say, a sweater hanging from a rack in Hermès—that it fulfills him or her has felt the erotic charge of the commodity's seeking to become his or her fetish.

An adventuresome reading of theories of the closet, then, can embark on extending our understanding of the metaphor of the closet to the erotically reified objects of consumption. Sedgwick's own limning of the closet derives from the "aegis-creating" (Sedgwick's term) work of D. A. Miller on the secret in *The Novel and the Police*, in which Miller tells us that "secrecy would seem to be a mode whose ultimate meaning lies in the subject's formal insistence that he is radically inaccessible to the culture that would otherwise entirely determine him."[10] By inhabiting the closet—not the ostensibly liberating act of departing it—the subject can pause, however briefly, for a moment of self-fashioning through the closeted commodity that the subject has closeted with himself. But, critical to my reading—and made quite explicit in the commodity-scape that is Harold's bath—is the sense that, partitioned as the subject may be from human social life, even within the bath, he is not alone in that space but sits alongside the products he has taken into the closet's interior with him. However much we can agree with Miller's definition of the secret, its eventual disclosure (even if only to oneself) both maintains the minimum of an autonomy from the socius *and* the need for disclosure of the commodity fetish and the consumer's relation to it; consumption "outs" the moment of privacy with the fetish and its perversions of the product's value codings. When Max Horkheimer and Theodor Adorno write that "the most intimate reactions of human beings have been so thoroughly reified that the idea of anything specific to themselves now persists only as an utterly abstract notion; personality scarcely signifies anything more than shining white teeth and freedom from body odor and emotions,"[11] the resonances with the bath—"body odor and emotions"—are hardly mistakable for what this enactment within the bath has to offer us. But if Horkheimer and Adorno would have us believe that absolute conformity is solely what is possible for the subject in the terms of the reified object—intimacy being relegated to an abstract notion that has no reified counterpart—the door of the closet (of both subjects and commodities) that Harold's bath and Michael's bedroom brings to light reverses the dialectic: this door reveals that the subject can reinvent the social life of queers from within the closet and then extend such reinvention to the larger world.

The disclosure of the commodity fetish—its outing—excites so powerfully that it should hardly surprise us that the drama of Harold's efforts to prepare himself for the world beyond his closet/bath organize the film after his appearance at Michael's front door.[12] Indeed, the shift in tone between the moments before and after Harold's arrival signals the movement toward *disclosure* (literally: unclosseting) of many things within the narrative: of memory, of desire, of subjectivity, of erotic attachment, and of loss. Harold's speech to Michael upon his arrival at the party is a monument to the closet and the drama of its departure—both for the subject and for the fetish. After Michael chides him for being late and for arriving stoned, Harold announces, "What I *am*, Michael, is a thirty-two-year-old, ugly, pockmarked Jew fairy—and if it takes me a while to pull myself together and if I smoke a little grass before I get up the nerve to show my face to the world, it's nobody's goddamn business but my own." Harold's speech reveals the countervailing tendencies of the closet, because Harold first bluntly describes those of his characteristics that are seemingly unappealing and then turns them to an act of witty self-naming: within the conventions of queer male culture, he is old at thirty-two, not conventionally handsome, Jewish, and, saving the worst for last, a "fairy." Second, he admits to the fact that, realistic as he is about these traits and their relative appeal on the marketplace of queer desire, preparing for the social encounter still demands the labors that we are now, as spectators, in a position to realize we have already witnessed at the film's earliest moment. It turns out that it is the spectator's "goddamn business" to know what is involved in preparing oneself for the social life of appearances and that, for the gay man of the 1970s, this ability to appear—to come out—will be conjoined with his ability to consume. *The Boys in the Band* makes apparent the *costs* of coming out, both in the sense of the price of things (and the labor required to purchase them—hence, Michael's lament about debt) and the knowledge of the commodity fetish that must be embraced *and* disavowed.

What is this costly knowledge? The second half of the film answers that question in several ways, all of them related to the disclosures made by the exchanges between the partygoers and Harold—and here I mean quite explicitly the exchanges of commodities that take the form of the gift. The characters bestow on Harold, variously, a dowdy sweater from Hank, garishly jeweled knee pads from Bernard, a large-scale graphic rendering of the Monopoly board-game token for the Boardwalk property from Larry, and a sexual encounter with the hustler Cowboy from Emory.

Before these gifts appear, though, Harold and Michael will set the terms of debt and gift giving in a conversation about the insights that each has about the other; the conjunction of the economic terms of debt and the anxiety of appearing appears, at last:

> MICHAEL: Standing in front of a bathroom mirror for hours and hours before you can walk out on the street. And looking no different after Christ knows how many applications of Christ knows how many ointments and salves and creams and masks.
> HAROLD: I've got bad skin, what can I tell you.
> MICHAEL: Who wouldn't after they deliberately take a pair of tweezers and deliberately mutilate their pores—no wonder you've got holes in your face after the hack job you've done on yourself year in and year out!
> HAROLD: You hateful sow.
> MICHAEL: Yes, you've got scars on your face—but they're not that bad and if you'd leave yourself alone, you wouldn't have any more than you've already awarded yourself.
> HAROLD: You'd really like me to compliment you now for being so honest, wouldn't you? For being my best friend who will tell me what even my best friends won't tell me. Slut.
> MICHAEL: And the pills! Harold has been gathering, saving, and storing up barbiturates for the last year like a goddamn squirrel. Hundreds of Nembutals, hundreds of Seconals. All in preparation for and anticipation of the long winter of his death. But, I tell you right now, Hallie, when the time comes, you'll never have the guts. It's not always like it happens in plays, not all faggots bump themselves off at the end of the story.

This fiery exchange offers a number of opportunities to discover the psychic damage of queer men—done not least by other queers to them—and most important for my discussion is that the cruelest accusation that Michael makes of Harold is that he has disfigured himself through the application, on the one hand, of apparently useless products ("ointments and salves and creams and masks") while simultaneously rendering visible on his face the wounds that reflect the violence lived by queer men. If Oscar

Wilde's Dorian Gray magically concealed such disfigurement by containing it within the hidden image of himself, all the while that he maintained his beautiful appearance, Harold's labors on his appearance have produced him as a vision of all that the larger world's sanctified notions of beauty reject.

Michael accuses Harold of, of all things, being a bad consumer because he uses the wrong products to address the wrong shortcomings in his life, while, by implication, Michael perceives himself to be a better queer man because of his comparatively sophisticated consuming practices—this, despite the fact of his earlier confession to Donald about his debt and alienation. Further, when Harold states that he sees Michael as thinking that he is giving Harold insight that no on else will or can ("what even my best friends won't tell me"), Harold reminds us that it is he who understands that the cruel insights about each other that are exchanged are in fact that—a form of friendly exchange that exceeds both sexuality and money—and Harold undermines this exchange by telling Michael that he will not give to Michael what he expects: gratitude for such apparent truths.

## The Debt and the Gift

With this sense of the reified commodity operating as a vehicle for queer affect to develop in *The Boys in the Band*, we can learn much about how the film's narrative continually combines and recombines the commodity and queer affect. Debts and gifts in the second half of the film demonstrate the conjoining of the economic and affective lives of these characters. This combination appears in three objects that will be exchanged at Harold's birthday party: the sweater, the photograph, and the hustler.

### THE SWEATER

When Michael corrects Donald in their earlier conversation for mistaking the sweater discarded onto the floor for cashmere—it is vicuna, he tells him—Michael asserts both that there is something more exotic and luxurious than cashmere and that he himself is so discerning a consumer as to be able to scorn such luxury as being, paradoxically, *not luxurious enough*. Michael does not simply change his mind about the sweater as an emblem of fashion, and his gesture—tossing it on the bathroom floor—at once relegates it back into a closet and deems it worthless. Worth recalling is that Donald has in the previous moment deemed himself nearly worthless—to his family and to himself—because he is scrubbing floors for forty-five dollars a week. The branded, luxurious sweater from "a clever little shop on the right bank" is concurrently of no value to Michael in his production of his own appearance while figuring as something unattainable to Donald in his own abjection and relative poverty. It is this dual ability of the commodity—to exist as both the least of things (Michael's scorn for it) and the most exceeding of things (the very epitome, by Donald's assessment, of that which appeals beyond the realm of necessity)—that situates it as the reified figuration of queer life itself: simultaneously useless and alluring for the impossibility of obtaining it.

The reified commodity, though, is mutable, and the sweater's reappearance in the second act realigns it as something on which no stable value, either monetary or sentimental, can be placed. After Alan assaults Emory for his provocative insinuation that Alan's erotic motives for inadvertently being at the party are not clear, a bleeding Emory exchanges his stained sweater for the one that Michael has left on the floor of the bathroom, and Donald playfully reminds the group that, of course, it is vicuna. For the rest of the film, Emory wears the sweater as a reminder of the earlier conversation.

That Emory should be the figure whom the sweater adorns tells of the possibility of the reified object to escape the matrix of labor and debt within which it has functioned. Emory's status as the effeminate man, the caregiver, the cook, the bitch, the sissy, strips the reified and fetishized dimensions from the sweater and replaces them with the elemental character of economic things, as an object of use, but in a jarring way: the sweater provides a comfort to Emory, its softness and its luxury providing him a solace after the attack by Alan. This is indeed a powerful conjoining of subjects and objects: the queerest of queer men embraces the rarest of rare commodities for its most basic possibility: to clothe, to cover, to nurture.

### THE PHOTOGRAPH

Repeatedly, *The Boys in the Band* stages friendly cruelty and hurtful intimacy in an oscillating and escalating scale of melodramatic affect, and underlying this pattern is the exchange of gifts. Given that the organizing event is Harold's birthday, the party itself is part of Michael's gift to Harold, and the food, drinks, fashion, music, and birthday gifts for Harold form a nexus of profit and debt that the opening act's conversation between Michael and Donald has announced as the film's metaphor for male same-sex desire.

A particular gift links the early scene of Michael and Donald's private conversation and that of the subsequent birthday party: Michael's gift to

Harold. In the first scene, Michael wraps this gift while discoursing on his debt and abjection, and later we will see Harold unwrap this gift; as he does so and is asked by Larry what it is, he cryptically responds that "it's a photograph of him in a silver frame, and there's an inscription engraved and the date." After Bernard is heard to ask, "What's it say?" Harold leaves off by vaguely commenting, "Just something personal." The photograph and its inscription remain unseen and unknown by anyone but Harold and Michael.

Here, the animus between intimate friends is transfigured into something that the film in quite graphic terms refuses to disclose to its audience, and for all the hurt that both Michael and Harold are capable of, we witness the limit of the reified object that is the commodity. We learn this limit through the paradoxical inability of the film to show us or the characters that which will not be reified or, in the terms that Floyd outlines earlier, that relation between men that will not condense within the object of exchange. Given all the emphasis in the conversations about sex in *The Boys in the Band*, it is the friendship among men that cannot speak its name and that Harold and Michael will not speak about or show.

Friendship takes the form of the photographed face, and that face, it is implied but not made knowable, is seemingly Michael's. In the aftermath of the earlier speech about waste that Michael made to his own portrait, the gift of his photograph to Harold allows for the image to be exchanged between the two men and for it to be, as the old phrase says, the *token* of their affection. This token, however, cannot have its equivalent shown or established; it is quite explicitly priceless and thus forms that thing that can defy the insistent logic of reification and of the commodity fetish.

## THE HUSTLER

The hustler remains an object through the explicit refusal of the narrative to give him a name other than that of "Cowboy," a name that has long-standing and pungent erotic resonances for male homoerotic fantasy and longing.[13] The fact that he arrives with an accompanying card inscribed, "Dear Harold: Bang, bang, you're alive. But roll over and play dead. Happy Birthday, Emory," underscores the exemption of this character from the status of friend, lover, rival, trick—all names for the social roles that these men play for each other. Cowboy, in fact, is the realization of the reified human in its nascent form, and the conversational exchanges he has with the other men in the film emphasize his function as an object of erotic desire and play by insisting on his being stupid, inarticulate, socially awkward, nervous, and devoid of insight about the queer world he has come to inhabit.

The first image of Cowboy, though, is not on a ranch but, rather, leaning on a wall among a string of male prostitutes who solicit Emory as he "shops" for Harold's birthday gift. The winks, crotch thrusts, and pouts that these men aim at Emory are, by the time Emory arrives at Michael's party, gone, and in their place, Cowboy's talk and gestures reveal him to be earnest, naïve, and curious. This transformation is worth remarking on because it tells of the effort by the partygoers to allow their desire for him to realize fully the manner in which the hustler is the site on which reification is most exerted. Further, this commodity does not labor—it simply exists—and is most desirable when it is rendered by the men around it as mute, unknowing, and socially unrecognized. In Harold's speech about Cowboy, he reveals to the group how much they are all hypocrites in their combined lust for him and concurrent refusal to admit it. When Emory asks Harold what he thinks of the slim, blond, muscular, and handsome Cowboy, Harold drawls, "Well, I suppose he has an interesting face and body but it turns me right off because he can't talk intelligently about art."

EMORY: Yeah, ain't it a shame?
HAROLD: I could never love anyone like that.
EMORY: Never, who could?
HAROLD: I could and you could, that's who could. Mary, she's gorgeous.
EMORY: She may be dumb, but she's all yours.

Friedkin stages this exchange cinematically by framing the depiction of Cowboy as awkward because he is expected to enact a fantasy of masculine strength and virile beauty while at the same time being feminized as an object of sexual attraction. Cowboy's slouched posture and sideways glances reveal just how much he has been presented as an object for Harold, and the partygoers' mocking and teasing of Cowboy stage him as both erotic fetish and object of scorn. Indeed, there is a vengeful and cruel dimension to their treatment of Cowboy that punishes him for the trait that has brought him to the party: his willingness to exchange access to his masculine beauty for money.

Leo Bersani describes this punitive impulse when he comments, "Anyone who has ever spent one night in a gay bathhouse knows that it is (or was) one of the most ruthlessly ranked, hierarchized, and competitive environments imaginable. Your looks, muscles, hair distributions, size of cock, and shape of ass determined exactly how happy you were going to be during those few hours, and rejection, generally accompanied by two or three words at most, could be swift and brutal, with none of the civilizing hypocrisies with which we get rid of undesirables in the outside world."[14] In the terms offered by Miller, what is the subject's formal insistence here? None other than the marked ambivalence of the commodity—here, Cowboy—as both reification of the many clichés about masculinity and the American West and the fetish that holds the promise of some kind of liberation. The bathhouse of which Bersani writes—explicitly not Harold's or Michael's bath—animates fantasies of new forms of erotic contact among men and then, in the reality Bersani describes, denies them.

## "Paid For"

At the end of the conversation in which Michael and Harold exchange cruel verities about their lives, Harold responds to Michael's suggestion about the final consumerist fantasy in which Harold will indulge himself—his death with "hundreds of Nembutals, hundreds of Seconals" by bitterly asserting, "What you say may be true, time will undoubtedly tell. In the meantime, you've left out one detail: the cosmetics and astringents are paid for, the bathroom is paid for, the tweezers are paid for, and the pills are paid for." Before Michael can respond, the topic is cut short by Emory bringing out the birthday cake and inaugurating the exchange of the gifts.

This final comment of Harold's telegraphs through the rest of the film's narrative because it confirms Harold's moral authority over that which follows. As the telephone game to which Michael subjects his guests is played out in the final third of the film, with each man tortured into a confession of desire to those who are present and those on the telephone receiver, it is Harold who presides over these activities with hauteur. Like Apollodorus in the *Symposium*, Harold becomes an observer rather than a participant, and what grants Harold this different status is his assertion that, regardless of all the things that he may be—ugly, pockmarked, Jewish, a fairy—he is not, contra Michael, in debt.

Why does Harold's speech about his finances matter? What difference does it make that he can claim a kind of sovereignty in economic affairs? I argue that he and Michael are the sole figures in *The Boys in the Band* who realize the connection between money and affect. This connection is expressed through, on the one hand, Harold's luxuriance in the world of the commodity fetish and his ability to self-fashion and, on the other hand, Michael's abjection of his aging and his sense of time that increasingly disappears in the service of debt (and, by proxy, shopping).

In this regard, *The Boys in the Band* proves prescient in the way that it knows that money is a deep and yet disregarded form of affect, not least in queer culture; indeed, as Andy Warhol, a queer man who knew much about both poverty and wealth, claimed, "money is the MOMENT to me. Money is my MOOD."[15] As we learn from Harold and Michael, though, money contains within it *many* moods and many *queer* moods: the lamentations of debt and the complacencies of ownership among them, and if *The Boys in the Band* continues to fascinate its audiences (in fact, to shock and titillate them), the film endures because it allows us to make sense of the deeply entwined forms of indebtedness (emotional, financial, sexual) that shape these queer men's lives.

## Notes

1. I am grateful to Barry Grant for pointing out that the Hermès brand was featured in a nearly contemporaneous film to that of *The Boys in the Band*, Jean-Luc Godard's *Weekend* (1967). In that film's most widely noted scene, which depicts a near-endless traffic jam in the French countryside that devolves into a carnage of dead bodies on the highway and burning cars all around, a woman is overheard to exclaim about the sight of her car as it turns into a bonfire, "My Hermès handbag!" Godard's trenchant critique of middle-class French values, in which objects like handbags take precedence over human life and its dignity, are all summed up in the concern over a purse in the midst of a shared emergency such as this.

2. There are important similarities between this scene and that of a sequence from Andy Warhol's 1965 film *My Hustler*. In both, bathing becomes the circumstance in which queer men share intimacies of the body and of language.

3. The film adaptation omits segments of Donald's speech in which he discloses that he has dropped out of Cornell and is presently living "over a garage and scrubbing floors in order to keep alive." Mart Crowley, *The Boys in the Band*, in *Forbidden Acts: Pioneering Gay and Lesbian Plays of the Twentieth Century*, ed. Ben Hodges (New York: Applause, 2003), 453.

4. Ibid.

5. Kevin Floyd, *The Reification of Desire: Toward a Queer Marxism* (Minneapolis: University of Minnesota Press, 2009), 17.

6. Ibid., 20.

7. The scene resonates strongly with the function of the portrait in Oscar Wilde's *The Picture of Dorian Gray*, about which Sedgwick comments that the innovation of Wilde's depiction of queer desire resided "in the relatively

modern terms, as slim rose-gilt Dorian's inescapably narcissistic mirror relation to his own figured body in the portrait." Eve Kosofsky Sedgwick, "Nationalisms and Sexualities: As Opposed to What?," in *Tendencies* (Durham, NC: Duke University Press, 1993), 150.

8. Eve Kosofsky Sedgwick, *Epistemology of the Closet* (Berkeley: University of California Press, 1990), 67; Karl Marx, *Capital: A Critique of Political Economy*, vol. 1, trans. Ben Fowkes (New York: Penguin, 1990), 163.

9. Sedgwick, *Epistemology of the Closet*, 68.

10. D. A. Miller, *The Novel and the Police* (Berkeley: University of California Press, 1988), 195. Sedgwick, *Epistemology of the Closet*, 67.

11. Max Horkheimer and Theodor Adorno, *Dialectic of Enlightenment* (New York: Continuum, 1969), 167.

12. Worth noting is that, in Crowley's stage script, Harold's arrival at the party forms the break between the play's two acts; thus, the secret that Miller theorizes gives form to the structure of the play itself. The film's organization turns on this moment as well: the first forty-five minutes of the film promise Harold's arrival, and we finally get it.

13. Two films that served to publicly and cinematically frame this fantasy—Andy Warhol's *Lonesome Cowboys* (1968) and John Schlesinger's *Midnight Cowboy* (1969)—appeared nearly simultaneously with *The Boys in the Band*.

14. Leo Bersani, "Is the Rectum a Grave?," *October* 43 (Winter 1987): 206.

15. Andy Warhol, *The Philosophy of Andy Warhol* (New York: Harcourt Brace Jovanovich, 1975), 136.

# 10

## The Tragedy and Hope of Love between Gay Men

### The Boys in the Band and the Emotionality of Gay Love in the 1960s and '70s

#### J. TODD ORMSBEE

> MICHAEL: Now! Who's going to play with Alan and me? Everyone?
> HAROLD: I have no intention of playing.
> DONALD: Nor do I.
> MICHAEL: Well, not everyone is a participant in life. There are always those who stand on the sidelines and watch.
> LARRY: What's the game?
> MICHAEL: Simply this: We all have to call on the telephone the *one person* we truly believe we have loved.
> —Mart Crowley, *The Boys in the Band* (1968)

I do not think I was gay until I fell in love. I was seventeen when I met Kyle, and I fell madly, teenagerly, in love; the force of the emotional connection I felt shook me, challenging everything I thought I knew about myself. For the first time in my life, I allowed myself to think that I might be gay. Such experiences are far from unique, but I reflect on them briefly here because they suggest a possibility for an expansion of our conception of gay male subjectivities and communities, to account for the role and force of emotional attachment in the development of sexual identities. Since the 1960s, our wide-ranging discussions about LGBTQ sexualities seem to have focused on sexual desires and deeds in ways that obscure the emotions that might lead to male-male sexual identities and communities. But more, interaction produces *feeling* subjects, and those feelings in turn push back on and shape desires, deeds, contexts, and subjectivities. It is this feeling subject who interests me here, the subject whose emotions compel social interactions, sexual deeds, and relationships.

In my book *The Meaning of Gay*, I attempted to tease out in detail the interactions among gay men in 1960s San Francisco, to describe how the social category of "out," liberated, public *gayness* came to be through interactional processes, over time, in a specific historical moment.[1] Here, I return to this period to locate the emergence of a new kind of *love*, the love between gay men. This *gay love*, I argue, played a key role in laying the foundation for post-1960s gay male culture, shaping subsequent politics and our responses to HIV/AIDS and our experiences of being gay, that is, our gay subjectivity. When examining gay love as it came to be understood in the 1960s and '70s, we begin with men whose love lives were thwarted by legal, religious, familial, medical, and interpersonal barriers. The importance of love-bonding (as opposed to friendship- or kin-bonding) among gay men should now come to the fore. The context of a dominating heterosexuality during the 1960s and '70s necessitated a heightened awareness of love, which in turn raised its significance among gay men. As their interactions were creating gay subjectivity itself, they were also working to make their love meaningful, to make *gay love* an integral part of gayness.

## The Significance of *The Boys in the Band*

The 1970 film *The Boys in the Band* serves as a cultural touchstone in the midst of the postwar years of the movement toward a public, visible, self-conscious political gayness. A tent pole in history with a decade before and after, the film represents and (re)produces not gay love itself but rather a fictional moment when a group of gay friends engaged in the *emotion work* necessary to create gay love.[2] The film winds the tensions among the group of friends and one interloper to a near breaking point at a birthday party hosted by Michael, a somewhat self-hating gay man. As the party progresses into the evening, Michael tightens the screws on his friends, insisting that they play a modified game of Telephone—in the play, he calls the game "Affairs of the Heart"—in which the participants must call the "one person whom [they] believe [they] have truly loved."[3] A surface-level reading of this, the film's climactic sequence, might highlight the dysfunction of gay male friendships and emotionality, perhaps revealing internalized homophobia or, less generously, the overall unhealthiness of gay men's emotional lives.

Mart Crowley wrote the original play *The Boys in the Band* in 1967, and by the time the play was being turned into a Hollywood film in 1969, gay men already disagreed about the play's representations of gayness. By the early 1970s, *The Boys in the Band* had become a shibboleth of the "old gays" and the closetedness, self-hatred, and dysfunction of pre-Stonewall gay male culture generally.[4] But as Ramzi Fawaz argues elsewhere in this volume, there is something far more complex going on here and something far more important than internalized homophobia or an unflattering representation of "bitchy queens." As a play and film produced during a rapid transition in LGBT history, *The Boys in the Band* is both a snapshot of a particular kind of interaction at a particular time in history and a window onto the emotion work gay men engaged in to fight against homophobia and to construct an emotionality for their love.

Two overlapping contexts framed the interactions of gay men during this period, including those represented on-screen, one of them an outward-facing process, the other an inward-facing process. Facing outward, gay men had to interact with a dominant culture that called gay love sick, sinful, and criminal and that marshaled institutions to enforce and contain gay love. Gay men had to make sense of their love in a context that denied its very existence; the dominant psychological theories of the 1950s and '60s argued that, given its pathological nature, healthy long-term love between men was simply an impossibility, an unnatural and deluded fantasy of a mentally ill person. At the same time, gay men faced inward toward each other and created gay spaces—both actual physical spaces such as bars and symbolic spaces such as the gay press. These spaces enabled the interaction necessary for the creation of an emotionality of gay love.

The complexity of this emotion work demands a multipronged approach for its study, a kind of triangulation of both method and evidence: textual interpretation of both play and film, archival research, and grounded theory interviews.[5] First, a critical, close reading of the dialogue, characters, and images of the film, intended for a wider audience, lays bare gay men's emotion work but leaves significant gaps. Rather than home in on issues of representation per se, I focus on underlying systems of meaning in the film.[6] Second, I have been gradually conducting interviews with gay men since October 2013 for another, longer project about gay men's emotionality after marriage equality. From among these interviewees, I have chosen five men who came of age between the release of the film version of *The Boys in the Band* and the advent of AIDS in the early 1980s. I conducted these interviews, coded them, and wrote memos following the current standards of grounded theory methodology.[7] Finally, I have gone back to the archival work of my previous research about the emergence of gay male culture in the 1960s, focusing on the gay publications of the San Francisco Bay Area between 1961 and the mid-1970s.[8] I ran this archival data through the same analytical process as the interviews to suss out the patterns in gay men's arguments about love as they are preserved in one region's gay press from the period.[9] Within the interview and archival data, I have looked for patterns of topics, ideas, images, and points of conflict and resistance that arose repeatedly throughout the period. These patterns serve as the groundwork from which I built the analytical frame I employ here to interrogate and explain gay love as it emerged through interaction among gay men, against the larger society within which Crowley wrote *The Boys in the Band*.

## Emotionality and Gay Love

In order to speak as precisely as possible about gay love and its relationship to emotions, beliefs, bodies, individuals, and societies, I divide emotion up into three constituent parts: *feeling* denotes the involuntary, embodied phenomenon, a somatic undergoing; *emotion* is used to describe what happens to the feeling as soon as it is brought into consciousness, where it is named, evaluated, and responded to in thought and behavior at the individual level; and *emotionality* is used to denote the entire social and cultural apparatus of a given emotion, including its history, social meanings, behaviors, interpretations, and values, as well as the social responses and interactions provoked by emotional expression. I think about emotionality by adapting George Herbert Mead's theory of meaning.[10] To wit, emotionality is constructed through interactional processes, that is, as humans interact with each other and with their environment within specific historical, cultural, and physical contexts. Emotionality in turn constrains the stimulus-response circuit at the heart of emotions, shaping both the perception of stimuli before they provoke a feeling and the cognitive and behavioral response to the feeling before it ever happens. In this way, emotions are a crucial link between the society (emotionality) and the "self" (feeling).[11]

Importantly, linguistic labels connect us to the cultural history and structure of our social environments; however, they constrain but do not determine emotional experiences of the world and the gestures and behaviors that accompany a given emotion.[12] Rather, emotions are the means whereby individuals knows if they are in sync with their social context; that is, emotions are a primary instrument of social control. In my analysis of gay love around 1970, this highlights the relationship between the dominant cultural definitions of love-emotionality in contrast to the emotion work that gay men were engaged in to make gay love meaningful.

Martha Nussbaum's thorough synthetic theory of emotion points to three aspects of gay love vital to my analysis here.[13] First, inasmuch as emotions signal a lack, pain, or need, emotions force us to acknowledge our needfulness, our unwholeness, our lack of control. In this way, emotions are both comforting and an "upheaval" of life, as emotions are thoughts about an object of desire combined with our thoughts about the *salience* of that object for our own well-being. In short, emotions are eudaemonistic, that is, *felt* evaluations of objects in the environment in relationship to our well-being. Gay love, then, can be seen as the emotional judgment that a given man would be good for or is necessary to another man's well-being. Second, emotions are usually habitual, having become automatic and unconscious from a lifetime of lived experience in a social context. But in a world that sought to foreclose gay love, indeed to suppress its expression through force, and where heteronormative emotionality of love defined gay love as a disease, gay love *could not become a habitual emotion*. It is in this foreclosure of habit and gay men's response to resolve the problem of their thwarted love that we will find the answers we seek to how and why gay men constructed the gay love they did.[14] And finally, Nussbaum offers a way to frame the relationship between sexual desire, sexual orientation, and emotion that distinguishes between *drives* and *emotions*. Whereas emotions are value laden and object specific (i.e., eudaemonistic), drives are object neutral, arising from the body, independent of the world. Sexual attraction and its concomitant orientation are *intermediate* between drives and emotions, says Nussbaum, in that they persist without an object present in the environment (drive) but also potentially direct toward a specific object (emotion). Nussbaum argues that *sexual orientation*, the desire for a category of gendered or sexed objects, is part of the drive, the push of the body outward into the world; for my purposes here, I assume that male-directed desires underlie gay love but are not the same thing as gay love.[15]

Because English uses the word *love* to mean so many different things, the anthropologist Helen Fisher uses the awkward term "romantic love," by which she means the emotional bonding of people who are not familial relatives, with significant sexual and social components structuring their emotions. By *gay love*, I want to connote a similar kind of sexual and social emotional bonding, but one whose emotionality is specific to men loving each other during a specific period that saw the rise of "gayness" in American culture. Fisher argues in her synthesis of the anthropological literature on "romantic love" that underneath the cultural meanings and social structures, romantic love manifests itself across cultures in three broad phases.[16] In order to describe gay love, I have modified Fisher's categories to reflect my working theory of emotion discussed earlier.[17] First, *lust* is sexual desire, which ebbs and flows with flexible objects; second, *besottedness* is a kind of obsession with the beloved, in which perceptions and preferences of the beloved merge with one's own; and third is *emotional bonding*, when the emotion has transformed itself into the background, habitual life, forming the bedrock of a long-term relationship with the ongoing presumption of the necessity of the beloved for one's well-being. Though imperfect, Fisher's model of the three phases of love offers a way to distinguish between important aspects of love that impacted directly gay men's emotion work during the 1960s and '70s.

Simon May, a critical philosopher of love, has laid out a useful hermeneutic of the kind of love that forms the understructure of dominant, heterosexual American love-emotionality. May builds a historical argument to support what he sees as the three primary manifestations of love in European cultural history, beliefs that govern emotionality of love in the United States: (1) that love is unconditional; (2) that love is transcendent; and (3) that love is selfless.[18] Whereas May's purpose is to critique those dominant definitions of love, his three-part frame illuminates the dominant strains of "romantic love" as a ground from which to analyze gay men's historical emotion work on gay love. In other words, the historical context of the 1960s functioned to make the traditional, ethical-religious, and popular romantic notions of love indicators of disease, crime, and sin when "romantic love" was felt and expressed between men.

All of these historical, sexual, and emotional phenomena converge on the movie screen, as the camera shows Michael's New York apartment, where he sets up the party game. When he says, "We all have to call on the telephone the one person whom we believe we have truly loved," he unwittingly conveys two contradictory beliefs about gay love. To humiliate his friends, he must believe that gay love is an impossibility, that his friends will be humiliated by the game; but the game itself divulges his perhaps-unconscious belief that gay men are capable of loving. This contradictory view of gay love was not invented by Crowley and indeed underlies the emotion work throughout the period.

In that fissure between the acknowledgment of gay men's experience of love and the fear that real gay love cannot exist, I have mapped out four key issues or problems around which gay men centered their emotion work of the period. First, confronting the dominant culture and their own oppression head-on, gay men spoke of gay love as both an act of freedom and an experience of freedom itself. Second, they took the notion of gay lust and transformed the role of lust within love so that it looked significantly different from the dominant culture's ideas of sex. Here, gay men broadened and deepened the meaning of sexual connection to the extent that it broadened and deepened the kinds of loving bonds they could experience with other men. Third, gay men sought to replace the dominant notion that gay love was pathological, immoral, and criminal with the assertion that gay love was in fact superior to heterosexual love, providing a model for ethical social behavior. And finally, and perhaps most darkly, in all of the three previous components of gay love, gay men of the period expressed an abiding fear that there really was no hope for them to experience real, lasting love with another man. This fear is a dark foil against which the other three parts of 1960s and '70s gay love must be measured.

## Gay Love as Freedom

> MICHAEL (to Alan): Have you heard the term closet queen? Do you know what that means? Do you know what it means to be "in the closet"?
> HAROLD (to Michael): You are a sad and pathetic man. You are a homosexual and you don't want to be. But there is nothing you can do to change it.
> —*The Boys in the Band* (1968 play and 1970 film)

> The first [major problem coming out] was finding a lover. . . . I was begging for love. I was so disgusted that I went back to try loving girls, . . . winding up by trying to make love to heterosexual boys.
> —Charles Thorp, "A Teenager Talks about Being Young and Gay" (*Vector*, November 1970)

> [By the time I was finishing up college] I had not yet been in love. Visualizing myself in love, the idea of love, I just couldn't see how that would happen in my life. . . . Up to that point, my gay identity was only an individual thing. I thought that having sex with a woman was easier than loving a man.
> —Butch, age forty-nine

In my reading of Michael, at the core of his game of "Affairs of the Heart" lies the almost-unbearable pain of his lovelessness. As he gets drunker and more belligerent, as his eyes dart around the room, he insists with more and more force that his friends reveal their *true loves*, and in doing so, he reformulates the closet into a wardrobe filled with unfulfilled possibilities for love, aborted connections, denied intimacy. The group of friends are all out gay men already, but Michael demands that they return to the closet and open its doors, not to "come out" but rather to reveal the heart of their gayness, the love denied them. In a key way, Michael's vicious game asks us to reassess the meaning of the closet itself and its emotional consequences, but it concentrates our attention on the emotional and psychological consequences of the closet, not on the homophobia or heteronormativity that maintains the closet's structure.

Around 1968, gay men began a long argument with each other over the meaning of being a "closet queen" and the dangers that secret homosexuals posed for the increasingly public homosexuality that had gradually arisen during the 1960s. In the years immediately leading up to the production of *The Boys in the Band* as a play, gay men were confronting their symbolic domination head-on, refusing to accept the frames of illness, sin, or criminality to describe their experience of love for other men, even as they were keenly aware of their oppression. For gay men living within the postwar context of legal, ecclesiastical, and psychiatric domination, love between men came to stand for freedom itself, both an institutional liberation they demanded and an experiential, consummatory *feeling* of freedom through loving other men. Gay love as freedom came to be located in a free expression of an emotion and its concomitant sex acts, almost an ontology of gay freedom within love.

In the play and film, we find only hints of the connection of gay love and freedom, primarily as the boys reject the terms of their oppression, what I refer to as the structure of the closet. Instead we get repeated moments when the struggle against internalized symbolic domination emerges,[19] that is, when the characters argue about the terms of their oppression. For gay love to *mean* freedom, indeed for it to mean anything, the terms of the closet's structure must be rejected. In Harold's ultimate rebuttal to Michael at the end of the film, he posits homosexuality as an unchanging state of being, an inescapability that cannot be denied. In the context of its time and considering the interactions of the friends who both belittle and bolster each other up in their oppression, it reads today more like a call to action. When Harold says, "You're a homosexual and you don't want to be. But there is nothing you can do to change it," he is calling Michael into the present and challenging him to open his own closet door in some way.

Over the course of the 1960s, before the release of *The Boys in the Band* on film, the activist gay men engaged in the fight for public recognition of homosexuality were in a way meeting Harold's challenge, embracing their gayness and confronting what open, public homosexuality would mean for their loves, sex, and relationships. In the '60s and '70s, gay men knew they were in the sights of the police departments, politicians, clergy, moral reformers, and busybodies; but they also were coming to see their sexual desires as inevitable and good. Gay politics in the decades preceding and following the writing and release of Crowley's play and film were internally combative and often acrimonious. The context, then, of gay men's emotion work was not merely oppressed from the outside but also included disagreement, anger, and hatred among gay men as they argued with each other about the meaning of *gay ways*, indeed, the nature of homosexuality itself. These internal political conflicts divided gay men on cultural-political grounds, between those who saw gay ways as the result of internalized homophobia and those who saw them as "authentic" (in the language of the period) expressions of men who loved men. When combined with the dominant heteronormativity and homophobia of American society, these internal conflicts made the realization of a coherent *gay love* nearly impossible.

Ultimately, during the '60s and '70s, gay men associated gay love with freedom in three different, overlapping, and often contradictory ways. First, starting in the early 1960s, there was a straightforward liberal-democratic argument for a *negative* freedom to gay love, that is, the freedom from the state's or anyone else's interference in one's right to choose whom one loved. Then by the mid-1960s, activist gay men incorporated their understanding of oppression into a more complex and personal notion of freedom, in which gay love was seen as part of a process of undergoing a subjective, individual, internal emancipation of one's gay selfhood. Finally, by the early 1970s, this personal freedom had been connected to gay love, and the experience of loving another man had come to be seen as a positive experience of freedom itself—that is, in feeling love for another man, one *felt* free.

Taken in this context, I propose that we see *The Boys in the Band* as a depiction of a small group of gay men engaged in a fraught and raw exchange about their own oppression through remembering their early loves and arguing about their present loves. This enables us to put the representations in the film into a dialogue with the cultural and political conflicts from the period, which demanded breaking out of internalized domination. Rather than seeing Crowley's boys as caricatures or stereotypes of closet queens, we can consider them as a public representation of the struggle to break out of symbolic domination. More importantly, in historical context, Michael's game reveals not the structure of the closet—the heteronormativity and homophobia that gay men were fighting against—but the deepest, most intimate secrets hidden in the inner nooks and crannies of the closet, dragging love denied, truncated, and abrogated out of the closet into the light of the party room, to be confronted, mocked, relived, felt, empathized with, and reshaped into something more, something new.

That some of Michael's friends agree to his sadistic game shows a trust in the group and its ability to hold the ensuing feelings and struggles, even with two strangers present (Cowboy and Alan). They could choose to resist or to refuse, but they play. Their acquiescence to Michael's power as host may expose a singular power of their own, the power to face the closet's denial of gay love and to share its painful memories. Their willing vulnerability is a sharp contrast to Michael's building fury. Harold, however, has refused to play and sits watching and listening, interfering only to add meaningful corrections and directives, keeping Michael in check without ever severing the ties that bind the friends together.

Outside the play/film, gay men had simultaneously fought for the freedom to love each other while often blaming each other for their failures in love. Inside the play/film, when the only couple at the party, Larry and Hank, try to play the game, they end up fighting about their relationship, again, in front of their friends, again vulnerable, again willing. Larry defends his promiscuity by avowing his love for Hank and connecting that love to "respect—for each other's freedom." *The Boys in the Band* presents a snapshot of an intimate space of argument and difficult emotional work, indeed, of an interactional space where we witness an actual moment in the construction of the emotionality of gay love, where the surface level reveals the failed gay love of the closet, but where the interaction relies on the unspoken hope, the deepest secret the closet hides, that there is something beyond the closet for gay men, beyond self-hatred, beyond isolation, beyond the pain of past loves. The 1968 play and subsequent screenplay are a window onto the historical moment when gay love was linked to freedom.

## Gay Love as Lust

> LARRY: Charlie is all the people I cheat on Hank with. . . . I love 'em all! And what Hank refuses to understand—is that I *love* them all. . . . It's my right to lead my sex life without answering to *anybody*. . . . Numerous relations is just part of the way I am.
> EMORY: You don't have to be gay to be a wanton.
> LARRY: By the way I am—I don't mean being gay, I mean my sexual appetite.
> —*The Boys in the Band* (1968 play and 1970 film)

> COWBOY: Well, I'm not like the average hustler you meet. I try to show a little affection—it keeps me from feeling like such a whore.
> —*The Boys in the Band* (1968 play)

> Sex for us [gay men] is more a matter of communication. And, through our experience with different people, we develop a wide range of skills and a broad perspective on sexual means of relating to people. . . . Gay men welcome the opportunity for intimate relationship with many people and experience is more highly valued.
> —Richard Nash, "Gay Love" (*Gay Sunshine*, April 1972)

With Bernard giving Harold a set of bejeweled knee pads for his birthday, the audience is brought into the campy and lighthearted way that gay men might have treated sex in the late 1960s. But the campy sex jokes and allusions sprinkled throughout the film are periodically interrupted by much more serious considerations of the connection between gay love and lust. Four central dramatic themes of lust in *The Boys in the Band* emerge as the points of meaningful connection between lust and gay love: the failure of gay lust within the context of the closet; the possibility of gay love in the context of sex work; lust in an ugly body; and the complicated connection between love and lust in a sexually open relationship between men.[20] Here,

I focus on the last of these to shed a light on the ways gay men had come to see lust in all its forms, with and against the dominating social structures of the time, which had created deeply conflicted and unsettled negotiations among gay men not only about when, how, and with whom they were allowed to have sex but also about what the connection between lust and gay love should be. *The Boys in the Band* shows us gay men as a group of friends working out their own lust and, significantly, their experience of being lusted after—or not.

Hank and Larry's conflicted, sexually open relationship does more than illustrate sexual negotiation in a couple. It is here that Crowley most explicitly connects lust to gay love. Interestingly, none of the friends is in the least bothered by Hank and Larry's ongoing struggle to define and understand the sexual and emotional boundaries of their relationship. Only Alan cannot abide their public negotiation of sexual boundaries, as it forces him to confront his delusion that Hank must be "like him," that is, not effeminate like Emory and not homosexual like the rest.[21] Michael uses the word "lover" when he tries to force Alan to accept that Larry and Hank are a couple. "They are lovers," Michael says. Both in Michael's use of the word and in the way the gay press of the 1960s used the word, *lover* among gay men is often juxtaposed specifically against anonymous sex. A lover is, in the parlance of the time, someone with whom one is in some kind of a relationship, and it indicates nothing about the relationship's sexual boundaries. Use of the word *love* as a euphemism for a sexual relationship may or may not be coincidence, but it is important for my discussion here that the meaning that gay men gave to the word during this period was that men who were lovers were, literally, *love*-rs—although the depth, kind, and boundaries of the love were likewise often left undefined. As Hank and Larry argue about their relationship, each uses Michael's "despicable game" to tell the other that he loves him, while they try to work out what their lust for each other, and their sex with each other and Larry's sex with other men, means for their love.

Larry's long discussion of his sex drive paints a picture of a complicated relationship between sex, love, and lust. When he fights against being called a "villain," a "home wrecker," and a "son of a bitch," Larry is pointing up stigmas against sexual promiscuity and open relationships. He stands in for a particular kind of gay male relationship that got practically no attention in the gay press of the day but that clearly existed, in which commitments and strong emotional attachments did not necessarily entail sexual exclusivity. Larry, then, becomes the mouthpiece of three related themes in the construction of gay male love. First, he is adamantly sex positive; that is, he insists on the importance and goodness of both lust (emotion drive) and sex (the acts). Second, he represents a thoroughly negotiated sexuality between gay male lovers. And finally, he represents a simultaneous untying of love from lust and a rearticulation of sex and lust in a different, significantly broader way. Of his many casual sexual partners, Larry exclaims, "I love them all!" By contrast, in the heteronormative model, lust must be contained and constrained within a single relationship—indeed, part of the selflessness that Simon May describes in his critique of Western cultures of love can be seen as the agreement to give up all other sexual contact. In the emotionality of gay love, the dominant way of linking lust and love within a single relationship can be rejected in favor of a new sexual connection that widens and deepens the possibilities of experiencing love and having sex with multiple men. In this new way of articulating lust to love, in broadening lust to encompass more love, Larry is in fact bringing back an older idea among male-directed men that goes back at least to the mid- to late nineteenth century in the United States, that lust and sex are expressions and experiences of love itself.

To understand what Crowley's boys are really doing with lust in the play, we must stand back and see the 1960s and '70s as a time when gay lust was publicly suppressed and severely punished with arrest, incarceration, institutionalization, and "corrective" medical procedures. The dominant culture of the time reduced gay men's emotions and relationships to specific sex acts, and gay lust was reduced to a misdirected sex drive.[22] The emotion work surrounding gay love, then, can only be all or in part a response to the pathologization, criminality, and sinfulness of gay sex and lust. It should also be clear that gay men, living as they did in larger America, had absorbed many of the dominant ideas about love and lust generally, and these romantic ideas often crept into their discussions, both as normatives and as foils.

Within this context, what ended up forming was an interactional knot made of multiple threads that never resolved or melded into each other: the repression of the state, church, and medical establishment; the historical breadth of gay men's sexual practices and lust, combined with an insistence on their fundamental difference from the heterosexual norm; the effort to embrace those historical practices and gay lust; the rejection of those historical practices as either self-hating or immoral; and the rejection of any normative difference between gay lust and heterosexual lust at all. These contradictory threads converged in arguments over a range of sexual issues salient to gay men: the criminality of homosexual sex; the power dynamics of S/M sex; idealized egalitarian gay relationships; cruising for anonymous sex; prostitution; pornography; and so on. Gay men from across the political spectrum moved back and forth in their arguments between supporting the dominant culture and advocating for their inalterable difference from the norm. In their criticism of anonymous gay sex, for example, sometimes gay men would slip into arguments that anonymous sex cannot be love and that love and wanton lust cannot coexist, echoing the dominant view of the connection between love and sex.[23] Others denied such constructions of love and defended anonymous sex and cruising as evidence of the ways that gay men connect, even through brief sexual encounters, creating real love.[24] Ultimately, what emerges in these arguments is a notion not only that gay male lust is broader but that the broadening of lust beyond traditional relationship models also broadens gay men's capacity to love. Gay men did not agree about any of this, clearly; but the idea of a broad gay male lust seems to have preoccupied gay men as they argued about sex and love through the 1960s, a preoccupation, I argue, that continues into the twenty-first century.

## Gay Love as Superior

> LARRY: I can't take all that let's-be-faithful-and-never-look-at-another-person routine. . . . But if you have to promise it—as far as I'm concerned—nothing finishes a relationship faster. . . .
> BERNARD: Yeah, freedom, baby! Freedom!
> —*The Boys in the Band* (1968 play and 1970 film)

> Homosexuality is the capability of two members of the same sex loving each other in a way which is determined consensual and mutual in feeling by both persons; and therefore expressed by love in sex that assures a metaphysical well-being for both in their principles and practice. We gay people do have our role hang ups, but are overcoming them through confrontation known as consciousness-raising sessions in groups and/or on a one-to-one basis.
> —Ralph Hall, "Rising Up Gay"
> (*San Francisco Gay Free Press*, December 1970)

> We aging gay guys can look back. I was immersed in leather culture and escorted when I needed money. There is power in breaking the rules and in taking risks. Straight people are hemmed in and controlled by the rules. . . . Gay love is free and lightly ruled.
> —Bobby, white, northeastern, age fifty-four

As we have seen, Larry and Hank stand in for a kind of gay relationship in which the bonds of emotion are clear—Larry declares in no uncertain terms, "I love you, Hank"—but the sexual boundaries and even the limits on loving other people are not at all clear. Their relationship represents just one part of a more general *negotiatedness* in gay love as it arose during the period; its shape and boundaries were worked out and fought over within relationships and even sometimes in anonymous sexual encounters. In an analysis of how love relationships are transforming and evolving during our post-Fordist, neoliberal era (since 1973), the British sociologist Anthony Giddens turns to same-sex relationships as a paragon of late-modern love and intimacy.[25] For Giddens, gay men, and to a lesser degree lesbians, negotiate the terms of their sexual relationships rather than following set scripts.[26] Although I find Giddens's idealization of gay love flattering, I am wary of it because, historically, those practices of sexual negotiation grew out of a context of intense oppression, in which gay men were denied the social recognition of their relationships and lust. In other words, regardless of the potential normative value of gay and lesbian practices of varying degrees of sexual negotiation, they grew up as a necessary response to a very tightly restricted and policed world of sexual legitimacy, from which they were excluded. Raising them up as an *idealized* way of loving risks erasing both the hard-fought battles that underlie the negotiation practices and their gayness per se.

That said, Giddens is not alone in idealizing gay love. Indeed, the idealization of love in general dates back at least to Plato in the European tradition and to ancient religio-poetic traditions throughout the Asian continent. So it should come as no surprise that gay men themselves would also engage in some idealization of their own, elevating gay love while gainsaying "straight" love. By the late 1960s, critical comparisons of gay love to heterosexual love, with gay love often coming out ahead, were becoming commonplace in the gay press. But there is barely a trace of such idealized gay love in either the play or the film version of *The Boys in the Band*. Here, then, the question arises, why is gay love so often and so profoundly idealized within the gay press of the 1960s and early '70s, and among my interviewees, but not in Crowley's play? Following the cultural development of the period, I argue that as gay men's and lesbians' publicity grew, and as the outward resistance to symbolic domination increased, gay men and women created new cultural space to evaluate their love vis-à-vis the heteronormative culture that surrounded them and that sought constantly to contain and control gay love.

In my argument, I have glossed the American (hetero)normative love as "romantic love," using the tripartite definition of idealized love in the European tradition from Simon May. In order to make gay love superior, gay men's emotion work had to compare it to the straight "romantic love" and judge its relative value to themselves and ultimately to society in general, in the eudaemonistic mode. From time to time, gay men in the 1960s did engage directly in a reproduction of a gay version of romantic love. A notable article from 1964 describes at length an ideal form of gay love that co-opts directly the dominant ideas of the time about heterosexual marriage: limited to two people; based on selflessness and mutual respect; demonstrated through quality time together and sharing.[27] More importantly, the writer describes "true love" as losing the self and becoming "one" with the beloved, an ancient trope of romantic love, as described by May. But even in this early article, the writer considers gay men's relationships closely and proposes an egalitarian vision of love between gay men that would eliminate all set roles and power differentiations. This pattern of borrowing from "romantic love" and then turning back toward a gay egalitarianism is a hallmark of the period; indeed, its possible egalitarianism was the earliest argument for the superiority of gay love to straight, romantic love, reflected both in the archival record and in my interviewees' descriptions of their understanding of gay love.

Moments of full-bore, uncritical adoption of heterosexual, romantic love turn out to be rare in the 1960s and almost nonexistent in the 1970s. Instead we find that gay men were reconsidering and reconstituting love between men, such that by the early 1970s they had graduated to a full-throated advocacy for the superiority of gay love over heterosexual love. Here, gay love was seen as more *authentic* and more *real* (echoing the language of the counterculture). The move not only reclaimed gay love as a good in itself but saw it as superior to heterosexual love as both more egalitarian and more authentic; the discourse of superiority became a weapon against the oppression of the pathologizing dominant culture, a weapon that gay men deployed to combat key legal and religious arguments. The call for *authenticity* in gay love was at its base a call for being honest about oneself and seeking the love that one actually wants. Gay love was, in short, an "out" love, or as I have called it elsewhere, a "public" love, and it was experienced as a superior, more authentic kind of love.[28]

As *The Boys in the Band* proceeds, there is little, if indeed any, idealization of gay love or love between men at all. The film contains no detectable moments of idealized gay love and only the slightest of hints through Larry's voice. The target of Michael's party game is the failure of gay love, its pain and humiliation, perhaps its impossibility. As the friends argue, yell, insult, and humiliate each other about their true loves, the play and film might help us to see a more honest and full view of gay love during the 1960s and '70s, one in which gay men hoped beyond hope that there was value and purpose, that there was *meaning* to gay love. *The Boys in the Band* offers us a view into the heart of a watershed moment in the development of American "gayness"; it might not show us an idealized gay love because it shows us instead the raw moments when gay men faced their fears that gay love was not possible, a world in which average gay men, not activists and writers, felt a strong longing for love and nursed the wounds of love denied, while doubting the reality, the very possibility of love between men at all. *The Boys in the Band* thus approximates cinema verité, documenting gay men's fears and anxiety about their love that existed underneath the public bravado that asserted gay love's superiority.

### Gay Love as (Im)Possible Consummation

> COWBOY: Michael, aren't you going to call anyone?
> HAROLD: How could he?—He's never really loved anyone.
> —*The Boys in the Band* (1968 play and 1970 film)

> I too wanted to meet and become friends with gay people in a way that bars and baths make difficult or altogether obstruct. For bars and baths, as we all know, are worlds where looks, superficialities, masks, and games force us all to compete for triumph, admiration, and love and where we all must be prepared to face defeat, humiliation and loneliness.
> —Dick Jones, "Gay Lib's Phallic Scale"
> (*Gay Sunshine*, June–July 1971)

> When we're growing up, we miss seeing the love and relationships around us. So when we try them ourselves, they are raw-er than [straights']. . . . They feel adolescent, underdeveloped to me.
> —Henry, white, southern, age fifty-four

In the decades before and after the release of the film version of *The Boys in the Band*, gay men seemed to have harbored a deep fear that their own self-loathing would prevent them from experiencing love—real, deep, authentic, unfettered love—with another man. This turns us back to the contradiction at the heart of Michael's game, the emotional opposition, if you will, in which his intention to humiliate depends simultaneously on the existence and impossibility of gay love. The setup for the game insists that everyone in the room has "truly loved" at some point in the past, affirming the possibility of love between men; but Michael's humiliating intentions also assume that no one has actually consummated that desire for love. I want to move the word *consummate* away from its modern, misogynistic connotations—transforming a virgin into a wife and mother—and return it to closer to its original meaning, to bring together to completion, to connote the full convergence of lust, besottedness, and a loving bond with another man (or men), supported by sexual and social structures of emotionality. In *Boys*, Michael knows that he and his friends are having sex with men regularly—that is, that none of them are gay-sex virgins (except perhaps Alan). Instead, he sees a world where gay love, love between men, cannot be reciprocated. Consummation of gay love, then, represents the confluence of all the phases of love—lust, besottedness, and long-term bonding—to effect the fulfillment of gay love. The fear of gay men in the 1960s and '70s, and of the boys in the play, was that consummation of gay love would prove impossible, despite all of their emotion work and their deepest wishes.

As discussed earlier, Bernard's and Emory's turns at the game uncover the darker underbelly of gay love, when its object is a straight man. Emory's campy aside, "I'd make someone a good wife," betrays not a repudiation of consummation but a desire to consummate a full-fledged gay love with Delbert Botts. A deeper wound is brought forcefully home when he describes how his classmates mocked him after he asked Delbert to be his "friend": "What they didn't know was that I loved him. And that I would go on loving him years after they had all forgotten my funny secret." It is in this moment in the film, with a close-up on Emory's face, eyes looking past the other men into an unseen world of the past, when the audience is invited to see through the eyes of the most effeminate and promiscuous faggot in the room, perhaps the most abject of all of the boys, and to feel his unconsummated love. Through Emory, the viewer might feel both a desire for the consummation of gay love and the fear of its ultimate impossibility.

In *The Boys in the Band*, there is never a clear resolution of the question whether the consummation of gay love is possible. Both the play and the film leave unresolved the question of gay love's possibility, and neither seems to hold out much hope for the consummation of gay love. And indeed, this fear of the impossibility of gay love arises continually across these two decades, concurrent and perhaps constituted in gay men's insistence that they *can* love and that their love is a *good* love against the dominant emotionality of "romantic love."

Even when lust, besottedness, and bonding did converge, gay men expressed the deep-seated fear that it was fleeting or fake, and they turned to the dominant culture's romantic love to express their fears. In these moments, the romantic myths irrupted into gay male discourse, seeing a transcendent love beyond gayness that was salvific, complete with American rituals of wooing and sexual exclusivity.[29] But what I have found difficult to discern is what precisely the fear was. Did they fear the impossibility of gay love per se, that it could not exist at all? Or did they fear the impossibility of consummating gay love, that is, of experiencing the confluence of love, besottedness, and bonding? Or did they fear that their performance of gay love with each other would never be sufficient to warrant acceptance in the dominant rituals of romantic love? What is clear in the film, the historical record, and in the interviewees' personal stories is that gay men had already shaped and defined a gay love that was itself evidence of escaping oppression and experiencing freedom, that was intricately tied to lust and sex in a broad way, that almost completely ignored besottedness other than to describe the pleasure of the feeling, and that construed bonding as an open, unofficial choice rather than a socially sanctioned ritual. So if gay men had already defiantly constructed a love that was their own, why do we find these irruptions of dominant romantic notions in the form of a deep and troubling doubt and fear?

At this point, my interviewees' recollections of their lives over the past forty-five years offer a stark contrast to the pessimism about gay love evident in the archival record and the film. Over the past forty-five years, these men have actually tried in their lives to connect lust, besottedness—interestingly theirs were the only detailed descriptions of besottedness in my research—and long-term bonding in ways that they felt had been a truly consummated gay love. Butch described besottedness in a way that explicitly connected it to the bonding phase of love. He described it as going "beyond other forms of love": "Your heart beats faster, and you're drawn as if by force.... There's this early visualization [of being with this one person] and a sense of urgency, the need to connect.... That love changes the relationship over time, but the need to connect remains in place for me." Julio credits his long-term bonding of seventeen years to the gradual dissipation of sexual jealousy and to open, constant communication. He further describes a complicated lust within his relationship: although the couple more or less stopped having sex after ten years, their love for each other now is stronger than it has ever been. So lust was present, is no longer present, and is not necessary to the long-term viability of gay love. Given the temporal distance from 1970 inherent in the interviews, the more hopeful view of the interviewees suggests both their own maturation and a possible shift in the dominant culture and in gay male cultures since the movie's release.

The worst imaginable possibility for gay love is staged in the film in Michael, in whom we observe the central contradiction within gay love that I have been exploring here. Harold's watchful eye and chorus-like powers of observation tell us that Michael has "never loved anyone," that he has not charm but "counter-charm." Are we to take Harold's diagnosis, that Michael is incapable of love, at face value? Is Michael the embodiment of gay men's darkest fears, that their own self-hatred will render them unlovable? What stunned me more than anything the first time I saw *The Boys in the Band* over twenty years ago was that all of the friends *stayed* with Michael. They pushed back, they fought with him, they corrected him. But they stayed for the game, endured Michael's meanness and anger, and made themselves vulnerable to his mockery and cynicism. There is a strong bond, some of it connected to lust and past sexual encounters, all of it real enough for the men to sit together and endure the pain of their emptied closets and exposed wounds. When the guests have all left, Michael, wounded from his own behavior, falls apart, and Donald, the last friend to leave, holds him—physically restraining him in the play's stage directions—to calm him down and comfort him. And Michael says aloud what the audience has known all along, the play's central theme: "If we could just learn not to hate ourselves so very very much." And Donald, as he sits down to read a book and drink bourbon, becomes the voice of hope, the glimmer of light in the darkness foreshadowing the experiences of the men I interviewed. He tells Michael that he is not as bad as he used to be and that he can get better if he wants to. Donald assures us that gay love might yet be possible.

## Eudaemonism, Political Valuation, and Gay Love

When Kyle moved away a few short months after I fell in love with him, I was left a bereft eighteen-year-old, knowing that I had fallen in love with a straight man and knowing that he was unattainable. In my rural, conservative environment of the 1980s, I landed in an emotionality not unlike that of *The Boys in the Band*. I knew that I had loved a man, but I also had experienced a kind of impossibility of gay love, one that haunted me for years to come. But I also hoped there might be something more to being gay than scrapbook porn and unrequited love; what I did not know at the time was that I needed to talk to other gay men, experience gay culture, experience love in a way that could build a gay-love-emotionality in its own right. One of my ends-in-view in writing this chapter was to move toward a revaluation of gay love that might lead us to a practical philosophy of love among men in a twenty-first-century context, with its quickly increasing structural equality and institutional recognition of relationships between gay and bisexual men.

If emotions are necessarily eudaemonistic, the *feeling* and *emotion* of gay love, and the *drive-emotion* of gay lust, direct gay men's emotional attention to how other men can be salient to their senses of well-being in the world. Gay men's emotion work during the 1960s and '70s, then, can be seen as a collective effort to make an emotionality of gay love—meanings, values, beliefs, responses, embodied gestures, and behaviors supported by social recognition among other gay men—that would enable its full consummation. Those men hoped gay love could withstand the barbs, diagnoses, arrests, beatings, and condemnations by a homophobic and heteronormative society. In a real sense, gay men's activism tried to transform their eudaemonistic world, tried to create a social environment that would correspond to their eudaemonistic emotions, in which their *feelings* of lust and love could correspond to emotions that could, in turn, increase their sense of meaning and wholeness in the world. But their fears revealed that the project of constructing an emotionality of gay love capable of consummating its constituent parts, while standing up to the dominating society, lay incomplete.

The emotionality these men created exists in various degrees among gay men today. But if the emotionality constituted in freedom, a broadened lust, superiority, and consummation arose in a context of heteronormative repression, what will become of it in the wake of *Obergefell v. Hodges*? In the 1960s, gay love was under constant assault and its eudaemonistic potential constantly denied. By contrast, the gay marriage campaigns of the past twenty years have consciously equated gay and straight love, with gay politics valuing the reformation of "romantic love" into a more gay-friendly version. Katrina Kimport found in her extensive research of gay and lesbian couples who have been legally married that most of the couples she interviewed viewed their marriages as challenges to heteronormativity, not capitulations to it, and that they engaged in practices such as negotiation that marked 1960s gay love as distinct from heterosexual "romantic love."[30] Yet the couples also reported wanting access themselves to the rights and privileges, structures, signs, and practices of heterosexual marriage, ultimately creating a contradictory picture of the state of gay love after marriage.

In the age of gay marriage, then, we have been bombarded with the images and rhetoric of "same love," that there is *no* difference between gay love and dominant heteronormative love. From news stories to sitcoms to advertising to pop music, gay love is being shoehorned into the twenty-first-century model of romantic love. Heterosexual love itself has changed significantly since the release of *The Boys in the Band*, following the rise of second-wave feminism and the 1960s version of sexual revolution and, if Giddens is to be believed, in no small part because of the gradually increasingly publicity of gay love since the 1970s. Nonetheless, most of the underlying structure of the idealized European traditional love and its romantic rituals as described by May remain in place, albeit perhaps in a slightly less gender-oppressive form. As Macklemore croons in our ears in his milquetoast, Seattle hip-hop that it is "time to raise up same love," I must wonder what is lost in framing sexual justice in terms of sameness and, per force, assimilation.

In my previous research about the rise of gay male culture in the 1960s, I argued that gay men tended to explain their experience of gayness (meaning the full range from same-sex desire to their relationships to gay institutions and social contexts) along a range of often-shifting values. From that historical data, I formulated two ideal types—in Max Weber's sense of an analytical concept constructed from empirical data against which individual cases can be compared[31]—as poles between which gay men seemed to move during this period. One end was an expansive, capacious gayness, experienced as infusing every other aspect of life, transforming and shaping perceptions of the world, values, emotions, indeed life in its entirety as *gay*. The other end was a minimal, parsimonious, tightly limited gayness, experienced as merely sexual desire for other men, constrained and focused on sexual activities alone and only possibly extending to one's most intimate, often secret, relationships. I suggested that any individual gay man might move back and forth between those ideal types, depending on his current experience of oppression or acceptance and in relationship to the values that drove other aspects of his life, for example, family, work, education, and religion. Significantly, in studying gay men's emotion work on gay love, I found very little evidence of these two extremes. Rather, gay men seemed to have come together to try to make their love intelligible and effective in the world, regardless of where they fell between a capacious and a minimized gayness. This seems to indicate that the centrality of the emotion of gay love was a sine qua non, the base from which capaciousness or minimized gayness could be worked out.

If gay love was indeed so vital, so axial to the whole idea of gayness, it strongly suggests that gay love may retain a strong significance even in the age of gay marriage. Whereas *The Boys in the Band* asked that we watch a representation of gay men in an intimate moment of conflicted friendship suffering the pain of gay love denied, and whereas gay men of the period wrote of gay love as a fundamental *difference*, the strength and basis for a political resistance to the heterosexual order, we now live in a context of enforced and normative *sameness*, ranging from Macklemore's well-intentioned ballad to same love to a liberal erasure of gay difference across social spheres and in which the most powerful LGBT political organizations have focused all of their resources on creating a context for gay sameness since the mid-'90s. Back in 1971, a reporter for the *Bay Area Reporter* wondered if "organizing homosexuals actually destroy[s] or replace[s] the intellectual camp engendered within the gay community."[32] Indeed, it has. I am actually less concerned about the legalization of same-sex marriage as such than I am about the ways that this equality has been won, by deprecating and marginalizing the capacious forms of gayness in favor of the minimal, limited gayness, the kind that appears to be the *same love*. Today, the contradiction at the heart of Michael's game comes back with an all-new force: gay men clearly lust after each other and continue to love each other, but is *gay love* still possible when we are expected to be minimally, parsimoniously gay and when our love is supposed to be "the same"? The question in the age of pathologization was whether gay men were even capable of love. In the age of sameness, the question is now whether gay men can continue to love each other in a meaningful, separate, different, outside, perhaps even abject way, or if all that is left is the tightly limited, contained homosexuality that so many gay men have been coveting for decades.

## Notes

1. J. Todd Ormsbee, *The Meaning of Gay: Interaction, Publicity, and Community among Homosexual Men in 1960s San Francisco* (Lanham, MD: Lexington Books, 2010).
2. See Arlie Russell Hochschild, "Emotion Work, Feeling Rules, and Social Structures," *American Journal of Sociology* 85, no. 3 (1979): 551–75.
3. Mart Crowley, *The Boys in the Band* (New York: Samuel French, 1968), 71.
4. See for example John Ferguson, "The Boys in the Band," *Vector*, October 1969, 22; "Boys in the Band," *Vector*, January 1970, 19; and Denis Altman, "Gay Liberation," *Vector*, April 1972, 13. See note 8 below for full list of period publications cited.
5. See Robert R. Alford, *The Craft of Inquiry: Theories, Methods, Evidence* (New York: Oxford University Press, 1998).
6. For a discussion of this analytical move, see Samuel A. Chambers, *The Queer Politics of Television* (London: I. B. Tauris, 2009), 85–104.
7. Grounded theory is a qualitative method from the symbolic interactionist tradition of qualitative sociology. The method seeks to theorize from the ground of evidence, rather than to begin with theories that function as hermeneutical "lenses," which risk distorting the evidence at hand. The method includes a systematic reading, coding, and organizing of data along with self-reflexive monitoring of the researcher(s). For an introduction to the current state of grounded theory, see Kathy Charmaz, *Constructing Grounded Theory: A Practical Guide through Qualitative Analysis* (Los Angeles: Sage, 2006).
8. For this work, I consulted the following gay publications from the San Francisco Bay Area, published between 1961 and 1975 (in chronological order): *LCE News* (1962–63); the *News* (1963); *Citizens News* (1964–65); *Town Talk* (1965–66); *Vector* (1964–72); *Vanguard* (1966–67); *CHF Newsletter* (1969); *San Francisco Free Press* (1969–70); *San Francisco Gay Free Press* (1970); *Agape and Action* (1970–71); *Gay Sunshine* (1970–72); *Ads Gayzette* (1970–71); the *Effeminist* (1971); *I Am: Oracle of Gay Emmaus* (1971); *Bay Area Reporter* (1971–75). *Vector* and *Bay Area Reporter* continued publication beyond these dates, but I did not consult later issues; the *Bay Area Reporter* is still in publication today.
9. It is important to highlight here that within the San Francisco gay publications of the period, there is a stark lack of voices of gay men of color; they are clearly present in photographs of the day and occasionally identify their racial and ethnic backgrounds in their articles and letters. But there is most often an unacknowledged whiteness. From the outset, this gap in the historical record points to further research necessary for future complications and criticisms of my work here in terms of race and ethnicity.

10. George Herbert Mead, *Mind, Self, and Society: From the Standpoint of a Social Behaviorist* (1934), ed. Charles W. Morris (Chicago: University of Chicago Press, 1962), 75–80.

11. See Jonathan H. Turner and Jan E. Stets, *The Sociology of Emotions* (New York: Cambridge University Press, 2005).

12. Despite ongoing debate, the general consensus among sociologists, anthropologists, and psychologists is that there is a set of primary emotions common among humans. See ibid., 2–21.

13. Martha Nussbaum, *Upheavals of Thought: The Intelligence of Emotions* (New York: Cambridge University Press, 2003).

14. For a full theory of the relationship between thwarted desires and conscious problem solving, see John Dewey, *How We Think*, rev. ed. (1933), in *John Dewey: The Later Works, 1925–1953*, vol. 8, *1933*, rev. ed., ed. Jo Ann Boydston (Carbondale: Southern Illinois University Press, 2008).

15. Please note that I am speaking of a kind of phenomenal, maybe even somatic, drive here. Sexual behavior is not the same as a sexual drive; a eudaemonistic or religious reason, for example, can motivate a sexual *act* (to satisfy particular needs, that is, to create equilibrium) without or in spite of the drive.

16. Helen Fisher, *Why We Love: The Nature and Chemistry of Romantic Love* (New York: Holt, 2005).

17. I am using different words from Fisher here to displace heteronormative assumptions about love and especially European and American received cultures of "romantic" love.

18. Simon May, *Love: A History* (New Haven, CT: Yale University Press, 2013).

19. See Pierre Bourdieu, *Masculine Domination* (1998), trans. Richard Nice (Stanford, CA: Stanford University Press, 2001). Bourdieu seeks to explain why oppressed people sometimes accept or even participate in their own oppression; he offers a theory of the internalization of *symbolic domination*, in which the symbol systems of the dominating culture are all individuals or groups have to work with to make their lives intelligible, which effectively functions as a kind of internalized coercion.

20. Much of this material was pared down for the film version; the film is a weaker representation of the construction of gay lust than is the play.

21. Gay men's gender often arose in these discussions about lust in disturbing ways, in both liberationist and earlier publications, as a repudiation both of the hypermasculinity of leather culture and of effeminacy and drag. No organizations at any point along the political spectrum during the period were immune from these problems of seeing gay male cultural practices as some kind of self-hating gender dysphoria.

22. Although the American Psychiatric Association declassified homosexuality as a mental disorder in 1973, followed by the American Psychological Association in 1975, the idea of the pathological homosexual has remained dominant in the public imagination, as reflected in most antigay literature and politics of the twenty-first century.

23. See "Our Bodies: Toilet Training," *Effeminist* 1, no. 2 (1971): 5, 12.

24. Stephen Ben-Mordechai wrote in an untitled poem, "I felt your soul and you shared mine. / It could have gone on forever, but they called your locker number." *Gay Sunshine*, March 1971, 5.

25. See Anthony Giddens, *The Transformation of Intimacy: Sexuality, Love, and Eroticism in Modern Societies* (Stanford, CA: Stanford University Press, 1993).

26. In interesting ways, this also dovetails with the philosophical correction to idealized love offered by Simon May (*Love: A History*), discussed earlier.

27. *Citizens News* 3, no. 25 (1964): 2, 10, 25.

28. See Ormsbee, *Meaning of Gay*, 11–42.

29. See May, *Love: A History*, 1–13, 38–55, 119–28, and 235–56. May traces the history of how, in Western cultures, love came to be seen both as the source of morality and virtue and as a transcendent purifying experience for lovers. He argues a sharp critique against this dominant through line in Western culture. Here, I am arguing that, because gay men's love was denied recognition, they were at least partly able to sidestep the dominant, transcendent view of love.

30. Katrina Kimport, *Queering Marriage: Challenging Family Formation in the United States* (New Brunswick, NJ: Rutgers University Press, 2015).

31. See Max Weber, "'Objectivity' in the Social Sciences" (1904), in *The Methodology of the Social Sciences* (New York: Free Press, 1949), 90. "An ideal type is formed by the one-sided accentuation of one or more points of view and by the synthesis of a great many diffuse, discrete, more or less present and occasionally absent concrete individual phenomena. . . . This mental construct (*Gedankenbild*) cannot be found empirically anywhere in reality." The ideal type must emerge from the empirical data but is not a representation of reality; rather, it functions as a way to see how an individual case relates to the complexity of a cultural reality.

32. William Beardemphl, "Comments: The Loss of Camp?," *Bay Area Reporter*, September 15, 1971.

# 11

## The Sounds of Silence

### Acoustics and Politics

**AMY VILLAREJO**

In 1969, AT&T executives hired a young documentary filmmaker, Nell Cox, to make a recruitment film for telephone operators. The telephony union, the Communications Workers of America, had waged an eighteen-day strike against the company the previous year, during which period AT&T executives themselves had served as operators. Through this nascent film project, they apparently sought to advertise the switchboard work, according to director Cox, as "interesting" through a movie that would appeal to young people.[1] Accordingly, the resulting fifteen-minute film, *Operator*, seeks to make the world of the telephone "cool" to its sixties audience, through elements such as an original rock score, solarization in its credit sequence, and a hip vérité style. And it had vérité cred, too: it was shot by Richard "Ricky" Leacock, one of the most significant documentary filmmakers of the twentieth century.

*Operator* trains its immersive gaze not just on telephone workers—many young women who testify to the satisfying and pleasurable nature of their labor—but on the world of telephone *talk*. While Leacock's camera caresses faces and surveys the cutting-edge AT&T telephone technology in exciting close-up, the filmmakers' microphones record interviews and intimate telephone conversations to intercut with the groovy score. What we *hear* is therefore a sampling of the discursive field of telephony at this particular moment in history, its audible range of affects and concerns: a woman distressed by a stranger at the door, a young boy who wants to speak with his grandmother, an impatient businessman, a jokester. In *Operator*, talk is thereby embedded into a range of social dimensions: privacy, sexuality, and family, alongside economy and labor. Through Cox's amusing insertion of found footage from D. W. Griffith's silent film *The Telephone Girl and the Lady* (1913) accompanied by solo piano, *Operator* also very clearly marks the domain of the telephone as that of melodrama. And although the film *Operator* ideologically aspires to make talk safe and appealing, it also, melodramatically, reveals moments of menace, malice, and alienation (all of which it seeks to contain quickly). "I love any kind of talking," an operator tells us, and we are meant to love talking, too, mostly for the profit and well-being of AT&T.

The year of *Operator*, 1969, is, of course, the pivotal year for historicizing *The Boys in the Band*, the play that opened in 1968 and was adapted for the screen in 1970 (in a film of course shot in New York City during the spring and early summer of 1969). As most of the contributors in this volume discuss, it is the year and very moment of the Stonewall Riots, an event that marks a caesura at least in the commonsense understanding of gay politics (from silence and self-loathing to coming-out and pride) in which both the play and the film are implicated. Stonewall, that is, is understood as a shorthand for a watershed shift in gay life, when liberation could be both proclaimed and heard; it is also a name for a particularly melodramatic understanding of history, as I suggest in reading the melodramatic flows of *The Boys in the Band*, with its trafficking in themes of privacy and the safety of the home and the telephone as a conduit to external threats. The year 1969 is also when Judy Garland died, and her mourning is intimately connected with Stonewall; identifying 1969 with her death gives us a window onto the broader queer world of entertainment in which *The Boys* is embedded, from Mart Crowley's Hollywood and New York connections to the celebrity circuits of its producers, publicists, directors, and actors. Linking all of these sites and scales is the mediated voice, figured through various electronic devices, especially the telephone (and the record player). These do indeed figure as key props in both the play and the film, but as my opening example of *Operator* suggests, they also open onto broader historical and aesthetic fields and concerns. In what follows, I examine the role of the mediated voice in *The Boys in the Band* in order to elaborate what gay liberation in that film *sounds* like, as articulated also in *Making the Boys* (2010), the subsequent documentary film by Crayton Robey. In doing so, I hope to reveal the limits of characterizing liberation as the end of silence by listening to the ghosts of *The Boys in the Band*. In my view, there is no *unmediated* voice to salvage in *The Boys in the Band*, no authentic enunciation of liberation unleashed by the vicissitudes of history but rather always an elsewhere that speaks through the characters and the film's own apparatus and space, including the acoustic chamber that functions as its primary setting. If "silence" is said to be what precedes the loud and proud declaration of gay liberation, I suggest in what follows that we can hear its traces in the postliberatory culture that *The Boys* heralds; just as clearly, we can hear the echoes of silence in the deaths by AIDS of those boys we preserve on film.

## General Organology

While I do not share all of Bernard Stiegler's dire assumptions about symbolic misery or societal malaise, I am inspired to think about the mediated voice initially through a theoretical framework elaborated by the French philosopher. I shall give a mere snippet of it here, but Stiegler's work can be accessed through his multivolume works *Technics and Time* and *Symbolic Misery*.[2] In his many writings, Stiegler has sought to explain a generalized sense of misery in hyperindustrial society, a misery that for him results from the synchronization of consciousness with mass-produced culture. In hypothesizing how a culture of mass consumption—particularly of images, symbols, and sounds—produces passive and impoverished subjects, Stiegler extends a line of thinking from twentieth-century philosophy that emphasizes the impersonal logic of economic productivity and the standardization of experience under what his predecessors, such as Theodor Adorno and Max Horkheimer, called "the culture industry."[3] But in Stiegler's revision to the Frankfurt thinkers' treatment of the psychodynamics of late capitalism and the negative dialectics that opposed them, hyperindustrial culture (media-info-digital) puts at risk our very capacity to develop as individuals through the mechanisms of primary narcissism. In Stiegler's view, our impoverished and standardized culture inhibits our ability to individuate, to attach to singularities, to recognize singular objects; it inhibits, that is, our capacity for *aesthetic* engagement.

In the realm of the aesthetic, Stiegler finds the resources for those singular identifications or attachments to singularities: the artwork affirms and promotes processes of primary narcissism insofar as it permits identification and differentiation. In place of negative dialectics, then, Stiegler proposes a revolution at the level of the interface between the body and technics, between one's sensorium and a technological extension or prosthesis. He argues, interestingly, that mass culture needs to be not simply negated but rather *invigorated*: since we share so much in common (from YouTube to national archives), we have to find ways for our own bodies to encounter and enliven aesthetic objects. Such a revolution would be *organological* (what Stiegler sometimes calls a critical project of general organology) insofar as it would interrogate and specify sites of interaction between the body and technics that allow for intervention, action, contestation, struggle, and indeed, revolution. Like other key thinkers of the intersection between technologies and bodies (Marcuse, Deleuze, and Reich, just to name a few), Stiegler links the refunctionalization of the aesthetic to a reconstitution of libidinal energy, so that our unconscious as well as embodied rhythms escape synchronization by the society of control and can be rerouted into new forms. What role has the mediated voice played in this interface between technics and sexual life? In short answer, a crucial one, especially in the historical interval of the late twentieth century, when the telephone opened new avenues for libidinal expression, new communities for sexual belonging, and new linkages for survival. At the same time, the telephone posed its own threats and problems, dramatized poignantly in *The Boys*.

## The Call Comes

In an essay titled "The Telephone and Its Queerness," Ellis Hanson begins to align the social history of the telephone with the vicissitudes of queerness, noting how the telephone has served as both a "site of sexual panic" and a lifeline.[4] The telephone, that is, quickly became a popular site (and therefore a highly regulated one) for erotic play, a safe electrical space for polymorphous pleasures to find narrative or descriptive expression, a technological role that intensified particularly during the HIV/AIDS crisis. The "gay hotline" (now LGBTQ hotline) has likewise historically provided a sympathetic or nonjudgmental ear, needed information, local resources, and all-around support to imperiled queer migrants and queer youth. Linking individuals to virtual networks, hotlines have long served diverse populations—gay youth without access to adult resources, survivors of abuse, addicts, and other people in crisis—such that the telephone functions as a coil of rope might to provide safety on deck during a storm at sea. As a prosthesis or as an extension of queer lifeworlds, the telephone enlarges but also complicates notions of connection.[5]

Key to both roles of the telephone, as Hanson outlines them—as site for sexual play and as lifeline—is the uncertainty of both identity and clarity in the call. The first is not simply a matter of anonymity, as much as anonymity has been crucial for certain types of queer telephonic exchange. The uncertainty of identity additionally involves the possibility of impersonation and/or the capacity for misrecognition and/or the potential for a disembodied voice to shift erotic direction, sexual object, or sexual aim. One can pretend to be someone, one can be mistaken for someone, or one can fall for someone or some part of someone one thought was something else. Disembodied voices can, in other words, become feigned identities and dispersed subjects. Similarly, telephonic static can obscure voices, while dropped calls or broken connections can disrupt otherwise smooth or seamless transmission. Or one can simply hang up. All of these thicken and describe aspects of what I have been calling the mediated voice.

Mart Crowley himself answered a call, and his answer became *The Boys in the Band*. The initiating voice was that of Stanley Kauffmann, whose 1966 article in the *New York Times*, "Homosexual Drama and Its Disguises," challenged the queer playwright to write not about straights but about queer worlds, "to write truthfully of what he knows, rather than try to transform it to a life he does not know, to the detriment of his truth and ours."[6] Kauffmann's article rankled and still does, for it implicated the three major American playwrights of the twentieth century—Tennessee Williams, William Inge, and Edward Albee, all gay men—in a dramaturgy of distortion. Nowhere, we should note, does Kauffmann mention their names: he summons them bafflingly and anonymously as "(reputed) homosexuals."[7] Due to the homophobic culture of the American stage, Kauffmann alleges, all three men (1) disguised queer life as straight life, embedding queer male characters, conflicts, and situations in portraits of the straight world, marriage, and women, and (2) therefore refrained from writing about what they *really* know. Although Kauffmann indicts these distortions, as well as the society that has demanded them, his particular form of condemnation is not particularly generous to the men who gave us, respectively, *A Streetcar Named Desire*, *Picnic*, and *Who's Afraid of Virginia Woolf?*, all magisterial treatments of gender and modern life. Essentially, however, he is less concerned with (1) than with (2). Here is Kauffmann: "To me, [the gay playwrights'] distortion of marriage and femininity is not the primary aspect of this matter, for if an adult listens to these plays with a figurative transistor radio simultaneously translating, he hears that the marital quarrels are usually homosexual quarrels with one of the pair in costume and that the incontrovertibly female figures are usually drawn less in truth than in envy or fear."[8] The figure of the transistor radio summons our attention. Somehow, it makes possible a kind of listening to what is straight as *really* gay, while at the same time it allows a "translation" such that female characters can be understood as distorted (by "envy or fear") rather than as truthful. The first translation unveils a distortion whose truth can be recovered; the second translation reveals the playwright as constitutionally unable to be truthful, to "know" women. This "figurative" mediation of a nonexistent radio for adults, in other words, allows us—viewers, readers, presumptively straight—to have it all, without contradiction. At once we can decipher the worlds of gay men through whatever apparently straight world is served up to us, while at the same time we can condemn queer writers for their specificity, for their particularity. What a difficult call for a playwright to answer, in seeking to write truthfully of the New York gay scene of the late 1960s. Mart Crowley answers, and in part his answer makes sense: write a world *without* women, a world in which femininity attaches only to gay male bodies and camp, such that the queer conflict need not be deciphered at all. It is there plain to see. Crowley aims directly for an *unmediated* voice, one without the static and interference Kaufmann condemns in the three giants of the American stage. But then why is it constantly mediated by electronic voices and sounds?

## Calling *The Boys*

William Friedkin's masterful opening sequence for the film version of *The Boys* receives due attention elsewhere in this volume. Here, let us notice how the lyrics to its musical score, Cole Porter's song "Anything Goes," locates the film within the very problematic of mediation we have been elaborating. For Porter, words were queerly married to sounds.[9] Compiling the shudders of urban mass culture, Porter's song concludes,

> Just think of those shocks you've got
> And those knocks you've got
> And those blues you've got
> From that news you've got
> And those pains you've got
> (If any brains you've got)
> From those little radios.

In traveling onto the streets of New York and in gesturing to the actual locales and milieus that are the context of the play's action, Friedkin gives his audience a visual compendium of the phenomenal social transformations that Porter's equally queer list presents. This compendium does not reflect just a generalized change, though, intimated visually and aurally: it is a set of particular changes accomplished through reversal ("black's white today"), surprise, deception, connection, and, crucially, the mediating forces of technology and mass culture.

The first diegetic sound that prompts a character's action in the film is, of course, a telephone: the phone ringing in Michael's apartment as he juggles his keys and packages in the stairwell outside. He misses the call, only to receive another one in short order: Donald (Frederick Combs) calls from a pay telephone in a parking garage, Michael (Kenneth Nelson) answers, and a circuit of identity already is put into play as Michael asks, "Did you just call a minute ago?" It was not, in fact, Donald who had just called but Alan (Peter White), whose entire character will be sketched through telephonic ambiguity. The film will pick up Alan's thread in a moment. Summoning Donald to the apartment, Michael quips a line of dialogue that exemplifies the film's camp capacity for contradiction and play around talk itself: "You're too early and hurry up. Goodbye eye eye." I read the latter as Michael's inclination toward sound itself, making a word into a lyric across multiple beats, making a quotidian expression into an occasion for invention, however minimal. Virtually all of the rest of the film takes place within the mise-en-scène of Michael's apartment and its terrace. From now on and until the bitter end of the party, there are inside (the world of out gay men, their pleasures and their deep pains, and mostly their *talk*) and outside (the straight world, hostile—and raging with storms—but also crucial to these men's identities). Linking and delimiting the inside and outside are the buzzer and the telephone.

I do not have a great deal more to say about the buzzer, but it does serve Crowley and Friedkin as a device for introducing the ensemble cast and for suggesting the unknown and often intrusive nature of "outside," which is to say the difficulty of preserving an "inside" that might represent a form of freedom. Donald's arrival is heralded by the buzzer, just before Alan calls Michael again on the telephone in some emotional distress; he is on his way over, setting a horizon of expectation, even menace, regarding the narrative motivations for his despair. Emory (Cliff Gorman), Hank (Laurence Luckinbill), and Larry (Keith Prentice) buzz and enter as a group, followed by Bernard (Reuben Greene), who enters alone. Whenever the buzzer buzzes, in fact, it seems to reverse expectation and to generate surprise, perhaps carrying that uncertainty from the outside in. After Bernard's entrance, in these first moments building the momentum of the party, Crowley introduces a "poesis of the ordinary," a "little world"—the helpful terms are Kathleen Stewart's[10]—of queer New York: camp and play, celebration and energy, fueled by drinks and cavorting. Notably, the loud fun drowns out the next telephone exchange, with Larry picking up the phone. Michael must retreat upstairs for the third call from Alan, who is now at a telephone booth on the street. He is apologetic and embarrassed by his earlier display of emotion, and we abandon our expectation that he will play a continuing role in the drama and let go of our fear that he might intrude. This is the beginning of the film's volley with address and expectation, though, not the end. This arc culminates in the "(Love Is Like a) Heat Wave" dance number on the terrace, only to be interrupted once again by the buzzer: enter Alan.

Alan quickly incites violence. His homophobic perceptions initially are based on appearances, yet they soon become reactions to ways, precisely, of talking. Drawn toward the manly Hank and his wedding ring, Alan alienates Hank's partner, Larry, and then attempts to communicate with Michael upstairs, out of earshot of the rest of the guests. For Alan, what is unbearable is Emory's speech: "I just can't stand that kind of talk. It just grates on me." "What kind of talk, Alan?" When Alan names it, calling Emory a pansy, we tremble, anticipating that verbal violence might soon convert to a physical attack, since the buzzer now signals the arrival of Cowboy (Robert La Tourneaux), the hustler who is, by definition, all idealized body and little speech. When Alan's rage culminates in his attack on Emory, we notice that Emory's wounds are concentrated on his mouth. Finally, the last buzz of the evening brings up Harold (Leonard Frey), the birthday boy, whose peals of laughter dissolve speech into mere sound.

At this point, almost halfway through the film, we have seen how the habitat of homophobia on the "outside" makes its impact on the gathering "inside" through the politics of speech and silence, plotted by Crowley and orchestrated by Friedkin. Through dialogue, we learn, for example, of raids on bathhouses and on the persecution felt most intensely by Emory, the queeniest of the bunch, when he opens his mouth. We understand that promiscuity and fidelity exert their own pressures, in ways that the second half of the film will elaborate, when Donald exchanges a silent glance with Larry, suggesting (rightly) that they have slept together. We delight in the proliferating camp references to mass culture, from Judy Garland and Bette

Davis (and Betty Grable and Victor Mature and Maria Montez and . . .) to Tennessee Williams himself. As Michael, however, "turns" from sobriety to searing hostility (a transformation discussed at length by Joe Wlodarz in this volume), his venomous talk threatens not only to destroy the fun of the birthday party but to annihilate whatever paths toward a shared lifeworld the friends are forging in their togetherness. The capacity to speak one's own truth, in other words, is already imperiled, if not violently constrained, by forces of regulation, containment, and, yes, self-loathing and overwhelming amounts of alcohol.

## Playing Telephone

Now assembled in these lines of allegiance and conflict, the group is ready for the second, rather different half of the action, when Michael announces, "Hey everybody. Game time." "We all have to call, on the telephone, the one person we truly believe we have loved. . . . Now, here's how it works. If you make the call, you get one point. If the person you're calling answers, you get two points. If somebody else answers, you only get one point. And if nobody answers at all, you're screwed. . . . And when you get the person you've called on the line, if you tell them who you are, you get two more points. And then, if you tell them that you love them, you get a bonus of five more points. Therefore, you can get as many as ten points and as few as one." While Michael belabors the rules and the point counting, the "game" functions in more significant ways as a narrative problematization of mediated speech, that is, as an investigation into mediation itself. Without marching through each man's "turn" with the telephone (funny that this important word might be appropriate here, too), I want to emphasize how a sense of telephony expands during the film's second half, so that the telephone itself is no longer required as an actual prop in order to arrive at a thickened sense of mediated communication resembling Stanley Kauffmann's figurative transistor radio. It is the goal of this section to clarify that sense and to derive something like a politics of queer speech from it, before I try to understand its afterlife in Robey's documentary.

Bernard makes the first call, with the telephone and its two buttons for multiple lines featured in close-up, and it reveals powerful racialized dimensions of mediated speech, so much so that the affect generated by Bernard's call spills onto the next "turn" by Emory. After some prompting by Michael, Bernard places (and redials) a call to the son, Peter Dahlbeck, of his mother's (white) employer, for whom Bernard also worked. Emory interjects some operator lingo, asking Bernard whether his first attempt resulted in "DA or BY," a choice between "doesn't answer" and "busy" that cannot contain the force of what erupts as a result of the call. Getting Dahlbeck's mother on the line, Bernard identifies himself as "Francine's boy," to which Emory responds, "son, not boy." In privileging the duo of Bernard and Emory in two-shot in this prolonged scene of Bernard's call, Friedkin aligns Emory's abjection and abasement at the hands of homophobes like Alan with the more diffuse yet clearly infantilizing effects of racism. As with the call Alan will soon make, Bernard's call becomes fixed on the coordinates of heterosexual marriage when Bernard offers, as an alibi for his interest in Peter, his sorrow over the breakup of Peter's third marriage.

Soon after hanging up with Mrs. Dahlbeck, Bernard expresses regret over the call that does not quite seem commensurate with the shame he might have experienced in placing it. He begins to moan, "Why did I call him?" Emory, again privileged in a close-up, asks, "Are you all right?" and Bernard again almost wails, "I shouldn't have called" and "Oh, I wish I hadn't called now." For Bernard, the "call" starts to take on more than it would appear to mean narratively as part of Michael's game of humiliation. That is, Bernard himself is called into racialized abjection, shattered by shame, and is doubly particularized as the only African American queer at the party. He finally *feels* it once it has been spoken, and at the same time, it overwhelms what can and cannot be said within the diegesis. While his character is marked as black from his first appearance, when Emory's line of dialogue announces his entry as the "queen of spades," it seems to me that it is this call, in other words, that puts the burden of racialization *on him*, and its weight is more than his character can bear. From this call, Bernard slides into an alcoholic stupor from which Donald will have to rescue him at the party's (and film's) end, a stupor that literally silences him for the duration, until he utters his last outburst, "Yeah, freedom, baby! Freedom." Sounding like a cliché of the civil rights movement or a non sequitur in the context of the party's cynicism, Bernard is nonetheless called toward a different political register than his compatriots, one that shuttles between the private pain of his conversation with Mrs. Dahlbeck and the convergent burdens of gay and black liberation. This movement, from the private to the public and from the individual to the societal, makes this feel like one of the most melodramatic moments of the film, emphasizing as it does the depths of the inexpressible.

Emory's moving recollection of his love for Delbert Botts provides the second instance of the telephone exceeding its physical status as a prop or game, and it provides another moment of emotional excess, too. (This scene is read with intense emotion by the understudy for Emory in the stage version of *The Boys* in Robey's documentary, corroborating how keyed this specific scene is to the work's overall melodramatic ambitions.) In the first moments of Emory's "turn," he recounts his fifth-grade crush on Delbert Botts, an older boy at school, who goes on to become a dentist. There is some nascent humor in the name "Delbert Botts" alone, as well as in the unexceptional profession of dentistry, but Emory is clearly serious, almost trance-like in his recollection as he caresses the phone in anticipation of calling Delbert. The call hardly matters: it is the affect generated from this story that takes center stage, rather than the call itself. The scene is shot to emphasize Emory's interaction with the telephone (writing Delbert's number on the plastic of the phone's body, balancing the phone delicately on his lap, gripping the handset as he prepares to call).

Emory's story about Delbert, of course, is about the risks of speech. When Emory asked Delbert to "be his friend," Emory already buried his love in a secret; when he bestowed on Delbert a cigarette lighter inscribed with Emory's name ("from your friend, Emory"), Emory already scripted the shame that would then overwhelm him when his secret became known. Unlike Bernard's story, Emory's is thick with campy description and detail, especially of the prom decorations (including the famous line, "Oh Mary it takes a fairy to make something pretty"), heightening the pathos of Emory's humiliation. At this point in the "game," the telephone no longer is required for the misdirections and indeterminacies of speech to take center stage. And so when Emory ultimately does place the call (one point) and gets Delbert on the phone (two points), he identifies himself as Delbert's friend only to have Delbert abandon the phone call. "He said I must have the wrong party," a double entendre that calls attention to the quite specific ways I have been detailing in which this birthday party is about being party *to* a broader mediated conversation about queer life.

The final two examples only drive home the point that speech is always-already mediated by political noise or, to put it slightly differently, that we falsely imagine the self-present and proud politics of liberation to sound clear and, er, straightforward. Hank, you will remember, calls his and Larry's own answering service and leaves a message that itself is important *insofar as it is mediated*: he asks the answering-service worker to deliver his declaration of love to Larry. Not so much the declaration of Hank's queer love for Larry but the insertion of that "I love him" into a public relay of telephonic communication freaks Alan out. Larry called Hank, Donald explains; "he just didn't use the telephone." It is then even more fun to watch Larry phone Hank to declare his love for him on Michael's apartment telephone—which, we know from the many close-ups, has *two* lines—thereby winning the game. Finally, Alan phones not Justin Stuart but his wife, Fran, and we tend to conclude that Alan's distress had been over marital problems rather than anxiety over the closet, inciting a rage from Michael, who cannot bear to hear the truth about his friend's straightness. Harold's famous final speech might be said to be his "turn," in the sense of having the final say and in "calling" Michael on Michael's own truth: "Now it's my turn. And ready or not, Michael, here goes. You're a sad and pathetic man. You're a homosexual, and you don't want to be. But there is nothing you can do to change it. Not all your prayers to your God, not all the analysis you can buy in all the years you've got left to live. You may very well one day be able to know a heterosexual life if you want it desperately enough—if you pursue it with the fervor with which you annihilate—but you'll always be homosexual as well. Always, Michael. Always. Until the day you die." In the best possible gloss one can put on this final "turn," Harold's love for his friend Michael compels him to speak the final word regarding their sexual identity, an identity that, for the first time on the American stage, is said to be a *truth*, enduring and shared, even if borne with great difficulty by those called by its names. Crowley's play might therefore be said to be proleptic: it inaugurates a trajectory toward the declaration of gay existence in American theater, and the film adaptation carries that desire forward. In the section that follows, it is time now to ask how Mart Crowley's call for this "truth" has been answered in the years since he penned these crucial words.

## Returning the Call of *The Boys*

Crayton Robey's documentary film pays deserved tribute to Crowley for his groundbreaking play and film adaptation, and what I like about the documentary is its confessed insistence on teaching history to our young queers today, like *Project Runway*'s Christian Siriano and a host of other celebrity white boys enlisted as talking heads for Robey's film. (The fact that Robey is African American makes the discussion of race—or the studious avoidance of questions about race in his film—even more complicated.) In so doing, however, *Making the Boys* significantly reroutes the complicated field of mediation I have been discussing into a more traditional linear historical story of our collective queer emergence from the silence of pre-Stonewall politics into the bright, noisy light of liberation. Here, I try to draw out some of the resonances of Crowley's accomplishment that Robey seems to me to disregard or to refuse to answer.

In my reading of Friedkin's film, I have tried to suggest that truth telling about queer life on American stages and screens is anything *but* a matter of proud, authentic, unmediated self-declaration. Through the film's ensemble, *Boys* instead tells a story of perilous community and precarious singularities, to return to a term privileged by Stiegler. In emphasizing the traffic between the outside world and the inner lives of queers on the cusp on Stonewall, Crowley crafts a complicated story about the emergence of politicized identity and mediated lifeworlds. Like Edward Albee, who felt that *The Boys in the Band* allowed straight audiences "to see gay people they didn't have to respect," I myself find Crowley's answer to Kauffmann dated and imperfect.[11] Upon reflection, however, I think I find Robey's film even more so, since it had the benefit of forty years of queer political and aesthetic energies that Crowley helped to forge, and yet the documentary seems to me to forsake flashes of history for the romance of hagiography.

Consider this: almost every one of the actors in *The Boys in the Band* died from AIDS, except for the alive and presumptively straight Laurence Luckinbill and Peter White and the very-dead-but-from-leukemia Cliff Gorman and the missing-in-action Reuben Greene—all of them: Kenneth Nelson (Michael), Frederick Combs (Donald), Leonard Frey (Harold), Keith Prentice (Larry), Robert La Tourneaux (Cowboy)—and not only the actors but also Robert Moore (director of the stage play) and Richard Barr (producer of the stage play). In *Making the Boys*, the dead are memorialized in a sequence showcasing their head shots and announcing their dates of death, accompanied by a soft-rock song called "Without the Wind," credited to Lucian Piane. The lyrics simply run, "we tried to set sail without the wind." Despite the presence of an apparent pause for mourning, what would it mean to understand Robey's film as enacting or repeating both a silence about AIDS and an aversion to race in its enthusiastic embrace of the gayness of *The Boys*? This reading introduces another facet of how silence nonetheless reverberates, if we listen carefully.

The deaths of members of the cast and producers of *The Boys in the Band* occurred in the late 1980s and early 1990s, as the AIDS epidemic decimated arts communities in every major city in the United States. According to Richard Barr's business partner, David Bixler, the news of Barr's illness was "particularly shocking to this group of producers and theater owners, despite the fact that AIDS was killing one major theater artist after another in the late 1980s: "I think a lot of people were frankly very shocked that he was sexually active. Knowing somebody is gay is one thing, but then finding out that they have AIDS or HIV is another."[12] This difference, between one sort of public broadcast and another, is crucial to understanding the resonance of *The Boys* as a political document, not just a *text* of its moment but a record of a later itinerary toward death that "the boys" followed. Part of its force, the retrospective call that it emits toward us, must come from the knowledge we have in watching these young men shimmy and "turn" that they will soon die. To paraphrase the late Jacques Derrida, *Boys* as a moment of cinema becomes an art of allowing ghosts to come back.[13] My sense of Robey's roll call of these deaths is that he tames this force through banality: the sequence he includes domesticates the sense of being-toward-death that only a blinkered viewing of the film could obscure. One need only compare Robey's memorialization to the gut-wrenching moment in the television adaptation of *The Normal Heart* (dir. Ryan Murphy, 2014), in which Tommy's telephonic mode of remembrance comes in a stack of Rolodex cards belonging to dead friends, his "collection of cardboard tombstones bound together with a rubber band."

The other enigma of the afterlife of *The Boys* is Reuben Greene, who is said to have severed all connections to the production of *The Boys in the Band* and its personnel. In Robey's film, Greene, like the men who have died from AIDS-related illnesses, is a ghost who haunts the celebratory story of post-Stonewall ebullience. If I am right in thinking that Bernard's "call" in the narrative of *The Boys* overwhelms its parameters and motivations, then perhaps it is not inappropriate to wonder how the affective force of playing a black gay man onstage and on-screen might have spilled into Reuben Greene's subsequent life and career. From that wonder might come a sense that the queer community celebrated by Robey's film was itself fractured by racial division as much as it was and continues to be haunted by forms of suffering that are not transcended by the declaration of liberation or pride. In Heather Love's words, Reuben Greene might disclose "what it is like to bear a 'disqualified' identity, which at times can simply mean living with injury, not fixing it."[14]

In celebrating Mart Crowley's achievement in both the stage and screen triumphs of *The Boys in the Band*, then, we would do well to hear a cautionary whisper, the sound of ghosts who remind us of the losses and antagonisms that Crayton Robey's film elides. It is, in fact, this whisper that may be Crowley's gift to us, for it reminds us of the mediations between our experiences and world building, never clear-cut or free from noise or static, never pure, never untroubled. If we are always haunted by the ghosts of *The Boys*, we are in the good company of men who struggled to make good on their end of the conversation, as we do on our end.

## Notes

1. Nell Cox, introduction to *Operator*, 8th Orphan Film Symposium, April 12, 2012, audio file at www.nyu.edu/orphanfilm/orphans8/audio8/04_12_2012_Orphans8.16_Cox.mp3.

2. See Bernard Stiegler, *Technics and Time*, vol. 1, *The Fault of Epimetheus*, trans. Richard Beardsworth and George Collins (Stanford, CA: Stanford University Press, 1998); and Bernard Stiegler, *Symbolic Misery*, vol. 1, *The Hyperindustrial Epoch* (London: Polity, 2014).

3. "The Culture Industry" is the title of the fourth chapter of Theodor Adorno and Max Horkheimer, *The Dialectic of Enlightenment: Philosophical Fragments*, ed. Gunzelin Schmid Noerr, trans. Edmund Jephcott (Stanford, CA: Stanford University Press, 2002).

4. Ellis Hanson, "The Telephone and Its Queerness," in *Cruising the Performative: Interventions into the Representation of Ethnicity, Nationality, and Sexuality*, ed. Sue-Ellen Case, Philip Brett, and Susan Leigh Foster (Bloomington: Indiana University Press, 1995), 36.

5. An earlier 1960s film that hinges on the social complications of crisis calls is *The Slender Thread* (1965), the first feature-length film directed by Sydney Pollack, starring Anne Bancroft and Sidney Poitier.

6. Stanley Kauffmann, "Homosexual Drama and Its Disguises," *New York Times*, January 23, 1966, 93.

7. Ibid.

8. Ibid.

9. Writers have observed the prevalence of pastiche in Porter's compositions, but I am after something more nuanced and, I confess, enigmatic, having to do again with the mediations of Porter's homosexuality that are traced in his lyrics, his appreciation of trained vocal ranges, and his genre adaptations. There is an affinity between Porter's aesthetic achievements and the ones that I am tracing here by Crowley.

10. Kathleen Stewart, "Weak Theory in an Unfinished World," *Journal of Folklore Research* 45, no. 1 (2008): 71–82.

11. Interview with Edward Albee in *Making the Boys*. Transcribed by me.

12. Quoted in David A. Crespy, *Richard Barr: The Playwright's Producer* (Carbondale: Southern Illinois University Press, 2013), 219.

13. Jacques Derrida, interviewed in Ken McMullen's film *Ghost Dance* (1983).

14. Heather Love, *Feeling Backward: Loss and the Politics of Queer History* (Cambridge, MA: Harvard University Press, 2007), 4.

# Contributors

**MATT BELL** is associate professor of English at Bridgewater State University, where he teaches courses in film, American literature, and queer studies. His articles have appeared in *GLQ* and *American Literature*, and he is presently completing a book manuscript titled "Riotous Plots: Gay Liberation and Narrative Form."

**STEVEN COHAN** is the Dean's Distinguished Professor Emeritus of English at Syracuse University. He is author of *Masked Men: Masculinity and the Movies in the Fifties* (1997), *Incongruous Entertainment: Camp, Cultural Value, and the MGM Musical* (2005), and, for the BFI TV Classics series, *CSI: Crime Scene Investigation* (2008). He has also edited or coedited *Screening the Male* (1993), *The Road Movie Book* (1997), *Hollywood Musicals: The Film Reader* (2001), and *The Sound of Musicals* (2010). He is presently writing a book on the backstudio picture and the branding of Hollywood.

**NICK DAVIS** is associate professor of English and gender and sexuality studies at Northwestern University, focusing in the areas of popular cinema, queer theory, and American literature. His book *The Desiring-Image: Gilles Deleuze and Contemporary Queer Cinema* (2013) theorizes a new model of contemporary queer cinema based on formal principles rather than identity politics, drawing heavily on Deleuzian philosophies of film, desire, and unpredictable production. He has published essays on Julie Dash's *Illusions*, Alfonso Cuarón's *Y tu mamá también*, John Cameron Mitchell's *Shortbus*, James Baldwin's *Blues for Mister Charlie*, and the performances and political activism of Julie Christie and Vanessa Redgrave. He is also the author of the film reviews and festival journalism at www.NicksFlickPicks.com.

**RAMZI FAWAZ** is assistant professor of English at the University of Wisconsin, Madison. He is the author of *The New Mutants: Superheroes and the Radical Imagination of American Comics* (2016), which won the Center for Lesbian and Gay Studies Award for best first book project in LGBT studies. His essays have been published in *American Literature, GLQ, Callaloo*, and *Anthropological Quarterly*.

**DAVID A. GERSTNER** is professor of cinema studies and chair of the Department of Media Culture at the City University of New York's College of Staten Island. He also serves as a member of the doctoral faculty at the CUNY Graduate Center. His books include *Christophe Honoré: A Critical Introduction* (co-written with Julien Nahmias, Wayne State University Press, 2015); *Queer Pollen: White Seduction, Black Male Homosexuality, and the Cinematic* (2011; *Choice* Outstanding Academic Title, 2012); *Manly Arts: Masculinity and Nation in Early American Cinema* (2006); *The Routledge International Encyclopedia of Queer Culture* (editor, 2006; New York Public Library "Best of Reference," 2007). His coedited works include *Media Authorship* (with Cynthia Chris) and *Authorship and Film* (with Janet Staiger). His essays have appeared in numerous anthologies and journals. He is editor of the book series Queer Screens at Wayne State University Press.

**J. TODD ORMSBEE** is associate professor of American studies at San Jose State University. His research focuses on interdisciplinary social scientific study of gay male culture. His first book, *The Meaning of Gay*, was an in-depth study of the emergence of modern gay male culture, using the San Francisco Bay Area as a case study. He is currently working on a project to describe the relationship between aesthetics of sound and political organizing and community development in the Queercore punk rock movement of the 1980s and early 1990s.

**RYAN POWELL** is assistant professor of cinema and media studies in the Media School and adjunct professor in gender studies and American studies at Indiana University. His recent publications include a chapter on cultural geography in Joe Gage's *Kansas City Trucking Co.* and *El Paso Wrecking Corp.* in the volume *Queering the Countryside* (2016) and a chapter on costume and set design in James Bidgood's *Pink Narcissus*, published in *Birds of Paradise: Costume as Cinematic Spectacle* (2014). He has also published articles in *Forum*, *Little Joe*, and *Sight and Sound*. He is currently working on a book titled "*Coming Together: The Cinematic Invention of Gay Life, 1968–1979.*"

**MATTHEW TINKCOM** is associate professor of communication, culture, and technology and director of American Studies at Georgetown University. He is the author of *Working Like a Homosexual: Camp, Capital, Cinema* (2002) and *Grey Gardens* (2011), as well as coeditor of *Keyframes: Popular Cinema and Cultural Studies* (2001). He is currently writing a book on queer theory and Ang Lee's *Brokeback Mountain*.

**STEPHEN VIDER** is an Andrew W. Mellon Postdoctoral Fellow at the Museum of the City of New York. From 2013 to 2015, he was the Cassius Marcellus Clay Postdoctoral Fellow in the History of Sexuality at Yale University. He completed his Ph.D. at Harvard University in the History of American Civilization, with a secondary field in Women, Gender, and Sexuality Studies in 2013. His writing has appeared in *American Quarterly*, *Gender & History*, and *Transition*, as well as the *New York Times*, *Avidly*, *Time*, and *Slate*, among other places. His current book project examines how American conceptions of the home have shaped gay identities, relationships, and politics since World War II.

**AMY VILLAREJO** is professor in the Department of Performing and Media Arts at Cornell University, where she is also jointly appointed in the Feminist, Gender, & Sexuality Studies Program. Her publications include *Queen Christina*, coauthored with Marcia Landy (1995); *Keyframes: Popular Cinema and Cultural Studies*, coedited with Matthew Tinkcom (2001); *Lesbian Rule: Cultural Criticism and the Value of Desire* (2003), which won the 2005 Katherine Singer Kovacs Book Award from the Society for Cinema and Media Studies; and *Film Studies: The Basics* (2007). Her newest book, *Ethereal Queer*, was published in 2014. Her articles on documentary film, activist media, television, and queer culture have appeared in numerous journals such as *New German Critique* and *Social Text*, and she has also contributed to a variety of edited volumes, including a coedited special issue of *GLQ*, and book projects.

**JAMES WILSON** is professor of English and theater at LaGuardia Community College and the Graduate Center of the City University of New York. Areas of research include queer theater and performance, African American theater, and pedagogy, and he is the author of *Bulldaggers, Pansies, and Chocolate Babies: Performance, Race, and Sexuality in the Harlem Renaissance* (2010).

**JOE WLODARZ** is associate professor of film studies at Western University. His work has appeared in *Camera Obscura*, the *Velvet Light Trap*, *Queer TV* (ed. Glyn Davis and Gary Needham, 2009), and *Hollywood Reborn* (ed. James Morrison, 2010). His book *American Macho* is forthcoming.

# Index

Abraham, Karl, 61, 83–84n13
accountability, 228, 230–31, 239
acidic intimacies, 223–28
Adorno, Theodor, 256
aesthetic, Stiegler on, 294–95
affect aliens, 72
*After Dark* magazine, 200–201, 202
"age of queerness," 91, 104
Ahmed, Sara, 58, 67–68, 71, 72, 82
AIDS crisis, 153–54, 155, 304–5
Albee, Edward, 4, 296, 304
alcohol
    altered states and rants caused by, 68–76
    expression and repression of queerness tied to, 57–64
    and gender identity, 84n21
    and screaming queens and queer euphoria, 64–68
    and unhappiness and self-loathing, 76–82
Alinder, Gary, 219
Allen, Pamela, 229, 233
Alpert, Hollis, 197
altered states, 68–76
Altman, Dennis, 12
ambivalence, of Michael, 233, 234, 237
anger, deeroticization of, 243–44
"Anything Goes" (Porter), 47–49, 95, 120, 297, 306n9

appearances, and consumerism, 248–49, 258–59. *See also* masculine self-presentation
Arendt, Hannah, 222, 237
Arnold, June, 229–30
assimilation, Jewish, 194, 203–4
AT&T, 292–93
Atkins, Robert, 171
Australia, reception of play in, 150–51

backward, feeling, 58–59
*Band Wagon, The*, 181, 189n53
Barnes, Clive, 64, 144, 145–46, 147, 160n24, 161n52
Barr, Richard, 304–5
bathroom-as-closet, theme of, 251–52
baths, 171, 262–63, 282
Beame, Abe, 166, 172–73
beauty, male, in opposition to camp, 40–44
Bell, Arthur, 58, 114, 172
Ben-Mordechai, Stephen, 291n24
Benshoff, Harry M., 54n2, 102
Bernstein, Robin, 211n16
Bersani, Leo, 116, 122, 262–63
besottedness, 271, 284–85
*Best Little Boy in the World, The* (Reid), 11

Betsky, Aaron, 96–97
Binkley, Sam, 108
*Birthday Party, The*, 119, 124, 127–30, 131–32, 142, 180
Bixler, David, 304–5
Bogdanovich, Peter, 113–14
Bono, Sonny, 118
boredom, and critical reception of *The Boys in the Band*, 19–20
Bourdieu, Pierre, 290n19
*Boys in the Band, The* (film). *See also* New York City trilogy
    as allegory of social combustion, 2–3
    conclusion of, 133–34
    context of, 88–90
    datedness of, 14–16, 39, 40
    death of actors in, 304–5
    description of, 3–4
    reception of, 4–6, 16–23, 35–37, 54, 57–58
    recognition for, 10
    reconsideration of representation in, 7–9
    returning to, 1–2
    scholarship on, 6–7, 11–14
    significance of, 267–69
*Boys in the Band, The* (play)
    allusion to Judy Garland in, 44–45, 47
    Altman on, 12
    audience of, 159–60n24
    datedness of, 142, 146
    Dunlop on, 35–36
    genesis of, 4
    influences on, 142
    as informed by film, 143
    as national and international brand name, 147–51
    new productions of, 157–58
    production history of, 142–43
    as queer play, 141–42
    reception of, 144–47, 199
    recording of, 159n21
    revival of, 6, 45–46, 151–54, 161n51
    significance of, 268
    staged as living movie, 155–57
    Yorktown Heights community theater production of, 161n44
"Boys In the Band: The Queer Life of a Gay Film, The" workshop, 24–25
*Branding New York: How a City in Crisis Was Sold to the World* (Greenberg), 163
Brantley, Ben, 151, 152, 156, 157
*Brokeback Mountain*, 7
Bronski, Michael, 202–3
Brooks, Daphne, 192
Bryden, Ronald, 149–50
*Bug*, 115, 119, 124–25, 131
bullying, 157
Burke, Tom, 70
Butler, Judith, 29n17
buzzer, 298–99
Byron, Stuart, 81

camaraderie, disaggregation of sexual desiring and, 41–44
camera movement, 96, 97–99
camp, 39–40
    antagonism to, 36
    Cohan on, 85n36
    communality conveyed through, 38–39
    defined, 55n9
    as evident in direction, 50–51
    as expression of queer masculinity, 55n13

historicity of, 52–54
as manifestation of queer communal pleasure, 66–67
and musical numbers, 47–49
and older movie icons, 44–47
in opposition to male beauty, 40–44
and politics of sexual visibility, 52
social function of, 44, 52
training in, for revival, 152–53
Canby, Vincent, 20, 197
capital, sexuality and, 248
Carrithers, Joe, 37, 39
Carson, Mark, 157
Carter, David, 14
Carver, Benjamin, 157
*Cat on a Hot Tin Roof*, 61–62
*Celluloid Closet, The* (Russo), 12–13
Champlin, Charles, 55n6, 67
Chauncey, George, 91
"The Christ-was-I-drunk-last-night syndrome," 233
Cinema Center Films, 4
Clagett, Thomas D., 136n7, 164, 183
claustrophobia, 116–17, 123–30, 131
Clementi, Tyler, 157
Clendinen, Dudley, 14
Clinton, Bill, 154
closet. *See also* coming out
and commodity fetish, 255–59
and economic lives of queer characters, 248–49
evolution of theorizations of, 134
reification and, 249–55
Sedgwick on, 133
closetedness, 101, 273
closet queen, 200, 273
close-ups, 37, 50, 55n6, 104–6, 121
Coe, Richard L., 85n33
Cohan, Steven, 85n36

Combs, Frederick, 153
coming out. *See also* closet; closetedness; closet queen
cost of, 257
and critical reception of *The Boys in the Band*, 18–22
emergence and meaning of term, 200
as freedom, 273–74
phone game and, 103–4
in pop psychology, 108–9
Committee for Public Safety, 167
commodity, 247–48. *See also* consumerism; consumption
closet and reification and, 250–52
combination of queer affect and, 259–63
rejection of branded, 253
commodity fetish, 251–52, 254, 255–59
communality
and camp humor, 39
and musical numbers, 47–49
consciousness-raising, 219–23, 227–30, 236–39
consumerism, 248–50, 258–59. *See also* commodity; consumption
consummation of gay love, 282–85
consumption, 255–56, 257. *See also* commodity; consumerism
Continental Baths, 171
Control hairspray, 251–52
Coppola, Francis Ford, 113–14
Corman, Roger, 102–3
Cory, Donald, 61
Cowboy, as gift, 261–63
Cox, Nell, 292
Crimp, Douglas, 154, 171
critical judgment, 222–23, 230–31, 233–35, 237, 240–41

Crowley, Mart
  on Emory's comfort with queer sexuality, 68
  and genesis of *The Boys in the Band*, 4
  Howard Jeffrey and, 197
  on living-movie staging, 156
  on Michael, 83n10
  on religion, 205
  on title of *The Boys in the Band*, 45, 56n17
Crowther, Bosley, 62
cruising, 183–84
*Cruising*, 114, 119–20, 183–85. *See also* New York City trilogy
culture industry, 294
Cummings, Jack III, 155, 156, 157

dancing, 66, 97–98, 171, 180–85
Davis, Bette, 45, 152
Davis, Mike, 163
*Daydreams from a Cross-Town Bus*, 93
death, certainty of, 127
debt, 252–53, 254, 258, 259–64
Delany, Samuel, 104, 172, 173
de Lauretis, Teresa, 29n17
Deleuze, Gilles, 125
D'Emilio, John, 173–74, 188n39
Denmark, reception of play in, 150
Derrida, Jacques, 305
de Villiers, Nicholas, 192
Dews, Peter, 175
Dietrich, Marlene, 45
direction, camp as evident in, 50–51
Directors Company, 113–14
disintegration, 175–77, 183
documentary films, 175
Doyle, Jimmy "Popeye," 117
drag culture, 44, 152–53
Drake, David, 81, 151

Dresser, Norine, 13
drives, versus emotions, 270
Dunlop, David W., 35–36
Dutoit, Ulysse, 116, 122
Dutourd, Jean, 150
Dyer, Richard, 39, 65, 80, 91

economic, recognition and misrecognition of sexual for, 254–55
Edelman, Lee, 29n14, 136n9
Eisenbach, David, 14
"Eli, the Fanatic" (Roth), 204
Elliott, Kenneth, 151
Elsaesser, Thomas, 63
emotional bonding, 270–71
emotional isolation, depicted through close-ups, 37
emotionality, 269–72, 286–87. *See also* feeling(s)
emotion(s). *See also* feeling(s)
  defined, 269
  and development of sexual identities, 266–67
  and gay love, 270
  and gay love as lust, 278
  and significance of *The Boys in the Band*, 267–69
England, reception of play in, 149–50
"enlarged thinking," 222, 237
eudaemonism, 286–88
euphoria, queer, 64–68
exclusion
  queerness as mark of, 29n17
  social, 250, 253, 254
*Exorcist, The*, 132

Faderman, Lillian, 14
Fawaz, Ramzi, 268
"Fear"/"Fear City," 163–64, 166–67, 173

feeling backward, 58–59
*Feeling Backward: Loss and the Politics of Queer History* (Love), 10
feeling(s). *See also* emotionality; emotion(s)
  defined, 269
  representation and legitimation of gay men's, 227–28
Feingold, Michael, 161n51
Felker, Clay, 165
*Fiddler on the Roof*, 190–92, 196, 207
Fisher, Helen, 270–71
flash, cinematic, 164, 175, 177, 179–81, 185
flashpoints, 2, 26–27
Floyd, Kevin, 253, 254
framing
  of *The Birthday Party*, 129
  coalescence of characters into collectives through, 120–22
  in Friedkin's New York City trilogy, 164
  and "gritty macho look," 176
  joint, 121, 130, 131
  and subject-object distinctions in *The Boys in the Band*, 130–31
  of *12 Angry Men*, 122–23
France, reception of play in, 150
freedom, gay love as, 272–76
free indirect cinema, 125
Freeman, Jo, 242
*French Connection, The*, 117, 176, 180–83. *See also* New York City trilogy
Frey, Charles (father of Leonard), 195
Frey, Charlie (nephew of Leonard), 203
Frey, Henrietta (mother of Leonard), 195

Frey, Leonard
  background of, 195–97
  death of, 153
  Jewish transparency of, 203–9
  negotiation of dual identities of, 194
  obituaries for, 190–92
  queer opacity of, 197–203
Frey, Sally (sister-in-law of Leonard), 195, 203
Friedkin, William. *See also* New York City trilogy
  chosen to direct *The Boys in the Band*, 4
  cinematic education of, 175–76
  claustrophobic effects in works of, 123–30
  masculine self-presentation in works of, 117–20
  resurgence of, 113–17
  and scholarship on *The Boys in the Band*, 6
  on Stonewall Riots, 27n1
"Fun"/"Fun City," 163–64, 165–66, 173

Gaines, Charles, 173
Gans, Herbert, 204
Garland, Judy, 44–45, 46–47, 152–53, 293
gay bars, 62–63, 95–96, 171, 183–85, 224–25, 282
gay bullying, 157
gay culture
  in New York City, 170–71
  New York filmmaking and, 169–70
gay hardcore porn, 93
gay health, 107–9, 111
gay icons, 45–47, 152–53
*Gay L.A.* (Faderman and Timmons), 14

gay liberation
  and criticism of *The Boys in the Band*, 11–12, 77, 81, 200
  and gay love as freedom, 274–75
  and gay negativity, 92
  Michael and, 74
  and refusal to accept homophobic injustice, 227–28
  sound of, 293–94
  and technology of gay visibility, 92–93
Gay Liberation Front, 221
gay love
  consummation of, 282–85
  and emotionality, 269–72
  eudaemonism and, 286–88
  as freedom, 272–76
  as lust, 276–79
  and significance of *The Boys in the Band*, 267–69
  as superior, 279–82
gay male heterogeneity, 237
gay male sociality, 90–99, 107, 224–27, 242–43
gay marriage, 154, 287
*Gay Metropolis, The* (Kaiser), 13–14
*Gay Power: An American Revolution* (Eisenbach), 14
gay visibility, 190–94, 197–203
gesture, 96–97
ghosts, 143
Giddens, Anthony, 280
gifts, 257–58, 259–63
Glaser, Milton, 165
Godard, Jean-Luc, 264n1
Goffman, Erving, 193, 199
Goldman, A. Bruce, 205
Goldmark, Sandra, 155
*Good Times*, 118
Gorman, Cliff, 86n37, 201, 304

Gornick, Vivian, 237
gothic spatiality, 88–90
  and Alan as different visual scheme, 99–100
  and Alan's arrival at party, 100–102
  and layering of gay visibility and queer sociality, 92–99
  and negotiation of spatio-temporal dynamics, 102–9
  and persistence of Harold, 109–11
  and positive framing of queer sociality, 90–92
Gould, Deborah, 80–81
Graham, Allison, 13
Grant, Barry Keith, 167
Greenberg, Miriam, 163, 166, 167, 168–69, 170
Greene, Reuben, 304, 305
Greenspan, David, 151
"gritty macho look," 176, 189n49
grounded theory, 289n7
group shots, 50, 122

Halberstam, Judith, 29n14
Hall, Ralph, 279
Halperin, David, 40–41, 44, 109
Hansen, Miriam, 175
Hanson, Craig Alfred, 92
Hanson, Ellis, 295–96
happiness, 58–59, 67–68, 71, 76–82
hardcore porn, 93
Haverkamp, Anselm, 175
Hawks, Howard, 136n7
"Heat Wave" dance scene, 47–49, 66, 97–98
Herberg, Will, 204
Hermès/Hermès vicuna sweater, 250–51, 253, 259–60, 264n1
heterogeneity, gay male, 237
heterosexual love, 280–81, 287

Hoberman, J., 14, 208
Hollywood Renaissance films, 62
*Homographesis* (Edelman), 136n9
homophile activism, 148–49
homophobia
    acidic intimacies and refusal to accept, 227–28
    Alan as allegorical figure for societal, 232
    bullying and, 157
    and consciousness-raising, 220–21, 222
    and gay love as freedom, 274–75
    gay visibility and, 191–92
    institutional, in New York City, 171–74, 187n24, 188nn32,40,42
    internalized, 5–6, 74–76
    judgmentalness as weapon against, 230
    and politics of speech and silence, 299–300
    racism and trauma of, 79–80
homophobic homophilia, 133–34
"Homosexual Drama and Its Disguises" (Kauffmann), 4, 296–97
homosexuality. *See also* queerness
    alcohol tied to expression and repression of, 57–64
    old and new, 70
    shift in perspective regarding, 154–55
*Homosexual: Oppression and Liberation* (Altman), 12
Hongisto, Richard D., 174
Horkheimer, Max, 256
hotlines, 295
Hummler, Richard, 158n3
Humphreys, Laud, 70–71
*Hunted, The*, 119
hustler, 261–63

Hyman, Stanley, 204
hyperindustrial culture, 294

"icks," 60, 76–82
idealization of gay love, 280–82
ideal type(s), 287–88, 291n31
identity, telephone and, 296
Inge, William, 4, 296
inside, delimited by telephone, 298
internalized homophobia, 5–6, 74–76
International Association of Chiefs of Police (IACP), 174
intimacies, acidic, 223–28
It Gets Better Project, 10, 157

Jackson, Peter, 149
Jay, Karla, 221, 229
Jeffrey, Howard, 197, 205, 207
Jewish visibility, 190–94, 203–9
"Jew Wave," 208–9
joint framing, 121, 130, 131
Jones, Dick, 282
judgmentalness, 228–36, 240–41
judiciousness, 235–36
Julius' (bar), 62–63, 95–96

Kael, Pauline, 8–9, 20–21
Kaiser, Charles, 13–14, 28n7
Kalem, Ted, 144
Kameny, Franklin, 5–6, 28n7, 194
Kantrowitz, Arnie, 5–6, 8, 9, 13, 28n8
Kauffmann, Stanley, 4, 19, 296–97
Kavka, Misha, 89, 102–3
*Killer Joe*, 115, 123
Kimport, Katrina, 287
Kissel, Howard, 152
Knight, Hilary, 46, 152
Knoebel, John, 229
Koch, Ed, 188n40

Kort, Joe, 109
Kracauer, Siegfried, 175
Kramer, Carol, 202
Kretzmer, Herbert, 149
Kroll, Jack, 144

Laffrey, Dane, 155
latency theory, 61
La Tourneaux, Robert, 153
*Lawrence v. Texas* (2003), 154
Leacock, Richard "Ricky," 292
Leary, Timothy, 86n42
Lewis, Emory, 187–88n30
LGBT activism, 10
LGBTQ hotline, 295
lighting, in New York trilogy, 176–77
Lindsay, John, 165, 168, 169–70, 187n24
location, and construction of gay visibility, 93–96, 99–100
*Logics of Disintegration* (Dews), 175
*Lost Weekend, The* (film), 61–62
*Lost Weekend, The* (Jackson), 61
Loughery, John, 7, 12, 13–14
love. *See* gay love
Love, Heather, 10, 58–59, 82, 144, 305
lover, 277
Luckinbill, Laurence, 304
lust, 271, 276–79, 285

*Magic Christian, The*, 201
*Making the Boys*, 6, 303–5
male beauty, in opposition to camp, 40–44
marginalization, 41–42
marijuana, 69, 71
Marx, Karl, 255
masculine self-presentation. *See also* appearances, and consumerism

and framing of *The Boys in the Band*, 120–22, 130–31
in Friedkin works, 117–20
mass consumption, 294
master suite, 132–33, 134
May, Simon, 271, 278
Maye, Michael, 188n32
Mayor's Office of Film, Theatre, and Broadcasting (MOFTB), 168
mediated voice, 293–95, 296, 300–303
Meyer, Richard, 96
Midler, Bette, 46, 152, 171
Miller, D. A., 256
misery, 294
*Mondo Rocco*, 93
money, and affect, 263–64
monogamy, 238
Montez, Maria, 45
Moore, Robert, 153
moral authority, of Harold, 263–64
*Mother Camp* (Newton), 44
multiple identification, 237–38
Muñoz, José, 143, 154
musical numbers, 47–49
*My Hustler*, 264n2

Nagourney, Adam, 14
Nash, Richard, 276
negativity, queer, 90–92, 111
Nelson, Kenneth, 153
new homosexuality, 70
Newton, Esther, 44
New York City
 disintegration and transformation of, 175–77
 as "Fear City," 166–67
 film industry and image of, 167–70
 as "Fun City," 165–66
 gay culture in, 170–71

institutional homophobia in, 171–74, 187n24, 188nn32,40,42
New York City trilogy
   and link between homosociality and homosexuality, 174–75
   mise-en-scène of, 163–65
   sexually uncertain men in, 177–85
   style of, 176–77
*New York* magazine, 165, 168
Nielsen, Ken, 150
Nightingale, Benedict, 149
*No Future: Queer Theory and the Death Drive* (Edelman), 29n14
nonjudgmentalness, 228–30
*Normal Heart, The*, 305
Nussbaum, Martha, 270

Ogren, Peter, 197
opacity, 192
*Operator*, 292–93
organological revolution, 294–95
*Other Side of Silence, The* (Loughery), 13–14
*Out for Good* (Clendinen and Nagourney), 14
outside, delimited by buzzer, 298–99

*People vs. Paul Crump, The*, 126–27
phone game
   and coming out, 103–7
   and consciousness-raising, 236–41
   and "enlarged thinking," 222
   and gay love as freedom, 273, 275
   Harold's role in, 263
   as mediated speech, 300–303
   and possibility of gay love, 271–72, 283–84
photograph, 236, 260–61
Piane, Lucian, 304
picture frame, 236, 260–61

*Picture of Dorian Gray, The* (Wilde), 264–65n7
"Planned Shrinkage," 166, 172–73
Poe, Edgar Allan, adaptations of, 102–3
political landscape for gays and lesbians, 154–55
polyamory, 238
Pop Art and Film, 169, 170
popular psychology, 108–9
porn, 93
porn-film theaters, 172
Porter, Cole, 47–49, 95, 120, 297, 306n9
Portnoy, Alexander, 206
poststructuralism, 175
Prentice, Keith, 153
Price, Vincent, 102–3
psychology, popular, 108–9
purgation, ritualized, 132

queer affect
   combination of commodity and, 259–63
   money and, 263–64
queer discourse, current, 10
queer euphoria, 64–68
queer negativity, 90–92, 111
queerness. *See also* homosexuality
   age of, 91, 104
   alcohol tied to expression and repression of, 57–64
   polarization between masculinist vision of gay health and non-normative, 107–8
queer sociality, 90–99, 107, 224–27, 242–43
queer utopian memory, 143, 154

race, 301, 305
racism, and trauma of homophobia, 79–80

Ralston, Vera Hruba, 45
rants, 68–76
rebellion, deeroticization of, 243–44
Reed, Rex, 141, 143, 144
Reid, John, 11
reification, 248–49
　closet and, 249–55
　and closet and commodity fetish, 255–59
　and combination of commodity and queer affect, 259–63
religion, 205
Renaissance films, 62
representation, 5–6, 7–9, 35
ritualized purgation, 132
Robbins, Jerome, 195, 196
Robey, Crayton, 6, 303–4
Rohe, Kathryn, 155
Roizam, Owen, 176
romantic love, 270–71, 281, 287
Rooney, David, 156
*Rope*, 142
Rosen, Steven A., 187n24
Roth, Philip, 204–5
Rotskoff, Lori, 61, 62, 83–84nn13,21
Russo, Vito, 12–13, 28n8, 58

same-sex marriage, 154, 287
Sarachild, Kathie, 219–20, 227, 229, 242, 246n21
Scheie, Timothy, 37, 159n23
Schiavi, Michael R., 158n5
Schickel, Richard, 20
screaming queens, 64–68, 75–76
Scroggie, William, 86n49, 223
secret/secrecy
　about commodity, 251
　of homosexual, 19–20
　Miller on, 256

Sedgwick, Eve Kosofsky
　on closet and closetedness, 101, 133, 255, 256
　on coming out, 19–20, 21
　on male-male desire, 247, 248
　on queer desire in *The Picture of Dorian Gray*, 264–65n7
Segaloff, Nat, 136n7
self-improvement, 108
self-loathing. *See also* shame
　alcohol and, 73, 76–82
　of Michael, 50, 53, 72, 73–74, 240–41
　and polarization between masculinist vision of gay health and non-normative queerness, 107–8
　and possibility of gay love, 283, 285
　and rejection of *The Boys in the Band*, 12
　Scheie on, 159n23
Sellers, Peter, 201
sexual, recognition and misrecognition of economic for, 254–55
sexual behavior, and critical reception of *The Boys in the Band*, 22–23
sexual desire
　disaggregation of companionship and, 41–44
　emotion and, 266–67, 270
sexually uncertain men, in New York City trilogy, 177–82
sexual openness, 37–38
sexual visibility, camp and, 52
shame. *See also* self-loathing
　alcohol and homosexual, 60, 72–75
　Love on pride and, 82
　produced through truth game, 237, 301, 302
silence, 299–300, 304

silliness, 67–68
Siskel, Gene, 21
sociality. *See* queer sociality
social landscape for gays and lesbians, 154–55
social problem films, 62
Sontag, Susan, 193–94, 211n16
*Sorcerer*, 114, 118
spectacular opacity, 192
speech
    homophobia and politics of, 299–300
    risks of, 302
*Star Is Born, A*, 44–45, 46–47, 56n17, 152–53
Starr, Roger, 166, 172, 186n10
Staub, Michael, 205
Stewart, Kathleen, 299
Stiegler, Bernard, 294–95
*Stonewall* (Carter), 14
Stonewall era, 67–68
Stonewall Riots, 2, 27n1, 36, 293
*Street Theater* (Wilson), 159n23
Streisand, Barbra, 209, 215n76
subject-object distinction, 130–31
Swanson, Gloria, 45
sweater, 250–51, 253, 259–60
symbolic domination, 273–74, 275, 281, 290n19

Teachout, Terry, 156–57
Teal, Donn, 78, 146–47, 159n24
technology of gay visibility, 92–94
telephone, 292–93, 295–96, 298. *See also* phone game
*Tell Me That You Love Me, Junie Moon*, 201–2
Terry, Jennifer, 61
Thorp, Charles, 272
Times Square, 172, 173

Timmons, Stuart, 14
Tinkcom, Matthew, 47
Tobias, Andrew, 11
*To Live and Die in L.A.*, 118–19
tourism, 169–70
transformation, 175–77
truth game. *See* phone game
"turning," 59, 68–76, 83n12, 86n42, 234
*12 Angry Men*, 122–23, 124, 131
Tyler, Parker, 102, 103
typecasting, 201–2

unhappiness, 58–59, 76–82
universalism, of Alan, 232–33, 234, 237, 238–39
upstairs master suite, 132–33, 134
urban planning, 166, 172–73
utopian memory, queer, 143

Vincentelli, Elizabeth, 156
virility, 43, 70–71
visibility
    and Alan as different visual scheme, 99–100
    and Alan's arrival at party, 100–102
    gay liberation and, 74
    gothic spatiality and limits of, 88–90
    layering of queer sociality and, 92–99
    and negotiation of spatio-temporal dynamics, 102–9
    and persistence of Harold, 109–11
    and positive framing of queer sociality, 90–92
Voss, Brandon, 156

Warhol, Andy, 169, 264
weakness, Jewish, 206
Weber, Max, 291n31

*Weekend*, 264n1
Weinberg, Thomas S., 62
West, Anthony, 145
West Side, 172
White, Edmund, 64
White, Peter, 304
*Who's Afraid of Virginia Woolf?*, 142, 144
Williams, Tennessee, 4, 296
Wilson, Doric, 159n23
"Without the Wind" (Piane), 304
Wittman, Carl, 200
Wlodarz, Joe, 184, 185

Wojcik, Pamela Robertson, 56n15, 65–66, 96, 103
Wolfe, Tom, 165, 169
women's liberation, 219–20
Wood, Robin, 58, 89
Worton, Michael, 183
*Written on the Wind*, 61–62

Yorkin, Bud, 164, 177
Young, Allen, 77, 221

Zerilli, Linda, 240
*Ziegfeld Follies*, 47, 181

www.ingramcontent.com/pod-product-compliance
Lightning Source LLC
Chambersburg PA
CBHW070259240426
43661CB00057B/2594